ECHOES OF A LOST VOICE

Echoes of a Lost Voice

Encounters with Primo Levi

Gabriella Poli
and Giorgio Calcagno

Translated from the Italian by Nat Paterson
Edited by Carole Angier

VALLENTINE MITCHELL
LONDON • CHICAGO, IL

English edition first published in 2018 by Vallentine Mitchell.
Reprinted in paperback in 2020.

Catalyst House,
720 Centennial Court,
Centennial Park, Elstree WD6 3SY, UK

814 N. Franklin Street,
Chicago, Illinois,
IL 60610 USA

www.vmbooks.com

British Library Cataloguing in Publication Data:
An entry can be found on request

ISBN 978-1-910383-46-9 (Paper)
ISBN 978-1-910383-44-5 (Cloth)
ISBN 978-1-910383-45-2 (Ebook)

Library of Congress Cataloging in Publication Data
An entry can be found on request

Contents

Notes on the Translation

Gabriella Poli constructed this book from a range of sources, many of which have already been translated into English. The books Levi published during his lifetime, which for the most part are quoted only briefly, are cited here as they appear in the 2015 edition of Levi's *Complete Works*, edited by Ann Goldstein. However, all the articles and interviews, to which much of Poli's and Calcagno's work is devoted, have been translated and edited by us. In some cases we have indicated where a published translation exists, mainly in the *Uncollected Series and Essays* sections of the *Complete Works* and in the selection of Levi's writings compiled by Marco Belpoliti, *The Black Hole of Auschwitz*, but there may be other translations we are unaware of. More details of Italian and English texts are listed in the 'Works of Primo Levi' section at the back of the book.

The interview granted by Primo Levi to Philip Roth, which took place in English, was quoted by Poli and Calcagno as it appeared in two interviews published in *La Stampa*. These interviews include passages missing from the version published in the *New York Times Book Review* and in Roth's collection of interviews with writers, *Shop Talk*. These passages have been back-translated, with the English and Italian sources referenced in endnotes, but without translated and original sentences being differentiated.

As a close friend of Levi's, Gabriella Poli believed that he had committed suicide, and her discussion of his death at the end of Chapter 13 takes this for granted (as do occasional remarks elsewhere in the text). Subsequently doubts were raised, first by Levi's cousin Rita Montalcini Levi, and later by other commentators and critics both inside and outside Italy. Both the main biographies of Levi so far, by Carole Angier and Ian Thomson, conclude that sadly suicide is almost certainly the right explanation. In any case, it should be recalled that Poli was writing out of her own experience and beliefs about Levi.

Levi's lively interest in language, literature and culture is manifested here in a number of literary and historical references non-Italian readers are likely to be unfamiliar with, as well as in terms from such languages as Piedmontese, Latin and French. These have been explained briefly in additional endnotes.

Acknowledgement

The Translator and Editor would like to thank Elena Poli for the original idea of making her sister's book available in English (and French), and for all her support.

Foreword by Giorgio Calcagno

For forty years, Primo Levi bore witness in the pages of his books. For twenty-five years, in his newspaper interviews or meetings with the public, he never refused to answer a question. Yet a complete portrait of Primo Levi does not exist. For many his image continues to be based on his first book; and even today a section of his readership wonders how such a writer could be born from a chemist, then from a concentration camp survivor. The man who had felt almost morally obliged to present *Natural Histories* under a pseudonym so as not to disturb his audience, had to come to terms with the indelible mark he had carried back with him from Auschwitz both as a man and a writer. Could he, Häftling number 174517, play with irony, experiment with incursions into fantasy, then attempt to grasp a history that is always changing? With his clarity, Levi saw himself as a centaur; for others, he remained an enigma.

The book we have conceived together, and which Gabriella Poli has written, attempts to retrace what Levi himself has said about his work, and to answer these questions. It is a self-portrait built up like a mosaic, bringing together pieces scattered in newspapers and magazines, radio and television interviews, conference reports, recordings of discussions, meetings with students, and memories of personal conversations.

They reveal a man consistent in his contradictions, coherent precisely because he is multifaceted, secure in his roots while curious about new developments. Around his atom's nucleus turn different kinds of particles, always in motion.

The element that is most striking, in this succession of testimonies, is the precision with which Primo Levi reveals himself and his relationship to his works. Everyone who met him, and above all those who interviewed him, remember the firmness with which he answered questions, even the least predictable ones, as if he had thought them all through beforehand. In his conversation you never sensed the ephemeral nature of the encounter, just the skeleton of his thought. And yet his answers are not all the same. This man, it emerges from these pages, knew how to look at himself with surprising clarity – 'Know thyself'[1] was programmed into him – but he also knew how to recognize the change that came about in the self that he observed.

Primo Levi is 44. Urged by the press, he begins to make public statements for the first time. He is a writer who is recognized if not universally acclaimed; his oeuvre consists of two books on the same theme. He is a chemist, a Jew, someone who works in a factory and writes in the evening. He knows that he plays three roles at the same time, and they are roles he has never stopped probing: he doesn't want to and can't give up any of the three. He shares with everyone who asks him the results of that probing, but the three characters mutate and combine in different ways.

More than any other writer in Italy, Primo Levi is *the* Jewish writer. But he was not a Jew before anyone else. His Jewishness is all the more decisive for having arrived late, having been discovered by force and defended with stubbornness. Whatever he talks about, whatever question he needs to answer, that element comes decisively to the fore, marked with clarity and especially with pain. He won it through the experience of the victim, reduced to a number, humiliated into an object.

'I became a Jew in Auschwitz, before I didn't feel like one', he declared in an interview for *Famiglia Cristiana*. 'The awareness of feeling *different* was imposed on me. Someone, without the slightest reason in the world, decided that I was different and inferior; as a natural reaction, I saw myself in those years as different and superior.' Despite this rude awakening, he maintains a kind of distance regarding his own identity. He considers himself a 'registered' Jew, who doesn't practice or even believe. 'My Jewishness is a purely cultural fact. If it weren't for the racial laws and the Lager, there would probably be nothing Jewish about me but my surname.' To Luciano Genta, who interviews him on his translation of *The Trial*, he says that he feels 'much less Jewish' than Kafka. And to Giampaolo Pansa, who met him in June 1982, after the Israeli invasion of Lebanon, he admits that 'Now it's harder than ever to be a Jew.'

But as well as the surname he knows that he has in him, and he defends, some of the most characteristic Jewish traits. Irony, for example, always a precious gift for the persecuted, and still more difficult self-irony, 'that extraordinary desire for joy through misery, persecution and massacre'. Wariness about his own states of mind, fear of an emotion that could overpower his rational vision of life tormented him ('I'm moved by the things which affect more or less everyone, children who suffer, elderly people who suffer…but perhaps because of my experiences I am quite hardened, I'm not moved easily.') The defence of reason against the distortions of barbarism, the insistence on always thinking for oneself, avoiding the watchwords of the crowd. ('Fascism openly discouraged reason. I force myself to have a rational view of the world.') But also the right to fantasy, the awareness that there is something beyond reason, the other half of himself he calls, in no uncertain terms, 'irrational'. ('It's a mechanism I don't know and which sets itself off unexpectedly.')

He defends the cultural heritage of Judaism. Answering a question from Giorgio Bocca on the meaning of a Yiddish saying, he reminds him that culture 'doesn't obstruct you, doesn't get blocked at customs, you carry it with you in any migration, from any country from which you were expelled… The terrible history of the Jewish people, a history of expulsions and persecutions, has obliged it to take refuge in the only moveable good that cannot be confiscated.' And at the very heart of his culture he defends the duty of memory, to which he has devoted his work as a writer; a duty 'especially for us, who have undergone the ordeal, and in a way also had the opportunity, of living through fundamental experiences. It would be more than a denial of duty not to pass on what we have lived through.'

Memory brings the author back from *Natural Histories* and *The Wrench* to his point of departure, the centre of his universe. Human history, for Primo Levi, can be divided into before Auschwitz and after Auschwitz; it can never ignore Auschwitz. But it must overcome it. The greatness of his testimony lies not in the memory but in the life he went on to reconstruct. 'This is the experience I have come out of and which I have been deeply marked by', he told a periodical run by Rosanna Benzi, a woman trapped in an iron lung. 'It marked me but it didn't take away my desire to live, in fact it increased it, because it gave my life a purpose, that of bearing witness so that nothing similar will ever happen again.'

The 'no longer human' protagonist of his first book, as he explained to an audience in Switzerland, regains his identity as a person precisely in that Jewish strength; he bears witness, and he lives.

Like the Jew, the writer in Primo Levi is born late, under the torment of an external condition. And he is born in the same place, the concentration camp. For many years Levi is himself unaware of it. He writes out of a sense of duty, not out of choice. 'The need to eat and the need to tell were on the same level of primal necessity,' he told a conference, 'because what I had seen and lived through was weighing down on me and I felt the urgent need to free myself of it.' He writes under the pressure of memory; he doesn't feel sure he is producing literary work and he doesn't even ask himself the question. So much so that he feels awkward in the company of professional men of letters. Questioned by three university lecturers on a television programme he is defensive: 'My theoretical ideas on literature are few.' And he almost feels the need to apologise, when he moves from the literature of memory to that of invention: 'My store is diminishing. I have no memories left. If I carry on writing, I will at some point have to invent.' But then he claims, with great lucidity, the right to stop being a slave to memory. And he shows his irritation with the critics who in *Natural Histories* and *Flaw of Form* look only for the continuation of his discussion of the Lager. 'I must admit that that controversy interests me very little. Writers draw on what they know. My sources are multiple and varied.'

In reality,this man with 'few ideas on literature' is acquiring an ever-clearer awareness of his 'second trade'. Ever since *If This is a Man*, he has known the attitude to adopt if he is to achieve maximum effectiveness. 'It seemed to me to be harmful, to the goals I had set myself, to adopt the state of mind of the lamenting victim. Because a lamenting victim arouses more pity than belief, and I wanted to be believed more than pitied.' But when he moves to the inventions of *Natural Histories* he discovers another dimension to his literary instrument. To the demands of the 1960s literary rulebook for politically engaged, even explicitly protest-driven narrative, he opposes the right of the author to make other decisions: 'Human genius is varied and unpredictable: between consumer literature and pure engagement there is a vast no-man's-land, from which a true and valid book could emerge, outside of any pre-constituted plan.'

The discovery of this land is his alone. In a period where there seems to be no room for anything but a politically oriented, prescriptive literature, and the verbal acrobatics of the new avant-garde, Levi proceeds by looking at his own resources, testing himself step-by-step on the ground of writing. He discovers that literary work is not a gratuitous act, but answers to an inner human necessity. In a chaotic world, he affirms to the man who would be his last interviewer that'Writing is a way of putting things in order'. He knows, with great self-awareness, that he needs to keep away from the literature of feeling. ('World literature is saturated with feeling. Why not try to beat different paths?'). He knows that writing requires a rigorous calculation, a precision of terminology almost at odds with the apparent freedom the author is granted. He recognizes that the 'decisive factor in the narrative process must be a shrewd balance between the necessary and the superfluous.' He accepts, indeed he declares his love for, works such as *Tristram Shandy* and Stefano d'Arrigo's *Horcynus Orca*; but for himself he makes other choices. 'My books, I think I can boast of this, don't contain anything that's superfluous. It comes spontaneously and naturally to me to refrain from adornment, from additions put there only to make the page look nice.'

And if he agrees, at a certain point, to stop being a slave to memory in order to enter the realm of the imagination, he also senses the danger of invention turning into arbitrariness. 'You, the author, find yourself gifted with unlimited powers, you can do with a character what you will, you can kill him, you can make him beautiful, omnipotent, perverse; you can make him suffer or be happy, and that for me has been quite a new experience, a feeling of childlike omnipotence. . . .' No novelist in Italy's writers' union would ever have expressed himself like this; the great creators of plots were able to invent only because they had never been aware of their omnipotence. At the moment when Primo Levi senses that unsuspected power, he also discovers its dangers and prepares antidotes against them. 'It's true: the child builds himself a universe where he can do what he wants. From that viewpoint writing a novel is a regression.'

It is precisely Primo Levi's awareness of limits that leads him to bring together the absoluteness of writing with the relativity of technology. It is not a coincidence that he is the first Italian writer to take on the computer. Levi doesn't distrust the new tool; he certainly doesn't reject the help it can provide. But, just as he has demythologized the freedom of fantasy, he demythologizes the slavery of software. The advent of the computer is the time to come to terms with poetry. It is the same Levi who in the 1960s had written the story of the 'Versifier' who in the mid-1980s, with computer mania raging, warned the followers of the new religion: 'A computer that produces valid, original poetry of its own accord will never be built. . Bad poetry, yes...'. Because 'poetry is greater than logic or chance: it can contain both of them within itself, but it is broader...The computer seems to me an excellent tool to carry out clear and distinct tasks, but poetry isn't such a task: it's fluid, oblique, continuous, bathed in halos and shadows.' This is the big departure, the surprise we weren't expecting. The author who confessed he lacked ideas on literature was the first to identify the essential role of poetry in the age of electronic communication. The rules of logic, the arbitrariness of chance will never be able to replace it. Because poetry is 'broader', and not only in quantity.

Such a comparison, in favour of poetry, could only come from someone who had always worked with the tools of technology and science. This is the third side of Levi, which can often appear to be the first. If the Jew and the writer in him came late, the *Homo faber*[2] comes early. And he will claim it as his first self-image throughout his life.

Against the prophets of doom, the apocalyptic preachers proliferating so freely in a literary world dominated by latter-day followers of Adorno, Levi the chemist believes in science, in its power to redeem humanity. He believes it with the calm of intelligence, without sanctimoniousness, always leaving the possibility of criticism open. Even in the laboratories of Auschwitz, he can never forget, men of science were at work. And new Strangeloves could always come onto the horizon. 'Anyone denying the benefits of machines isn't speaking in good faith,' he tells Claudio Toscani in 1972. 'But it is equally clear that a technology that has sprung out of control, or been taken over by the interests of a single class, can lead the world to a catastrophe or a slow cancer, whereas science, as the daughter of reason, can liberate the human race from many of its afflictions.'

To this concept of science as the daughter of reason he will remain forever faithful, even in those years when the political role of science is called into question on many fronts. Levi, *homo politicus* at heart, ready to enter the arena wherever there is a side to be taken, doesn't let himself get entangled on this point. Is it possible for science to be neutral, he was asked by an audience member after a conference at Turin's Carignano theatre. Yes, it is not only possible but right that it should be, the writer replies firmly, while acknowledging the risk that science can lose its independence. 'But if technological education is combined with moral education man should not let himself be subjected. I don't believe that there is a right wing mathematics opposed by a left wing mathematics. Scientific reality is one, and if it's not, it means that someone has corrupted it. When science isn't neutral it's because it's someone's bad science.'

His is a faith that is not easy, not a passive faith of the Enlightenment, but a faith in the most hidden resources of mankind. His concept of progress is full of uncertainties, nuances, even contradictions; but it remains fundamental, right across this autobiography of ideas. Levi confesses as much to the interviewer who was the most difficult for him, a young journalist for *Lotta continua* in 1979. He senses, in this interviewer, a legitimate distrust of 'mankind as a chemical system' and admits, in part, to sharing his worries. But he defends the development of knowledge, which has grown exponentially in recent times: 'We have learned more in the last ten years than we have done since Plato.' And despite the uncertainties in which he wraps his answer, he ends with a statement of trust in the future: 'I can see a goal to aim for, and for that reason I am not an outright pessimist.'

This humble, positive, when necessary sceptical faith does not translate into presumptuous statements of principles, but into a daily attentiveness to a value forgotten more and more in today's society, and defended, when it was most difficult to do so, by Primo Levi: work. Levi believes in work, the fruit of science and technology, as a man, but he believes in it even more as a writer. Time and again in the interviews he gave, the author of *Natural Histories* and *The Periodic Table* defends his chemical training because chemistry teaches clarity and concision, and only with clarity and concision does the writer work with the knowledge that he is doing a service for his readers. 'My trade has also been useful to me in my style of writing', he declares in a discussion on his book dedicated to the chemical elements. And in a radio conversation he defends the right of readers to understand every hidden corner of the text. Levi calls it, understatedly, 'access to communication'. For every writer this is a duty; for him, it is a need. 'It must be a working telephone, the written book, and I think that chemistry taught me those two qualities: concision and clarity.'

It is from this that Primo Levi's writing is born: determined, certain, the sentence divisions carefully organized, the vocabulary clear, every word fitting neatly into its box. But from this too is born his most extraordinary narrative discovery: Faussone, the worker hero in *The Wrench* who makes his job as a rigger the centre of his universe. Levi admits to basing his adventures on technical reports published in specialist journals, but he also acknowledged, not long after, that he wrote about him only when he realized that 'Faussone had enough blood and skin and bone to last a whole book'. The character is completely new in Italian literature; he allows the author to establish, for the first time, a bridge between 'those who work with their brain and those who work with their hands'. Through Libertino Faussone, Levi has chosen to put into a book 'the way that 80 per cent of human beings live', but which novels have always overlooked. 'Novels take on refined existential themes, books are often full of violence and sex. But how much of people's everyday lives are taken up by violence, sex and existential crises? Eight hours of work a day take up a lot more space. I write about the problems of those eight hours.'

Faussone salvages work at a time when the 'vanguards' of social movements held it in contempt, and this from an author who was always connected with the political left – and the pages Gabriella Poli dedicates to that relationship, in the seventh chapter of this book, are illuminating, not just from the standpoint of Levi's work. But Faussone also salvages a language, which moves from daily reality into writing for the first time. And this is not the least important aspect of *The Wrench*, for some it is even the most original. Salvage or discovery? 'It's a literary operation, to be sure', Levi tells Giorgio De Rienzo, 'but it has a basis in truth: this is in fact the language that the educated Piedmontese labourer uses when he speaks. I wouldn't say that it's a fake or a fraud. If anything, it's a restoration. Popular language has exceptional resources; it uses delightful metaphors; I felt the need to put them down in writing.' With results that attract the astonishment of critics and the admiration of linguists. In him, they seem to come naturally. Only Primo Levi could plunge into the waters of his experience of work, and emerge reborn with such a dazzling invention.

But it is not only the chemist who explains the uniqueness of the writer. We get the measure of Primo Levi in his attachment to his soil, which he never tires of mentioning. Levi is, we must never forget, a son of Turin, who lived all his life in the house where he was born, bound to a society whose most ancient values he represents. Clarity of judgement, rationality of thought, a taste for geometry to the point of transforming it into fantasy, love for one's profession: these are just some of his typically Piedmontese traits. 'I am very fond of my small homeland', he replies to a lecturer from Bern who wants to know how much his origins have influenced his writings. 'I love the city, its dialects, its streets, its cobblestones, boulevards, hills, the mountains that surround it and that I climbed as a young lad. I like the rural and mountain origins of its people, the conscientiousness of its labourers, the flair of its artisans, the rigour of its technicians.' In other words, all the qualities that combined in the man who was Primo Levi.

Is it this character that gives birth to his distrust for big messages, his wish almost to minimize his role? Perhaps. Precisely because he knows how important his testimony is, Levi doesn't want to disperse it in the fog of ideology; he defends it from the standpoint of universal values. The man who trained in a paint and varnish laboratory orders his words to the rhythm of the everyday; history can wait. 'I don't write to improve the human race', he tells a young man who questions him during a debate, and he speaks not out of lack of confidence but out of realism. He recalls how few people even the most widely published book can reach. He recalls the German readership for the first edition of *If This is a Man*, fifty thousand in a population of fifty million. 'I received thirty letters from Germans who told me that reading the book had left them "improved". Thirty!'

He is aware of his mission; he doesn't tire of recalling its limits. In the last interview he gave, published posthumously on 26 April 1987, Levi asks the interviewer not to confuse him with a seer or a prophet. 'They're the plague of our age, prophets. Or maybe they're the plague of every age. Because it's almost impossible to distinguish a true prophet from a false one. The language is the same.'

Yet all Levi's work has a warning quality, which can often be interpreted as prophecy. History, which the man wanted to escape, has chosen him to be its mouthpiece, and the writer has done his best not to walk away from his task. The enemy of false prophets has, without using the same language, issued the only acceptable prophecy in our time, and has proclaimed it throughout his life. A prophecy which he is unable to conceal; hard, often unpleasant, but necessary. And he has proclaimed it with the humility of the man of science, with the understatement of the Piedmontese, welded to the sense of tragedy and the painful irony of the Jew. These are the characteristics that make Primo Levi a unique, irreplaceable figure in Italy's literary world.

This book is the product of a long friendship between Primo Levi and the two journalists who collaborated on the text, despite having contributed to it in different proportions.Gabriella Poli, then a journalist for *Avanti!*, first met the writer in 1954, on a train taking a delegation of ex-deportees to Buchenwald for a ceremony organized by the International Federation of Resistance Fighters, on the ninth anniversary of the camp's liberation. Primo Levi acted as a guide for the delegates of the various countries,and he helped to introduce them to survivors so that their tragic stories could be told. I met Levi in 1966, when I was managing *La Stampa*'s theatre section and Gianfranco De Bosi was directing *If This is a Man* at Turin's Teatro Stabile.

The two friendships continued in parallel through the years, meeting at *La Stampa*, where Poli had long been a reporter and to which Levi started contributing in 1975. Gabriella's work often led her to attend ceremonies, debates, demonstrations on the themes of deportation and the Resistance, at which Levi was almost always present. My work, especially after I moved to *Tuttolibri*,[3] allowed me to approach him, to ask him for articles, to interview him on his most recent publications. When he came to the paper to hand in an article, Primo always came to say hello to at least one of us.

Together with the newspaper interviews, the radio and television texts, the documents of his public meetings which Gabriella Poli has patiently been collecting, we have been able to bring together a precious series of personal testimonies.[4]

'Each of us carries the imprint/Of the friend met along the way', Levi wrote in his poem 'To My Friends'. This book seeks to preserve the memory of that imprint as well.

Notes

1. A Greek aphorism inscribed on the porch of Apollo's temple in Delphi, most famously used by Socrates in many of Plato's dialogues.
2. 'Man the Maker', a phrase coined in Latin literature and used in anthropology, philosophy and literature ever since.
3. The literary supplement to *La Stampa*.
4. These were private conversations between Gabriella Poli and Levi, details from which she integrates into the narrative of *Echoes of a Lost Voice*.

I

The Centaur

Sixteen years of silence punctuated by the republication of *If This is a Man* and, occasionally, by the appearance of his name in some newspaper or magazine; then, the unexpected move into the open with the second book of memoirs, *The Truce*, in which he told of his rise from the depths and the odyssey of his return home from Auschwitz, across Poland, Russia, Romania, Hungary and Austria. The 17th Strega Prize, announced on the evening of 4 July 1963, saw *The Truce* in the running right until the end. The shortlist two weeks before put Primo Levi third among the six finalists and predictions on the eve of the event were uncertain. But the survivor-Proust, as someone that night described him, did not leap into first place, despite the predictions of many and the book's 'inherent values and determined supporters'.[1] In the final vote he was beaten by Natalia Ginzburg with *Family Sayings* and Tommaso Landolfi with *Rien va*; far behind were Renzo Rosso with *The Hard Thorn*, Beppe Fenoglio with his posthumous *A Day of Fire*, and Giorgio Saviane with *The Finger in the Candle Flame*.

On the trio of lead candidates, the *Stampa* news team noted:

> The prize has brought to the final writers entirely unlike the 'newsflash' literati (that is what they are called for the vice or at least the weakness they are said to demonstrate turning up again and again in the pages of glossy magazines and filling the gossip columns) to the extent of making us think that a fashion for the shy, bad-tempered, isolated writer is being born [...] Primo Levi, who is a chemist, has never even made writing his profession, nor defined himself as a writer.[2]

He was too kind-natured to ever be seriously called 'bad-tempered'; but the adjectives shy, isolated, reserved, modest and solitary accompanied every piece of writing he had anything to do with from then on.

The qualities of the man and the uniqueness of the writer help to clear up, at least in part, a small mystery. *If This is a Man*, a great book destined for a strange fate, was born twice in ten years: first, almost in secret, in 1947, then successfully in 1958. It had already been translated into English (published both in Britain and in North America, where it was retitled *Survival in Auschwitz*), French, German and Finnish, and had been greeted with universal acclaim by international critics, by the time *The Truce* was published in Italy. But no journalist had been curious enough to get to know better this survivor who had written a masterpiece of European concentration camp literature and who then, as though his need to write had been satisfied, returned to his day job in chemistry and disappeared from the literary horizon. Nor did it ever happen, even later, that he was interviewed about that book, which unlike his others was never awarded a prize – another strange part of its fate. Yet to make up for this everyone was talking to him about it, and for decades he was constantly asked about the history, motivation and circumstances behind it. It fell to Levi himself to point this out, sometimes with a a hint of frustration, almost of mild annoyance. In one of his last interviews, in March 1986, he told the journalist Gianni Milani:

> With *If This is a Man*, I have an almost competitive relationship, because it is a book that still holds out well after so many years. And while in one way that makes me happy, it is also a challenge. In fact, I often ask myself whether I will ever be able to write a book like that again.[3]

But with the incongruous appearance of a disoriented Turin chemist in the worldly pomp of Rome's Villa Giulia palace, on that sweltering night when he failed to walk away with first prize, the interest in him revived. The 'real discovery', the 'big story' of the 17th Strega Prize, people kept repeating, was the lively critical interest in *The Truce*, with dozens of positive reviews, and enhanced sales figures. It was a book people liked, which left them both moved and entertained, and translations were being prepared.

At the start of August, the correspondent Pier Maria Paoletti met the author in Turin. 'Short, slender, much thinner than you might think, seeing him as he appears on the book cover, with his Allied army jumper and his partisan's expression' was how Paoletti described him to readers of the newspaper *Il Giorno*.[4] From the short sleeves of his summer shirt 'emerge two nervous, shiny little arms. On his wrist is an old-fashioned quadrant watch and a bit higher up his bronze skin is marked by the barely faded deep blue of a registration number – 174517, a number which burnt through his youth and marked his destiny as a writer.' And which today is engraved on his tomb, under the shade of two red maple trees.

Conversation with the man whose moral uprightness has mellowed 'into a mild, modest expression' proves 'calm, amiable, consisting wholly of facts, people, things, told without bitter personal grudges, so that they are not filtered by the irony which he often, with obvious enjoyment, uses to make grotesque caricatures [...] out of the human monsters or rather, as he puts it, the zoological specimens he has met in his appalling past'. And naturally the interview begins with *The Truce*:

> I didn't suffer, you know, over the Strega Prize. If I won, I was happy, if I didn't win, I was happy all the same. I had to be: I'd said what I needed to say. Still, it was my first entry into the world of literature in flesh and blood. But I realized that I was a foreign body. Why did I write it? *The Truce* is the story of tales I've been telling for years, again and again, to the few friends I have here in Turin, old school friends, over coffee in a bar, at my house, on walks along the banks of the Po, and they always asked me why I didn't publish them. Until the day came when the equation between free time, the will to act and pressure from others was perfect. Two hundred hours *The Truce* cost me, a chapter a month. If you consider that I can only write in the evening after finishing work at the company and that I need a good hour to change my skin, let's say that the book was born over three hundred, four hundred days, in other words in a year.
>
> *After the unexpected success of* The Truce *and the reprinting of* If This is a Man *how do you see yourself? As a writer who is also a chemist or as a chemist who has written two books?*
>
> Ah, as a chemist, let's be very clear about that and have no misunderstandings. And the two books I wrote, I wrote by chance.

At the time, he is technical director in a paint and varnish factory. His real job is one he feels passionate about, he lives and fights in the laboratory.

> He tells me that one client might ask for a particular resin which is in line with certain mechanical, technical or electrical requirements. Another might ask for a paint, let's say for the radiators of ocean liners, which will be able to resist salt attack at a certain temperature for a certain number of years, and he has to study that. Then, in the evening, he goes back, in his old Lancia Appia, to the big Art Nouveau house on Corso Umberto where he has lived since his childhood, to his cool, tidy study, with his favourite books all neatly arranged. His favourites are a great many, but what dominates are works of paradoxical, rebellious fantasy: Villon, Rabelais, Swift, Conrad. [...]Then, as he reiterates, he changes his skin and he becomes a writer.

Levi tells Paoletti:

> Look, maybe now I find writing more enjoyable than being a chemist, although another aspiration, one to cultivate in secret, would be to find a meeting point between the two, if I may put it that way: I mean to tell the public the meaning of scientific research, with a

> fictionalized, but not too fictionalized, account of what happens behind the closed doors of a laboratory. Which really means revealing man's oldest, most mysterious emotions, in the hour of uncertainty when he doesn't know whether he will kill the buffalo or not, whether he will find what he is looking for or fail to find it. There is a whole narrative tradition, you see, which tells us about the lives of miners, or doctors, or prostitutes, but almost nothing on the spiritual exploits of a chemist.

The plan, the purpose and the outline for *The Periodic Table* have already taken shape in the secret world of the author's mind. Between the first publication of *If This is a Man* and *The Truce* Levi's writing has moved in an unexpected direction: towards science fiction stories, the most disturbing of which have been published in *Il Giorno*.

> *Will you write more of these stories? Will you put them together in a book?*
>
> In science fiction, there are a great many themes which I enjoy and find exciting. I see science fiction stories as moral tales in disguise. I scribble down a fair few of them in the time I have available, or rather the time I *make* available, with great effort, as much as the work of a factory manager allows. I wouldn't mind making a book out of them at all: in a few years' time, of course. Now, with *The Truce*, it would make for a very confusing pair.
>
> *Have you completely finished telling the story of your experience in the Lager?*
>
> Oh yes, not one more word. Nothing. Everything I wanted to say, I've said.

But he hasn't. With time, many fragments will re-emerge from memory and be turned into new Lager stories. Most of all he will manage, in his last book *The Drowned and the Saved*, to sound out the aspects of the phenomenon which had remained in darkness, which the Auschwitz prisoner, dominated 'by a huge edifice of violence and menace', could not recognize or understand 'because his eyes were glued to the ground by the needs of every minute'.[5] That will take more than twenty years; for now, he is convinced that he has nothing else to say. But the characters remain and the questions remain: why all this happened 'is a mystery', Levi says, 'which up until now no revelation has shed light on'. He confides in the journalist that he has made and continues to make attempts to diminish this mystery. For example, Doktor Pannwitz from Commando 98, who subjected him to the surreal chemistry exam in *If This is a Man*: 'He looked for him for years after the war, persistently, meticulously, untiringly, all across Europe: not out of a desire for revenge but rather to resume the interrupted dialogue, to understand what he was made of, what human or inhuman processes were at work in the intimacy of his mind. Then finally he discovered that Pannwitz was dead.'

Together with the tragic or unsympathetic characters of *If This is a Man*, the 'human, eccentric, mad, picaresque figures' of *The Truce* have stayed inside him too. He recalls some of them with affectionate tact. He speaks of Cesare, of whom he wrote in the book: 'a child of the sun, a friend of the whole world. He didn't know hatred or scorn, he was as varying as the sky, joyful, sly, and ingenuous, reckless and cautious, very ignorant, very innocent, and very civilized.'[6] Now he says:

> He isn't really called Cesare, but don't write his real name please: he lives in Rome and he has a position of grave moral and financial responsibility. My book could damage him. Just think that once he wrote me a letter saying that Romans are too intelligent and that it is difficult to work in Rome: you know, to work as he understands it. He said he wanted to move to the north and for me to look for a wife for him. After *The Truce,* he hasn't written to me again. Maybe he didn't understand, maybe he was offended. But don't write his name, I beg you; I wouldn't want to cause him problems.

As for his Greek 'of …tall stature' and 'red of hair and skin', wise and despotic, cunning and bad-tempered, he says:

> He lives in Thessaloniki and naturally he isn't called Mordo Nahum, but don't put that down please, maybe now he has a respectable profession.

He would happily go to look for him, but he is afraid he would not recognize him, that he would find him faded, 'that he might have acquired all the residues of civilian life'.

On the night of 3 September 1963 on the Venetian island of San Giorgio Maggiore, fully lit up for the occasion, Primo Levi, barely turned 44, won the first Campiello prize with *The Truce*. The decision was agreed by the 'Great Jury' (246 signed and sealed ballot papers from readers secretly selected across the whole of Italy) together with the 'Little Jury' made up of nine writers including Bonaventura Tecchi, Giovanni Comiso and Michele Prisco. From the stern, bureaucratic office where the counting took place there was a leak: that the nine had voted unanimously for the writer from Turin, who had known for months that he was expected to win the prize which took most account of the views of ordinary readers, and who had met the knowledge with a kind of dismay. Levi was afraid, he told an interviewer for *Il Giorno*, of somehow offending the Belloncis, the founders of the Strega Prize, that 'they who had been so kind' would take it as an insult. He hastened to say:

> I've had nothing to do with it, you know, I really haven't. It all happened without my wanting it, without my even knowing about it.

He gave few reactions to this first official recognition, apart from the few words in his acceptance speech. Prizes, in any case, never excited him very much. But now, whether he liked it or not, and despite his continuing to define himself as a 'foreign body', he was part of the literary world. The writing germ had entered his blood with the second publication of *If This is a Man* (this time with Einaudi), when he burst onto the literary scene with a bang after an 'apparent death' of ten years.

> After this 'rebirth' I felt – how can I put it – promoted. Like a chemist who has, along with his laboratory, an extra instrument, flexible, precise and well-adjusted. It seemed appropriate to bring over into my new job the method of my old one: to weigh, separate and unite.[7]

Journalists, who can be good hunting dogs, have got his scent. Alfredo Todisco makes a stop in Turin to add Primo Levi to his *Viaggio nell'Italia delle Lettere* [Journey in Literary Italy], a survey of Italian writers he is publishing for *Corriere della Sera* and which has got to its fifth episode. He sketches this profile:

> A chemist by profession, he works in a varnish factory. If I'm not mistaken, this is the second case in our literature of someone in the paint industry grappling with a pen in his leisure hours: the other was Italo Svevo. The man I've been speaking to lives eight hours a day in an authentic research laboratory, in between test tubes, Bunsen burners, centrifugal extractors, acetic acid vapours [...] He's small, shy, a quivering flame. The experience of the concentration camp has marked his face with a sadness, a cosmic gloom that no moral cleansing will ever be able to remove[...] He has nothing 'technical' about him, nor any of the rhetoric that raises ex-homines fabri to the level of present-day heroes. But he's equally far removed from the behaviour of the writer and the man of letters and the often very fussy behaviour of the career intellectual. As was the case with Fenoglio [...] he belongs to the Piedmontese branch of the writers *du dimanche*[8] [...] In a hundred years historians who want to examine our age are likely to learn more from the testimonies of the outsider Primo Levi, written in a traditional form, than from the ultramodern texts of many literary innovators, which will appear even more

> pointlessly indecipherable than they already are. Levi wrote his extremely important books because he had something urgent to say, without devising any defensive theory on writing style, without setting up in advance a series of 'stylistic features' and 'syntagmas'. The only principles he believes in as a writer are clarity, truth and responsibility for every word he consigns to paper, and these are all sides of the same coin. Born of a need to be told, the books of this intelligent chemist have found a sincere language in which the facts and the characters of the hell of the concentration camps will not easily fade away.

Levi accounted for *If This is a Man* at every meeting, even chance meeting, with the public, students or television, prompted by their questions on his appalling experience. *The Truce* he talked less about, and only once at length, on 6 September 1986, during one of the most important interviews of the many that took place in the house where he spent all his life and where, just seven months after the meeting, he would decide to die.The writer Philip Roth had come specially from America to speak to him, willingly agreeing with one of the most authoritative and influential of his country's literary magazines, to probe the mind and literary toolbox of the man he admired and the colleague he valued most. Roth says:

> *Your sequel to* If This Is a Man *(*The Reawakening *as it was unfortunately retitled by one of your early American publishers) was called in Italian* La Tregua, *the truce. It's about your journey from Auschwitz back to Italy. There is a real mythological dimension to that tortuous journey, especially in the story of your long gestation period in the Soviet Union, waiting to be repatriated. What's surprising about* La Tregua, *which might understandably have been marked by a mood of mourning and inconsolable despair, is its exuberance. Your reconciliation with life takes place in a world that sometimes seemed to you like the primeval chaos. Yet you are so tremendously engaged by everyone, so highly entertained as well as instructed, that I wondered if, despite the hunger and the cold and the fears, even despite the memories, you've ever really had a better time than during those months that you call 'a parenthesis of unlimited availability, a providential but unrepeatable gift of fate'.*
>
> *You appear to be someone whose most vital need is, above all, for rootedness – in his profession, his ancestry, his region, his language – and yet when you found yourself as alone and uprooted as a man can be, you considered that condition a gift.*

A statement, more than a question. Primo Levi agrees, but now that he can look at his book from a distance he expands on it:

> A friend of mine, an excellent doctor (he was a brother of Natalia Ginzburg: do you know her books? She's a Levi too, but not a relative of mine), told me many years ago, 'Your remembrances of before and after are in black and white; those of Auschwitz and of your travel home are in technicolor.' He was right. Family, home, factory are good things in themselves, but they deprived me of something that I still miss: adventure. Destiny decided that I should find adventure in the awful chaos of a Europe swept by war.
>
> You're in the business, so you know how these things happen. *The Truce* was written 14 years after *If This Is a Man*: it is a more 'self-conscious' book, more methodical, more literary, the language much more profoundly elaborated. It tells the truth, but a filtered truth. There were already many oral versions of these stories, by which I mean that I had recounted each adventure many times before, to people of many different cultural levels (to friends mainly and to high school boys and girls), and I had retouched it en route so as to arouse their most favourable reactions. When *If This Is* a Man began to achieve some success, and I began to see a future for my writing, I set out to put these adventures on paper. I aimed at having fun in writing and at amusing my prospective readers. Consequently, I emphasized strange, exotic, cheerful episodes – mainly with Russians seen close up – and I relegated to the first and last pages the mood, as you put it, 'of mourning and inconsolable despair'.
>
> As for 'rootedness', it is true that I have deep roots, and that I had the luck not to lose them. My family was almost completely spared by the Nazi slaughter, and today I continue to live in the very flat where I was born. The desk where I write occupies, according to family legend, exactly the spot where I first saw light. When I found myself 'as uprooted as a man could be' certainly I suffered, but this was far more than outweighed afterwards by the fascination of adventure, by human encounters, by the sweetness of 'convalescence' from the plague of Auschwitz. In its historical reality, my Russian 'truce' turned into a gift only many years later, when I purified it by rethinking and writing about it.[9]

It does not happen often, but when it does it is always a happy coincidence for an author's own analysis of his work to coincide with the interpretation by another writer, and a friend and companion at that. Italo Calvino, one of the most enthusiastic of *The Truce's* first readers, wrote on the jacket flap a judgement that coincided with the one Levi expressed in the Roth interview:

> The entire span of the book takes place under these two signs: the persistence, in a hundred open and secret ways, of the 'pestilence that

> had flattened Europe to the ground'; and the discovery of a new Russia, seen at first hand and from the inside, by turns smiling or tragic, picaresque or epic or Oblomovian, far from any ideological framework and much closer to the famous accounts of Pushkin, Gogol and Tolstoy. But in this 'lively and colourful story of a no longer hoped-for springtime of freedom', the most heart-rending note is that of 'a stab of anguish from a sorrow that can no longer be cured'.

The writing of *The Truce* took place over 1961 and part of 1962. About this period, just as his interview with Philip Roth was being published in the US and then in two episodes in *La Stampa*, the author was heard to observe:

> They were the years of Krushchev, Kennedy and Pope John XXIII, of the first thaw and of great hopes. In Italy for the first time one could talk objectively about the Soviet Union, without being accused of communist sympathies by the right and of reactionism by the powerful Italian Communist Party.

That is, it was the right time, in his opinion, to put to the test the flexible, precise and well-adjusted instrument (which on other occasions he called fine and sensitive, pleasant and sweet-sounding) which he found in his hands. And to use it to tell the story of his long return from imprisonment across 'the land, so rich in humanity, of Poland and the Soviet territories during the spring of liberation and the great summer of 1945'.[10] The book was still hot off the press when he explained to his friend Paolo Spriano from *L'Unità*:

> It was a summer of 'truce' for all humanity, as it emerged from a terrible massacre and prepared to enter the hard environment of post-war reconstruction, a summer in which human beings, together with nature, were becoming protagonists of a mythical period that could never be repeated.

And recalling the genesis of his book, he also said, during the discussion following one of his lectures in Switzerland in November 1976:

> Nobody had ever written about what the Soviet Union was like then. It was a no-man's-land, trampled on, destroyed, tortured, devastated, massacred in its villages and communities, but exceptionally rich and fertile, abuzz with activity like the earth after the flood. For many years after the war nobody could go there; nobody was allowed to look around and understand. I had the experience of seeing from the inside this vast country drunk with victory, despite the 20 million dead behind it. I wanted to try to give shape to this extraordinary experience of mine.[11]

The Truce is certainly a book on 'a rising note', as the author often loved to repeat. But its exorcism was not enough for him, the shadows of his past continued to assault him. They came with that 'dream full of horror which does not cease to visit the survivor: a dream within a dream, in which resounds the dawn command of Auschwitz, a foreign word, feared and expected: get up, Wstawàc'. And around him, in the world, there were new danger signs. Therefore, when he received a letter from Radio Canada around the middle of 1963, informing him that they had made a radio version of *If This is a Man*, and when not long afterwards he received the script and the tape recording, he greeted the idea it gave him with joy. 'Maybe', he wrote,

> I had never received a more welcome gift; not only was it an excellent piece of work but for me it was a genuine revelation. The scriptwriters, who were distant in time and space and who didn't share my experience, had taken from the book what I had enclosed in it, and also something more: a spoken 'meditation' at a high technical and dramatic level and at the same time scrupulously faithful to the reality as it was. They had understood very well the importance in the camp of the absence of communication, intensified by the absence of a common language; and on that theme, the theme of the Tower of Babel, of the confusion of languages, they had courageously built their work. The thesis, the finished product and the radio medium itself, which was new to me, excited me. A few months later I submitted to the RAI an adaptation of the book which, while not retranslating the Canadian version, developed the episodes that seemed to me most suitable and maintained, as far as possible, that technique of multilingual dialogue that struck me as essential.[12]

The RAI immediately accepts the offer from the author who has already written the screenplay; it assigns the production to its Turin studios with Giorgio Bandini as director, moves quickly (we are at the start of 1964) and decides to transmit the work on RAI Radio 3 on the evening of 24 April, for the anniversary of Italian Liberation the next day. Mirella Appiotti of *La Stampa* surprises Primo Levi at Brozolo, in the hills around Turin, where he regularly attends the recording of the outdoor scenes, and finds him prepared to accept, without reluctance, the role his books have fixed him in.

> It would be impossible now to separate me from the character of the 'veteran', the Auschwitz survivor, but that doesn't bother me. Unlike many friends who have lived through the same offence, I am the 'veteran who talks'. At first I needed to do it to break free a little and find a new equilibrium, then later I considered it a kind of duty to tell of the mad things we witnessed. That's why I wrote my books.[13]

And that is why, now, he takes on the new challenge:

> There were two main difficulties in the 'dramatic' adaptation of *If This is a Man*: making 'dramatic' what was a long monologue, made up in large part of a soliloquy; and recreating that atmosphere, or at least trying to.

Thanks to the collaboration of a group of foreigners living in Turin (among others a Polish industrialist who speaks fluent Yiddish and four Germans who play the parts of the SS), they have managed to reconstruct with a certain realism the dissonant voices of the camps. 'But is it really true that the Germans cast in the thankless role of the SS are looked at with suspicion by everyone working on the play?'

> It's true, I can't escape the effect myself. I hope they'll forgive me, but they're unsympathetic to me through no fault of their own. They prompt memories and reactions that I can't control.
>
> *Do you find Germans in general unsympathetic?*
>
> In general, no. Still, when I go to Germany (and I often do because of my work) it is difficult for me to establish a cordial relationship with them. When they hear that I'm an Auschwitz survivor, the elderly go on the defensive. The young don't know much about what happened. Those who do know condemn it, in general, and they write to me. What can I say to young Germans? I try to enlighten them but all the same it's difficult for me to speak to them. Can I tell them that the Germans are, or were until recently, a people possessed by the devil?

For three years now he has been collecting in a folder the letters addressed from Germany to 'Herr Doktor Primo Levi'. There are more than 30 of them, but they have not been enough to appease his anxiety about 'understanding the Germans'. It is an anxiety that has dominated him since the time of the Lager and that he hoped to be able to appease after *If This is a Man*, in the excellent translation of Heinz Riedt, an Italianist and expert on Goldoni ('as much an enemy of the Nazis as I'), had started to be distributed in Germany, when he thought that finally:

> [...] the time had come to settle accounts, to put my cards on the table. Above all, the time had come to talk [. . .] My task was to understand them. Not the handful of great perpetrators, but them, the people, the ones I had seen up close, the ones from whose ranks the SS soldiers had been recruited, and also those others, those who had believed, who didn't believe but had kept quiet about it, who hadn't mustered

> the feeble courage to look us in the eyes, to throw us a piece of bread, to whisper a kind word.[14]

He hadn't wanted to write a Preface to the German edition of the book so as not to distort the nature of the testimony. Instead he suggested to the publisher Samuel Fischer that he put at the start of the text an extract from the letter of 13 May 1960 that he had written to the translator thanking him for the collaboration. In this extract his wish took a definite shape:

> I have never harboured any hatred for the German people [...] I cannot understand, I cannot bear to see a man judged not for who he is but for the group he happens to belong to [...]
>
> But I cannot say that I understand the Germans. Now, something that one does not understand becomes a sore point, a sharp pain, a permanent itch that demands to be scratched. I hope that this book will have some kind of echo in Germany, not only out of ambition but also because the nature of this echo will perhaps allow me to understand the Germans better and to calm this itch.[15]

His German correspondents, all but one of whom were young, showed that they had read *If This is a Man* carefully, the Preface included, and they tried to reply as they were able (or willing) to the author's urgent request. But the mystery remained unsolved. Primo Levi referred to it with regret in his last book, quoting passages from some of the most important of these letters. Even Mrs Hety S, the only German reader 'with clean credentials'(from Wiesbaden, an employee of the Hesse Ministry of Culture, she had been expelled from school for her opposition to Nazism, and her father had been sent to Dachau) who kept up a long correspondence with him, had her own way of disillusioning him, in the first of around 50 letters which she sent to him over 16 years: 'You will certainly never succeed in understanding the Germans, not even we Germans can. So much happened in those years that should never have happened at any price.'[16]

But in the spring of 1964 Primo Levi has still not entered into contact with Hety S. He tries eagerly to 'understand the Germans' through the words of those who write to him after reading his book. And he tries, precisely, to enlighten them. He will summarize the contents of the replies he received from Germany in an interview in 1986 with the writer Ferdinando Camon:

> They all go out of their way to say that they themselves, as young Germans, don't understand themselves, still less understand their parents, because there's an insurmountable wall between them. Still others speak of [...] the devil. I've kept these letters and now I'm going over them for a chapter in this book, *The Drowned and the Saved*. Only

> one of all those who wrote to me wasn't young. A curious letter. He doesn't give his age, but you can see he's not young from what he writes. This one defends the Nazis. He's the only one. He says he's not a Nazi, but declares, 'We had the choice between two abysses, one was Communism, the other was Hitler; we'd seen the revolution of 1919 in Germany, the Spartacist revolution, and we chose to defend ourselves. But we were betrayed. We're not a people of betrayers, we're a betrayed people; because Hitler promised things he didn't do and didn't promise the things he did.' Then this German goes on to tell me that it's not the first time there've been massacres in the world, and he maliciously mentions a massacre I didn't know about: the massacre of the Goths by the Byzantines under Belisarius. As if to say, you Mediterraneans have also done something against us. Then he concludes: 'Let's let bygones be bygones, I've fallen in love with Italy and Italian literature, and I have Dante, Petrarch and Boccaccio in my library.' It's a two-page letter. I answered him that in my library I have Hitler's *Mein Kampf*, where Hitler promised exactly to do what he did do, so didn't betray anyone; if you can say one thing for him it's precisely that he wasn't a betrayer. Enclosed with this man's letter, his wife had written a short letter of three lines. She says: 'When the devil is loose in the village, a few people try to resist and are overcome, many bow their heads and the majority follow him with enthusiasm.' The wife had slipped this note in the envelope without telling her husband.[17]

To the excuse that the wife of 'this non-fanatical but opportunistic' Nazi had devised, Levi replied harshly 'that no church offers indulgences to the devil's disciples or accepts as an excuse blaming the devil for one's sins. That a person has to answer for his sins and errors, otherwise every trace of civilization would disappear from the face of the Earth, as in fact it did disappear during the Third Reich.'[18]

This is a fundamental principle that he will never stop insisting upon, in public as well, that everyone is individually responsible for their actions. At the end of 1976, he replied to an audience member in Zurich who was questioning him on the extermination of the Jews and trying to find extenuating circumstances for the perpetrators by putting all the blame on the highest officers of the state:

> It's terrifying to watch Hitler's rallying of the crowds and to see the spectacle of a monolithic, possessed Germany, where every opposition is snuffed out, where violence begets violence in a chain reaction. But to delegate all responsibility for what happened to a single man and consequently to cancel all individual responsibility is madness. The guilty existed, from high to low and from low to high, even if on high

there was a Hitler, a tyrant capable of brainwashing, raping, molesting, bestializing a mass, a crowd, ultimately a people.

Ten years later he developed these thoughts in his interview with Ferdinando Camon, while dissenting from Camon's interpretation of a particular aspect of *The Drowned and the Saved*. Camon had read in it 'a continual probing of the irruption of the demonic in history, of the absence of "god" and of the possibility of a true justice'.[19] He read in it, as in Levi's other books, an invitation to probe 'not just one moment in the history of the Germans, but a long governing principle, running through the mythology of the Germans since the time of the Teutons, their conversion, their Lutheranism, their sense of salvation and perdition'. It is here that Levi interrupts him:

> If you don't mind, I disagree with that interpretation. The Germans of Goethe's time weren't like that.
>
> *Still, in the moments when their great moral and religious movements restart , they always draw on a reservoir of perdition, of damnation, of...*
>
> Of the demonic?
>
> *Of the demonic, which implicates and cancels divinity itself.*
>
> Yes, the devil is a fundamental presence in their upbringing.

The Catholic writer persists:

> *...so that there's not a glimmer of good and the demand for their salvation can't avoid a hatred directed at God, which is found even in Luther [...] The kind of pedagogical operation that you perform with your narrative, for example in* If This Is a Man, *consists in leading the reader by the hand to experience a certain reaction, to pronounce a certain condemnation. Without saying it yourself. For your part, you use the technique of suspending not only condemnation but judgement as well.*
>
> It's true that I abstained from formulating judgements in *If This Is a Man*. I did so deliberately, because it seemed to me inopportune, indeed importunate, on the part of the witness, that is myself, to assume the position of the judge. So I suspended any explicit judgement, whereas the implicit judgements clearly are there. But I sincerely don't think that I share this judgement of yours about the Germans [...] I absolutely don't feel the equivalent of the anti-Jewish aversion of the German created by Hitler.

Camon is surprised by this neutrality. But Primo Levi will not be budged. He says:

> It's odd that here I am defending the Germans and yet it falls to me to do so. I don't think that even in Hitler's Germany there was widespread anti-Semitism at first. The weight of Hitler's personality was the determining factor in everything, even in this. I don't much believe in Tolstoy's thesis of history emerging from below, from the tide on which the Napoleons bob like corks. Because experience has shown me the opposite: I had a distinct impression, witnessing the rise of Nazism in Germany and experiencing it at first-hand, or reading about it later; the impression of a curse, of something demonic – you spoke of it a moment ago, of the devil as a constant in German culture – being embodied in Hitler.

'That's a heroic conception of history', Camon objects, 'history is made by the few, the heroes whose will shakes the world like a wind, and all the people can do is cower'.

> Yes, I'm well aware that many don't share this conception, but it seems to me that, at least in cases like this, one must realize that the personal power of people like Hitler and Stalin (and not like Mussolini) have weighed heavily. Because there's a qualitative leap between Germany before Hitler and Hitler's Germany. Anyone who's seen films at the cinema or on TV of Hitler's speeches to the crowds has witnessed an appalling spectacle. A mutual induction was formed, as between a cloud charged with electricity and the earth. It was an exchange of lightning bolts. Hitler responded to the reaction that he himself provoked. And he exulted in it. I think, if such an observation can make sense, that if another man had been in his place, things would have gone differently.[20]

****

The success of the radio experiment with *If This is a Man* has stimulated him. But he doesn't wish to remain anchored to his memories. He wants to set sail, to find a different means of communicating with people, and he has already started to do so with stories suspended between satire and irony, fable and metaphor. Some have found a place in newspapers, and he is adapting others for the radio. Other stories, and a few essays, most of them written after careful rereading, are piling up on his desk. At the end of 1965, together with Massimo Scaglione and his 'Teatro delle Dieci' [Theatre of the Ten] company, he plans to stage three one-act plays, three of the *Natural Histories*, as he calls them, which the RAI commissioned from him after the success of *If This is a Man*: first *Sleeping Beauty in the Refrigerator* and *The*

Versifier, which the RAI recorded in September and October, and then *The Sixth Day*, which he had planned as far back as 1947 and written ten years later. To the half incredulous, half scandalized question of *Unità* journalist Edoardo Fadini 'From the author of *If This is a Man* and *The Truce*, two high expressions of the tragic experiences of war and the concentration camps, who expected science fiction?' he replies calmly:

> No, they're not science fiction stories, if by science fiction one means futurism, cheap futuristic fantasy. These stories are more possible than many others. So possible in fact that some of them have even taken place. For example, that of 'The Versifier': a commercial poet purchases a verse-writing machine, to serve his client base better; the machine then turns out to be the author of the very play we're watching. The attempts, some of them major attempts, already made in that direction are well known. Yes, these are stories that occur on the margins of natural history, which is why I gave them that title. But they are also unnatural, if they are looked at in a certain way. And the two meanings obviously cross over.[21]

The second question, whether there is a link between the concentration camp survivor and these stories of poetry machines, women in states of hibernation and bureaucratic creators, leads him to have recourse to an image he holds dear. He will always be fascinated to see his reflection in the mysterious ambivalence of the centaur:

> I am an amphibian, a centaur – I have even written stories about centaurs – and it seems to me that the ambiguity of science fiction mirrors my current fate. I am divided in two halves. One is the factory half: I am a chemist, a technician. The other is completely detached from the first, and is the half I write in, reply to interviews in, work on my past and present experiences in. They really are two half brains. It's a paranoid split (similar, I think, to that of Gadda, of Sinisgalli, of Solmi).[22] And the two parts of myself are so separate, that the first part, the factory part, my pen and my imagination cannot work on. I have tried to make stories out of my life in the factory. They're my worst. No, I will never manage it. It's the other world that comes out in my books. The world that includes my teenage experiences, racial discrimination, my attempts not to differentiate myself from my schoolmates, then my rediscovery of Jewish tradition (and Judaism is opposed to fascism, as freedom is to terror, because I also discovered that many of the principles of freedom are part of the purest Jewish tradition). Then there is the partisan war and finally the Lager, and having written about this monstrous distortion of the human. All this belongs to my first books and the renown they've given me and the

> new people I've met and new dimensions I've gained as a person. But all this happened 'outside' my day-to-day existence. In this situation, it seems natural to me that one should write science fiction. These *Natural Histories* are also propositions of science and technology as seen by the other half of the self in which I find myself living.

These words suggest the content of his future books, from the one that is already almost ready to those maturing in his unconscious, from the *Periodic Table* to his last, in which he will let the harshest truths about 'the monstrous distortions of the human' emerge from the depths.

The three stories adapted for radio, together with another twelve 'entertainments' collected under the title *Natural Histories*, constitute Primo Levi's third book, which Einaudi published in 1966 under the pseudonym Damiano Malabaila. This is the second small mystery in the writer's life, but the jacket flap is illuminating. It consists of an extract from a letter to his friend the publisher, in which he explains that he has written twenty stories 'for the most part in one go' and that he doesn't know whether he will write any more, 'trying to give narrative form to a pointed insight [...] that is not rare today: the perception of a flaw in the world in which we live, of a large or small crack, of a "formal defect" that thwarts one or another aspect of our civilization or moral universe'. He adds that he feels, in the act of writing these tales, 'a vague sense of guilt, like someone who is consciously committing a small transgression'. And to explain this he formulates two hypotheses. The first is that one who is aware of a 'defect' should not free himself from it by writing a story. The second is that when one has entered ('unexpectedly', he clarifies) the world of writing with two books about the concentration camps, serious books dedicated to a serious audience, 'isn't it a commercial fraud' to offer this audience a series of joke-stories, of 'moral traps'? Anticipating criticisms of this kind – and inevitably there were some – he says of his *Natural Histories:*

> I wouldn't have published them if I hadn't realized (not straightaway to tell the truth) that between these stories and the concentration camp a bridge, a continuity exists: the camp, for me, has been the biggest of the 'defects', of the distortions I spoke of earlier, the most threatening of the monsters produced by the sleep of reason.

Il Giorno, in which some of the stories now collected have appeared under the author's real name, allows Levi to explain more fully by asking him three questions:

> *Why did you want to hide behind a pseudonym?*
>
> 'I may have erred', replied Renzo to Don Abbondio:[23] it may have been a mistake, we'll soon see. In short, I felt a slight sense of embarrassment,

maybe also of reserve towards a certain part of the readership of my two previous books: those who perhaps were affected personally and in their families by the tragedy of the concentration camps, who read my stories in *Il Giorno* and then said to me 'How can you, coming from Auschwitz, write about these things?' It's an opinion I don't share (otherwise I wouldn't have written the *Natural Histories*, or at least I wouldn't have published them) but which I do respect. So, to mark a gap, a differentiation from the author of *If This is a Man*, I accepted the publisher's suggestion of using a pseudonym. From my own point of view I don't feel any contradiction between the two themes and I honestly don't believe I've betrayed anything or anyone; I believe on the contrary that it's not difficult to find, in any of the stories, the marks of the concentration camp, the acceptance of evil, the 'preposterous' cosmos, the geometric madness: for example, in 'Versamine' and 'Angelic Butterfly', which not coincidentally came to me as set in Germany.

What are the reasons that led you to choose a name like Damiano Malabaila?

I thought I had chosen at random: it's the name of a shopkeeper whose store I pass twice a day on the way to work. Then I realized that between the name and the memories a relationship exists, an allusion grasped and understood by one of those deep layers of the subconscious that are now the subject of so much discussion. Malabaila means 'bad wet-nurse':[24] now it seems to me that from many of my stories there wafts a vague odour of spoiled milk, of nourishment that is no longer nourishment, in fact of adulteration, contamination and black magic. Poison in place of food – and on that note, I would like to recall that for all of us survivors the concentration camp, in its most offensive and unforeseen aspect, appeared to us as just that, a world turned upside down, where 'Fair is foul and foul is fair', where teachers work with a spade, murderers are the team leaders and, in the hospital, there's killing.

Are you preparing any new stories, any new books?

Nothing for now. But I'm tempted by an amazing story, the true story of another return, of another salvation across the whole of wartime Europe. It was told to me, and it is so full of adventure and necessity, of tragedy and surprise, that it would be a shame if it remained unwritten. But it requires calm, inspiration and lots and lots of time.

This is the announcement of *If Not Now, When?*, his first and only real novel, to which he will dedicate himself, joyously and in a pioneering spirit, in 1981.

The 'marvellous story', which he diligently noted down after a meeting with his friend Emilio Vita Finzi, is for the moment compressed into ten lines (with abbreviations, as was his usual practice) of a memo pad left to go yellow in the dark intimacy of a drawer.

A month later, the most widely read Italian weekly, *Famiglia Cristiana*, publishes a major report on Primo Levi's complete works, edited by Gabriella D'Angeli[25] and illustrated with beautiful photographs, one on each page, taken during a recent conference of ex-deportees at which Levi was guest of honour together with Father Roberto Angeli, himself a survivor of the camps and author of *Vangelo nel Lager* [Gospel in the Lager]. The starting point for the article is a curiosity: a young priest has taken for the subject of a sermon one of *If This is a Man's* most powerful figures, Lorenzo, the civilian worker from Fossano who for six months risked his own life bringing the Auschwitz prisoner a piece of bread and what was left of his ration 'because he was good and simple and did not think that one should do good for a reward',[26] and because for him 'a Jew was like any other Christian soul'.

In the interview Primo Levi tells of Auschwitz, which no one should have left alive; he evokes again that desolate, paradoxical, upside-down world where for the victims reduced to suffering and need, there is no why; where a Kapo,[27] identical to all the other Kapos, can – but without hatred and without mockery – wipe his grease-stained hand on the shoulder of Häftling 174517, who graduated *summa cum laude* from the University of Turin. And where, alongside physical extermination, an equally atrocious crime was perpetrated: the dehumanization, the moral death of millions of human beings.

'I'm twenty years old and I'm a hundred' says the survivor, a prisoner of memory, concluding the page on the Lager. Then he talks about factory work and about the stories in *Natural Histories*, those elegant moral traps in some of which man is resigned in the face of the relentless advance of his own catastrophic inventions. He has a wife and two children, a chemistry laboratory and a writing career.

> *Where do you find time for everything?*
>
> Writing also creates free time for me. When I don't feel the need to write, free time doesn't exist, because I've always got something to do. When I feel able to write, time expands: I sleep less, I jot things down anywhere. Except in the car, where I need both hands for driving.
>
> *And why the nom de plume?*
>
> The pseudonym indicates the distance between one group of my works and the other. But in my view there's an intimate link between this last book and my previous work. In both man is enslaved by a

thing, the 'thing' that is Nazism and the 'thing thing', the machine. The sleep of reason always produces monsters. [...]

When you wrote because you 'had to', you defined yourself as an 'occasional writer'. How do you define yourself now after Natural Histories?

Still as an occasional writer, because I am one and I think of myself as such. I don't earn a living out of writing, I wrote the *Histories* for fun.

He returned to the subject of his pseudonym for *Natural Histories* in November 1976 in Bern, after a discussion entitled 'Experiences of a writer'. An audience member had asked him:

Reading the covers of your books of stories I had the impression that you'd experienced a moral crisis in moving from your first tragic theme to a very different one, that you felt the need to excuse yourself to your readers but also to yourself and that for those reasons you chose a pseudonym for Natural Histories. *Is that correct?*

That's true. I felt uncomfortable and I experienced almost a sense of panic at the thought of appearing before my ex-deportee friends in another skin. I felt a bit, how can I put it, like a deserter. Already when I published these so-called science fiction stories in some newspaper, I'd get puzzled and even disheartened letters from them. They wanted me tied, as was right and proper, to the theme of the concentration camp, it seemed to them that I couldn't write about anything else, they said they even felt a touch of anger towards me, they thought (rightly) of my books as belonging to all of us, as if they were their books too. I liked the idea of bringing the stories, those that were already published and those that weren't, together in a volume so they wouldn't be lost, but I realized this could hurt their feelings: it could seem like a betrayal, a desertion, or at the very least a distancing of myself from them. I replied, in person and by letter, to the objections they raised with me. I spoke of the joyful liberation of writing and of the seed of these stories that had matured in the laboratory. Then I published my two books of stories, the first under a pseudonym, the second under my own name. Some people may have liked them, others may have disliked them. I think they have the right to a life of their own. I refuse to be pigeon-holed as a writer of the concentration camps. I've come out of them, I've written about them and perhaps, in fact definitely, I've not finished writing about them, but I think I can also say something valid outside that theme.

The last time Primo Levi mentioned Damiano Malabaila was in October 1982 in a radio interview. He described the pseudonym as a compromise, a way to dodge a problem. He added:

> The result has been that nobody has read this book except when it was republished fifteen years later under my own name. Poor Damiano Malabaila (I later learned that the Malabailas are an aristocratic family from Montferrato, I hope they weren't offended) has had no luck.[28]

With the public, maybe not. But with the critics he did. The jury of the 31st Bagutta Prize, chaired by Riccardo Bacchelli (it also included Eugenio Montale and Dino Bunazzi), meeting in Milan on the evening of 14 January 1967, cast most of its votes for the invented name of Damiano Malabaila who, amidst the curiosity and impatience of those present, outdistanced Sciascia and Palazzeschi. The correspondent from *La Stampa* wrote:

> Right up to the last minute the name of the winner had remained secret. It was revealed to the crowd of guests, journalists, writers, painters and elegant ladies, at the end of a convivial gathering, in the loud voice of Riccardo Bacchelli as he called the writer to his side to present him with the 100,000 lire cheque crowning him 'Writer of the Year'. A confused Primo Levi, stunned by the applause, said a few words for the occasion, and was flooded by a sea of outstretched hands from friends and attendees eager to show him their support.[29]

Notes

1. Carlo Laurenzi, 'Sei scrittori in corsa per un premio letterario' [Six writers in the race for a literary prize], *Corriere della Sera*, 4 July 1963.
2. *La Stampa,*'A Natalia Ginzburg il Premio Strega' [The Strega Prize goes to Natalia Ginzburg], 5 July 1963.
3. Gianni Milani, 'Al chimico va stretta la memoria del Lager' [Lager memory constricts the chemist], *Piemonte Vip*, March 1986, p.1.
4. Pier Maria Paoletti, 'Sono un chimico, scrittore per caso' [I'm a chemist, a writer by chance], *Il Giorno*, 7 August 1963.
5. P. Levi trans M. Moore, *The Drowned and the Saved* in Goldstein, A. (ed.), *Complete Works of Primo Levi* (Liveright: New York, 2015), Vol.III, pp.2,420.
6. A. Goldstein (trans.), *The Truce* in *Complete Works of Primo Levi*, Vol.I, p.278.
7. Gabriella Poli, 'L'alfabeto della chimica' [The alphabet of chemistry], *Tuttolibri (La Stampa),* 6 December 1976.
8. 'Sunday writers'.
9. Philip Roth,' A Man Saved by His Skills', *New York Times Book Review,* 12 October 1986, reproduced in *Shop Talk: A Writer and His Colleagues and Their Work* (New York: Houghton Mifflin Company, 2001) pp.1-17. Parts not present in the English originals retranslated from 'Salvarsi dall'Inferno come Robinson' [Saving oneself from hell like Robinson], *La Stampa*, 26 November 1986 and 'Il mio western degli ebrei ribelli' [My Western about the Jewish Resistance], *La Stampa*, 27 November 1986.

10. Paolo Spriano, 'L'antifascismo al Premio Strega' [Anti-fascism at the Strega Prize], *L'Unità*, 4 July 1963.
11. On his return from Switzerland – where from 8 to 12 November he had given a series of lectures on the topic 'Esperienze di uno scrittore'[Experiences of a writer] on a tour organized by the Dante Alighieri Society and by the Swiss Association for Economic and Cultural Relations with Italy (ASRI) – Primo Levi delivered to *Tuttolibri* a typewritten list of the questions asked by the audience at the University of Zurich and then at St. Gallen, Aarau, Bern and Chur. On request, he dictated to the typists' office a summary of his answers to the main questions. It was our intention to reconstruct from it a 'Helvetic dialogue', but nothing was done about it; in the meantime, other meetings and discussions had taken place in Italy, after which the writer gave an interview to *Tuttolibri*. The statement he made at Chur, reported here, and those quoted afterwards, which relate to Primo Levi's conversations with his Swiss audiences, are taken from the above-mentioned typewritten text.
12. From the author's introductory note to the dramatic version of *Se questo è un uomo* [*If This is a Man*], (Turin: Einaudi, 1966), p.7.
13. Mirella Appiotti, 'Sulla collina torinese risuonano le voci del Lager di Auschwitz' [On the Turin hills the voices of the Auschwitz Lager resound], *Stampa Sera*, 22-23 April 1964.
14. *The Drowned and the Saved*, in *Complete Works of Primo Levi*, pp.2,540.
15. Ibid, pp.2,541.
16. Ibid, pp.2,560.
17. Ferdinando Camon, 'Ma allora Dio non c'è?'[So then there isn't a God?], *Panorama*, 25 May 1986.
18. *The Drowned and the Saved*, in *Complete Works of Primo Levi*, pp.2,549.
19. Camon, 'Ma allora Dio non c'è?'.
20. The conversation from which we reproduce the extract concerning the 'people possessed by the devil' is included in F. Camon, *Autoritratto di Primo Levi* [Self-Portrait of Primo Levi], (Padua: Edizioni Nord Est), published in May 1987, about a month after the writer's death. In the preface Camon alerts the reader to the fact that the text of the dialogue has been checked, and supplemented in many places, by Primo Levi himself. But for the passage used here, the modifications and additions were marginal. There is an English translation by John Shepley: *Conversations with Primo Levi* (Marlboro: Marlboro Press, 1989).
21. Edoardo Faldini, 'Primo Levi si sente scrittore "dimezzato"' [Primo Levi feels like a 'halved' writer], *L'Unità*, 4 January 1966.
22. A joking reference to three other writers with a scientific background.
23. A quote from *I promessi sposi* [*The Betrothed*] by Alessandro Manzoni, the classic novel Levi was much influenced by and cites on numerous occasions in this book.
24. In Piedmontese.
25. Gabriella D'Angeli, 'Il sonno della ragione genera mostri' [The sleep of reason produces monsters], *Famiglia Cristiana*, no. 48, 27 November 1966.
26. S. Woolf (trans.), *If This Is a Man* in *Complete Works of Primo Levi*, Vol. I, p.113.
27. A prisoner in a Nazi concentration camp who was assigned by the SS guards to supervise the slave labourers or to carry out other tasks. Kapos were usually chosen from among criminal prisoners, and most were notorious for their cruelty.
28. From the interview granted to Dina Luce for the programme 'Il suono e la mente' [Sound and Mind] broadcast on RAI Radio 2 on 4 October 1982.
29. *La Stampa*,'Levi sotto falso nome vince il premio Bagutta' [Levi wins the Bagutta Prize under a false name], 15 January 1967.

II

A New Incarnation

On the evening of 19 November 1966 Primo Levi had been regaled with, and perhaps moved by, another round of applause, when the audience of the Carignano theatre in Turin gave a standing ovation for the author of *If This is a Man*. Produced by the Stabile di Torino theatre company, the play was co-directed by Gianfranco De Bosi, Giovanna Bruni and Marta Egri, with Gianni Polidori as stage designer. Levi himself had collaborated with Pieralberto Marché in adapting his first book, of which Norberto Bobbio wrote:

> Before it came out, what the Nazi extermination camps were was already well known. But only after the book were they 'understood' in the full sense of the word, in the sense that to understand means to grasp the essence, the deep meaning, the reason why they were unique, not as *an* event but as *the* monstrous, perhaps unrepeatable, event in human history.[1]

The theatre version had taken two years of intensive work and close collaboration between author, adapter and director, as well as a long preliminary period to translate the book into theatrical language. Forty days had been taken up with rehearsals; 53 actors were involved, including many from the theatre companies of seven nations. The play should have been performed at Prato's Metastasio theatre on 9 November, during the second international festival of the Stabili theatre companies of Florence. But the disastrous flood of a few days before (which flooded the warehouse where the remaining 600 copies of *If This is a Man* in the 1947 De Silva edition were stored) prevented the work from being staged there. To avoid the meticulous preparations going to waste, the organizers decided to perform in another venue, and chose Turin's Carignano theatre.

On the eve of the preview, Primo Levi had wanted to meet journalists, accompanied by Marché and De Bosi. He was anxious that his decision to present his book in this new incarnation, which was neither easy nor painless, should not be misunderstood. The original idea for the adaptation had in truth been put forward by his friend Marché and at first Levi had been opposed to it. Analysing those initial qualms he wrote in the introductory note to the theatrical text:

> It seemed to me that *If This is a Man* had already changed its skin too many times, that I'd already cooked it in too many sauces. I was afraid of tiring the audience. I was also afraid of the theatre itself. The audience that reads, even that which listens to the radio, is far off, hidden, anonymous; but the theatre audience is there, it looks at you, it lies in wait for you, it judges you. But it was a case, once again, of telling; this time in fact of telling in the most immediate way, of making things be relived, of inflicting our experience, ours and that of our vanished companions, on a different and wider audience. Of seeing, of measuring their reaction, of testing it[...]

In short, an irresistible urge for the witness torn between 'the obvious dangers and a certain sense of violated reserve'.[2] He explained to a journalist:

> Above all I had doubts when I was afraid that people would think of this as a kind of personal exhibitionism. For this reason, I also changed the name of the protagonist, who in the play is called Aldo, because I didn't want to emphasize the autobiography but rather the shared tragedy. Indeed the dramatic version of *If This is a Man* is intended not as the story of a single victim, but the voice of a people, of millions of victims. Nor does it seek to represent the suffering of Italians alone, but of all those swept away by the terrible ideology of death. I wanted to make a European play, and the opportunity for international collaboration – to which theatre groups from different countries replied immediately – underlines that commitment.[3]

His doubts receded for another, essential, reason:

> I accepted when I had Marché's central idea clear in my mind. It didn't need to be a horror show. The drama of the concentration camp prisoners wouldn't be represented with an excessive realism. Marché and I have tried to transform it above all into a drama about the lack of communication between the deportees. Anyone arriving in Auschwitz found himself not only in a hostile world but in a world where he couldn't understand anything because there was no common language. When I got there the main languages were Polish and Yiddish. Then there was the surge of Hungarians. But Dutch, French and Russian were also spoken. Even the guards didn't communicate in a single language. Together with the German SS, there were Kapos of all nationalities present in the camp. For the Italians in particular this situation increased their suffering. I remember my anguish at not being able to establish a dialogue, my awareness that they wanted to destroy our humanity by forcing us to remain silent because of the impossibility of communication.[4]

To give authenticity to the desperate trauma of the concentration camp they had undertaken a daring experiment: the actors would speak in their own languages.

> It was a question of realizing on the stage, with the maximum possible authenticity, the anguish of the prisoner who couldn't understand or make himself understood. For me it was a frightening experience then. There are those who perhaps don't need communication, who are able to endure solitude and manage all the same. I on the other hand needed to talk, to find answers that confirmed to me that I hadn't become an object. And that went beyond the immediate problem of grasping orders, when not understanding could cost you your life. It was very difficult to achieve a theatrical balance in the text between what is Italian, and therefore comprehensible, and what is foreign and so for many incomprehensible. We think we have succeeded in reconstructing that Tower of Babel atmosphere that made our lives even more monstrous, without falling into an excessive realism.[5]

The SS do not appear on stage. Their orders come from loudspeakers and their savagery is impersonal, detached and even more appalling precisely for that reason.

> What needs to be understood is obviously said in Italian. The other speeches have the function of pure sound. The audience isn't called to make any interpretative effort, because our aim is to make them understand the absolute isolation of a man in Auschwitz, his invincible anguish.[6]

What is generally judged to make *If This is a Man* inimitable, setting it apart from the hundreds of other concentration camp testimonies, is that the author refrains from describing specific appalling details. His approach is discussed in this extract from the book's Preface, recited at the raising of the curtain for the first act:

> Many people, many nations, can find themselves believing, more or less consciously, that 'every stranger is an enemy'. For the most part this conviction lies buried in the mind like some latent infection; it betrays itself only in random, disconnected acts, and does not lie at the basis of a system of thought. But when that happens, when the unspoken dogma becomes the major premise in a syllogism, then, at the end of the chain, stands the Lager. It's the product of a conception of the world carried out rigorously to its logical consequences with relentless consistency; as long as the conception

> subsists, the consequences remain to threaten us. The story of the death camps should be understood by everyone as a sinister signal of danger.[7]

From this lucid realization of the Nazi project arises the prisoner's hope to survive in order to tell. The book had almost written itself, crystallized from the stories the survivor had repeated hundreds of times in a few days to relatives, friends, enemies and strangers with the same tumultuous urgency as the 'ancient mariner in Coleridge's ballad, who goes into the street and buttonholes guests on their way to a party in order to inflict on them his sinister story of evil doings and ghosts'.[8] But to present such a searing subject in the theatre it was necessary 'to decant it, channel it, to bring out its civil and universal significance, to guide the spectator to a conclusion and a verdict without shouting it in his ears, without handing it to him ready made'.[9] Primo Levi explains during the press conference:

> One of the concerns Marché and I had was precisely to avoid sentimental adhesion to incidents in the camps, and to re-establish as everyday – because that is what they were, absurdly, frighteningly everyday – the terrible work, the absence of food and clothes, the everyday slaughter. In the book a large part of all this was entrusted to the reflective passages; here we've tried to adapt it into dialogue where possible and then we've introduced those choruses, which don't have the function of the Greek chorus but are rather multi-vocal discussions which the actors, the prisoners, open with the audience. In this way, we wanted to develop even the marginal elements in the life of the Lager, the moments of reconsideration, of dreaming, almost of holiday; those that allowed us to show the human substance that still survives in the victims, even as it is worn down every day by the clash with its wild, inhuman environment: Auschwitz.[10]

Now that all the decisions have been made, the author's hopes grow:

> I hope to spark in the consciousness of the spectators a reaction against and a condemnation of the ideology that led to the concentration camp as a means of destroying man. In a certain sense I can say that the work is aimed precisely at an audience that won't go to see it. That is, at a generation who don't like talking about these things because they feel responsible in some way, if nothing else than because of their sins of omission in the face of what was happening. What I wouldn't want to happen, on the other hand, is a sentimental attachment to the tragedy of the deportees. I wouldn't want anyone to leave the theatre saying 'The poor things!'[11]

By a curious coincidence *If This is a Man* went on stage at the same time as *The Investigation*, which the playwright Peter Weiss based on the proceedings of the Frankfurt Auschwitz trials. Although the two works were very different Primo Levi smilingly admitted the possibility of a 'competition', but the director De Bosi had no doubts as to its significance. 'I believe that this staging constitutes a fundamental moment in the evolution of the Turin Stabile's work, a point of arrival and at the same time of departure in the research we've been doing for years on the essential themes and questions of contemporary history.'[12] Marché agrees: 'We haven't done a documentary work, we've sought to address the issues Primo Levi's experience presents, that is to say we've tried to make the audience reflect, think again about what happened as something that could happen again and that humanity needs to take precautions against.' History has shown that the effort to bring to light every nuance of meaning from Levi's now famous text succeeded. It would only take another 48 hours. But like every author at his debut, Primo Levi fretted:

> To me it seemed impossible to transfer my diary to a stage. It still seems almost impossible to me now; but the fervent persistence of Marché has succeeded in overcoming my doubts and now all that's left is to wait for the curtain to rise…[13]

The curtain rose and the packed audience followed the horrifying drama. The lights came back on and the audience, glued to their seats by 'You who live safe/In your warm house…', after a moment of stunned silence, broke out in rapturous applause. A few months later, in Saint-Vincent, the work received the Institute for Italian Drama [Istituto del dramma italiano] prize for the best first play.

The play's tribute to the duty of testimony unleashed a wave of approval for the author, in the form of dozens of letters. Letters from Italians this time, and some of them dense and problematic. His friends asked him why he did not publish them. He was evasive:

> It's not right. These are things which, if anything, others will do, the ones who are left. Afterwards. I think that I will end up clearing my files of correspondence and keeping only what's important, and that's not much. Readers write, comment, thank, ask questions – even on the title of *If This is a Man*. I answer all of them, briefly. With few exceptions they don't tell me anything very important, even if some of them show they have understood what I wanted to say.

We do not know whether Primo Levi also wrote to the audience member who after the performance of *If This is a Man* asked him for a clarification of the title. If the letter existed and escaped the clear-out he had scheduled, it probably still lies in one of his files. We do know, however, the answer he gave the audience in Zurich in 1976 and then in St. Gallen, when they asked him why he chose that title and what it meant:

> *If This is a Man* are words taken from the poem that serves as an epigraph to the book. In truth I wanted to call it *The Drowned and the Saved*, which has remained as the title of one of the chapters. It was Franco Antonicelli, a highly cultured man and authoritative figure in the Resistance, who entitled it that way, and I'm grateful to him for it. The meaning? The oppressor is not a man, nor is the oppressed. The theme of the book is being 'no longer a man'. The dehumanizing is parallel, in the sense that the inhumanity of the perpetrator has led the victim to become inhuman. When we arrived in the Lager (those who did get there were around a fifth of the members of each convoy, the others were selected for the gas chambers straight away), they took our luggage, our clothes, our hair, our names, everything. Then they marked us with a number. Essentially they said to us, 'You're no longer a man.' It's no longer a man who's had his loved ones, his home and his language torn away, who no longer owns even what a beggar owns, who is forced to compromise his dignity and morality in order to survive. And it's no longer a man who inflicts total demolition on other men and in whose eyes those men have become objects. It wasn't by chance that the SS chose to use in the gas chambers the same disinfectant used to clean out ships infested by mice. It was another way of saying to a nation that was being exterminated 'You're not men'. This is what I wanted to explain throughout the book, this is what the title means: that victims and perpetrators are dehumanised alike, marked by a wrong which can never be healed. I took up that theme in the first pages of *The Truce*. We felt shame because it was men who had made Auschwitz and men who had suffered it. We felt shame because they had destroyed us even when they hadn't succeeded in killing us. Their crime had contaminated us. It's in this, and only this, that we should see the paradoxical victim-perpetrator analogy that's so often talked about now, or shown in some films which may be blockbusters, but are gravely offensive to us.

A little more than four years separate the theatre version of *If This is a Man* from Primo Levi's fourth book, *Flaw of Form*, published by Einaudi in 1971. These were years filled with intensive reading; foreign travel (in 1965 he returned to Auschwitz for the first time); contributions to newspapers with news articles, reviews and stories. With the success of his books of memory, first *The Truce* and then *If This is a Man*, both became standard reading in Italian middle schools. He had begun a dialogue with students, who wanted to hear from the man himself details of the events he related, through interviews and questioning. They were the questioners he preferred, and he described them as 'naïve or knowing, emotional or provocative, superficial or profound'.[14] To the teenagers, who saw the events of Auschwitz 'as if they'd happened 3,000 years ago, and are amazed that there's somebody alive, or at least not quite an old wreck, who has lived there'[15] he never said no, even if their requests involved exhausting journeys. He judged these open forms of contact to be necessary. It is to these young people that he addressed the idea summarized in the introduction to the German reprint of *If This is a Man*:

> I think that I perceive in the criminal tragedy of the Third Reich a unique event that is an example and a symbol, but whose meaning has not yet been made clear. Perhaps one can read in it the warning of a greater catastrophe that looms over humanity, which can only be averted if we all truly succeed in understanding the past, and so drain it of its threat.

The stories in *Flaw of Form* are new moral traps from the 'centaur'. They are born of anxiety over impending technological catastrophes:

> Let's say that they had been sizzling inside me, because of my work, ever since I wrote *The Truce*. Let's think of them as a bridge, as a debt paid to technology, to its distortions and its wonders. The stories are all, more or less, children of that flash of insight in the laboratory.[16]

Claudio Toscani, for *Il Ragguaglio Librario,* asks:

> *How on earth, in a tradition as rich in thought and imagination as ours, have you and other writers been able to withhold your moral attention from the future, the warnings necessary for the physical and spiritual survival of the human race?'*

Levi answers declares his freedom to write:

> You're a prohibitionist. True, we Italians have a noble philosophical and literary tradition. We tend to say that it adorns our life and maybe it does; but does it help us to solve certain urgent problems? Or predict the future? And was anxiety about the future, about positive and negative utopias, alien to the great figures of the past?

The interviewer is struck by the implications of the story entitled 'Heading West'. In it Levi asserts that life is essentially useless, although there is a genetic will for it; and he dwells on the philosophy of suicide. Why does the stubborn life instinct of lemmings (who decide en masse to kill themselves) turn against the species? Is the parallel with the tribe which lets itself die meant to indicate the apex of civilization, or the opposite of civilization?

> Lemmings really exist, they aren't my invention; the mystery of their collective suicide intrigues and fascinates not only me, but many serious zoologists and ethologists.[17] I don't know on the other hand whether the Arunde [the tribe in Levi's story] exist, but in both cases I intended to represent neither a civilization nor an anti-civilization, but a state of mind, which in many people, and in me, alternates with the other, which one tends to describe as 'normal'[...] few people possess sufficient qualities to give a purpose to their lives. So, for most of us, the feeling that life is pointless is justified, and so too is existential anguish despite its 'truces'. But an undefined natural providence (maybe a Darwinian one: whoever doesn't possess it is unfit to live and his line becomes extinct) acts so that the normal person, in normal circumstances, is not aware of that immense pointlessness.[18]

Flaw of Form, which in its title takes up the legal formula already used in the introduction to *Natural Histories*, did not thrill the critics. Some accused it of an excessive optimism, of being a graceful satire. Some would have preferred, from the author of *If This is a Man*, an authentic 'engagement'. On this question Primo Levi had already, calmly, taken a position, when Mario Miccinesi, editor of *Uomini e libri*, had asked him whether in the face of the great problems of the day (the interview took place in 1968) the writer can avoid taking up a position of protest in his books. And he had added:

> *In your view, can protest limit itself to being purely literary, or must it involve the writer in taking a position that amounts to a clear and conscious protestation?*
>
> Without doubt the writer who, in his work and in the example he sets in his life, he's reached a position of lucid criticism, or at least of awareness, of the great problems of today's world is to be praised and approved. All the same, I don't think this direction should take the form of a prescription or a preclusion; it is good that there should be participation and good that it should be clear and aware, but why shouldn't it also be unaware and vague, or aware and allusive, or describable with any other pair of adjectives? Every prohibition is dangerous, and the human race mustn't mutilate itself; should we

> perhaps banish a work like *Joseph and His Brothers* by Thomas Mann because it doesn't contain a political message or a protest, despite having been conceived in an age full of terrible omens? [...] Denunciation is welcome, and let it be brave and unequivocal, but if it doesn't contain a proposal together with the protest, it isn't worth very much. Human genius is varied and unpredictable: between entertainment and engagement there is a vast no-man's-land, from which a true and valid book could emerge, outside of and against any pre-constituted plan. If protest is the only safety net, it can't be very sturdy or viable.[19]

Levi never changed his mind on this question. Controversies leave him unmoved. With calm assurance he stays in the centre of the storm, faithful to his task of communicating. Even the stories of *Flaw of Form* were written to communicate facts, anxieties, images, insights; poetically, ironically and with a different kind of engagement. His faith in the word is unshakeable, whatever tent it may camp under in this 'vast no-man's-land'. He tells Piero Bianucci, who is writing about the crisis of the novel for the *Gazzetta del Popolo*:

> The novel holds firm: it can hold firm even today, threatened as it is by the rising tide of instant information, written or otherwise. Even the novel informs, of course, but often in a subtle and imperceptible way, without the knowledge of the reader. Each of us harbours still, deep within him, the child-like wish to be told a story: each has in his own life holiday interludes (childhood, illness, retirement), holidays from rushing around, I mean, that can be filled by a good book. It doesn't matter if it's a classic, or experimental, as long as the experiment isn't so daring as to harm the communication, the transmission of facts and images.[20]

At the basis of the inspiration for *Flaw of Form*, over which the consequences of an irresponsible use of the wonders of technology and the widening 'fissure' in the social fabric cast their shadow, there is moral seriousness and recognition of scientific progress, provided it does not become distorted and corrupted by the aberrant use of its conquests. Progress is never condemned *per se*: such a Luddite argument would be incompatible with Levi's firmly rational way of thinking.

> Anyone denying the benefits of machines isn't speaking in good faith, but it's equally clear that a technology that's become out of control, or been subjected to the wishes of a class, can lead the world to a catastrophe or to a slow cancer, whereas science, as the daughter of reason, can liberate the human race from many of its afflictions, and

> within certain limits it has already shown that. [...] I think that technology is like Achilles' spear, which wounds or cures, depending on how it's handled, or rather, on the hand that holds it.[21]

Statements such as these were not intended to calm the criticism or to resolve the question, constantly put to him, of the relationship between the writer of the Lager and the writer of fantasy stories. Questioning him years later on his relationship with criticism, Professor Giuseppe Grassano discovered that he shared the thoughts of Beppe Fenoglio, who had admitted 'his surprise at what the critics managed to find in his work, though he was equally surprised by what they hadn't been able to find'.

> I agree. Fenoglio put it very well. It's true, often they've helped me to clarify myself to myself and often they've found things I didn't know I'd put there, or hadn't really put there. I would say that quite a typical case is the controversy that has followed me for as long as I've been writing, about the relationship between my first two books (of memoirs) and my other two books of stories, *Natural Histories* and *Flaw of Form*. It's something that is clearer to my readers than to myself. I think that the Lager really has little to do with today's world. I don't entirely agree [...] that the alienation of today's world is no different from the alienation of the Lager [...] It has the same effect on me when I see written on a wall 'PS=SS'. The police [Public Security] forces are unpleasant, but the SS really were different [...] On the other hand it's likely that the reader will find in my stories features of man as prisoner that I didn't know I'd put there. It's likely. In some stories it's obvious. In 'Versamine' and 'Angelic Butterfly' certainly I've consciously reconnected to old experiences. In other stories there might be such a connection, but I didn't mean to make one. Clearly, the experience of the Lager is traumatic and trauma is carried inside and comes out in a way that isn't perceived by the writer.[22]

He pointed again to the 'typical polemic' following him at a lecture held in Zurich, saying of his two books of stories:

> A true battle has flared up between critics on the relationship between my books of memories and the others. They've wondered whether *Natural Histories* and *Flaw of Form* are a continuation of the discussion of the Lager; whether it's a question of allegories, of symbolic stories where, from a different point of view, the oppression by man of man is represented. I must admit that that controversy interests me really very little. Writers draw on what they know. My sources are multiple

> and varied. Faced with these questions, I say with sincerity: I can't give a precise answer. I can only say this: of course, Auschwitz re-emerges in some stories, but as something profoundly embedded, not as a deliberate intention.

Four books, two major prizes, interviews, photographs: fame. Talking about this period in the lectures in Switzerland he said:

> Now I could no longer reject the label of writer. There was no way out of it any more: I'd been categorized. A pinned butterfly. So it seemed to be time to honour the vow: I wanted to complete the crossbreeding of the everyday job with the Sunday job. And *The Periodic Table* was born, a title that means something to chemists, but for one who is not a chemist is vague and indefinite.

Notes

1 N. Bobbio, *Trent'anni di storia della cultura a Torino (1920-1950)* [Thirty years of history of culture in Turin (1920-1950)](Turin: Cassa di Risparmio, 1977), p.104.
2 Primo Levi, *Se questo è un uomo: Versione drammatica* [*If This is a Man*. Dramatic version], (Turin: Einaudi, 1966), p.8. An English version of Levi's 'Note to the Theatre Version of *If This is a Man*' is available in P. Levi, ed. M. Belpoliti, trans. S. Wood, *The Black Hole of Auschwitz* (Cambridge: Polity Press, 2005), pp.23-7.
3 Guido Boursier, 'Primo Levi rievoca la barbarie dei Lager nazisti' [Primo Levi re-evokes the barbarism of the Nazi Lagers], *Gazzetta del Popolo*, 17 November 1966.
4 Giuseppe Del Colle, 'Attori di sette nazioni per il dramma di Auschwitz' [Actors of seven nations for the drama of Auschwitz], *La Stampa*, 17 November 1966.
5 Boursier, 'Primo Levi rievoca la barbarie dei Lager nazisti'.
6 Del Colle, 'Attori di sette nazioni per il dramma di Auschwitz'.
7 P. Levi, trans. S. Woolf, *If This is a Man*, in A. Goldstein (ed.), *The Complete Works of Primo Levi* (Liveright: New York, 2015), Vol. I, p.5.
8 P. Levi and P. Marché, *Se questo è un uomo: Versione drammatica*, p.6.
9 Ibid, p.8.
10 Boursier, 'Primo Levi rievoca la barbarie dei Lager nazisti'.
11 Del Colle, 'Attori di sette nazioni per il dramma di Auschwitz'. See also Giorgio Calcagno, 'Primo Levi spiega perché ha accettato la riduzione del suo libro' [Primo Levi explains why he agreed to the adaptation of his book], *Il Nostro Tempo*, Year XXI, No.47.
12 Del Colle, 'Attori di sette nazioni per il dramma di Auschwitz'.
13 Nino Ferrero, '*Se questo è un uomo* in scena a Torino' [*If This is a Man* on stage in Turin], *L'Unità*, 17 November 1966.
14 *If This is a Man* in *Complete Works of Primo Levi*, p.168.
15 Reply to an audience member in Chur.
16 Gabriella Poli, 'L'alfabeto della chimica' [The alphabet of chemistry], *Tuttolibri (La Stampa)*, 6 December 1976.
17 Scientists who specialise in animal behaviour
18 Claudio Toscani, 'Incontro con Primo Levi' [Meeting with Primo Levi], *Il Ragguaglio Librario*, No.3, 1972.

19 Mario Miccinesi, 'Inchiesta sulla letteratura come contestazione' [Inquiry into literature as protest], *Uomini e libri*, n.18, April 1968.
20 Piero Bianucci, 'Tanti atti di fede nel romanzo' [So many acts of faith in the novel], *Gazzetta del Popolo*, 20 November 1971.
21 Toscani,'Incontro con Primo Levi'.
22 From the interview granted by Primo Levi on 17 November 1979 and reported at the beginning of G. Grassano, *Primo Levi* (Florence: Il Castoro/La Nuova Italia, 1981).

III

The Welding

The Periodic Table, twenty-one stories each named after an element in Mendeleev's table, appeared in bookshops in the spring of 1975. It was not a chemistry treatise, the author explained in the concluding chapter, nor was it an autobiography 'except in the partial and symbolic limits within which every piece of writing, in fact every work produced by humans is an autobiography: but it surely is history [...] a micro-history of a trade and its defeats, victories and sufferings.'[1]

Without doubt this unusual book is all this and much more. It is also a pedagogical poem, a picture of a generation and a cultural history. From the perspective of literature, Italo Calvino judged it 'an extraordinary work', which mingles 'fact and fiction, history and anecdote [...] to illuminate the human condition'.[2] From the perspective of science M. Piattelli Palmarini called it a shining example of the interpenetration of science and narrative,[3] and Carlo Mussa Ivaldi, a lecturer in chemistry and physics but also an expert on classical literature, declared that with this work 'Primo Levi takes the credit for having confronted the key issue of the welding of science and the arts, building one of the strongest and most original bridges of our century over the unfortunate division unknown to Empedocles and Lucretius.'[4]

The Periodic Table, despite its title, was an immediate success. Readers were intrigued by the novelty of its theme, amused by its elements with human qualities and flaws and struck by the talent of the writer who, 'navigating among pestles and foul concoctions', was able to create 'from a micro-reaction, with a miniscule kit, the universal truth of the human condition'.[5] Before the wave of reviews (thirty in less than six months), Ernesto Gagliano from *La Stampa* and Professor Giorgio De Rienzo interviewed the author.[6]

Your book could be considered the autobiography of a chemist?

In one respect yes, but a book that has only one aspect, that can only be read in one way, is in my view a poor book. In this case my intention was that, behind the condition of the chemist, would be hidden the human condition as a whole.

You've talked of a contest between man and matter? What is that relationship?

> Even the relationship between man and matter in this book is ambiguous. Matter is mother, also etymologically, but at the same time she's an enemy. The same can be said of nature. Yet man too is matter and is in conflict with himself, as all religions have recognized. Matter is also a teacher, the real teacher. Fighting against her one matures and grows. It's a fight one sometimes wins and sometimes loses, and in which matter can be felt as cunning or obtuse without there being any contradiction, because she has both aspects.
>
> *Your prose is smooth, a lucid construction that is calm and detached. How have you managed to believe in the triumph of reason, after experiences such as persecution and the Lager?*
>
> Believing in reason means believing in one's own reason, but it doesn't mean that reason governs the world, nor even that it governs mankind. Having witnessed the wreck of reason – and here I refer not only to Nazism but also to fascism here in Italy – should not and will not make me surrender. I'd say with Calamandrei[7] that for our generation there is no leave of absence. There is no leave for reason either, she can't go on holiday. For my part, I regard any absence of reason with suspicion. I therefore consider all trades which exercise reason healthy, and mine is one of them. It is not by chance that I constantly compared my trade to hunting in this book. Humanity became humanity by hunting; that is, by exercising reason.

Fascinated by the 'overflowing Hylozoism'[8] of *The Periodic Table*[9], the interviewers wanted to find human features in other elements, maybe in all of them. The answer dampens their enthusiasm:

> Let's not exaggerate, samarium and gadolinium are for now generally perceived as purely alien and hostile. But it's a question of time and getting to know them, as with people. Other elements (for example iron, gold and sulphur), those that have a long history, undoubtedly have human features, an anthropomorphic character. I've exploited that character, for example, in the story about iron, but it wouldn't be difficult to do so for oxygen or for copper. It wouldn't require a chemist to do it either.

'You believe in the pleasure of work. Why?' The answer to this pertinent question looks forward to *The Wrench*:

> Not all work is pleasurable. It's a sad and obvious truth. It would however be a good thing for the individual, and therefore also for society, if the work a person chooses were among those that can

become pleasant. Anyone who manages this has some chance of knowing happiness, if only occasionally. It seems to me inane, and also base, the common masochistic vice of considering work as a biblical condemnation. One quickly concludes from it that working is suffering and so it's better not to work. Now, it's not like that, or not necessarily like that. Already the work of today, one thinks of work in the fields for example, is much less damaging than forty years ago, and it can become less damaging in all sectors. In this book I've tried to put the spotlight on the nobility of our work, its educational and formative value, disputing the ideology that prevails even today in our country, according to which the only sure route to culture and maturity passes through Latin, Greek and aesthetic analysis, whereas mathematics and physics are abstruse pursuits which are either useless, or useful only as trades, only as breadwinners. You will have noticed the absence of shame, indeed with what pride people often say 'I've never understood algebra', whereas no-one ever admits to not knowing Italian spelling or grammar, even if in fact they don't. I've tried to show that a science or a technology can not only be the subject of a book, but also a school of thought, and therefore of writing. I'd be happy if a physicist or a biologist were to imitate me. As for doctors, they have already been thinking about it for a long time.

The first public launch of *The Periodic Table* took place in Turin on 4 June in a crowded room of the city's cultural union, organized by Carlo Mussa Ivaldi and the historian Paolo Spriano, both friends of Primo Levi. The first had witnessed his struggle to make his way under the racial laws; the second the arrest of the Jewish partisan, who had left for the mountains the day after Italy's armistice with the Allies on 8 September 1943.

In the book the elements play different roles, but for the most part they refer, symbolically, metaphorically or concretely, to the event or the character in the chapter where they appear. But there is one chapter, that on cerium, where the element provides the story. Levi tells of how he saved himself from starvation in the laboratory of the Lager by stealing small grey cylinders which, at the risk of hanging, he and his friend Alberto trimmed into flints which they exchanged for bread.

Why didn't you include 'Cerium' in If This is a Man, *a book in which chemistry has no role despite having contributed to saving your life?*

I'll tell you why, thinking of what I've written here, in the book: One of the old names for chemistry, in German, is *die Scheidekunst*, the art of separating, from *scheiden*, to separate. Now, for us it's a bit of an instinct, keeping things separate. And for that reason, I wanted

> to write *If This is a Man* as a story of a fall into the depths, which chemistry had very little, indeed nothing, to do with. Or rather it had nothing to do with it except by pure chance, even if it saved my life. It's not negligible, the aspect of a practical job that is useful in all circumstances. Not that I'd chosen mine for that reason, let's be clear. But I must recognize that chemistry is something that is useful for everything. It's useful for improving one's mind, it's useful for growing, it's useful for entering into the world of concrete things; all in all, it's useful for educating oneself. Going back to 'Cerium', what I wanted to say is that I kept this episode out of my first book in order not to contaminate it, because this story is happy. Happy [...] well, it has a backdrop that isn't happy at all of course, but it's a tale of victory, of a daring and even reckless enterprise, carried through to the end. And so it would have clashed with that other canvas which is a canvas of defeats, a canvas of tragedies, a tragically intense canvas. It's not exactly that I thought it through in this way, but instinctively it seemed to me I shouldn't tell it in that other context, whereas in this one it fits well.

'You've often told me', Mussa Ivaldi interjected, 'that they ask you how on earth a chemist can write books, and write them well. Anyone who's read *The Periodic Table* should turn that question around and, if anything, ask a good chemist, physicist or biologist why he hasn't managed to write a book that is comprehensible and interesting even for those outside the profession.' Primo Levi grabs the ball in mid-air and for the first time reveals the tools of his trade:

> It seems to me that the answer I always give to the question 'Why are you a chemist who writes?' (as if it were a scandal for a chemist to write: he isn't an authorized member of the profession) is that I write *because* I am a chemist, and this is an answer given in good faith. Without its being a necessary condition for writing, it's nevertheless a sufficient condition. I think, I don't know whether out of pride or modesty, that my writing is more or less imbued with the road I've quite consciously chosen. Maybe a bit prematurely, because fourteen was a bit young to decide, but in short I've never had doubts: I've chosen it, I've followed it and I still follow it; my real trade is as a chemist. Now, for at least two reasons my real trade has helped me to write. First of all, because it's given me the raw material, the point around which stories are told: in *The Periodic Table*, essentially, the things I have written about are chemical. At least, that's what I wanted to do. Then I crammed the book a bit, because I like telling stories and sometimes I make them burst under the strain, but I take liberties. In any case, I wanted to write stories of militant chemistry and that to a

large extent is what I have done. I note in passing that it isn't necessary to go too far back to take up themes going back centuries and millennia, but that one can tell stories, which I think are interesting and comprehensible to all, drawing on that mysterious, dangerous, suspect, arid thing which non-chemists see in chemistry. If I knew I'd convinced some young person at the age of choosing to take that road rather than another, I'd be happy.

So that's in terms of the raw material for things I've written. But my trade has also been useful to me in my style of writing, seeking clarity and precision. I believe that chemistry is a good school in that regard. I've hinted at it, in the book, in the discussion of qualitative analysis and the task that is assigned to students in their second year. They're each given a gram of powder, which they need to study, proceeding with a certain established method or as they see fit, inventing their own path. But, at the end, they need to produce a report, an account where they write: this thing is this, this other thing isn't. And one can't say 'I think so' or 'maybe' or 'it gives every appearance of being'. One must write precisely 'it is' or 'it isn't'.

I say this because I remember even now that it was something new. From the first year of primary school onwards, we'd never found ourselves set a task so precise, so responsible, so alien from the culture that filled the air, which was fascist culture. It was, I repeat, something totally new: man facing matter, a young lad facing matter, what is more a defenceless lad, totally unprepared. The task of breaking up, analysing and then answering, not with nice rhetorical phrases but with a 'yes' or a 'no', with a 'more' or a 'less', had immediately seemed to us, at least it had seemed to me, something extremely clean and responsible. Like a foreign body, exactly, in the fascist culture that had been administered to us in the course of our studies. And perhaps I secretly dedicated this book to us as we were then. So that, by free choice, I've left in my book a certain close impression of that period. I've dedicated many pages to few years and few pages to many years: three elements, forty pages, for the years at university. They're important for everyone, but for us they were especially so. And I'd like to say that they were so particularly for me. It was a case of taking on, in one go, two adversaries: one was chemistry and the other was the racial laws. One needed to find a path, to resolve the problem which, it didn't take much to understand, was about to become a tragedy. Most of all we were faced with an anguished choice, we who were denied identity, social belonging, a homeland: you're not an Italian anymore, you're something different; we've taught you up to now that you're a citizen like the others, now

> you're not any more. All this, thinking about it again, seemed to me so important that the book escaped my grasp and pages came out that weren't in the programme.[10]

In *The Periodic Table*, Auschwitz is recalled not only in 'Cerium' but in the chapter 'Vanadium', which returns to the theme of the Lager with such intensity as to hint that the survivor still has more to tell. At the beginning of the summer Professor Giorgio De Rienzo went to find Primo Levi in his factory, the Siva factory in the suburb of Settimo Torinese, accompanied by a photographer. From this meeting came another long interview, centred around the recent past, published by *Famiglia Cristiana*[11] and illustrated with haunting images of the camp and of Primo Levi in a white coat in the laboratory or in front of his desk. These are among the first photos in which the author, up to then clean-shaven, appears with 'those sideburns and that goatee halfway between a rabbi and an Alpine soldier'[12] which is already lightly sprinkled with white. 'There is', De Rienzo wrote, 'a great sweetness in his eyes.Whenever anyone speaks to him, listens to him, speaks to him and hears him listen, it communicates a feeling of trust'. Levi's readers are instinctively inclined to regard him as naturally superior, but, De Rienzo writes, 'Levi rejects this idea decisively, without false modesty'. He says in fact:

> There is an upside-down debate between me and my readers, who are convinced I've survived Auschwitz because of my moral strength. They're convinced, I'm not. I escaped, rather, by pure chance and I challenge anyone to show me the opposite [...] When I left I weighed little more than I did on my return: the most banal secret of my survival perhaps lies in that simple fact. The first to die, among those who were not sent immediately to the gas chambers, were the strongest: the scarce food, the tiny calorie content of the soup we were given, was endured with less sense of privation by those, like me, with moderate eating habits. In fact I missed food less than so many others. Beyond that, though, my curiosity may have had an influence, my knowing how to listen and my desire to speak: all of this perhaps helped me to feel less alone.

He often returned to the theme of the factors which had saved him, in public and during interviews. He indicated some, hypothesized others. He certainly never omitted curiosity, of which he said this to a young audience:

> Perhaps human curiosity, which I've always had, played in my favour. In parallel to its tragic, negative aspect (because seeing hundreds of friends die around one, finding oneself a target for destruction, suffering cold and hunger are things that are profoundly traumatising)

> it was that which for many of us, but for me especially, made the Lager an observatory. That is, another way of storing experiences. Experiences are always positive, they're the bricks one builds with. Now, the Lager, as well as a 'bone mill' as it was technically known at the time, meant for me also a store of experiences. And of such a richness that I can still draw on them today.[13]

It was above all the writer Philip Roth who induced him, with a clear critical examination, to rummage in that curiosity, which is nothing else than the inexhaustible thirst to know in order to understand, to understand in order to make understood. Roth says:

> *Survival in Auschwitz* concludes with a chapter entitled 'The Story of Ten Days', in which you describe, in diary form, how you endured from January 18 to January 27 1945, among a small remnant of sick and dying patients in the camp's makeshift infirmary after the Nazis had fled westward with some 20,000 'healthy' prisoners. What's recounted there reads to me like the story of Robinson Crusoe in hell, with you, Primo Levi, as Crusoe, wrenching what you needed to live from the chaotic residue of a ruthlessly evil island. What struck me there, as throughout the book, was how much thinking contributed to your survival, the thinking of a practical, humane, scientific mind. Yours doesn't seem to me a survival that was determined by either brute biological strength or incredible luck, but was rooted, rather, in your professional character: the man of precision, the controller of experiments who seeks the principle of order, confronted with the evil inversion of everything he valued.
>
> Granted you were a numbered part in an infernal machine, but a numbered part with a systematic mind that has always to understand. At Auschwitz you tell yourself, 'I think too much' to resist, 'I am too civilized'. But to me the civilized man who thinks too much is inseparable from the survivor. The scientist and the survivor are one.

Levi agrees with his logical friend, despite indicating that amongst the factors of his survival was chance:

> Exactly – you hit the bull's-eye. In those memorable ten days, I truly did feel like Robinson Crusoe, but with one important difference. Crusoe set to work for his individual survival, whereas I and my two French companions were consciously and happily willing to work at last for a just and human goal, to save the lives of our sick comrades.

> As for survival, this is a question that I put to myself many times and that many have put to me. I insist there was no general rule, except entering the camp in good health and knowing German. Barring this, luck dominated. I have seen the survival of shrewd people and silly people, the brave and the cowardly, 'thinkers' and madmen (for example, Elias whom I described in *If This is a Man*). In my case, luck played an essential role on at least two occasions: in leading me to meet the Italian bricklayer, and in getting sick only once, but at the right moment.
>
> And yet what you say, that for me thinking and observing were survival factors, is true, although in my opinion sheer luck prevailed. I remember having lived my Auschwitz year in a condition of exceptional spiritedness. I don't know if this depended on my professional background, or an unsuspected stamina, or on a sound instinct. I never stopped recording the world and people around me, so much so that I still have an unbelievably detailed image of them. I had an intense wish to understand, I was constantly pervaded by a curiosity that somebody afterwards did, in fact, deem nothing less than cynical, the curiosity of the naturalist who finds himself transplanted into an environment that is monstrous, but new, monstrously new.[14]

He preserves the events and images of the hellish world in his mind in such detail that during the interview with De Rienzo in July 1975 he recalls two vivid unpublished episodes. Only years later would he find the time to publish them. The first is the story of the Lithuanian doctor[15] who on the day of Yom Kippur, on which observant Jews are obliged to fast and to refrain from work, presents himself to the Kapo of the barrack, who is handing out the soup, and tells him 'I can't not work, because you'll kill me; I can however not eat'. And the Kapo, a Communist political prisoner 'by now turned to stone by eleven years in the Lager' looks at him in astonishment and promises him 'I'll keep your soup for tomorrow'. Primo Levi commented:

> This was a very rare act of humanity in the Lager, but a salutary example of human respect , even more salutary because it was between two people as ideologically far from each other as that believing Jew and that Communist. A true glimmer of light in the thick darkness of the Lager. These episodes, even if rare, were very useful to me then, and afterwards too.

The writer is not a believer. To the question 'But did you feel the lack of faith in the Lager?' he replies:

> Of course, I greatly regretted my lack of faith in the Lager, though not to the point of creating for myself a faith I didn't have. Believing Jews, Jehovah's Witnesses, Catholic priests escaped more than others. The Lithuanian doctor in the episode I've just mentioned was much less unhappy than the others, precisely because he believed in a destiny that was unknowable, impenetrable, but just. That's it. He had the certainty that his destiny would be indisputably just: he didn't feel, as the others did, the victim of a monstrous injustice. He didn't rebel, and to rebel, in the Lager, meant to die. What's more is that in him, as in all believers, there was also a helpful habit of internal discipline.

That said, he went back to telling his stories. The second episode, as yet unpublished,[16] is that of the pitiful end of the only parcel that came to him in the Lager, 'by an extremely complicated procedure, of planning and subterfuge and with the help of an Italian bricklayer, Lorenzo, who worked in the factory near his camp'.

> Together with the letter I'd also got a packet of provisions: with biscuits, chocolate. Capital of inestimable value, there in the camp. I couldn't eat all of it; I'd die I'd be so full. And then it was important to know how to manage such capital in the Lager: using it as goods for barter, for example. So I placed the contents of this packet in my legal and illegal jacket pockets. The next morning, like every morning, we had to wash, and in order to wash we had to strip to the waist. I hung the jacket on a nail close to the wash-house, and while I was leaning over to wash myself I saw my jacket fished with a rod from the small window at the top: I saw it rise and then disappear into nothingness. My treasure had been fished by someone who had been very attentively spying on me. Not only did I despair over the loss of the package, but I also had to suffer the blows given for losing a jacket, which was the property of the Lager, not the prisoners; and not only that but in the course of a quarter of an hour I had to get myself a new jacket and sew onto it the number torn out of the trousers, so as not to suffer worse punishments. This was the norm in the Lager: besides fatigue, cold, thirst and hunger, the annihilation of men, the deprivation also of every feeling of solidarity.

It is written in *If This is a Man* that 'Sooner or later we all discover that perfect happiness is unrealizable, but few of us pause to consider the opposite: that so, too, is perfect unhappiness.' Why did anyone who was in the Lager understand that truth immediately and instinctively?

> The material discomforts, the fatigue, hunger, thirst and cold tormenting our bodies, paradoxically managed to distract us from the very great unhappiness of our spirits. One waited for the few moments of truce, of freedom from work, as if for a liberation, and then the pleasure of that freedom turned into a great unhappiness: the privilege of thinking, for a few minutes, became a torment. And yet even that torment was, in its turn, a relief. Because it was perceived as a superior, nobler unhappiness, which distracted from the material one.
>
> *So it wasn't possible to be perfectly unhappy?*
>
> It's demonstrated by the fact that in the Lager suicide was very rare. Suicide is a philosophical act, it's determined by a faculty of thought. Urgent daily needs distracted us from thought: we could want to die, but we couldn't think of making ourselves die. I have been close to suicide, to the idea of suicide, before and after the Lager, but never in the Lager.

Referring to the years of fascism, Primo Levi spoke of 'providential racial laws'. How can that expression be interpreted?

> The racial laws were providential for me but also for others: they constituted the *reductio ad absurdum* of the stupidity of fascism. The racial laws were the symptom of a farce: people had forgotten by then the criminal face of fascism (that of the Matteotti crime,[17] for example); its idiot face remained visible. In my family, an ordinary bourgeois family without firm anti-fascist roots, fascism was accepted, with some irritation. My father had joined the party reluctantly but he had still put the black shirt on. And I was first a *balilla* and then an *avanguardista*.[18] I could say that the racial laws restored, to me as to others, my freedom of judgement. And with freedom of judgement came the capacity to choose.

But the tone with which the author tells of his brief partisan adventure in 'Gold' seems to be one of ironic distance. Why?

> We had gone into the mountains without the slightest preparation. We didn't even know how to mount a sub-machine gun; we were without the most basic military knowledge; we really didn't know a thing. We had to invent our resistance: being a partisan was also a profession to be learned. All the same, even without preparation, maybe without sense, what mattered was that we were in the mountains.

With one exception (when he was chatting to Massimo Mila), Primo Levi preferred not to linger on the subject, neither then nor later. When Paolo

Momigliano, president of the Aosta Valley Istituto Storico per la Resistenza [Historical Institute for the Resistance] wrote asking him to commemorate in an article the events that led to his arrest, together with other 'rebels' in the area around Amay on 13 December 1943, he replied:

> My period as a partisan in the Aosta Valley was without doubt the most lacklustre of my career. I wouldn't tell it willingly: it's a story of young people with good intentions, but with no preparation and no sense, and it's better forgotten. The references in *The Periodic Table* are more than enough. I don't mind at all if they're republished, but saying more would be too much, it wouldn't be an example even of what not to do.[19]

So the conversation, begun in the laboratory, returns to the laboratory. With *The Periodic Table*, Primo Levi affirms, 'I wanted to demonstrate that a science can be a school of thought, as well as a source of poetry.' And he insists on the concept that is dear to him: of chemistry as the adventure, hunt, battle, mistress of rationality and existential parable.

> The chemist begins a fencing match, a two-way game between himself and matter [...] One thing is very important in this fight. The chemist can never lose the lucidity of his own reason, he can never abandon himself to satisfaction with the elegant and unproved hypothesis: he must always check what he discovers, whatever his little victory might be. That, more than anything else, teaches the chemist to keep his reason always on guard [...] When reason surrenders, Nazism and fascism are born.

The book of the elements, like *The Wrench* later, is founded on a Conradian conception of existence. Professor Giuseppe Grassano identified it in a later interview, observing to the author:

> *The reference to unruly matter refusing to bend to man seems to me to underline how science repeats the struggle, the human effort, that is necessary in every field, to rule oneself and one's environment.*[20]
>
> That's well put and all I can do is to confirm it. I found an expression like that in Russell, in *The Conquest of Happiness*, where he says that there's no happiness without effort. And that is for biological reasons, because we're just made that way [...] as hunter and gatherer mammals. If we lived in the land of Cockaigne, where one lies down and receives food from above, we'd probably die, or we'd get ill, at least mentally, or we'd become very atrophied and stupid. Exercising oneself, confronting oneself with others and with

> the material world, although it costs fatigue and pain, is indispensable. One can't imagine a life without confrontation, and therefore without defeats.

On 12 September 1975 Arrigo Benedetti, president of the jury at Prato,[21] standing alongside ten writers and critics including Mario Tobino, Diego Valerini and Geno Pampaloni, announced that the 26th prize for narrative had been awarded to *The Periodic Table,* observing that:

> [...] the series of stories, besides having an intimately autobiographical meaning, has its own very precise historical depth. It's the mirror of Turin in the last years of fascism, in which the seriousness of the scientific enterprise, despite the backwardness of the tools and prospects with which it was conducted, constituted in and of itself the feeling of a certainty that could not be attacked or corroded by the rhetoric of the regime.[22]

Two days later Primo Levi, a little uncomfortable, is under the spotlight for the first time in a television broadcast dedicated entirely to him. For the programme 'Settimo Giorno'[Seventh Day] which he presented on RAI 2, the *La Stampa* critic, Lorenzo Mondo, asks him the ritual question:

> *How do you link your work, which is that of a chemist, with the work of writing? How on earth can a man of science dedicate himself simultaneously to the written word?*

The reply retraces and synthesizes, even if it is less sharp, the explanation given at the cultural union:

> Unfortunately, I am no longer a man of science, I am a man of technology: that makes some difference. But in either case, whether it is by destiny or by choice that someone happens to work in science or technology, I don't see a contradiction in writing: that is to say that I think the job of telling stories, which is the fundamental job of anyone who writes, can draw on almost any root, on any source. In my case I have the impression that my job, which I chose quite consciously even if for unusual reasons, has been useful both in providing raw material to tell stories about and for the manner of the telling. I have the impression that my way of writing (which I don't know very well what it is, just as every writer doesn't know very well what his own way of writing is) shows signs of the 'account', of the technical or even scientific report. The taste for concreteness, for the definite, for the exact word used to communicate, comes to me precisely from my job as a chemist.

Over the screen passes footage, recorded by Antonio Debenedetti and Emilio Greco, illustrating the life and work of the author, from the now famous pages of *If This is a Man* to his last work. Why, asks Mondo, have you chosen *The Periodic Table* as the title of your book? Would you like to explain what it is to those who don't know?

> You can see it in the footage: it's that table hung in the great hall of the chemistry institute, which represents the discovery of a Russian chemist, Mendeleev. He had realized that, if one organizes the elements in ascending order of atomic number, one obtains parallels which to him seemed very mysterious and which have now been explained. That is to say that one obtains an order which was lacking before and which, as often happens in our profession, turns up and one notices it. Suddenly. Like when one lights a lamp: first there was dark and now there is light. After Mendeleev it was clear that matter is ordered, it isn't disordered, and so we have reason to believe that the whole universe is ordered and not disordered. For that reason, I liked this ambiguous title, even if it doesn't say much to many people, and I chose it to order these stories.

So, Mondo observes, an absolute need to rationalize a past, a universe, an existence. Readers and critics have stressed the aspect of wounded memory in *The Periodic Table*, but the author rejects a discussion of his book which sticks too closely to the re-evocation of the Lager. Could he clarify?

> Auschwitz isn't forgotten, it's not deleted easily, but I wouldn't have wanted the centre of gravity of this book to be moved onto the concentration camps. I would have liked to put it precisely on the dialectic, on the confrontation between man and matter, between man and necessity we could say (which is very ancient, as ancient as humanity itself and from which humanity was probably born). That is, on a parallel that fascinated me, with man the hunter: not the hunter of today, the hunter of back then, when one hunted bison; when it was dangerous to hunt; when the act of hunting, the act of throwing the arrow, meant life or death for hunter and victim. And also on another parallel, another confrontation of man with matter that has also always fascinated me: that of Conrad, that of the journey in which one is abandoned to gigantic forces which can nevertheless be controlled: there it is no longer the hunter, but the sailor […] Maybe I haven't succeeded, but the book was born from these two stimuli.
>
> *And you've sought to merge the vein of testimony in* If This is a Man *with the wholly invented, wholly fantastical stories of* Flaw of Form *on the basis of these two stimuli?*

> I've forgotten them a bit, those fantasy stories, because they seemed to me to lead to uneven, untrustworthy ground and I preferred to return to the memoir vein. I felt more comfortable and for that reason I've tried to fish out of my memory recollections relating to events which just after they'd happened seemed rough and prosaic and yet, looked at again after many years, have allowed me to grasp in them meanings that had escaped me before.

To the questions of Professors Valinotti, De Castris and Bàrberi Squarotti who want long, articulate, philosophical answers, Primo Levi, although kind and modest, is evasive: 'My theoretical ideas on literature are few.' It seems to him that his interlocutors want to lead him into a field that is not his own. He does not recognize himself much, and he says so, in the assertions being made about his book. He clarifies:

> I wanted only to make it understood that no human experience is unworthy of attention [...] even the experience of a career that seen from the outside is dry, exhausting, difficult even, disappointing and frustrating: that is the career of a factory technician [...] I've tried to illustrate that experience in its positive and negative sides and to reveal how even the negative ones are fertile [...] and to show how the adventure of confronting problems and resolving them is essential [...] a good symbol in fact of the human condition as a whole.

Bàrberi Squarotti found in *The Periodic Table* an attempt to 'leave the decisive and in some ways conditioning experience of the Lager; to reach a new, freer form of literature'. The presenter of the programme asks whether the author has anything to observe on this.

> Yes. Bàrberi Squarotti has pointed to some pages that flew out of my hands, I'm not saying without my wanting them to, but without my having predicted it. He's caught me red-handed in the act of invention, because it's true that some pages are clearly invented. They contain old mineral stories written when I couldn't do anything other than dream. 'Lead' or 'Mercury', for example, refer to remote events, centuries and millennia ago. But also some of the other stories are invented: they are those in which in my turn, like the mad protagonist of 'Uranium', I've broken constraints and shattered meridians and parallels; in which I've tried to ride symbols and like Astolfo[23] to set off on horseback astride those symbols (which to me seemed interesting, new, fun, maybe unexploited) contained in the names, character and spirit of the chemical elements, which for me constituted my daily bread. Every one of them, seen in a certain way, has taken on an anthropomorphic character and

> has served as a springboard. This experience moreover is not only mine, it's the experience of the alchemists. For how many centuries did the alchemists perceive human meanings in matter? Still today iron and gold are teeming with human content of which we are not always aware [...] Now, for most people, for the layman let's say, the anthropomorphic elements are a dozen, for the chemist many more. [...]

After the television discussion, the invitations for the author of *The Periodic Table* to speak in schools, and participate in roundtables, conversations or meetings, become more frequent. Except to the schools, he usually says no. The post, every morning, brings him ever-bulkier piles of letters from Italy and abroad, but also numerous manuscripts by young people wanting his judgement and asking to be received by him. One by one old school, work or holiday companions, especially those who have recognized themselves in the book, contact him by telephone or in writing. On the street people stop him to talk, to ask him for an autograph, maybe on the back of a tram ticket. He says: 'Fame gratifies me a bit and bothers me a bit. I'll end up by cutting off my beard.'

A Dutch couple knock on his door. They are making a film at their own expense on a theme that is difficult but of great interest to Primo Levi, on how the truth becomes distorted among both the perpetrators of the Lager and the victims. They've travelled halfway across Europe, they've collected among others the testimony of an SS who's had the gall to affirm, 'To some of those poor people I gave bread, not to all. How could it have been possible?' For balance, they have already listened to a highly traumatized French female survivor. Now they would like to hear from the author of *If This is a Man* who of course makes himself available. He remembers well some desperate distortions of the truth, for example by one of his fellow prisoners who, when the SS 'selected' his father, that is took him from the crowd to send him to the gas chamber, pushed reality away by simply denying the 'selections' existed.

At the end of September the director of the publisher Adelphi Edizioni called Levi to Milan to assign to him the translation of *Die Nacht der Girondjinen*[24] by the Dutch writer Jacques Presser. Levi agreed. He would write in the Preface: 'I came across this story by chance, a few years ago: I read it and reread it many times, and it didn't leave my mind after that.'[25] First because it is a true story, almost a record of the deportation of Amsterdam's Jews to Auschwitz; then because it is the harrowing tale of the identity crisis of the Western Jew; and finally because it is an unprejudiced book, which puts at the centre the savage figure of a Jewish collaborationist.

> To be reminded that at Westerbork a man such as Cohn lived and operated burns like cauterized skin and is worthy of comment. Such

> individuals did exist, and certainly still exist among us in a virtual state: in normal conditions they're not recognizable [...] but merciless persecutions develop them and bring them to light and to power. It is naïve, absurd and historically false to hold that a demonic system like National Socialism sanctifies its victims: on the contrary, it degrades them and dirties them, assimilates them to itself and all the more so they are willing, blank, lacking a political or moral backbone [...]There exists a contagion of evil: the non-man dehumanizes the others, every crime radiates outwards, proliferates, corrupts consciences and surrounds itself with accomplices won over by fear or seduction [...] from the opposite camp.[26]

For the next year, *Night of the Girondists* took up nearly all his time. When the work was finished he confided in us:

> The whole time, I felt a violent emotion. Westerbork was the camp the Dutch had made for the Jews who'd escaped Poland; under the Nazi occupation, it had become a transit camp from which the convoys set off for the East. Translating, I relived Auschwitz. And writing the Foreword cost me a lot. But it's time to confront these subjects, even the ones that are burning hot. The space between torturers and victims is a grey zone, not a desert.

He will wield his scalpel into the 'grey zone' later and investigate it pitilessly in *The Drowned and the Saved*. Now, in the Preface to Presser's story, he writes:

> Only a Manichean rhetoric can maintain that this space is empty: it's not, it's crammed with sordid, wretched and pathetic figures (sometimes they possess all three qualities at the same time) whom it's indispensable to get to know if we want to know the human species, if we want to defend our souls should a similar test return.

This last quarter of 1975 is a very intense period. Levi has left the management of the factory a few months before, but has remained an active consultant; he writes pieces for *La Stampa* and others to put away in his drawer to think about further; he devotes himself to the council of his old school, the *Liceo Classico Massimo D'Azeglio*, of which he is the president; he is translating Presser and also Heine; he continues to go into schools. Most of all he is preparing for publication a selection of the questions students ask him when he meets them to discuss his books in dozens and dozens of middle schools in Piedmont, Lombardy, Veneto, Tuscany and Liguria. Together with the questions he is also summarizing the answers he gave.

Both will appear in advance in *Tuttolibri*[27] the following February, and will be put in the Appendices to the Italian editions of his first two books, which Einaudi had included for years in its series for middle school students and which from then on will find a place in their German, English and American editions.

Among the answers, the one to the question 'How can the Nazis' fanatical hatred of the Jews be explained?' is the most challenging. He outlines the history of anti-Semitism ('one particular case of intolerance') from the Romans to Hitler, from the persecutions to the massacres, the extermination. But none of the many hypotheses provided by historians to explain 'the furious anti-Semitism of Hitler and of Germany behind him' seem adequate. He writes:

> Perhaps what happened cannot be comprehended, or rather, *shouldn't be* comprehended, because to comprehend is almost to justify. Let me explain: to 'comprehend' a human intention or behaviour means (etymologically as well) to contain it, to contain the author, put oneself in his place and identify with him. Now, no normal man will ever be able to identify with Hitler, Himmler, Goebbels, Eichmann and innumerable others. This burdens us, and yet it brings us relief, because perhaps it is desirable that their words (and also, unfortunately, their deeds) should not be comprehensible to us. They are words and deeds that are not human but, rather, counter-human, without historic precedent, barely comparable to the cruellest events of the biological struggle for existence. War can be traced back to this struggle, but Auschwitz has nothing to do with war; it is not an episode of war, it is not an extreme form of war. War is an everlasting terrible fact, it is deplorable, but it is in us, it has a rationality, we 'comprehend' it.

'But there is nothing rational', he continues:

> [...] about the Nazi hatred: it's a hatred that is not in us; it's outside of humanity, a poisonous fruit arising from the deadly trunk of fascism, but outside and beyond fascism itself. We can't understand it; but we can and must understand its roots, and be on our guard. If understanding is impossible, recognising is necessary, because what has happened can happen again, conscience can again be seduced and obscured; even our own.[28]

Just when he was busy writing these things, he received a pressing invitation from the Leo Club in Cuneo: the young people of that town wanted to question him, particularly about *The Periodic Table*. The organizers of the meeting were the president of the Club Dr Massimo Martinelli, his father

Professor Claudio Martinelli, Cuneo's director of education and the writer Luigi Baccolo. The introduction is warm and affectionate, highlighting the figure of Primo Levi the anti-fascist, who entrusts his persecutors to the democratic legal process, a calm champion of the saving power of hope. Martinelli points out the book's enlightenment inspiration, its Ariostan imagination, its Lucretian poetry. Then it is the author's turn to speak, with his disarming simplicity:

> I would just like to make some small additions to this book. I'd made myself a plan, which was, essentially, for an educational book. That is to say I wanted, as I wrote in the story called 'Silver', to make non-chemists understand 'the strong and bitter flavour of our occupation'. Not because it's special, or privileged, but precisely because it is a 'trade'. If I'm allowed to quote myself, it's 'a more strenuous version of the occupation of living'. I'm convinced that all jobs done with the hands or with the brain possess, potentially, that substance, that flavour which mine possesses. I'm convinced, because it's already been experienced many times, that any serious, concrete human activity can harbour stories with the flavour of those I've written. And that's all I'd intended. I realized later, or rather my readers made me realize, and I've already admitted it in public, that the book had escaped my control. A book is a bit like a child: you have a strong desire that it take a certain path. Then it deviates, it takes its own path. Now, in *The Periodic Table* a bit of everything came out. Even scraps of my not strictly professional experiences. Whether it's a good or a bad thing I couldn't say. But it's a fact that, I don't say without my knowledge but certainly against the plan I had traced, there emerged a cross-section of a generation and of a history. How much the book is worth I don't know, because an author never knows how much what he does is worth; at least for me it's very difficult to judge the things that I do. I hope though that the book really does contain more hope than despair and that particularly the young people who read it will perceive that. One of the things I've learned is that between hope and despair it's better to bargain on hope, because it yields much more. Despairing is nice, it's masochistically satisfying, but in the long run it yields little. It yields little for the one who despairs, and it yields very little, indeed nothing, for others. It seems to me that one of the conclusions one can arrive at from a war service such as mine in my profession, which is that of measuring oneself up against things, is that despairing is really no use at all. It's much better to take on a certain fighting load, for which one doesn't resign oneself to things that don't work, and often they don't. It's rare, in all the jobs in the world, for things to go smoothly; in mine in particular they rarely go the way they should. There's a theory, of course, but it doesn't always work: there's often an

> incident, something unexpected against which one must mobilize, take precautions. Now, it seems to me that faced with a problem of that kind the state of mind of the despairing man is truly one of the worst, because it doesn't lead to any result. If other things appear in this book, besides the stories 'of the solitary, unarmed, pedestrian chemistry, on a human scale' (excuse me if I quote myself again), I'd like to say that I am not to blame. That is, that it wasn't planned. There's even a chapter which, as has recently been pointed out, could appear in *If This is a Man.* It's a story of the Lager, that on Cerium, but one in which there is no despair; and in *If This is a Man*, where there is little hope, it wouldn't have been in the right place. But it seemed right to me, with the distance of time, after the downward road, to tell also of the upward road. And I think therefore that the story has found its place in *The Periodic Table*, which in my view is an optimistic book. I'm not ashamed to say it even if it's been thrown back at me. In an age where optimism is little rated, it's an optimistic book.

The questions rain down from the audience. The first speaker quotes two reviews of *The Periodic Table* that had just appeared in the monthly publication of the Jewish Community of Turin, *Ha Keillah* [The Community]. One asserts that the book is the triumph of reason. The other claims that the 'extraordinary talent' of the book is deeply rooted in Jewish tradition and constitutes a classic of that culture. But according to the second reviewer, the dominant theme to be emphasized is a message about the love of work, which Primo Levi hopes to communicate to the young. Yet now, for too many, the possibility of accessing work no longer exists, and many of them, reading the book, felt more than anything a 'lump in their throat' and a bit envious. What did the author of *The Periodic Table* think of these observations?

> That the book is the triumph of reason, unfortunately not: it would be too easy if one succeeded in making reason triumph with a book. That it is however a vote in favour of reason and against non-reason: yes, I agree perfectly. Indeed, one of the reasons for the gratitude I feel towards my profession is precisely this: that it trains one to reason, and not only in the laboratory, but also outside it. I've written that in some of the pages. For us, for my generation, for my friends let's say, for my colleagues, the study of chemistry and physics has been a defence. An island of reason in the middle of the non-reason of fascism. Fascism, as it was administered to us, that is to say fascism already victorious, confirmed, installed, triumphant, openly discouraged reason. Our fascist history or philosophy texts were full, crammed to the brim, with the discouragement of independent reason. And we'd found, each in his own way, some in maths, some

> in geometry, some elsewhere (I in chemistry) an island of reason that was like firm ground on which to drop anchor. That's for the first point. As for the second, that is the implicit criticism that effectively says, it's a very fine thing, work, but we can't find any work. There too I can only agree. Maybe my optimism has been excessive, exaggerated. It's true that it's not enough to love work in order to find it; it's true that the current situation, especially for intellectual young people, is very serious. That 'lump in the throat' you mention I well understand. It's a sad fate that hangs over today's youth, over our children. For this I wouldn't know how to find a cure, that's clear, it doesn't depend on us: the cure must be found on a world scale, or at least a European or national one. I'd just like to say that one mustn't, in my view, give in too early, lay down one's arms too early. And I think that awareness of the objective difficulties mustn't coincide with a devaluation of work, for the reasons I've given before. That is to say that work, almost all kinds of work, I can't say all, is a good teacher it's good to turn to.
>
> Now we come to the judgement of the reviewer who would make me nothing less than a representative of Jewish culture. No, that seems to me decidedly exaggerated. I am too ignorant of Jewish culture to be called a writer in that tradition. It's true that I'm a Jew, that I've never been ashamed of being one, that I've learned something as a Jew, that reading the Bible interests me, that reading books belonging to the stream of European Judaism has always appealed to me. It's even true that a chapter of *The Periodic Table,* 'Argon', is dedicated to our legendary and mad Piedmontese Jewish ancestors. But I think that it would be immodest on my part to class myself as a classic figure of Judaism; that I'm not. I'd like to be, but I'm not.

A doctor, the father of a secondary-school student, is struck by 'the religious sense' of deep humility that one has, reading of the young Levi who, having taken his first steps in chemistry and reached as far as the third or fourth year, realizes that he is in a desert, in the sense that the truth is far distant. And so he resolves to go back to the origins, following mathematics and physics to their sources of 'strenuous clarity'. But he escapes also from physics, ending up rejecting university, as it was then, in a state of decay. 'I'd like to know', says that father:

> *[...] whether the hope that you've infused into your book is something that can give certainty to our children. That is whether, on the basis of your experiences, the study of the so-called exact science subjects has a meaning for life, even today when we find ourselves faced with the*

absolute relativity of science, because what was science in the 1950s isn't science any more.

I understand. First of all, the humility you've noted in the book is a personal humility of mine. It's because I studied so poorly, for reasons outside my control, that I couldn't help feeling humble. That is, feeling myself to be 'profane', in the etymological sense of one who stands outside the temple and can't come in. It's not that I rejected university, it's university that rejected me. That is, I had to study in the margins. I realized halfway through the chemistry course that it would have been better to have studied physics, for what I wanted to know: that is, it was a better stepping-stone, a better path, to follow physics rather than chemistry. It was, precisely, more 'exact'. If I didn't do it, it's not because I didn't want to; I would happily have taken that road later, but even later it wasn't possible, because it was post-war and there was bread to be earned.

As for the other part of your question, I think that things haven't changed very much. I think that even today, despite the exact sciences and also medicine and chemistry expanding at a speed that those outside the field can't even imagine, all the same one can undertake these studies to great advantage, with the certainty of finding oneself on the crest of the wave. In the last ten years more things have been learned about the solar system that in the previous four thousand, in fact in all previous years; every month truly amazing discoveries mount up, discoveries to leave one with bated breath, discoveries on the solar system, or DNA; the discussion of the genetic code is in fast development: if one thinks of all of this, truly it seems to me that any young person who has an appetite for these things, must be encouraged not discouraged. There's space for everything, despite the difficulties you mentioned earlier. I think that if there are students here who are uncertain about their choice, one can truly say that there are subjects that repay themselves, also financially. Whoever wants to, whoever seriously intends to enter the field can be sure not to waste his time, and also that he will find a position. On this I believe there is no doubt. Of course, it's necessary that the person who chooses, has a minimum of talent, and above all of willingness, but they won't be disappointed. If I were younger I'd happily start again myself, in fact. If that's what you wanted to ask, I can confirm it. What was said in your time is still valid.

The debate became animated when some audience members offered further penetrating questions, such as: 'Your book is a successful synthesis of scientific and humanist culture. Tell me, can one attempt, with analogies and parallels, to understand humanity by applying the laws of physics and chemistry to them? It seems to me that you've done so, is that right?' Another question is: what debt does the writer owe to the chemist?

> I would have liked to apply the laws of physics to something as complicated as mankind – but I'm not capable of it, and at the moment no one is. It's a well-known fact that the laws of physics are yet to be successfully applied even to a cell. Not that it's impossible; it's likely that in the next ten or twenty years one will succeed in applying at least a bit of mathematics to a simple cell. Now certainly not, still less to mankind. My trick, let's say, is much tinier, much smaller: it's about applying similarities. I've made use of the similarities I liked, which seemed fun to me, which also seemed to me to be more than superficial, a bit deeper. For example, the concept of purity, which is easily transferred from chemistry to mankind. As also the concept of combinatorial analysis: it can be and is done. Sociology, in large part, is an application of statistics and combinatorial analysis to the human sciences. Now I'll answer your other question.
>
> I said before that I'm grateful to my trade because it's provided me with a certain way of reasoning and expressing myself. I must also add that I am grateful to my trade for a second thing: because it's provided me with a remarkable amount of raw material. The individual elements, the laws of chemistry and physics, the terminology itself, seem to me to be extremely useful for one who intends to write, or for one who ends up writing, which is what happened to me. I found myself writing by chance, as is common knowledge; it wasn't my intention. I wanted to be a chemist and I have been one. I found myself going over to the other side, deserting in fact, going over to the side of the writers, because I had things to tell. But in this exercise of writing, the possession of other concepts, other terms and other experiences (also in the strict, laboratory sense of testing through experience and observation) is a richness, a supply, a true storehouse one can draw on. Among the reviews this book has had, there is one very beautiful one by Natalia Ginzburg, who is not a chemist at all, in fact she is on the other side. Natalia, with whom I am great friends, is a woman of great imagination, but lacking in scientific knowledge, despite being the daughter of a famous anatomist. Now, despite all that, she has hit home saying that I'm a chemist and that she's always been jealous of me for being one. I understand that perfectly. Because, truly, when I find myself writing, it seems that the patrimony I've inherited with four years of study but above all with twenty-six years in the chemical industry, is a heritage that is useful. Useful not only in writing, but also in understanding things and men.

Then Primo Levi was asked to comment, one by one, on all twenty-one chapters of *The Periodic Table*. 'The first', observes someone in the middle of the room,

> *[…] is one of the most beautiful. Having read 'Argon' I leapt greedily on the following ones and I certainly can't say that I was disappointed. But I found something completely different. Even if they're on the same level of perfection, the first chapter is completely different, a kind of legendary and at the same time clearly real re-enactment of an archaic past. Nona Bimba, Barbabramìn, Uncle Gabriele, all this extraordinary world of your ancestors. Don't you think that it could be the first chapter in a new book that you could write from the thread of memory? 'Argon' has made me discover some of the most beautiful pages in today's literature. It left me with pleasure, with desire, with the need to go on. Will it find a sequel and be further developed?*

> No, I don't think that one can. I don't think that I'm capable of writing much more on that theme. That first chapter, whose heterogeneity compared to the rest of the book I am well aware of, is almost an ex-voto. That is to say it's a vow fulfilled; the vow that I would not throw away, would not let fall into nothingness that little cupboard of Lares and Penates,[29] lopsided, comical, ungainly, pathetic, but alive, in their way, with an emotional life, which would be a shame to leave to waste away. And so it seemed to me that I needed to perform a work of piety, by preserving them in twenty pages. But I've been through my collection, there are no more. Unless I provide myself with more. I've collected the whole history, or legend, or myth, as it was told to me. It's clear that the detail of these stories is in inverse proportion to the distance in time. The furthest characters are collected in an image, in a central image like that of Nona Bimba who'd ridden up the ice-covered Po. It's certainly false, but that's how Nona Bimba's story came down to her great grandchildren. Whereas for Barbaricô, for example, whose story takes up two pages and is very well-structured, I met him myself and he was just like that, I've neither added nor taken away anything. I would very much like to write more on the subject, but I've finished, the material is all there. I've resigned myself to being a writer of memory. And memory isn't invented. It can be polished, cleaned, filtered, but it can't be created out of nothing. Even the chapter that concludes the book is an ex-voto. It matured from an old idea, conceived in fact when I was in prison in Aosta, condemned to death, and it seemed a great shame to me to be executed without being able to write the story of a carbon atom[…] It saddened me for other reasons, that's clear, but this was one of them, I remember it very clearly. It was naïve, but that's how it was. I will add, to conclude,

> that on the theme of the interaction between matter and mankind, I still have two or three things to say and I hope to have time to say all of them before that other death sentence that awaits us all. And that is to say other stories of the same genre as these, taken more literally; other questions of the endless battle between mankind and matter, in the multitude of forms it has taken over time: from prehistory, which fascinates me and which I've tried to draw out of nothing, up to what is happening today. What's happening today has many deplorable aspects we are all aware of: exploitation, pollution, urbanization and so on. Technological civilization, we well know, has many disastrously destructive sides. But I also know positive ones, and I'm not ashamed to say that I appreciate them, and that it seems to me a curious form of masochism not to tell about them. In fact, now that we live in the middle of technological civilization, it's fashionable to speak very badly of it. The reasons exist, and are many and undeniable. Yet faced with the prodigiously intelligent, patient and also heroic work that is done more or less everywhere in the world (a little bit, not much, also in Italy) one can only show respect. There are those who really fight on the front line, for example against illnesses, with methods those outside the field rarely imagine, because of the extreme sophistication, the extreme amount of intelligence and patience they demand. It makes me sorry that this isn't said and known, and even though I don't know the subject very well, I would like to deepen my knowledge and tell the story.[30]

He did not have time. The 'death sentence that awaits us all' came first. But the aim, the promise, shine through the words he spoke that night at the Leo Club of Cuneo, when it seemed the audience's curiosity could not be satisfied.

Notes

1. P. Levi trans. A. Goldstein, *The Periodic Table*, in A. Goldstein (ed.), *Complete Works of Primo Levi* (Liveright: New York, 2015), Vol. II, p.941.
2. P. Levi trans. R. Rosenthal, *The Periodic Table* (New York: Schocken Books, 1984), jacket flap.
3. M. Piattelli Palmarini, 'Quando il romanzo "parla" la scienza' [When the novel 'speaks' science], *Corriere della Sera*, 17August 1979.
4. From the 'Incontro con Primo Levi' [Meeting with Primo Levi] on 4 June 1975, organized by the Unione Culturale di Torino [Turin Cultural Union] in Palazzo Carignano, Turin, recorded by Cesare Vai.
5. Palmarini, 'Quando il romanzo "parla" la scienza'.
6. Ernesto Gagliano and Giorgio De Rienzo, 'La ragione non può andare in vacanza' [Reason can't go on holiday], *Stampa Sera* books column, 13 May 1975.
7. Piero Calamandrei, a famous anti-fascist soldier, jurist, writer and academic.

8. The philosophical doctrine that matter is alive.
9. Cesare Cases, introduction to the first volume of the Italian edition of Levi's complete works, which includes *Il sistema periodico*[*The Periodic Table*] and *I sommersi e I salvati* [*The Drowned and the Saved*] rather than *Natural Histories* and *Flaw of Form*: *Opere di Primo Levi*, Vol.I (Turin: Einaudi, 1987), p.xvii.
10. 'Incontro', 4 June 1975.
11. Giorgio De Rienzo, 'In un alambicco quanta poesia' [How much poetry in a still], *Famiglia Cristiana*, No.29, 20 July 1975.
12. Stefano Jesurum, *Essere ebrei in Italia* [Being Jewish in Italy] (Longanesi: Milan, 1987) p.5.
13. Meeting with Primo Levi organized by the Leo Club of Cuneo, Autumn 1975, recorded by Franca Veglia Grosso.
14. Roth (see Translator's Notes and note in Chapter 1).
15. Published in *La Stampa* in July 1978 with the title 'Il cantore e il veterano' [The cantor and the veteran] and then included in *Lilith and Other Stories*, published in Italy by Einaudi in 1981, and in English translation (by Ann Goldstein) with the title 'The Cantor and the Veteran' (*The Complete Works of Primo Levi*, Vol. II, pp.1,379-84). There are few changes from the original version as told to Di Rienzo. The protagonist is not a doctor now but 'a watchmaker by trade, a cantor on Saturdays, in a remote Lithuanian village [...], the heir to an ancient, sorrowful and strange tradition, whose core consists in holding evil in abomination and in "making a hedge around the law", so that evil does not flood in through gaps in the hedge to drown that very law' (pp.1,381-3).
16. It later appeared as the title story in *L'ultimo Natale di Guerra* [The last Christmas of the War], illustrated by Imre Reiner (Lugano: privately printed, 1984); the story 'Last Christmas of the War' is included on pp.55-67 of P. Levi trans. R. Feldman, *Moments of Reprieve*, (Summit Books: New York, 1986) and on pp. 2,687-94 of P. Levi trans. A. and F. Bastagli, *Uncollected Stories and Essays:1981-1987* in *The Complete Works of Primo Levi*, Vol. III.
17. Giacomo Matteotti, leader of the United Socialist Party, was killed outside Rome by fascists on 10 June 1924 after publishing a book and making speeches in Parliament attacking the fascists.
18. Levi was a member of two fascist youth organizations, first the Opera Nazionale Balilla [National Balilla Operation] for boys between 8 and 14, and then the Avanguardia Generale Fascista [Fascist Youth Vanguard] for boys between 14 and 18. The girls' section was called the 'Piccole Italiane', 'Little Italians'.
19. *La Stampa*, 'Così fu arrestato Primo Levi partigiano' [This is how the partisan Primo Levi was arrested], 21 April 1984.
20. G. Grassano, *Primo Levi* (Florence: Il Castoro/La Nuova Italia, 1981) p.9.
21. A town in Tuscany where three prestigious literary prizes (for poetry, narrative and essays) were awarded each year from 1948 to 1991.
22. *L'Unità*, 'Il Premio Prato assegnato a Donini e a Primo Levi' [The Prato Prize awarded to Donini and Primo Levi], 13 September 1975.
23. A paladin of Charlemagne who, in Italian romance epics such as *Orlando Furioso*, sets off on a magic horse that can run faster than an arrow.
24. *Night of the Girondists*, trans. B.Mussey (London: Harvill, 1992). The English edition also includes a translation of Levi's Foreword.
25. Levi, Foreword to Jacques Presser, *La notte dei Girondini*, [The night of the Girondists] (Milan: Adelphi, 1976) p.11.
26. Ibid, pp.13-4.
27. With the title 'Ma perché Auschwitz?' [But why Auschwitz?], *Tuttolibri (La Stampa)*, No.8, 28 February 1976.

28. P. Levi trans. S. Woolf, 'Appendix to *If This is a Man*', in *The Complete Works of Primo Levi*, Vol. I, p.190.
29. Guardian and ancestor deities in ancient Roman religion.
30. At the end of the meeting organized by the Leo Club, there were naturally some questions on the Lager. The main ones are quoted in this book in chapter VIII, 'If We Keep Silent, Who Will Speak?'

IV

Poetry, A Strange Infection

In the autumn of 1975, All'insegna del Pesce d'Oro, a small Milanese publishing house run by the journalist and art critic Vanni Scheiwiller, quietly published a slim volume of poems entitled *L'osteria di Brema* [*The Bremen Beer-Hall*], its author Primo Levi. It contains 66 pages, including the index; there are only 27 poems, written over more than 30 years. The first two poems are mirrors of the Lager, casting singular reflections over the abyss. In all or nearly all there is a core of pain that must not be suppressed or silenced 'because it is one with life'. And around this core – which features metaphysical desolation, terror, pity, anxiety, irony and solitude – grows a poetic construction fed by the curse of memory, diluted by a nostalgia that is 'fragile and tender suffering' and pain, even if 'limpid and clear'. Three poems of the collection were already widely known as the epigraphs to *If This is a Man* ('Shema', a glittering Biblical tirade), *The Truce* ('Reveille', dense with anguish) and *Flaw of Form* ('They Were a Hundred', pervaded by sinister omens). The other poems in the collection, though written many years earlier, were known only to a close circle of friends (23 poems, published privately, anonymously and without a title in 1970 in Turin, with a print run of 300).

After the books on the abyss and the escape from it; after the only apparently liberating flight into fantasy and the worrying reflection on the errors of technological progress; after the recent stories of militant chemistry and the precious fusion of the two cultures; after all these there was a new project. Primo Levi wanted to give his readers a poetry collection, with his usual modesty ('In exchange, I'll leave you nebbish lines like these') [nebbish is the Yiddish word for pathetic, useless, of no importance]. Why, they often asked him, did he feel it was the right moment to share with the public 'an isolated and probably marginal experience of his'?[1]. He defended himself. The answer he didn't give is perhaps in 'Farewell', which ends the brief collection: 'It's grown late, dear ones'. Late for the past as a lesson for the future; late because of the widening flaw threatening our moral universe. For anyone who has faith in reason it is high time to be alarmed. It's been said that 'There is no poetry except in the concrete'[2] and, for Primo Levi, the concrete had two sides: memory and science. With *The Bremen Beer-Hall* he offered both to the most careful 'five or seven readers': the recovery of the dark season ('I'd like to believe something beyond/ Beyond death destroyed you') that is, the group of 'concise and bloody' poems written just after his imprisonment, even before *If This is a Man* took shape from his 'telling the story at breakneck speed'; and the discomforting relationship with the architects of the sky ('The sky is scattered with horrible dead suns [...] And all of us human seed we live and die for nothing'). Between the two lies the black shadow of the crow ('What is the number of your days? I've counted them'); the pallid light of Lilith; the spectre of the 'abandoned creature' Eichmann; the grim foreboding of the past that returns with 'the familiar clang of iron feet' outside the door. Let mankind be on the alert before it sounds again.

When the poems had grown to more than sixty (not counting translations , which he defined in a note as 'more musical than philological, and amusements rather than professional works'), he wrote an ironic justification on the jacket flap of the new volume.[3]

> In all civilizations, even those without writing, many people, both illustrious and obscure, feel the need to express themselves in verse, and subject themselves to it. Hence they secrete poetic material, addressed to themselves, to their neighbours, or to the universe, material that can be full-blooded or bloodless, eternal or ephemeral. Verse was certainly born before prose. Who has never written poetry?
>
> I'm a man. I too, at irregular times, 'at an uncertain hour', have given in to this urge. It appears to be written into our genetic heritage. At times poetry seemed to be better suited than prose for getting an idea or an image across. I don't know why and I've never worried about it. I know very little about poetic theory. I read very little of other people's poetry. I don't believe in the sacredness of art and I don't even believe that these poems of mine are excellent. I can only assure the reader that in certain rare instances (on average not more than once a year) individual stimuli have taken on, *naturaliter*, a certain shape that my rational half continues to consider unnatural.

And Giovanni Raboni[4] would say this about the justification of a 'true poet' to his readers:

> Let me say straightaway that the modesty or caution of Levi (which is admirable, and should be shared, though in fact it isn't by many famous prose writers when they make their legitimate forays into the field of poetry) turns out, when measured up against the facts, excessive to say the least [...] I wouldn't take for granted by any means that the poetry of Primo Levi represents, as he seems to suggest, a necessary but marginal activity, a sort of *violon d'Ingres*[5] played with passionate discretion. Right from the start, from 'You who live safe', it seems to me that Levi's poetic writings have the same moral acumen,

> the same power of memory, warning and piety that makes his prose so substantial, so to the point and so naturally memorable.[6]

There were several reviews, but no interview at the first appearance of Primo Levi as a poet. They would come later, after he began to publish poems regularly on the third page of *La Stampa*, and after he finally decided to collect all the poems written from 1943 onwards in a volume, to satisfy the readers who constantly questioned him on it, asked him for explanations, expressed approval or disapproval, but always interest and curiosity, submerging him in letters and also telephone calls. He said on one occasion to the journalist and writer Giulio Nascimbeni: 'I get the impression that poetry is becoming a prodigious tool of human contact.'[7] Before then he rarely talked about his poetic work. Another occasion was around a year after the publication of that slim, elegant little book with the greenish cover, in reply to the question of an audience member in Zurich:

> *When and why did you write* The Bremen Beer-Hall?
>
> The first poem goes right back to 1943, when after my first work experience in Balengero, a town near Turin, I had accepted another at the Wander laboratory in Milan; fifteen are concentrated around 1946, before and during the writing of my first book, when I was working at the Duco factory in Avigliana; the following ones I wrote, sometimes with a gap of years, between 1949 and 1974. That's for the when. As for the why, well I don't, of course, feel guilt or shame about writing poems, but it's part of a mental process I don't know very well and have little control over. I'm a writer 'from the neck up'. in that rational part of me that ignores, disregards and suppresses all the rest. The poems are points of emotionalism which it's very difficult for me to analyse. As a writer, I've forced myself to be scrupulously clear; I'm not sure that I've lived up to that in my poetry. What there is underneath our rationality we don't know, we're made of ego and id. Inside us we have depths we ourselves know little of. It could be that poetry is the product of two right hands: and if it isn't certain that an author is completely aware of what he has written, if it isn't certain that between his lines there's something that comes from other places than the brain – for poetry, at least as far as I am concerned, I think it's definitely the case.

Shortly after that statement he spoke about poetry to the audience at the Carignano theatre in Turin, during the discussion following one of the Italian Cultural Association's 'Literary Fridays'. A spectator had asked him why, in his summary of his works, he had not included *The Bremen Beer-Hall*. He replied:

> For a number of reasons. Most of all because it's a very small book and the majority of the poems collected in it all collect around – at least a good half of them do – the period immediately following the end of the war and my return to Italy, after a year in Auschwitz and nine months of the absurd and tortuous return journey. That is, they were born like *If This is a Man*, from the urgent need to write. Then because, at least in some of these verses, I've expressed in poetry what I later wrote in prose. Finally, while I answer for every word written in my prose books, I don't answer for my poems. In fact, I have no rational answers; poetry has caught me red-handed, things that were weighing down on me inside broke the floodgates and came out like that, in verse. I've chosen to write with the head and not the heart; the poems have shown me that I don't always succeed. Allow me too to have a shred of 'id'.[8]

He returned to his poetic compositions and the manner of their birth in September 1979, answering the question of a scholar.

> *What is the value, what are the meanings of the poems which sometimes appear in* La Stampa?
>
> In my view, very little. My natural state is that of not making poems, yet every now and again that strange infection wells up, like a disease that comes out in a rash. I'll never apply myself to composing poems methodically. It has happened that I've written five or six in the course of three days, like those that open *The Bremen Beer-Hall.* It still happens to me, for reasons I don't understand, maybe because I've got more spare time, but it's a completely uncontrolled phenomenon. At a certain point one finds in one's body the core of a poem, the first line or another line, then all the rest comes out. Sometimes it stands up, sometimes I throw it away, but it's a phenomenon I don't know, don't understand, that I'm unable to theorize, even the workings of which I reject. It isn't part of my world. My world is that of thinking about a thing, of developing it almost like a [...] fitter, that's it, building it a bit at a time. That other way of producing in a sudden brainwave astonishes me. And in fact I've written only thirty poems in forty years.[9]

Notes

1. Lorenzo Mondo, 'Dal Lager non si esce' [One doesn't get out of the Lager], *La Stampa*, 19 December 1975.
2. By the collagist and graffiti artist Mimmo Rotella.

3. *Ad ora incerta* [At an Uncertain Hour], (Milan: Garzanti,1984). Translated by Jonathan Galassi as *Collected Poems* in A. Goldstein (ed.), *Complete Works of Primo Levi* (Liveright: New York, 2015) Vol. III, pp.1,865-2008.
4. A poet, literary critic and translator from French into Italian.
5. 'Occasional pastime', from the story that the painter Ingres preferred playing his violin badly to visitors rather than showing them his paintings.
6. Giovanni Raboni, 'Primo Levi poeta vero ad ora incerta' [Primo Levi a true poet at an uncertain hour], *Tuttolibri*(*La Stampa*), 17 November 1984.
7. Giulio Nascimbeni,'Levi, l'ora incerta della poesia'[Levi, the uncertain hour of poetry], *Corriere della Sera*, 28 October 1984.
8. From the shorthand notes taken by *La Stampa* at the discussion in the Carignano theatre, 19 November 1976.
9. G. Grassano, *Primo Levi* (Florence: Il Castoro/La Nuova Italia, 1981), p.15.

V

From the Laboratory to the Writing Desk

By the start of 1976 *The Periodic Table*, having reached its fourth Italian edition, had sold more than 40,000 copies. It would also be favourably received abroad, particularly in East Germany and in the United States, where it would be a bridgehead for all Primo Levi's works. Its success was accompanied by the thirtieth reprint of *If This is a Man*. This had already sold 220,000 copies, and by the end of the year would reach 30,000 and it was now translated into seven languages including Japanese. Entered into encyclopedias, respectfully discussed in books of contemporary literary history, all that was left for Primo Levi, as he put it, was to 'sign the capitulation' and publicly recognize his official status. He did so with a kind of irony, choosing as his theme for a lecture at Turin's Carignano theatre on 19 November 1976 'Lo scrittore non-scrittore' [The non-writer writer]. He had accepted the invitation of the Associazione Culturale Italiana [Italian Cultural Association] to take part in their 'Venerdì letterari'[Literary Fridays] series of lectures and discussions, on condition he was allowed to speak under that 'simultaneously shy and proud banner, which presented an attempt at self-analysis rather than a desire to communicate new theories on the nature of literary expression'.

On that foggy November evening the Carignano was packed. The meeting with the ex-'outlaw' of letters aroused people's curiosity; the ambiguity of the theme was stimulating. Primo Levi presented 'the notes for a sort of map of the motivations for his writing'.[1]

> It's not my intention to say that to write a book one must be a 'non-writer', but simply that I acquired that status without choosing it. I'm a chemist. I acquired the status of a writer because, captured as a partisan, I ended up in the Lager as a Jew.
>
> My first book is the story of my year in Auschwitz and the book has a long and strange history. I'd forced myself to write, despite my fear, from the time of imprisonment itself; a few lines, annotations, notes for my loved ones written with a stub of pencil and immediately destroyed, because there was no way of preserving them, except in memory. Being found with them on one's person was tantamount to an 'act of espionage' and that could mean death. But so great was my need to pass on the experience I was living through, to make others

acquainted with it, in other words to tell, that I had already started to do so there. I hoped, we hoped, to live to tell of what we'd seen. The desire wasn't just mine, it belonged to all of us and it was reflected in a dream, the same dream for many of us; recently I came upon it in the book of a French female deportee. It was a double dream. In the first one dreamed of food – fat, juicy, delicious-smelling food – but always, at the moment we brought it to our mouths, something happened: either it disappeared, or it was taken away by someone, or between the hungry man and his food a kind of barrier fell that made the act of eating impossible. The other dream was that of telling, generally to someone close to us, but here too the act was not completed. The person was indifferent, didn't listen and at a certain point shrugged their shoulders, went off, disappeared.

The symbolism of the double dream was very simple. I say this to underline that the need to eat and the need to tell were on the same level of primal necessity. The food that disappears and the story that isn't finished take on the same anguish of unsatisfied need.

In my case, I took that primal, violent impulse to tell with me when I came back, and I wrote it down straight away, building the story around those lost notes, for two reasons. First: because what I had seen and lived through was weighing down on me and I felt the urgent need to free myself of it. Second: to satisfy the moral, civil and political duty to testify. Of us Italian Jews, who had ended up in the Lager together with millions of other Jews from all over Europe for the sole crime of having been born, only a few dozen out of the 8,000 deported (in my convoy, 15 out of 650) were lucky enough to survive. People knew little of the truth, or knew only vaguely. I myself at the time didn't know the scale of the extermination being carried out on the basis of a mad ideology that sought the suppression of the other simply because of his otherness.

But in writing *If This is a Man* I didn't have literary ambitions, I didn't intend to make a book out of it, still less to become a writer. So much so that I wrote the chapters in order not of logic but of urgency, starting with the last ones, and I didn't even take care to structure it or to deal with its fragmented nature. When it was done I went, or rather went back, to being a chemist. For ten years. Only in 1958, when *If This is a Man* was republished, did the desire to write come back to me. As for the book, which was published with a print run of 2,500 at the end of 1947 by a small publisher after others had turned it down, it was very well received by the critics. But after a year, or not much more than that, it had been forgotten though especially here in Turin, it continued to be talked about by those affected by the events it related in *If This is a Man*. If you think about it, it was understandable that it hadn't been judged readable and that it hadn't got much of a hearing. The times were harsh. People were struggling to live, the wounds of war were wide and deep, people's only preoccupation was to rebuild the ruins; they just wanted to forget and move on. But already in 1955-56 the climate had changed. People had read Vercors, Russell, Poliakov and many others, they had seen the documentaries filmed at the liberation of the camps; and a broader interest in the Lager phenomenon was starting to take shape.

A prestigious publisher agreed to reprint *If This is a Man* in 1958. It was translated straight away; young people read it and took an interest in it. They called on me to speak about it, explain it, they asked me questions. It was the birth of my third trade, which, if I'd granted all the requests that came to me from schools, would have stopped me doing anything else. That fact has put me in contact with a new reality, with the generation that is setting out on life. I ended up by collecting them, the school students' questions, at least those that have answers, in another, school edition of *If This is a Man*, which will be published soon.

Faced with a book that was making its way in the world, I realized that I had my hands on a new tool, made to weigh, divide, verify; similar to those of the laboratory, but agile, quick, gratifying. I had told my story once, why not do it again? The germ of writing had entered my blood. Thus *The Truce* was born, which told of the return from Auschwitz. In the first book I had paid attention only to the material I was writing about; in the second I was aware that I was capable of transmitting experiences, but with a purpose. I wrote clearly, to seek contact with the audience. It doesn't pay, it isn't very useful to write and not to communicate. That was the present given to me by the first book and by the hearing it had obtained: understanding that though obscure speech may speak to posterity, to be understood by the people you are addressing, the important thing is to be clear. Writing serves to communicate, to transmit information and also feelings. If it isn't comprehensible then it's useless, it's a cry in the wilderness and a cry can be useful for the one who writes it, but not for the one who reads it. So maximum clarity and, second rule, minimum bulk: that means being compact, condensed. The superfluous also damages communication, because it's tiring and boring.

Contact with the reader has enriched my life, it brings me joy. But there is a very wide spectrum of readers. I've imagined myself an 'ideal' one, which relates to the real reader like the 'ideal gas' defined by the physicists, a gas that is that follows simple laws, relates to real gas. I write for and to that reader, not for the critics who are forced to be readers, nor for myself. I feel them next to me when I write, that typical reader, who comes to me willingly, who follows me and I follow them; I want them to receive what I transmit to them without it fading or being lost on the way. At the same time as *The Truce* and even earlier, I wrote stories, using for each of them a technical idea, born in the laboratory or the factory. The world that surrounds us is extraordinarily fruitful and I hoped in this way to achieve a 'crossing'[2] between writing and my experience as a chemist. On the subject of the stories, many people have asked me whether in giving narrative form to the big and small fissures in our world and our civilization I wanted to allude once again to the Lager. My answer would be: certainly not deliberately, in the sense that deliberately writing about a reality in symbolic terms is not part of my plan. As to whether or not there is continuity between the Lager and these insights; maybe, there could be, but I don't know precisely, it doesn't depend on me. 'I', as Palazzeschi[3] said, 'am only the author'.

Even when I was writing stories I was writing about my personal material. But I felt in debt to my everyday profession. It seemed to me that I'd wasted an opportunity to talk about the experience of a job many think of as arid, mysterious and suspect. It seemed that I was discovering a certain bias in the books that I read. It was an impression I kept locked away for a long time but that kept finding new evidence to confirm it. Everyone knows how a corsair, an adventurer, a doctor, a prostitute lives. But of us chemists, transmuters of matter, a profession of illustrious ancestors, there isn't much of a trace and it seemed right to me to plug the hole. Thus *The Periodic Table* was born. The title and the titles of the chapters, which are each given the name of an element, are undoubtedly provocative. But it seemed appropriate to me to exploit the chemist's relationship with matter, with the elements, like the nineteenth century Romantics exploited the landscape: chemical element-state of mind, like landscape-state of mind. Because, for anyone who works, matter is alive: mother and enemy, indolent and an ally, stupid, inert, dangerous at times, but alive as the founders knew well; they who worked alone, unacknowledged, without reason or imagination to support them. We are no longer alchemists, but anyone who has dealt with matter knows these things. Why then not create a drama where the characters are the elements of which matter is composed? Young people write to me: 'If chemistry were as you tell us it is, I'd be a chemist.' It's one of the compliments I hold most dear. Entering the literary field as a chemist, I also fulfilled a vow. I owe my life to my profession. I wouldn't have survived

Auschwitz if after ten months of hard labour I hadn't entered a laboratory, where I continued to be a labourer, but under a roof. Having the status of a chemist, having my name at the time, that is my number, entered in the workforce of the Buna factory managed by IG Farbenindustrie may also have kept me safe from the 'selections' because chemists were considered 'formally useful'. And chemistry has provided me with the subject for a book and for two stories. I feel I possess a reservoir of metaphors: and the more distant the other term, the more effective the metaphor. Besides it isn't just a quirk of mine. Huxley and Proust did it too. The fact is that anyone who knows what it means to reduce, concentrate, distil, crystallize, also knows that the operations of the laboratory have a long symbolic shadow.

That's one insight into my workshop. I'll add that my writing model is the report one writes in the factory at the weekend. Clear, essential, comprehensible to everyone. It would seem to me a great discourtesy to the reader to present him with an account he can't understand. That is not to say that the language of my unconscious is the language of the reader's unconscious. But I think it's right to transmit to him the maximum possible amount of information and feeling.

I'm in debt to my profession also in the way that it makes a person become mature: through success and failure, succeeding or failing to succeed, the two experiences of adult life (the expression isn't mine, it's Pavese's) necessary in order to grow. For the chemist who works in the laboratory both are needed; the militant chemist needs both of them: getting it wrong and correcting oneself, taking blows and returning them, confronting a problem and resolving it or emerging defeated and immediately re-starting the battle.

So my chemist also has a long symbolic shadow: in measuring himself against matter through successes and failures, he is like Conrad's seaman, measuring himself against the sea. And also like a primitive hunter. In the evening, when he draws the structural formula of the molecule he must build tomorrow, he carries out the same propitiatory rite as the hunter of Altamira who 50,000 years ago drew the elk or the bison he would have to kill the next day on the walls of his cave: to take possession of it, to make the rival his. Both are sacral gestures. I am almost certain that the experience of the chemist is the same as man's remote past, guided by the same purpose that led him to set out on the long road that would lead him to civilization. That's why, as I've said many times, whenever I'm asked 'why are you a chemist who writes?' I reply, 'I write *because* I am a chemist'. My profession helps me to communicate experiences.[4]

He would sometimes say cheerfully, 'The audience is anthropophagous, they want to know everything you've done, who you are, what you do, what you think.' But he was always prepared to accept questions and objections 'with that Etruscan smile' Paolo Spriano wrote of, 'and that calm courtesy that his friends know'.[5] That evening too the stalls bombarded him with questions. We'll quote from some of them:

> *You wrote* If This is a Man *to analyse what happened in the Lager, so that your testimony could contribute to avoiding any repetition of the tragedy you lived through. Faced with the re-appearance of the Lager phenomenon in Latin America, Greece, the Soviet Union, Vietnam; faced with the shrinking of the area of disagreement and with spreading conformism; faced with the misdeeds of the 'sorcerer's apprentices': how do you experience the darkening of the horizon?*

> That's several questions in one. I'll start with the question about what attitude I take, faced with the reduction of the area of freedom to disagree. Well, I experience it like everyone and perhaps even more intensely because of my experience. Faced with the brutal fact of the return of concentration camp rule I can make use of my first book, with a certain cynicism, I admit, as the demonstration of a theorem. Although Auschwitz, and this must be said, has not returned. The monstrous Nazi madness, 10,000 deaths a day in Auschwitz, has never had its equal even if there are those who try, today, to lay doubt on that fact. It's true on the other hand that the Soviet, American, Greek, Chilean Lagers, if they are not like this, nevertheless constitute an approximation. They are an alarm signal that invites us not to throw away the torn and worn-out freedom we possess. I make use of my first book to show where one gets to when one takes the road of intolerance, when one starts to violate man, when consciences let themselves be seduced and obscured, when one delegates one's will and abdicates one's judgement and sense of morality before the principle of authority.

> And we come to the 'sorcerer's apprentices' and to their misdeeds, as you called them. I find the position of the 'new Arcadians',[6] who faced with the serious and undeniable damage they observe would like to return to a civilization without detergents and without insecticides, absurd. Those who created DDT certainly didn't imagine it spreading as far as Antarctica; fifteen or twenty years ago one didn't think about population explosion, about the increase of carbon dioxide in the atmosphere, about the pollution of our water and soil, about the poisonous siege by our own waste. But scientific and technological progress, if it can't progress indiscriminately, shouldn't stop either,

still less be moved backwards, without a price that would be catastrophic. The damage that technicians and chemists have done and are doing, only technicians and chemists, not politicians, can repair; confronting the problems one by one, urgently, as they present themselves. But this requires intelligence, preparation, honesty. It's up to a class that knows what it's doing to attempt to repair, the damage caused to the biosphere and to humanity, and also the damage we don't know about yet but that could reveal itself in the future. And the means exist. I think that only a wise technology, can make up for the consequences of a badly used technology or of our infinite improvidence; not emotionalism, not words. Certainly we are in a critical phase and the water we are navigating is full of dangers: for that reason, the task awaiting the technicians is immense. Our survival is in their hands.

Despite the things you have lived through, seen and related in If This is a Man *and in part in* The Truce, *trust in man shines through your writings. Do you still have it?*

I do. I've always had it instinctively, it's congenital. The Lager was not enough to destroy it. Not that one must have trust in all men unconditionally. On the contrary, some are to be deeply distrusted. But starting from trust, even to get to distrust, seems to me to be a good thing. I believe in fact that it's better to start from trust, even at the risk of being wrong, rather than from distrust and pessimism. It's a gamble. Optimism too is a gamble. Optimism, although irrational, seems to me a way of betting on the right horse, even if later it doesn't win.

A young man wanted to know if a book like *If This is a Man* can improve the world and if it had been written for that reason. Didn't the author think that being published in Germany had had positive effects?

I take responsibility for every word I write, But I don't write to improve the human race. Even successful books reach only a certain number of people, so I don't believe they can have a wide effect. But if I see that a book has been beneficial to someone, that makes me happy. Of course, *If This is a Man* will have done some good through being translated into German, but not a huge amount. Fifty thousand copies sold in a population of 50 million isn't a lot. I received 30 letters from Germans who told me that reading the book had left them 'improved'. Thirty! It means that a book can do no great good, but no great evil either.

What judgement do you make of the recent decision by the Rome military tribunal on whether to grant Kappler conditional release?

I can't judge the legal aspect of the question. However, the crime is so great that, in my view, Kappler[7] should have stayed in prison. I'm not thinking only of the Ardeatine massacre, but of the vile fraud against the most defenceless, the Jews of the Roman ghetto. He demanded 50 kilos of gold within 36 hours for the promise of 'impunity' to those who were guilty only of being Jewish. He got his gold, but on 16 October 1943 the Jews left the ghetto in sealed goods wagons. All of them. And almost none came back. That act alone means that he deserves a lifetime of imprisonment. There has been talk of his repentance. If I were the judge, I would want to find out how he redeemed himself, in what words and actions his self-criticism showed. We'll see from what he does and says when he returns to Germany whether those 28 years have really changed him or whether they've left him as he is.

An elderly audience member asks:

How have you managed to save yourself from hatred against Germans? How have you managed to preserve such an objective vision, not to let yourself be contaminated by hatred, to preserve your calm clarity? Even though you wrote in The Truce, *excuse me if I quote from memory, that the scars of the outrage remain, that the offence is incurable, and that it's also a fount of evil because it perpetuates itself as hatred among the survivors.*

Yes, that's true. I've written that and I am profoundly convinced of it. But I think that hatred should be foreign to human nature. Animals hate; the cat hates the mouse. Man can and should judge; he is bound to judge. But not to revenge himself. I've felt and still feel the desire to judge; I felt little hatred then and I don't feel any more today. Do you remember Genesis, the episode of the righteous of Sodom? When the messengers who were sent to find out what is happening in Sodom go away and Abraham remains alone with the Lord who is determined to punish the corrupt city? Abraham approaches Him and says (I too quote from memory): 'Will You destroy the righteous as well as the wicked? Perhaps there are fifty righteous men in the city; will You not forgive it for the sake of the fifty righteous men who are in its midst? Far be it from You to put to death the righteous with the wicked, so that the righteous will be like the wicked. Will the judge of the entire earth not deliver justice?' The Lord agrees: if he finds fifty righteous

> men in Sodom, he will forgive the whole city for their sake. Abraham persists, putting forward ever narrower hypotheses: and if in Sodom there were forty, thirty, twenty, ten righteous men? And the Lord says: 'I will not destroy the city for the sake of the forty, thirty, twenty, ten.' Well, I can't manage to hate the Germans. Three or four are even dear to me: one is the translator of *If This is a Man*, Heinz Riedt, who deserted the Wehrmacht to fight alongside Italian partisans. I've known Auschwitz, I've been a Häftling, but as a rational man I must reason in the same way as Abraham did for the righteous of Sodom. I want to understand the Germans; I don't have a spirit of revenge against them, even if for me it doesn't make sense to talk about forgiveness. In schools the students often ask me: 'Have you forgiven?' No, I haven't forgiven: I can't forgive en masse just as I can't hate en masse. I couldn't even forgive an individual, unless he showed with deeds and not words that he'd mended his ways. But then he would no longer be an enemy. So I don't think that a general punishment should be applied. But if I were a judge, I wouldn't forgive: I'd deliver justice. In fact, I want, we want, only justice. On the other hand, the judge isn't an injured party, and neither is a witness when he is in the act of bearing witness. I am the witness, so I must express myself with the language of the witness in court, calmly and soberly, and not with the language of the persecutor, or the avenger. The witness offers the judge the means of judging. And the judge is you.

A teacher asks Levi what he wants to say or is able to say to the young of today? What advice can he give to the new generation?

> I don't feel authorized to give a lecture. Besides if I think about it, I've already done so. I've given advice with my first and with my last book. With the first I've emphasized the importance of never 'slipping backwards' on the road to freedom. The downward path that starts from the denial of equality between men ends in the loss of freedom and in the Lager. With the last book, which began as a collection of chemistry stories, though it grew into something more, I tried to emphasize the value of a trade. Chemistry is only an example, but it's the one I know, whose daily events reflect the confrontation of man and matter, because (if I'm allowed to quote myself) 'to conquer matter is to understand it, and understanding matter is necessary to understand the universe and ourselves'. Describing the victories and inevitable defeats of work I thought of the discomfort spreading among young people who despite having a qualification can't find a job, or among those racked with profound scepticism, as if no job were a worthy experience: whereas any job, whether it leads to victories or defeats, remains the essential experience of mankind.

You've spoken about your books but you've omitted the stories of Natural Histories *and* Flaw of Form. *Why?*

I have spoken about them, in fact, as a first attempt at crossing technology and science with the trade of the writer. The stories are born from an idea or impression often coming from the laboratory or the factory, and I've built a story around them. They are meant to raise surprise, questions, wonder. For this reason, I consider my two books of stories less important, but not less legitimate, than the other books I've written, which rather than raising questions forced themselves to give answers to questions.

You are a researcher. I want to ask you if it is possible for science to be neutral.

I will reply though I am not a researcher but a technician. Yes, I think that science can and should be neutral. I think that the danger exists that science could be enslaved. But I think that if technological education is combined with a moral one, people won't let themselves be subjected. I don't believe that there is a right-wing mathematics opposed by a left- wing mathematics. Scientific reality is one, and if it's not, it means that someone has corrupted it. When science isn't neutral it's because it's someone's bad science.

In your opinion what responsibility does the researcher have for the applications that are made of his discoveries?

There is research that is criminal *ab ovo*,[8] and in this case the researcher is extremely suspect. Then there are other lines of research that *a priori* are innocent. For example, creating a dye. Between the two extremes, of guilt and innocence, there are the ambiguous cases. And that of the atomic bomb is one of those. There was a war going on… that should already have been enough of a deterrent, it seems to me. However, it also seems to me now that no one can deny that the survival of humanity depends on the development of nuclear energy. This is the problem we find ourselves most unprepared for, loaded as it is with worrying associations (atom=Hiroshima, right?), with contradictory assessments, with inpenetrable mazes at the centre of which giant financial interests are operating. It's up to us, to our generation, to resolve the problem. The world has a desperate need for the prediction of that famous technological physicist, who is also the author of science fiction classics, to come true. His name is Arthur C. Clarke. Around 1960 he calculated that the production of energy from nuclear fusion, clean energy that is, could come in the nineties.

> Prophesying is a dangerous art; let's hope Clarke didn't get it too wrong.

He had already been asked years earlier about the writer's duty of engagement, and he had already expressed then his opposition to every restriction on the 'varied and unpredictable' human genius. To the question 'How do you see the non-engaged writer?' he replied:

> Everyone is free to write as he thinks best. Disengagement exists and in my view must be tolerated. The most disengaged writer still testifies, even in a negative sense, don't you think? Did the Arcadians teach us nothing about their age? A valid book can grow from any ground. The writer can write what he wants and how he wants. Imposing laws on him, prescribing rules for him, is damaging or at best useless.

After his meeting with the Turin audience, the 'non-writer writer' followed it up with others in Florence, Milan, Rome and Bari, as was the custom of the Italian Cultural Association. He was greeted warmly and assailed with questions everywhere. On his return, *Tuttolibri* invited him to clarify:

> *Whom do you write for?*
>
> It would be more accurate to ask 'to whom'. In completing the crossing between my everyday trade and that of writing, I've created for myself the image of the 'ideal' reader, who I feel is beside me and whom I write to, as one writes a letter to a friend, drawing only on what I know: my mine of memories, my profession of chemist and my inner life of course.
>
> *It is often said that your writing is based on balance, moderation, restraint, rigour. Above all on clarity: and in fact, everyone understands it. Is that also a choice?*
>
> It's a deliberate intention. It doesn't suit me to write in code. From *The Truce* on, I have resolved to make my language as clear as possible, in the hope that the information gets un-degraded to my readers, who in buying my books have signed a contract with me. It would seem to me a commercial fraud not to provide them with what they expect, and a discourtesy to write to them something they don't understand. And for this reason too, I impose maximum clarity, as well as minimum obstruction, on myself. For this reason, I have also agreed to speak orally with them. Meeting them, explaining myself to them, makes me happy.

> *You showed a good deal of courage, and also of trust, in addressing to your 'ideal' reader a book entitled* The Periodic Table, *but its success has proved you right. What was the inspiration for this additional testimony of yours?*
>
> For some time I harboured the wish to transmit the flavour of my trade; to convey to the non-chemist the experience of our encounter with inanimate matter, which has a thousand sides and is the whetstone we sharpen ourselves on. Today a good fellow-traveller, tomorrow an enemy. My chemist goes off hunting every morning and sometimes it goes well for him and sometimes not. [...] The title of the book is provocative, I recognize that. But I wanted to bring to the reader the experience of my daily work, because daily work is mankind's destiny: it takes up all our active life; with its victories and defeats it makes us adult. I think that my trade is beautiful and intelligent, even if my adversary can be dangerous. And I think that it's a battle that never ends. Isn't all this perhaps the symbol of something vaster? Of the permanent struggle of man on earth?[9]

Clarity: the first commandment of his Decalogue as a writer. He had repeated it in all the lectures of the Swiss cycle and of the Italian one. But that was not enough for him. He was reading Paul Celan, the Jewish-German poet just published by Mondadori, 'upon whose shoulders fell burden after burden, grief after grief, culminating in his suicide at the age of 50 in 1970'. But, he did not succeed in penetrating many of his lyrics (even if he would say of 'Death Fugue', 'I carry it inside me like a graft'). Reading it disturbed him, but at the same time confirmed his faith in the clear word: he felt the need to repeat that 'To write is to transmit'.[10]

On 11 December 1976, his essay 'About Obscure Writing' appeared in *La Stampa*: a real manifesto, a declaration of intent, a protestation of honesty. Starting with the absolute freedom of creative writing, and having recognized the existence of the unconscious, of the 'mute and faceless brother' whom we carry from crib to grave who is co-responsible for all our actions, as well as for our writing, in which it expresses itself in its necessarily obscure language – despite this, Primo Levi maintains that the unconscious is not the best or only source of expression. The 'language of the heart' is at best a vernacular, an argot, and can turn out to be indecipherable. Because writing 'is there to communicate, to transmit information or feelings from mind to mind, from place to place and from time to time. Someone who is understood by no one transmits nothing.' And if the reader does not understand, he must be reassured: 'the fault is in the author, not in you. It is an author's responsibility to be understood by whoever wishes to do so.'[11]

The essay gave rise to a heated debate with Giorgio Manganelli, who accused Primo Levi of hiding under a civilized and enlightened veneer 'a brutal ambivalence, terrorism and anguish'. Manganelli is indignant: 'I wonder how it can enter a writer's mind that he is a typical case of rationality triumphant.' He is vexed: 'I am deeply dismayed by the use of the word irrational in a solely negative sense.' To him, he maintains, the statement that 'the healthy is better than the unhealthy, the effable is preferable to the ineffable and human speech to an animal's whimper', 'sounds like a typical case of social welfare terrorism'.[12] His article is essentially a commendation of obscure writing as an expression of that disorder to which we are all heir, which Primo Levi had recognized in no uncertain terms while yet denying 'that a chaotic written page is the best symbol of the ultimate chaos to which we are destined'. To believe so was, on the contrary, 'a typical error of our insecure age'.[13]

Levi was championed by another writer-scientist, Roberto Vacca, with an article as thundering as his low voice: 'I believe that this debate is not about technique or literary preference, but about being civilized and honest. I find that speaking about terrorism to refer to what Primo Levi writes and says is offensive, ridiculous and above all wrong.' How can terrorism apply to a man who simply, 'in his usual, not very categorical or assertive way' presents 'certain thoughts of his' in order to say that in his view one should not write obscurely?

Vacca's harangue is full-blooded, skilful and generous. He judges Primo Levi 'the best contemporary Italian prose writer'; who is therefore doing something useful when he tells people what he considers good writing. And Vacca concludes: 'I prefer to read someone who writes clearly, perhaps even didactically – I can learn something from that – to someone who writes vaguely and confusedly, and perhaps expects that deep meanings will be put there by the reader; that way he makes less effort in writing.'[14] If Vacca returned Manganelli's blows in kind, Primo Levi replied with witty ripostes. Unfortunately, his reply appeared very late, and confined what's more to the *Corriere della Sera* letters' column, and so it escaped many people's notice. We reproduce it here as further proof of that subtle irony with which Primo Levi often dressed up his most deeply rooted convictions, so as to present them to the reader not as an imperative precept but as an attractive hypothesis.

> I'm sorry that Giorgio Manganelli (*Corriere*, 3rd January) has suffered a crisis over my piece 'About Obscure Writing' that appeared in *La Stampa*, and I thank him for calling me a friend: but why one across a divide? Separated or not, this is the first time that I've let myself be involved in a battle of words. But it's not a fair battle, as it's easy to see. In fact, given our respective arguments, Manganelli has the right to

be obscure (and in fact he is); whereas I have the duty to be clear. But let's try anyway.

Manganelli defines me as a 'social welfare terrorist' (which is a charming example of contradiction in terms, and therefore of obscurity, but there you are: he has that entitlement and I don't) because I prefer the healthy to the unhealthy. He asks what it means to be healthy. I admit that both terms are ambiguous: I've used them in reference to Ezra Pound, who seemed to me unhealthy in all the usual senses of the word. By contrast, I would define as healthy anyone who enjoys full mental and bodily function; hoping that Manganelli doesn't ask me (because if he did he would break the rules of the game: he shouldn't ask for clarifications) what 'full' and 'function' mean, and insisting on my personal preference for health. In effect, the unhealthy person, as defined above, suffers, and I don't like suffering, neither my own nor other people's. I am, therefore, a social welfarist, I admit, but why a terrorist? I don't believe I have ever instilled terror in anyone, least of all with the piece in question.

I admit just as readily that I was wrong to equate 'clear' with 'rational'. However, it still seems better to me to be clear, because an obscure message can be abused (as happened to Nietzsche) and because the obscurity of politicians is one of our national afflictions. It's nice and (in the circumstances) strange that Manganelli and I should find ourselves in agreement that 'no author deeply understands what he has written'; but for him that not understanding seems normal, indeed desirable, while for me it is either a danger, a failure or a nuisance.

Manganelli was not the only writer to side against Primo Levi's on the topic of clarity. Two years later Paolo Volponi took issue with Levi in a public debate on the subject. Levi discussed this debate with the essayist Professor Giuseppe Grassano, confirming what had always been his position. Grassano had presented his question in a rather more complex way:

> *You've upheld your commitment to clear writing many times, linking it to your identity as a chemist who writes, someone therefore who is used to scientific clarity, to weighing and verifying on the page as well as in the lab. Doesn't such a position acquire an obvious political significance in our world, as a rejection of ambiguity, as the defence, let's say, of a civil role for the writer who wants to be understood by others?*

And this is the answer, Franciscan in its simplicity:

> Recently I was invited to Milan for the *Festa de l'Unità,*[15] where I took part in a debate in front of an inattentive audience: they were thinking about the nibbles and not about us. My interlocutor was Paolo Volponi and we also talked about this theme. He disagreed with me. He said that a writer must position himself as a driving force with respect to his readers: not on the same level, but on a higher level. The writer must tow them along, must provide them with information and also with a personal education. So the writer can, indeed in Volponi's opinion must, speak a language freely chosen as he sees fit. If he feels that he must speak in a language that is intricate, abstruse, he can do it, indeed he must do it. And it's up to the reader to catch up with him. I am against any prescription for anyone who writes. I've chosen this path of clarity for myself and I wouldn't presume to prescribe it to Volponi, for example. I believe that anyone who writes must write as he wants. As far as I'm concerned I've chosen a road not for didactic, pedagogic reasons, but for reasons of my own internal clarity. I maintain that, when the idea is clear, it's automatically also expressed in clear language [...] Many people say to me: 'I want to express the confusion of today and therefore I write in a confused language.' It seems to me that that doesn't resolve anything, it leaves things as they are. We know that the world is confused and it doesn't add anything to describe it confusedly. Despite all this, I must say that I like some obscure writers very much. For example, I like Joyce. It would be complicated to say why, but it seems to me that his is only an outward obscurity. With a certain effort I succeeded in penetrating him, and then I liked him.

To an audience member in Bern who asked him whether he wrote with ease from the moment he put pen to paper, whether the page looking back at him was always crystal clear, he declared:

> I write to seek a contact with the reader; for that reason, I set myself the task of being clear, as clear as possible. Sometimes I succeed immediately; sometimes I don't. But I have the habit of giving everything I write to a small, honest and trusted group of readers. I await their judgement anxiously and I accept it with humility. If, in the view of even one of them, I haven't been clear enough, I rewrite the page as many times as it takes. I want the readers, whoever they are, to understand what I say to them.

Amiably ironic, and without hesitating to include two 'obscure' writers, Celan and D'Arrigo, among his favourites, Primo Levi summarized thus his private Decalogue:

> Your writing shall be concise, clear, composed; you will avoid whatever is willed and over-elaborated; you will be able to say of every word you use why you used this one and not another; you will love and imitate those who follow the same path.[16]

He was always clear, even dealing with complex questions, like those which arose in a discussion organized by the journal *Uomini e libri* in the spring of 1977 on the condition of writers in the Italian political context. Mario Miccinesi posed three questions: What was the condition of writers today? To what extent were they capable, today, of having an impact on a reality in flux? How did society respond to their work? Levi's response starts with a question echoing the one recited at the Seder, the Passover feast:

> In what way does this today differ from all our yesterdays, and from the yesterdays of our forefathers? Does it differ because of the fact that today the west is in crisis? It's been in crisis for a hundred years and was certainly in crisis even before, in the eyes of contemporary observers: there is no age that is not one of crisis. Only future historians, with the wisdom of hindsight, will be able to plot the ebbs and flows of this permanent crisis. Therefore, I don't think that the function of the writer has changed very much in the context of the current political situation. Writers of today, like writers of all times, must not forget that they're like everyone else, they've been conditioned (by the environment, by the time in which they live, by the class to which they belong, by the traumas to which they've been personally exposed); that they have no advantage over non-writers, except that luck, or their trade, has allowed them to communicate with a vast audience; that they must commit themselves to trying to overcome the conditioning influences we've mentioned, in order to arrive at a vision of the world which is broader and more vital.
>
> Certainly writers' work can have more impact on reality today than in previous times, but only because the means of mass production and the publishing industry allow him a louder voice now: not because today's reality really accentuates the process of detaching itself from power. It's doubtful that that is happening: even if in the short term that seems to be the trend, it's imprudent to be optimistic and it could just be a ripple on the graph. The fact remains that the written word can have an impact on political reality: but often that happens to an extent that is different (even opposed to) what the writer desires or plans. A book flies out of the hand of the person who writes it: it says more than its author intends. Being the product of an age, it provides evidence about that age: even when the author does not wish it to,

> even when he wishes the opposite. In this sense every book is engaged, even if its author declares himself disengaged.

Words which repeat an ancient conviction. As for the third question, about the weight that should be attributed to the writers' work, Primo Levi says:

> If one means 'writer' in the strict sense, today's society responds to their work with less enthusiasm than before, because of the obvious competition from radio, TV, cinema etc. As for the second part of the question, how does one formulate rules? As a writer, I'd be happy if many people read many books and derived benefit from them, or even just amusement, and I would favour reading over other activities, but at the same time I think these preferences could just be team loyalty. Writers aren't seers or prophets, and they aren't always right: the weight that should be attributed to their work varies greatly from case to case. It's up to the reader to learn to distinguish the original and honest writer from the faker and the sycophant.[17]

Notes

1. *L'Unità*, 'La parola al chimico' [The chemist's turn to speak], 20 November 1976.
2. In English in the Italian text.
3. The Futurist writer Aldo Palazzeschi.
4. Text and shorthand notes provided by *La Stampa*. A copy, on request, was delivered to the writer, who had spoken from his notes.
5. Paolo Spriano, 'L'avventura di Primo Levi' [Primo Levi's adventure], *L'Unità*, 14 July 1963. An Etruscan smile is a term taken from sculpture, meaning a simple, not always visible, smile.
6. The 'new Arcadians' are those wanting to rebuild Arcadia, a region of Greece celebrated in Renaissance literature as an unspoiled, harmonious wilderness. DDT is an insecticide used in the 1940s and 1950s before being discovered to be toxic to humans.
7. Herbert Kappler was head of the German police and security forces in Rome, responsible for the notorious Ardeatine massacre, which Levi mentions in his reply. This was a classic Nazi reprisal, in which over 300 Italians were murdered, one for each of 33 German military policemen killed by partisans the day before. The tribunal rejected Kappler's appeal for release, but he escaped and died in Germany in 1978. At the time, he was detained in a military hospital to which he had been moved from prison.
8. 'From the beginning'.
9. Gabriella Poli, 'L'alfabeto della chimica' [The alphabet of chemistry], *Tuttolibri (La Stampa)*, 6 December 1976.
10. P. Levi trans. P. Forbes, *The Search for Roots: A Personal Anthology* (Chicago: Ivan R. Dee Publisher, 2001), p. 198.
11. 'About Obscure Writing', in A. Shugaar (trans.), *Other People's Trades*, in A. Goldstein (ed.), *The Complete Works of Primo Levi*, Vol. III, (Liveright: New York, 2015), p. 2075.
12. Giorgio Manganelli, 'Elogio dello scrivere oscuro' [In praise of obscure writing], *Corriere della Sera*, 3 January 1977.
13. P. Levi trans. A. Shugaar, *Other People's Trades*, p.2066.

14. Roberto Vacca, 'Manganelli nell'oscurità' [Manganelli in obscurity], article published in both *Il Resto del Carlino* and *La Nazione*, 15 February 1977.
15. An annual celebration organized by the Italian Communist Party to raise funds for its newspaper, *L'Unità*. The debate being referred to, entitled 'Il romanzo e il lavoro' [The novel and work], took place on the evening of 9 September 1975.
16. P. Levi trans. P. Forbes, *The Search for Roots*, p.xi.
17. Mario Miccinesi, 'La condizione dello scrittore nel contesto politico italiano' [The condition of the writer in the Italian political context], *Uomini e Libri*, No. 63, March-April 1977, p. 20.

VI

Holiday Interlude

In Primo Levi's literary work, every now and again a 'holiday interlude' opens up. That is how he defined those light and surreal stories, often written on the same wavelength as *Natural Histories* and *Flaw of Form*, which alternate with the ones inspired by his memories. Readers like them, so the RAI, always attentive to its audience's tastes, broadcasts *The Versifier* and *Retirement Package* (performed by actors including Grassilli, Foà, Cucciolla, Didi Perego and Romano) on the radio. Massimo Scaglione had already been appointed by the broadcasting company to direct *The Versifier* for television; and at the end of 1976 he was chosen to film three one-act plays Primo Levi had based on his books – *Sleeping Beauty in the Refrigerator*, *The Sixth Day* and *The Brokers* – in the RAI's Turin studios. The author said:

> These are science fiction stories and science fiction is a bit of a holiday. Besides, I'd been determined for a while not just to be a writer about the Lager, because that was something that seemed limiting to me. Having had the good fortune to return to life, I feel authorized to see it in all its aspects.[1]

Ugo Buzzolan wrote: 'These are surreal, mischievous, grotesque adventures, when not openly humorous and reduced to the level of intellectual amusements.'[2] The director had already brought two of the works to the stage of the 'Romano' theatre in Turin and was used to Levi's active collaboration. But for everyone else, actors and technicians, the keen mind and inexhaustible curiosity of the man who took part in their every struggle was a revelation. They listened to his suggestions; they pressed him with questions. As for Levi, the television world fascinated him and he was almost always present, although he was now working hard on the script of *The Truce* for the next radio adaptation, to be directed by Edmo Fenoglio.

The shooting finished in mid-February 1977 and the journalist Bona Alterocca announced the news in *La Stampa*. She thought the director a bit preoccupied by the difficulty of translating the author's language dramatically, but Primo Levi seemed to her to be satisfied. He had told her that he liked the television experience because 'it's inviting to watch your creations brought to life', but that for him it was a secondary activity. He still preferred the written page.[3]

The year went by without the adaptations being broadcast. Only in 1978 did RAI decide to air them, across three Friday evenings: on 13, 20 and 27 of January. The Wednesday before the series opened, Primo Levi watched the preview of *Sleeping Beauty in the Refrigerator* in RAI's Turin offices. The television critics for the main newspapers were there, one of whom Levi had come to count as a true friend, Ugo Buzzolan. He told everyone: 'This is my holiday.'[4] At the end he was interviewed by Gabriel Bertinetto, correspondent for *L'Unità*:

> *When did you start writing these stories?*
>
> In 1952. I wrote one story then, published together with others in *Natural Histories*, which was set in 1975. Given the futuristic character of the story, I had to change the dates, moving the chronological setting to the twenty-first century and beyond.
>
> *It's been said that the television adaptation of your book belongs to the science fiction genre. Isn't it more like a comedy set in the future?*
>
> Maybe so. In any case, if it is science fiction, it's second generation science fiction: not the kind steeped in optimism and faith in progress, belonging to a long literary tradition stretching from Verne to Wells, but today's kind, which no longer believes in itself and often imagines disastrous futures.
>
> *The tone of this* Sleeping Beauty *is deeply pessimistic, despite its lack of a tragic ending, isn't it?*
>
> Yes. Behind the apparent normality of their behaviour, the characters are inhuman. Various people gather to celebrate the annual 'defrosting' of a girl, who had willingly had herself frozen into hibernation a couple of centuries earlier, and the only feelings they are able to show are curiosity, if not indifference. They eat, drink and chatter like they would at any party. The thought that repeated rapes hide behind this occasion doesn't even cross their mind.
>
> *Not even the victim of this abuse escapes though, it seems.*
>
> Indeed. Even Brunilde,[5] the young girl in the fridge, is a negative character. She herself says clearly that she accepted the freezing for financial gain. At the moment of the final thaw she intends to sell her memoirs, with a detailed account of her amorous meetings with important men during her brief 'revivals' over the centuries.

Why is the adventure set in Germany?

Obviously there are autobiographical reasons why Germany has remained the country of violence for me. Setting a story of this kind there is also a civilized form of retaliation.

The situation could however be adapted to other historical and geographical realities.

Certainly. The unconscious cruelty and egoism of the Thörls, of their friends, of Brunilde, is the same undercurrent of perversion, of internalized Nazism that so many people carry inside them and which in certain historical and political conditions leads to tyrannies.[6]

To the correspondent from *Il Giorno*, who had asked him a similar question about *The Sleeping Beauty*, he replied:

The text started as a kind of civilized revenge against Germany, but then it was entertainment that prevailed and the political allusions moved into second place.[7]

So that viewers could understand the three grotesque stories, the RAI had decided to precede the broadcast with an introduction by the author who 'simply and amiably, in conversation with the director and the other film-makers, clarifies the meaning of his stories'.[8] The main question the team posed to Primo Levi was the one that had pursued him since *Natural Histories* and *Flaw of Form* had come out.

You are known above all as the author of If This is a Man *and* The Truce. *Is there a link between these two books and the three stories that will be shown on TV, and if so what is it?*

At other times he had replied 'Maybe there could be a link' or 'Yes, otherwise I wouldn't have published them' or 'Not deliberately'. Now he says:

This is precisely the last question an author generally knows how to answer; the one about his inner working as a writer that is. I can say this: that there certainly is a link, even if it isn't very apparent. I think, indeed I hope, given how these three one-act dramas have been produced, that the link will come out in the end. And that link is the abuse of human beings. The beauty in the fridge is abused: because she's in the fridge, because she's reduced to the status of a block of ice and waits to return to consciousness and awareness once a year. Humanity is abused, *a priori*, in *The Sixth Day* (the allusion is biblical, it's the day when mankind was created) because human beings are treated like car engines. Finally, violent abuse appears also in the last play, though much more indirectly, because man is still to be born, so the abuse is perpetrated by the propagandists who lie about the range of fates that await everyone who is born on earth.

The style of these three one-act pieces seems to me rather different from the style of If This is a Man *and* The Truce...

I no longer know who it was who said that style is the subject.[9] I would say that yes, it's a different subject and it's a different style. But I think that here too there is something in common. I believe that, even if these three one-act pieces aren't easy (at least the second and the third aren't all that easy), they're not obscure: on the contrary they're very clear. A minimum of involvement and attention on the part of the spectator are enough for their meaning to come out clearly. If that weren't true I'd be very sad, because in the two books you've named, as in these plays, I've always made myself base my style not only on the subject but on the spectator – the willing spectator, I mean. Not the lazy kind of spectator obviously. On the one who watches and wants to penetrate the things he is watching.

The character in The Brokers *asks to be born provided that he is like any other man, in other words, accepting all the good and all the evil in the world. The Nazi Lagers were a period in which human cruelty raged, but what is happening now doesn't give us much hope either. I wonder how a man who has lived through Auschwitz can still display optimism.*

Norberto Bobbio wrote in a recent book that the Lagers were not *an* episode but *the* episode defining this century.[10] I must say this: if I'd written *The Brokers* in 1945 when I came back from Auschwitz, I would probably have written it differently or I wouldn't have written it at all. But I wrote it almost thirty years later, around 1970, and it's the product of a varied experience: that of the Lager, yes, but compensated by that of the return, which was positive; by the experience of having found a country, Italy, which was battered, yes, but still a country one could live in; of having found life itself again, of having willingly and actively entered into life. On the other hand, I must still say that the optimism of the protagonist of *The Brokers* is a conditional optimism. That is to say that he accepts the world, but on

> a condition, which is to be born without privileges; and it would also be necessary to add other conditions. His is an instrumental optimism; that is, it's an optimism one can't do without. I agree with you: the symptoms of violence exist, only a blind man could fail to notice them or disregard them. On the other hand, we must be optimistic, because otherwise we just sit there and what's waiting for us? There's talk of the N bomb…

The series of one-act dramas ended on the evening of 27 January. Gabriel Bertinetto wrote: 'The irony that makes these works of fantasy enjoyable does not lessen their deeply thoughtful and pessimistic tone'. He concluded with the statement that the 'unborn' man's refusal of an experience conditioned by privilege constitutes, according to Levi, 'the implicit acceptance of the Christian message that counters the objective tragedies of history with the will to continue to love and hope'.[11]

Primo Levi also played a constant part in the recording and the editing of *The Truce*, which took place at the start of that year. He spoke with the director Edmo Fenoglio, with the Italian actors and most of all with the group of foreigners, Belarusians munching sunflower seeds, German Jews speaking Yiddish, Austrians, Poles, Greeks, Hungarians, French, Romanians, Slavs. A little world turned the RAI studios into a happy Babel and, with its multitude of souls and tongues, brought to life the backdrop to his novel. 'It's a beautiful experience', he said, 'thrilling even'.

On 25 April Ugo Buzzolan wrote in *La Stampa*:

> Tonight at ten past five on Radio 1, the seven-part adaptation of *The Truce* starts, almost secretly. I say almost secretly, because none of our news bulletins, usually so ready and eager to inform of the most minor things, has taken the trouble to announce it. This is, to say the least, curious, since the broadcast seems to me very significant, and of considerable literary and radiophonic importance.[12]

All the more important because the radio has bravely tackled a project that quite a few directors (among them Marco Ferreri) had given up on one after the other 'presumably because of the impossibility of recreating the vast settings' that *The Truce* demanded in describing 'the gigantic odyssey of the obscure, endless masses who in 1945 wandered across the immense plains of Europe' driven on by chance, by necessity, by political calculation and by bureaucratic blindness.

The radio drama turned out as Buzzolan predicted: though atmospheres and landscapes were also rendered through word and sound, dialogue was logically privileged: listeners were above all assaulted with that great chorus of voices, like 'a chant of hope after the blind violence and hatred of war'.

Two years passed before the writer's next encounter with the theatre. It happened on 20 May 1980 at Turin's Teatro Nuovo, again with Massimo Scaglione, again with the 'Teatro delle Dieci', again with *The Brokers* now rewritten and renamed *Nascere sulla terra* [Being born on Earth]. Guido Davico Bonino, who had recently become the theatre critic for *La Stampa*, told the Primo Levi International Study Days[13] that on the evening of the première he found Levi sitting next to him and that the writer almost apologized to him, for 'the slight piece' he was about to see.

The hall was packed, the applause was warm and shouts of 'Author' rang out more than once in reaction to Levi's 'dry and hectic, witty and compassionate writing, his knowing how to smile with disenchantment at our ills: without scepticism, rather with an unconfessed hope, because anyone who has escaped from hell can't stop hoping'.[14] But what can be said about those two endings 'which appeared one after the other, suddenly and surprisingly'? Heading with him towards the theatre exit, Davico Bonino asked Levi which ending he preferred.

> I prefer my ending, the young S's choice to be born on earth, but by chance, like any one of us, without privileges, accepting everyone's fate.

The last work by Primo Levi to be destined for a theatre adaptation was *The Wrench*, which appeared on stage at the end of May 1986 at Turin's *Centro Piero della Francesca*[15] with Flavio Ambrosini as director, costume and set designs by Pasquale Barbano, music by the *Quartetto to Spirale*[16] and staging by *Gruppo Teatro Studio*, a group of workers and students. It was a very special performance and one in many languages: dumb-show, music and dance. Lionel Lingua and Guido Quarzo, who managed the company's press office, were sent by *Teatro Studio* to interview the author of *The Wrench* before the actors even set to work.

> *What do you think of this theatrical adaptation of your novel?*
>
> It makes me happy. In general, I have had very little contact with the theatre world. I remember that I enjoyed myself when a stage version of *If This is a Man* was put on, despite the sadness of the subject matter. I'm a kibitzer, as they say in America, using a Yiddish word that has come into widespread use, somebody who has fun watching the card players while they are playing.
>
> *How do you judge the character of Faussone, the novel's protagonist?*
>
> I would say that he's a sympathetic character. He's no angel, certainly. He has his faults like everyone. On the other hand, Faussone is a

compilation of real people I've known. He's nice in his own way, bearing in mind that the 'nice' man, by which I mean nice to everyone, doesn't exist. He's a fiction.

The central theme of your book is the relationship between man and work. Recently Sciascia has written that work is doing things one doesn't like doing. What do you think of that definition?

It's a great generalization. Sciascia is doing work he likes, when he does the work of a writer. In my case and also Faussone's, work is doing precisely what one does like doing. Naturally we mustn't idealize too much: the moments when we'd prefer to be doing something else are unavoidable. Still, I certainly didn't want to make Faussone into a typical case, as if to say: this is what a labourer is like. He's one of the many possible labourers and his is one of the many possible relationships with work.[17]

Notes

1. G. Grassano, *Primo Levi* (Florence: Il Castoro/La Nuova Italia, 1981), p.15.
2. Ugo Buzzolan, 'Come scongelare la bella ragazza dopo cent'anni' [How to defrost the beautiful girl after 100 years], *La Stampa*, 13 January 1978.
3. Bona Alterocca, 'Fantascienza in tv con Primo Levi' [Science fiction on TV with Primo Levi], *La Stampa*, 16 February 1977.
4. *La Repubblica*, 'La favola del prossimo secolo' [The fable of the next century], 13 January 1978.
5. This is the name of the girl in the adaptation. In J. McPhee (trans.), *Natural Histories* in A. Goldstein (ed.), *The Complete Works of Primo Levi* (Liveright: New York, 2015), Vol. I, pp.399-572, she is called Patricia.
6. Gabriel Bertinetto, 'La fanta-violenza di Primo Levi' [The fantasy-violence of Primo Levi], *L'Unità,* 13 January 1978.
7. *Il Giorno*, 'Bella da sgelare una volta l'anno' [Beauty to be defrosted once a year], 13 January 1978.
8. Ugo Buzzolan,'Come scongelare la bella ragazza dopo cent'anni'. The interview that follows was broadcast on RAI 2 on 13 January 1978.
9. This is a statement by Voltaire, 'Le style c'est la chose' [Style is the thing] in response to Buffon's claim that 'Le style c'est l'homme' [Style is the man]. Levi is saying that style depends on the subject described and not merely on the author.
10. N. Bobbio, *Trent'anni di storia della cultura a Torino (1920-1950)* [Thirty years of history of culture in Turin (1920-1950)], (Turin: Cassa di Risparmio, 1977), p.104. The same passage is quoted more fully in Chapter 2.
11. Bertinetto, 'La godibile ironia di Primo Levi' [The enjoyable irony of Primo Levi], *L'Unità*, 27 January 1978.
12. Buzzolan, 'Il diario di un uomo che è tornato alla vita' [The diary of a man who has come back to life], *La Stampa*, 25 April 1978
13. Primo Levi International Study Days, Piedmont Regional Council Offices, Palazzo Lascaris, 28-29 March 1988.

14. Guido Davico Bonino, 'Scusi, le piacerebbe nascere sulla terra?' [Excuse me, would you like to be born on earth?], *La Stampa*, 22 May 1980.
15. A huge business complex still under construction at the time.
16. A jazz band.
17. Levi, *Il teatro mi mette allegria* [The theatre makes me happy], playbill distributed on the first night. The quote from Sciascia is our translation of a note to the Italian edition of *La Strega e il Capitano* (Milan: Bompiani, 1986), translated by Ian Thomson as 'The Captain and the Witch' in *Death of an Inquisitor and Other Stories* (Manchester: Carcanet, 1990).

VII

The Watershed

Primo Levi's sixth book, *The Wrench*, was published by Einaudi towards the end of autumn 1978, another dark year of lead,[1] as violent debates inflamed factories, and split unions grappled with permanent unrest, with absenteeism and with the thorny issue of the division of labour. The book's protagonist is a rigger, Libertino Faussone, in love with his work and so talented that he's in demand even from beyond the mountains and seas of his own land. Faussone the builder of cranes and bridges is in conversation with the builder of molecules who has become a writer, and who is therefore able to extract the story from the facts. The book has an intriguing title, explores an unfashionable subject and uses a distinctive kind of language. The interviews (more than fifty in less than six months), the diatribes and interviews come thick and fast.

The first interview appeared in *Paese Sera*.[2] After a conversation with Primo Levi lasting several hours, the correspondent Giorgio Manzini wrote:

> The wrench is like a master key for a mechanical rigger [...] a symbol, despite its modest and familiar appearance, or perhaps precisely because of it. Did Primo Levi call his last book *The Wrench* for symbolic reasons? [...] He says he liked the sound of the name and that he chose it for that reason only. If there's a message behind it he can't say, at least not now, on the spot. Probably there is one, because the book seeks to have a clear, explicit meaning.

The author appeared definite, even passionate, when he responded:

> Isn't it in work that man finds his most solid and most long-lasting experience of happiness? Certainly, it isn't everyone who will find fulfilment in work: the door isn't wide but perhaps it's the only door, especially now, in this period of confusion and uncertainty in which religious faiths are fading, together with political ones.

So, a panegyric to work. But which work? The work of the man of the laboratory, as Levi was, or the free work of the protagonist of *The Wrench*? What of the assembly line, then? The author replied:

> The opening is narrow, there aren't many who get past it, but it's there, it exists; and perhaps it's the only one that leads to the road to salvation. Even in the Lager possession of a trade – whether as a cobbler, watchmaker or chemist – could reduce the harshness of our slavery.

'It's precisely his experience in the Lager', the journalist reports, 'that gave the ex-deportee his first notion of work that saves'. And *The Wrench* has at its core that idea conceived in the darkness: of 'work as the only road that can confer a meaning on life, the only tool that can put the world in order'. However, Primo Levi is painfully aware that the security of 'everyday toil'[3] is lacking for many young people, 'and it is this that poisons hope and makes every inner richness wither'.

The book represents the point of no return for the chemist who has gravitated towards literature despite himself. Manzini notes, summarizing his questions and Primo Levi's answers together: '*The Wrench* marks a watershed in his activity as an amphibian writer, until yesterday closer to the other shore, his factory, than to that of writing. For a year and a bit[4] he's been retired by choice, because he could very well have continued with his job'. Instead he chose to write, and to brush up his German in order to read what he had not yet had the time to:

> [...] even back then the days weren't filled up with the factory, because the time available to someone is flexible: if you want to do something you find the time, but if you don't want to, or only pretend to want to, then you are pressed for time.

'Another profession of optimism?' the correspondent asked him.

> Optimism and pessimism aren't so clearly separated: you can be an optimist one day and a pessimist the next. But there's no life without optimism, and even in the Lager hope – the hope of escaping the barbed wire, the hope of freedom – wasn't entirely extinguished. It's another guiding light that many young people lack, another richness that seems to be disappearing among our youth.

Manzini:

> Levi says that the idea for the character came to him in Togliattigrad, where he'd happened to stay for a long time because of work. In this city that appeared out of nowhere in the middle of a forest there were hundreds of Faussones then, people sent out by Fiat. These were quite special guys, almost all Piedmontese, workers

> who knew how to deal with every situation. Why not give literary form to this character, who appears abroad as the typical Italian, one who always copes with everything? But not just for that reason, also out of a kind of local pride, to rediscover Piedmontese speech, 'Fiat speech': degraded, with a limited vocabulary, with a jumble of metaphors taken from the world of industry, which even Calabrians use, once they've set up roots in Turin.

Many later interviews revolved around more or less the same themes as the first, focussing now on one, now on the other; but with his range of answers the author was able to corroborate or challenge the judgements that were piling up. *The Wrench* was called a Conradian existential model, a new frontier of the dignity of man, a modern adventure story, a test piece, a linguistic invention. Or: a challenge to the widespread desecration of work, an essay with a moral that swims against the tide. And also, *tout court*, as an anachronism (some said a fortunate one, others, on the extreme left, an unacceptable one). All in all, an explosive book. Its genesis had been long and subterranean. Towards the end of 1976, questioned on his intentions after the success of *The Periodic Table*, the writer had announced:

> For me books come as twins: first two on the Lager, then two of stories. *The Periodic Table* is on its own. I mean to give it a companion: other stories about chemistry, organic chemistry this time. The title's already there, *The Double Bond*; the book not yet.[5]

And he went on sketching in a school notebook the first adventures he planned for the protagonist of *The Double Bond*. Here is the first sentence: 'For fifteen years Z lived in sin, and he knew it; but his was an invisible sin, impalpable and compensated by a full and vigorous professional life.' Z was a chemist, the boss of a small factory which produced objects of faux tortoise shell such as combs, spoons and frames for glasses. Z's sin was ecological (he poisoned the water and soil with toxic waste from his production process); the remorse that tormented him was deep and his wrong was particularly difficult to redeem. Despite its superb style and suspenseful atmosphere, this openly autobiographical story never saw the light of day. Or rather, with Z's sin and remorse removed, it eventually appeared in a different form in *The Wrench*, which at that point Primo Levi had not even conceived. He had suddenly changed course as a writer. 'About thirty-five years old, tall, slender, nearly bald, tanned, always clean-shaven', his first fictional character had forced his way into the writer's life. Libertino Faussone, rigger, appeared with all his characteristics (language and tics included, proper name not yet) in a story entitled 'Meditato con malizia' [With Malice Aforethought], published on 13 March 1977 in *La Stampa*.[6] Some people observed that it was the only moment of truce in a journal thick, that Sunday, with terrible news.[7] But Levi found the juxtaposition appalling. For a while he abandoned the character, but he continued to suffer his silent siege. In the middle of the summer he announced that *The Double Bond* had run aground, but that it seemed to him that he had what it took for his rigger Faussone. Another of Faussone's adventures had already appeared in *La Stampa*: 'La Coppia Conica' [The Bevel Gear].[8] We thought, then, that the imaginary would be his route of escape (and of salvation) from the tragic times we were living through and which tormented him. We also thought that the time had come to which he had ironically alluded, and which had been preoccupying him when he said:

> Up until now my career as a writer has been an exercise in memory. First the Lager and the return from it gave me material for stories, and after that my experience as a chemist. But now my store is diminishing. I have no memories left. If I carry on writing, I will have to invent, and to invent stories that seem true. For me that will be a fascinating experience, even if I find becoming a falsifier quite disturbing. I'd be very embarrassed towards my future readers, knowing I was swindling them in some way, making them see and live unseen and unlived things.[9]

Falsifier: he said and repeated the word many times, condensing literary invention into that harsh term. In fact, he was a curious kind of falsifier, constructing with pieces of reality (known directly or indirectly, but always scrupulously investigated) this creature of his, to whom he gave Turinese citizenship, peasant-artisan ancestors and the task of telling, in his 'understatement and elliptical speech',[10] his own work-destiny. Which is solitary, reckless, patient, obstinate, made with hands and brain, because Faussone puts his soul into every job, 'even the stupid ones'; 'actually the stupider they are', he says, 'the more I put my soul into them'.[11]

Levi revealed the secret of how he had constructed his invented character at the end of the book, citing Conrad's 'Author's Note' on the protagonist of 'Typhoon'. And so that younger readers especially would be clear, in the school edition of *The Wrench* he explained that, just as the English novelist '[n]ever saw' Captain MacWhirr, so he never saw his Libertino Faussone in the flesh either. Like Conrad's Captain, Faussone is imaginary but at the same time 'perfectly authentic', since he is a conglomeration, a patchwork of numerous people the author has known, similar to each other in their character, virtues, singularity and vision of work and the world.[12] The journalist from the radio programme *Personalmente* asks:

> *Does the key to understanding the book's genesis, its meaning, lie in that description?*

> Without doubt. And I would say so in two respects: both in its genesis, that is to the idea that it starts from, and in its literary aspect. I've tried to carry out an operation – I don't know whether it's bold, maybe it's not very bold and not very new either – which interested me. That is to introduce into literature a type of character I see in today's world, not only in Italy, in whom literature doesn't take much interest. I'd alluded to something similar in a previous book of mine, *The Periodic Table*. Now, in homage to my past as a man of technology, I enjoyed giving life to this Libertino Faussone, mechanical rigger.[13]

'So Faussone doesn't exist in the flesh?' Professor De Rienzo asks, incredulously:

> He doesn't exist, he's a complete invention of mine. I took his adventures from technical reports I read in specialist journals.[14]

But not just from those. Also from conversations with experts, from chats with friends and from personal experiences. For example, he told us he had taken 'With Malice Aforethought' from a real incident (which actually took place in Lombardy, not in the Middle East where he set it), that had been told to him with extraordinary vividness by Giovanna, daughter of Alessandro Galante Garrone.[15] The technical material used in 'The Bridge' he owed to his close friend Livio Norzi, an engineer from a family of engineers (Norzi's father, Primo Levi told us, had built the stadium where as a young lad he went to compete with Guido, 'a statuesque young barbarian').[16] He said he had taken one of the most amusing stories, 'Cloister', 'from a drama he'd personally lived through', and that he had first written it as the opening to *The Double Bond*, the story he'd never finished. He talked about 'Cloister' in detail, with the correspondent from a specialist journal, Enrico Boeri of *Tecnologie chimiche*:

> The episode of the 'sick tower' is entirely autobiographical. The acetic acid separation tower is Siva's, which can be seen on the Milan-Turin motorway, just before the toll booths, on the right. I conceived this tower myself: I taught the workers how to manage it and I spent a lot of nights near it. The original designer was a Milanese architect, on the model of the characteristics of another tower which still exists. Perhaps the first tower was filled with metal rings. In any case the Siva tower's lower rings, which were made of clay, couldn't bear the weight and they pulverized. When it filled with steam the tower gave up the ghost [...] and to resolve the problem we had to re-mount the distillation plates one by one, precisely as they do in the book.[17]

Just as with his previous books, *The Wrench* was preceded by an account in oral form. Levi spoke, half jokingly and half seriously, of this habit of his of telling stories first and then writing them, to Professor Grassano, who was writing a study of him and had asked him:

> *How are your stories born?*
>
> They are born as verbal stories for the most part. Those about Faussone are almost all stories either of adventures someone has put me through or adventures I've attributed to Faussone [...] I'd say that I'm built that way: I like telling my stories aloud. And I do, most often those that really happened to me, but also those that are told to me. In telling them it seems to me I'm following a tradition thousands of years old, which goes right back to the oral storytellers of Africa or Asia. If you ask me why, please speak to a psychoanalyst, because I don't know what the root of this is, in us humans. It's by no means just me who takes pleasure in telling stories: many people do [...][18]

'He was a marvellous conversationalist: precise, meticulous, making frequent and significant memory associations',[19] remembers Ferdinando Camon, who had several meetings with Primo Levi between 1982 and 1986. When the equation Levi had alluded to at the time of *The Truce* – between free time, will to act and pressure from others – became perfect and he was ready to write, he gave free vein to the 'liberating joy of recounting'[20] in the many stories of *The Wrench*, stories which enriched his life as a writer. This time the unknowns were harder: the construction of the character; the material to be researched; the time involved, which had to be unlimited. The only known term was his determination: it was there and it was intense.

Primo Levi had met quite a few riggers, in his own and other factories, like the one he had seen at work on Siva's 'sick tower'. But it was during his two business trips to the Soviet Union that he was able to meet many Faussones, to listen to them, to speak to them. And to admire them. He said one day:

> I'd been storing up for a while the idea of writing something about this type of work, which is very similar, for that matter, to my work as a paint chemist and to all jobs that take initiative and where one runs a certain risk. I was stimulated by the quite maverick idea of speaking again about human responsibility, which shows itself everywhere and in particular at work. But I'd say that the real act of conception of the book occurred in Togliattigrad, where I went on paint business and where I met, I won't say Tino Faussone who doesn't exist, but dozens

> like him. They were all specialists from Fiat and associated companies, who were there to build the Zhiguli plant.[21]

Another decisive influence had come to him, he added, from that strange story of the plant where a 'curse' was cast, a story he had been fascinated by.

> So the idea came to me to write a story where the narrator was a witness: I then realized that Faussone had enough blood and bone to last for a book.[22]

Indeed he became so believable, authentic and concrete that he tricked many people into thinking he was real.

> [...] some journalists thought that this character really existed. Probably because the stories I make him tell are all true, apart from the one about the little monkey. [...] And then, if Faussone is invented, his father isn't, for example. I borrowed him off a copper-worker employed in my factory. His father was a panel-beater; I'd met him years ago. And when I needed to give a father to Faussone, I asked the copper-worker to tell me his father's story. He understood straight away what 'telling the story' meant. I gave him the drafts to look at and he corrected two or three technical terms.[23]

Thus the story 'Metalwork' was born, a portrait of a vanished world and a lament for it: 'a second after the factories arrive, nobody needs copper buckets anymore' and the father dies with his hammer in his hand. The generation 'of able and creative craftwork' is passing.[24] Levi portrays Faussone and those like him as its heirs.

If the stories of Faussone are all true (except one), so are those in which the first person narrator changes identity, and Primo Levi, having left the passive role of narrating witness, becomes a protagonist and narrator in his own right. The reason for this role reversal is to be found in the book's structural demands as much as in its technical and narrative rigour. In the minor role of a friend who listens to the main character, the writer has total freedom not only to tell of his own adventures at work (something he very much liked to do), but also to take on some demanding aspects of *The Wrench* without running the risk of didacticism. Firstly, to tackle the dominant theme of work as destiny, by showing the close, even philosophical, relationship between the trade of the rigger and the two trades of Levi the 'centaur'. Secondly, to give space to autobiography, showing how far the chemist travelled when he abandoned the career he had chosen with such determination in his youth (although the life-choice he made in his maturity was just as determined, and of equal value).

To the correspondent of *Il Quotidiano dei lavoratori*, Francesco Poli, who claimed that 'there are two protagonists in this book' and asked, 'Did you want to analyse your situation as a chemist-writer, as a person simultaneously engaged in two activities?', the author replied:

> I wouldn't want to misrepresent myself as a 'planner': I was one by necessity in the factory, but I'm certainly not one as a writer. This book was born in quite a casual way: as it went on I realized the main character needed to be given a counterweight, for reasons of balance and to vary the discourse. What's more, I also wanted to tell my own stories because, as I've already said, it seemed to me that there was a certain affinity between Faussone's work and mine.[25]

He indicated another reason for the alternation of narrators to the critic who observed that 'In *The Wrench* you are obviously the author, but you are also directly involved, a narrator-character, insofar as you intervene in your rigger's world, you come to life in his world.'

> That's certainly true, because I'm a bit of a Faussone, as often happens to writers. Many things I've done, would have liked to do or would have enjoyed doing, are reflected in him. For example, I've travelled too, but much less than Faussone. Especially not in strange countries, like him.[26]

Not in the East, nor in Alaska. But in the Soviet Union, yes. Invited years later to outline his professional career he affirmed:

> [...at Siva] I was hired first as a laboratory chemist, then became technical manager and finally general manager. And I remained in this company for 29 years, up to 1977. However, back in 1975 I had announced my resignation in advance: it didn't seem right to me to leave the factory in the lurch, given the friendship that connected me and still connects me to the owner. So I gave them two years' advance notice to find a substitute, and that's what happened. I've already written about this period. Even if the reason for the business trip was different from the one I invented (the varnish for the inside of anchovy tins), my journey to Russia in *The Wrench* is autobiographical. I changed quite a few specific details because it didn't seem right to me to give away the company's internal affairs.[27]

All the same there were still paint matters to attend to. Boring problems, long periods with many empty hours to meditate on the future that his 'advance notice to leave' had opened up. It was as if this Russian episode 'was in some ways', he wrote, 'a watershed, a key point on my earthly journey'. The chemist's last adventure: 'I'd had enough. With a sense of nostalgia, but without regret, I would choose another path, the path of the storyteller, since I had the ability to do it and I still had the strength.' Besides, he noted, 'a curious destiny had determined that my life's most decisive moments would occur in that great and strange country'.[28]

He did not just meet his character in that 'great and strange' country. By deciding to dedicate his time to writing, he also resolved another way to perfect the equation from which *The Wrench* would be born. Once the shift happened, once he had definitively taken that other path and bid farewell to the ineradicable experience of his thirty-year job, a book like *The Wrench*, when looked at closely, was an obligation, something almost required of him. Another ex-voto. It seems to us that we can interpret in this way his declarations to 'Segnalibro' [Bookmark], a feature on the RAI 3 TV news. Guido Davico Bonino summarized the varied activity of the writer:

> *There's a Primo Levi of* If This is a Man *and* The Truce, *the two great canonical books of the concentration camp experience, extremely popular even in schools. Then there's a Primo Levi the chemical narrator:* Natural Histories *and* Flaw of Form. *Then there's a third Primo Levi, whom we could say is immersed in the world of work:* The Periodic Table *and* The Wrench. *What do you say about those classifications? Are they correct?*
>
> Yes, indeed. Now, we could discuss whether they are two, or two and a half, or three. In any case they mirror a fundamental division in me: I'm made of different parts, as happens a bit to everyone, but especially to me, because I've been a chemist for thirty years and at the same time I've written books, so I'm an amphibian, essentially – I like to breathe a bit of air and a bit of water. Now I'm exploring a new field. I don't know whether I'll continue, but I've tried to explore it in two books: *The Periodic Table,* in which I've spoken about my work, and *The Wrench*, in which a rigger tells me about his. I'm trying to give literary form to an experience which few have attempted to show readers. I've tried in these books to force the doors a little, to pick locks essentially: to set before readers, even though they may not want it, something that exists, which is the world of work of today. In my view it's very different from how it's represented in the press, as 'work that ennobles' at one extreme and 'work that's a torment' at the other.[29]

What is work, what should it be, according to Primo Levi? We're at the heart of *The Wrench*, face to face with the inner life of the author, with one of the aims of the book and with the origin of all the controversies that shot up around it. Talking to Philip Roth, Primo Levi had no difficulty in admitting that, at the beginning, work was just a kind of compensation for him. But after the Lager it became an all-absorbing experience which – and this is the linchpin of *The Wrench* – every normal human being is 'biologically built for'. Roth had expressed a judgement and asked for its confirmation – this is one of the distinguishing features of his long interview. Primo Levi gave him that confirmation unequivocally. Roth:

> In The Periodic Table, *your book about 'the strong and bitter flavor' of your experience as a chemist, you speak of a colleague, Giulia, who explains your 'mania about work' by the fact that in your early twenties you are shy of women and don't have a girlfriend. But she was mistaken, I think. Your real mania about work derives from something deeper. Work would seem to be your obsessive subject, even in your book about your incarceration at Auschwitz.*
>
> *Arbeit Macht Frei [Work Sets You Free] are the words inscribed by the Nazis over the Auschwitz gate. But work in Auschwitz is a horrifying parody of work, useless and senseless - labor as punishment, leading to agonizing death. It's possible to view your entire literary labor as dedicated to restoring to work its humane meaning, reclaiming the word Arbeit from the derisory cynicism with which your Auschwitz employers had disfigured it. Faussone says to you, 'Every job I undertake is like a first love.' He enjoys talking about his work almost as much as he enjoys working. Faussone is Man the Worker made truly free through his labors.*

Levi:

> I do not believe that Giulia was wrong in attributing my frenzy for work to my shyness at that time with girls. This shyness, or inhibition, was genuine, painful and heavy, much more important for me than devotion to work. Work in the Milan factory, which I described in the chapter 'Phosphorus' in *The Periodic Table*, was mock-work which I did not trust. The catastrophe of the Italian armistice of 8 September 1943 was already in the air, and it would have been foolish to ignore it by digging oneself into a scientifically meaningless activity.
>
> I have never seriously tried to analyze this shyness of mine, but no doubt Mussolini's racial laws played an important role. Other Jewish friends suffered from it too: some 'Aryan' schoolmates jeered at us,

> saying that circumcision was nothing but castration, and we tended to believe it, at least at an unconscious level, with the help of our puritanical families. I think that at that time work was actually a sexual compensation for me rather than a real passion.
>
> However, after the camp my work, or rather my two kinds of work (chemistry and writing) played and are still playing an essential role in my life. I'm convinced that normal human beings are biologically built for activity aimed at a goal, and that idleness, or aimless work (like the *Arbeit* in Auschwitz) leads to suffering and atrophy. In my case, and in the case of my alter ego Faussone, work is identical with problem-solving.
>
> At Auschwitz I observed a curious phenomenon. The need for *lavoro ben fatto* – 'work properly done' – is so strong as to induce people to perform even slavish chores 'properly'. The Italian bricklayer who saved my life by secretly bringing me food for six months hated Germans, their food, their language, their war; but when they set him to erect walls, he built them straight and solid, not out of obedience but out of professional dignity.[30]

Solzhenitsyn had made a similar observation, Primo Levi reminded Ferdinando Camon. They were discussing the difference between Nazi and Soviet Lagers, and the discussion had turned to the Russian refugee, whom Camon did not consider a great writer. Levi told him:

> For *Ivan Denisovich*, I'll come to his defence, at least in this[…]: I found all the material details very well told: the way of eating the soup; the way of dressing; the way of hiding things if a search came; the way of working; even that curious point about the pride of building your wall straight. Even in these conditions, work can be redemptive when the perception one has of it is useful. I remember a fellow prisoner […] who wanted us to work well, in order to feel some gratification at the end of the day. I understand that. The Germans understood it too though, even if in previous experiments they had made us do useless work such as shovelling earth from here to there or digging trenches and then filling them in […] When the scarcity of the workforce began to make itself felt, they gave up on that use of work as an affliction. It remained very hard but not useless.[31]

Despite this, despite everything, real work it never was, not for Häftling 174517, nor for anyone else:

> It was a pure torment. And not even a Biblical torment: 'With the sweat of your brow you shall earn your bread.' There, the bread sweated for was eaten by others. The relationship between cause and effect, the work which gives nourishment, was entirely absent. That wasn't work, it was like taking lashes.[32]

Since keeping things separate was for Primo Levi a mental habit derived from his trade, he also denied that any link whatever could be made between *Arbeit Macht Frei* 'work' and the work-freedom which is the central theme of *The Wrench,* even by presenting the freedom of the one as redemption from the shame of the other. 'Lager work' always sounded to him like an ambiguous, offensive oxymoron. And to the interviewer who objected 'But work can also save: for you, in the camp, your work as a chemist became your salvation' he replied:

> For completely extrinsic reasons [...] I should clarify something. We survivors have all been exceptions by definition, because the Lager was where people died. Anyone who didn't die [...] was saved, in one way or another, by a miracle: he's an exception, a one-off case, not general, indeed totally specific. I worked in a laboratory as a chemist. I escaped by the skin of my teeth, through an unpredictable destiny and certainly a different one to that of the majority, which was to die: dying at work was predicted. So this destiny of mine absolutely doesn't carry weight [...] Even those very few who managed to become plumbers, for example, or cooks, in the Lager system, didn't feel that these jobs gave them relief; or rather, they gave them relief only in an external sense, not an internal one. It was work with which they still didn't identify. So I would leave out the work of the Lager.

In the upside-down world of Auschwitz, the 'non-man' had been destroyed by means of 'non-work'. Philip Roth observed rightly that his Italian friend could very well have called his new book, which tells of work as confrontation and responsibility, of the dignity of man the maker, *This Is a Man.* But among the many titles Primo Levi had considered, this possibility had not occurred to him. He had thought of a quotation from Manzoni, *vile meccanico,*[33] but on the advice of the publisher he ended up discarding it.

The deeper we get into *The Wrench,* the more the experiences of the rigger and the chemist become inseparable from those of the writer, until Primo Levi tells his readers that 'on good days, all three of our professions, my two and his one, could provide satisfaction'.[34] But saying 'satisfaction', which implies pleasure in 'work properly done', was not enough for him. He wrote that loving one's work 'is the best, most concrete approximation of happiness on earth';[35] and that being competent in one's work, and therefore taking pleasure in carrying it out, is 'perhaps the most accessible form of freedom, the most subjectively enjoyed and most beneficial to the social order'.[36] There was enough in the tense climate in which *The Wrench* came out to arouse fierce reactions to this. Primo Levi faced them calmly and with firmness, whether he was speaking to journalists or debating with unions or students.

'It seems to me that Faussone, with his religion of work, is an old-fashioned character,' observed Professor De Rienzo in one of the first interviews. The reply is a profession of faith:

> It's true, I chose him precisely because of that. I believe in work: I believe that it's not just a punishment, but also a virtue. One must be brave and, even at the risk of causing outrage, confront these stereotypes about work as a negative situation. Love of work is not as rare as it is thought to be and someone who loves work isn't necessarily a reactionary. Of course, repetitive, unpleasant work exists. But one can try to escape it, by organising it differently: so many energies wasted in protest could converge around this aim, to eliminate repetitive and alienating work.[37]

A journalist from the radio show 'Amico libero' [Free friend] surprised him while he was dining in the Ristorante del Cambio, the Turin restaurant frequented by Cavour: 'Today when there are protests against work, here is the fortunate anti-topicality of your book, here is a sort of moral. It seems to me that *The Wrench* stands against the neo-indifference of our times.' Primo Levi admits it:

> There's an underlying, never emphasized moral in this book: that the possibility of finding gratification in one's work exists. Unfortunately, we know very well what the neo-indifference is born from: it is born from political and economic factors that are overtaking us, that are bigger than us. But I think and hope that there's still a way out of it, this way for example.[38]

'Do you think that, with a book like *The Wrench*, you are responding to the fears, the uncertainties of today?' asked the correspondent from *La Repubblica*, Silvia Giacomoni. The writer countered the implied scepticism by affirming a principle:

> Yes, I think the discussion on work is important [...] It seemed very abstract to me, the discussion of work by the '68 generation. I think of the drawing-room trade unionists, for whom the world is composed of slaves on the assembly line and evil bosses. In reality, the world is

> more structured: between those two extremes, a zone exists where work is neither punitive nor alienating. Like the work I did for so many years, managing a small factory. They weren't wasted years. In work I found a Conradian image of life: the importance and positive values of anyone who struggles towards a goal. I saw the acceptance of responsibility in contrast to the refusal of responsibility as a way of becoming an adult.[39]

He would take up the argument again even in response to debates that had already died down, stimulated by one of the many questions on the 'anti-topical, or at least maverick' ethics of Faussone. To one interviewer it seemed that the book had had 'the luck' of coming out at the right time, when some models for understanding work were under debate. Levi replied animatedly:

> But it isn't luck: I knew it very well. I myself was fed up, like many people were, with a certain inane position: work is to be refused! If work is to be refused and everyone refuses it, we all starve to death. It's about negotiating. A position like mine doesn't exclude battles for work by any means. I haven't attributed a trade unionist position to Faussone, but I could very well have done. And besides I've worked in a factory and I know well that the best in their specialities are the best unionist fighters. Often, if not always. One does not exclude the other.

Maybe not even for Faussone, though his many battles do not include this one. In fact, Primo Levi replied to Giovanni Tesio, who asked whether the memory of an ideologically engaged Turinese tradition was at work in creating the rigger:

> No. Faussone doesn't contribute anything, in trade union terms. He acts on his own. He's the bearer of other values. He's that kind of character.[40]

****

It's the start of 1979. In an Italy of disaffection and rage, of economic crisis and unemployment, where a book that deals with love for work can cause outrage, but where 'timidly or aggressively, depending on the circumstances, the myth of "work properly done" returns',[41] *La Stampa*'s Stefano Reggiani involves Primo Levi in a discussion with union bosses and an economist. The theme of the interview is the 'civilization of competence', as it's called in the book.[42] Because it is a fact: 'The success of *The Wrench* coincides with a rediscovery, or nostalgia, for professional jobs.' Taking part in the debate are

Pierre Carniti from the Cisl[43] ('professionalism now seems to me to be a magic word, suitable for all uses'), Professor Sylos Labini ('it's more a question of an old concept that needs re-adapting'), Giorgio Benvenuto of the Uil[44] ('here's a goal for which the union must fight') and Primo Levi, who hazards, 'a little disconcerted':

> Maybe all that happens is this: people need something concrete, they want to feel pride in something.

The dream of a world in which everyone works at their best is returning precisely at the moment in which 'the generation that doesn't know how to do anything [...] they haven't been taught' is coming out of mass schooling. Primo Levi reflects:

> Certainly the state today doesn't prepare young people: the professional schools teach little; those who want to learn have to do it on their own, to pull their own socks up, as the character in my book says. Of course, I told an individual story; I didn't illustrate a political line, one can't generalize. Pride in the work one does has very distant sources, maybe local or regional pride. My worker is a Piedmontese mountain-dweller; stubborn, disposed to patience and to taking risks. There is regional pride in even the hardest jobs. In fact, what I mean is that competence and the taste for 'work properly done' are not qualities that can be imposed. They are born from favourable circumstances, either personal or to do with one's environment. My character is a rigger of cranes, of metallic structures. They call on him from all over the world. For him, at the top of the crane with his monkey wrench, it's a challenge every time.

It is right to claim competence for all independent professions and for autonomous work like Faussone's, thinks the secretary of the Cisl metalworkers.[45] 'But in the factory [...] How does one go about asking for love of work from people who carry out repetitive acts, without contact with the product, from people on the assembly line?' Levi responds:

> There isn't just the assembly line. I think that at Fiat, for example, only 45 per cent are employed in assembly work. But the others? I wanted to speak for once about the others, about the autonomous people who make their own way with hard work and competence.

And when the economist-sociologist observes that competence is also having something of a revival at university, 'where there are more people studying who believe in the chance to study', the writer takes the cue:

> [...] the competence one acquires in studying is useful in every case, even if it seeks to question competences or to be involved in active politics: a good physicist is a good politician, a good Hellenist is a good politician.

It falls to the general secretary of the Uil to underline the potential contained in the Faussone phenomenon, while being realistically aware of the need to rescue it from being exploited in any underhand way by the unions' opponents. 'I fight', Benvenuto says, 'for the value of professionalism to be recognized; the union must abandon some falsely egalitarian prejudices, we represent the best and the most capable people, as well the most competent. Let's not give them away to the conservatives'. *The Wrench* has become an 'incident' and there are those who insist on considering it a political book. The author declares on TV:

> Whether there is or there isn't a political aspect I couldn't say. Or rather there certainly is. It's not intended, but everything is political. This character of mine represents an attitude that is typical of today's world, but wasn't common thirty or even twenty years ago. It's essentially a case of the revolt of the technicians, who remake the world outside or beyond the wishes of the politicians. Those who are building the new world, maybe without knowing or intending to, are characters like this one.[46]

But do they exist? Or is the rigger Levi claims to have assembled from many people he knew an anachronism, an imitator of the old aristocracy of Turinese labour? This suspicion is advanced by Guido J. Paglia of *La Stampa*. Primo Levi denies it and makes a prediction:

> Who says that the Faussones are a species on the verge of extinction? If anything, the opposite is true. I don't have precise figures, but I believe that in Turin alone there are thousands of artisan-labourers with a technical professionalism like Faussone's. They're little known, it's true, but they are destined to increase, because industrial society will have ever greater need of people who work with their brain and their hands simultaneously. The robot-man on the assembly line is no longer worthwhile for the manufacturer: he doesn't give enough of a return. The reason? Because the worker starts to feel sick of what he's doing, he wears himself out, he hates his trade and he tends towards absenteeism. [...] To me it was interesting to underline a few points: manual work, if done competently, can be more rewarding than intellectual work; it takes dedication, study and sacrifice to master a trade; work isn't an unavoidable biblical curse,

> it can become interesting; if someone hates work he's in danger of also hating life.[47]

The interviewer from the radio programme 'Amico libero' looks for his impression to be confirmed. 'Your super-specialized worker seems quite distant from all the contradictions and controversies of today. Is that true?' Primo Levi agrees:

> Yes, he's outside of them. It's a theme which I deliberately didn't want to explore. On the other hand, it could be a defect in Faussone, this being distant from current and local political problems. But it's explicable: he travels; he sees many countries; he doesn't confine himself to the Italian situation of today.[48]

With the correspondent of an extreme left-wing newspaper,[49] Primo Levi openly confronts the diatribes roaring around his rigger. He recognizes straight away:

> He has that kind of energetic morality which Massimo D'Azeglio, in his *Recollections*, attributed to the old Piedmontese corporal.[50] Politically he could be for the Communist party, but it isn't stated.

'Isn't there a risk', prods the interviewer, 'that this individualistic and autonomous character could be taken as a model to be followed?'

> He could be, yes. I recently read a letter in *Lotta continua*[51] from a worker who talks about my book in irritated tones [...] He says: how has Primo Levi given himself permission to make one of us speak? Instead of that Faussone, who is a saved man, one of the privileged few, he could have made someone on the assembly line speak, or one of those from the IPCA who are dying of cancer.[52] [...] I could have done this, indeed many have already done it. But I was interested in exploring the work you can recognize yourself in: work which exists, if only rarely.

The danger that *The Wrench* could be taken for a right-wing book is there. Primo Levi admits this to his young interlocutor, and when asked 'On what basis could it be exploited by the right?' he replies:

> Because of the fact that it talks about duties and not so much about rights. I realized there was that risk, but I wrote the book anyway. It's certain though that daring to measure up to things is neither right-

> wing nor left-wing. It is part of the workings of the human animal and it must be recognized as such. This fact is also being realized by the unions: that work isn't necessarily punitive by nature.

In Levi's view – *The Periodic Table* and *The Wrench* are both indirect arguments against those who deny it – work even possesses 'a redemptive power':

> Which is part of human civilization, in my view. I'd say that the source from which I've derived this concept of work is in fact the books of Conrad, which indeed I quote in depth: because I've always sensed a certain analogy between his work and mine, which is very different from that of a sea captain, but similar in that it leaves a wide margin for error. Anyone who does a job where one is never wrong is outside the human condition. Anyone who does a mechanical, repetitive job also stands outside it. [...] But I wanted to write a different book. I wanted to describe a condition that isn't the widespread condition in today's world of repetitive working, but rather the condition of those who follow an ancient destiny, a destiny that has always existed: the destiny of the man who measures himself against the outside world through his work and exposes himself to being wrong, to repeating a test infinite times, until finally he gets it right, finds the answer, hits the target. My work is a destiny, a human condition.[53]

Would they, the young people, understand this intention of his? Because in his heart he had dedicated the book to them. He said so on the radio:

> My ideal reader, in the case of *The Wrench*, is a young reader. Out of love for the young: to show all of them who read this book that not everything is lost, even if much is.[54]

He repeated this dedication months later, replying to the *Stampa* reporter who had asked him 'To whom are your words addressed?':

> Above all to the young: they're words with a good dose of optimism, despite the negative background of today's society.[55]

Between the two declarations there had been an attack from *Lotta continua* (an attack that seven years later he described as 'savage', and against which he claimed absolute freedom for the writer, rebelling against any form of censorship).There had been some meetings with students, for many of whom Primo Levi had represented a point of reference ever since they had read his books in middle school. Now some young people felt perplexed and disturbed by 'the character and ideology of this representative of the aristocracy of labour'.[56]

One of those meetings, in a dusty lecture theatre in Palazzo Nuovo,[57] was packed with twenty-year-olds looking darkly into their futures. 'Tell us, is Faussone pointing out a road to us? Is *The Wrench* a recommendation of specialized work? Does the book contain a message? If so, how should we read it?' They kept on coming, these quick-fire questions and quick-fire replies. On one side the young, on the other their writer-father, and it could be seen, from their tension and his affectionate concern, that they had formed a bond. Primo Levi denied having consigned a message to his latest creation.

> I wouldn't say a message: the word is too strong, it doesn't suit me. Things are much simpler. I'm getting a tangible sense of the pessimism of young people grappling with serious problems. So I simply wanted to make my character say that in life we all need a trade we are masters of. That those with a trade make a better start. Fear and rage are not enough.[58]

He expressed a similar conviction to the *Quotidiano dei lavoratori* [Workers' Daily], conscious of the audience he was addressing:

> I believe that today it's dangerous to expect support from a welfare state which the state can never give you: that is, for the state to pluck you from the cradle and deliver you to the world of work prepared and armed. It's necessary for a young person to provide for himself, also to some extent where preparation for a profession is concerned.[59]

He was worried by the pessimism of the young, by their lack of confidence, by certain attitudes of refusal, of scepticism, of apathy. Someone remarked to him, 'Your character isn't alienated, he's the precise opposite of Calvino's Marcovaldo',[60] and asked him: 'This healthiness of Faussone's, the way he moves easily through building sites and through life, what is it for you? The ideal of a world different from this one? A source of hope?' Levi answered:

> It's a source of hope. But it doesn't represent a world different from this one. It's just one aspect of this one, which is rarely thought about and which is without doubt a source of optimism. That was a deliberate choice on my part: which I made precisely because there is alienation, there is a terrible wave of pessimism, especially among young people, and I thought it the right moment to show that everything is not lost, that ways out do exist, that work itself, which is

> often alienating, can also not be alienating. It can in fact be an aim in life. This isn't rhetoric, it's not the pathos-filled moralism of De Amicis. It's enough to look around us.[61]

He felt optimism as a duty: it accompanied him everywhere, that ability to communicate the love of life that Antonicelli had noted in *If This is a Man*. To anyone who reminded him of it he said:

> It's true. In part it's in my nature: I was born fairly optimistic. In part it's deliberate. It seems to me that it's a bad service to readers [...] to boost their pessimism. Being a pessimist essentially means holding up one's hands and saying 'let's all go to ruin'. Since the risk of ruin exists, the only remedy is to roll up one's sleeves. And to undertake something, to defend oneself from something, one needs to remain optimistic, otherwise one wouldn't enter the battle. And there is a battle. One can't go to war convinced that one will lose, and here we are going to war [...] Of course, it isn't always easy to be an optimist. It has to be kept in proportion; but at least where it's possible, I think it's a duty.[62]

Questioned on Faussone's philosophy, the writer supplied this reading of the character:

> I think that there's a bit of everything in him. First of all, he's secular. I've attributed some metaphysical temptation to him in two or three passages, when he gazes at the starry sky for example, but his reaction to everything outside his work is one of fear. He's only comfortable with concrete things. Secondly, he's a bit of a stoic, though that's perhaps too strong a word. Essentially his philosophy is that of reflecting himself in his work; of aiming to measure himself against it, of needing to measure himself, maybe because he's also vaguely neurotic.[63]

'He's a man', observed Davico Bonino in a television interview, 'who has a kind of restlessness (if I've understood rightly) that forces him to travel constantly and to test himself in work experiences which aren't different, since he's always practicing his trade, but are in different contexts'.

> Correct. And in this respect, I think that he's a character who's not only modern, but mirrors a human type that exists all over the world: in particular, and maybe this is chauvinism, in Turin. This Turin of ours is a curious city, which revolves around Fiat, but at the same time houses an ancient artisan tradition which comes from the valleys, which has put down roots in Turin, which has assumed ever more

> modern forms, indeed very modern ones, while still conserving those ancient roots. And I've tried to construct a character who doesn't exist in the flesh, but who reproduces the features of so many people I've met.[64]

He said 'features' deliberately, convinced that a man's trade marked his face and eyes and hands. The process of assembly that gave birth to Faussone had worked so well that, in the course of writing Levi saw Faussone all around him, heard him speak. And one evening he even met him. Levi had been invited to the town of San Mauro Torinese to give a lecture:

> [...] At the end an elegant young man came up to me. 'May I introduce myself? I'm Faussone', he said in a pure Piedmontese accent; and seeing that I thought it was a joke he took out his identity card. Then he said, 'Guess what trade I do', and I said 'You'll be a rigger.' *Propi parei*, he replied, exactly right. The book had just come out and I suggested to him that we appear together, the author and his character, on a TV broadcast they'd offered me. But he refused, saying – and these are his exact words – that this wasn't serious, whereas his was a serious trade.[65]

This was a reply, Levi remarked to his friends, perfectly in keeping with the protagonist of *The Wrench*: who apart from the trifling fact of being called Tino and not Carlo (like his flesh and blood counterpart) had the same attitudes, the same dialect inflections and what is more the same surname as the young man from San Mauro. It was precisely this surname that a RAI journalist had objected to: 'If I'm not mistaken, in Piedmontese Faussone means "big fake". Why give him that name out of *commedia dell'arte*?' Primo Levi understood that his disappointed interlocutor had in mind the offensive stereotype of the 'false and courteous' Piedmontese,[66] and hastened to reconcile him to 'Faussone'.

> I called him that because it's a typical Piedmontese surname, which goes back almost certainly to some ancient nickname, that's all. My character is anything but fake: he has a surprising naivety, he's almost infantile in his enthusiasm.

To which the relieved radio commentator replied: 'Quite so. I was astonished that the name could allude to something else, quite outside the character's personality. Which you profoundly admire, don't you?'

> Yes, that's true. Not pretend admiration, but real admiration that I learned in over thirty years of factory work, seeing around me people like Libertino Faussone, who is extremely intelligent without being

> educated, who you might say has his brain more in his fingertips than in its anatomically appointed place. People like that are capable of grasping with amazing speed problems that would take minutes or hours for an armchair technician. They're people, I'd say, much better known abroad than inside Italy.
>
> *Do you know any literary relatives of your character?*
>
> Clearly Captain MacWhirr whom I cited in a note, and many other Conradian characters. Conrad starts writing, it seems to me, after more than twenty years of sailing on commercial vessels, and he draws absolutely all his characters from life, from his companions and colleagues. It's also obvious that there's an extreme admiration and gratitude in him for those models who in his hands become literary characters.

The author realized that this irascible creature of his was liked by most people, but also had the necessary depth to be misunderstood or even to attract violent antipathy. For him Faussone was prodigiously alive (he told us that the character had sharply asserted himself during the writing of *The Wrench,* and that more than once, when he had wanted to impose his own way, the character had deserted him); so that it fell to him to defend him, as one does for an absent friend, to avoid misinterpretations. When it was observed that in describing these 'golden-handed' fellow-citizens of his, Levi might have added a 'touch of hagiography',[67] he objected, saying that love of work and study, competence and dedication

> [...] are qualities firmly rooted in our people of working class, peasant and mountain origins. From that point of view Faussone is Turinese to his fingertips [...] he's also the image of the average Turinese, with his virtues and his faults [...] he's limited, sometimes boring, he has a vocabulary that's reduced but drawn from his world.

When the journalist felt he could detect 'a little nostalgia for the Turinese character that is about to change, for this Faussone who is so honest, timid and stubborn, so respectable and individualist', Levi explained that it was not nostalgia but the choice of a calculated target:

> I limited myself to drawing one section of the city and one type of fellow citizen [...] the Faussones are among us, they walk with us along Via Roma, Via Po: you just have to know how to recognize them.

To those struck by other aspects of the protagonist, by his curiosity and thirst for knowledge, Primo Levi explained:

> His curiosity is also longing, dissatisfaction, the desire to measure himself, to prove his own identity. Faussone is a man of our time, with the dissatisfaction and the identity crisis of that man. I recognize myself in the character: I too love tests, proofs of my own identity.

The Wrench is a test and a proof of the writer on many levels, starting with the bridge between the two cultures:

> [...] As a writer I don't give up on my training as a technician. There's always been a split in our culture between the intellectual and the technician, between those who work with their mind and those who work with their hands. I'm trying to build a bridge over that split. For example, putting the way that 80 per cent of human beings live into a book. Novels take on refined existential themes; books are often full of sex and violence. But how much of people's everyday lives are taken up by sex, violence and existential crises? Eight hours of work a day take up a lot more space. I write about the problems of those eight hours. If I'm opening up a new path in our culture, I must say that I simply found it on my doorstep.

He had often talked of that unfortunate 'split' at the time of *The Periodic Table* and had written of it in an amusing review of *Parliamo Itang'liano*,[68] which concluded: 'to anyone who is interested in seeing the wall that separates the so-called two cultures breached, that wall which atrophies both and which in Italy is higher and firmer than elsewhere, this book will be useful and enjoyable reading'. He returned to the subject on numerous occasions after *The Wrench*, spontaneously or in answer to questions. One of these was: 'Debates and controversies have burned themselves out on the literature and science-technology-industry relationship. What's your position?'

> [...] I don't want to prescribe anything to anyone. A writer may very well exist who is totally ignorant of science and technology and yet is a valid and excellent writer [...] But it seems to me that it would be a good thing if he didn't live in an ivory tower, or let's say a passage, that starts from Dante and goes on to infinity; and if he didn't move only in that passage, without ever seeing the world around him. If we live in a world impregnated with technology and science, it is ill-advised to ignore it; also because, apart from existing and necessarily being mirrored in one way or another in the written word, technology and science are, at least for me, amazing stimuli. It seems to me that anyone who is ignorant today of what for example astrophysicists do with their instruments, or even more spectacularly with artificial satellites, with the Explorers and so on – anyone like that puts himself on a level that

> has regressed even beyond the time of Kant, for instance, who had studied astronomy before writing his books of philosophy. That seems to me to be a voluntary blindness. It means losing the measure of the universe we're living in [....]The fact that there are two cultures is harmful from the start. There should just be one: Galileo had one culture, and so did Spallanzani, and so did Magalotti. They didn't feel, they didn't perceive, any gaps. Galileo was a very great writer precisely because he wasn't a writer at all. He was someone who wanted to display what he'd seen.[69]

He gave a similar answer to the question 'What relationships do you think a writer can establish today between science and technology on one side and literature on the other?'

> I think one must establish, or reinforce, or renew, a relationship of mutual exchange, with advantages on both sides, as happens in animal symbioses. Science and technology can constitute a rich mine of 'raw material' for anyone who intends to write about them, naturally after an adequate amount of research. I say 'renew' because in fact this relationship has always existed: but at one time it had much less impact on everyday life. Today it pervades the daily existence of the great majority of the active population of industrialized countries; anyone who ignores that fact tends to build up a distorted image of the world in which he lives. By contrast, a literature that is attentive to work (of work as it is, not idealized or demonized, but seen from the inside) could achieve a result which up to now has never been reached, and that is to ensure that books are no longer the property of a narrow elite, but come to interest readers belonging to the working classes, because they see themselves depicted in them.[70]

He maintained that part of the trade of anyone who writes is 'to succeed in penetrating, capturing, conquering' that type of reader:

> [...] one of the aims [...] of the bets I made against myself in writing *The Wrench* was precisely this. A bet that succeeded, because I learned that the forty-six riggers of a factory, here in Turin, have all read *The Wrench*. Now, if they've all read it, it's because they've passed it on to each other. And that fills me with joy, because I don't mean to say that I've saved souls, but I've introduced into the world of books a group of people who had never been there before.

No sooner was that group confronted with the 'conglomeration and mosaic' that was Faussone than it had recognized its own world of iron in this world of paper, and felt at home immediately. As had happened, he told us, to the riggers of the Peyrani transport company in Turin, 'who had read *The Wrench*, curious, amused, even flattered'.

In a 1984 study of Italian writers' relationships with science, Ernesto Ferrero wrote in *Tuttolibri*[71] that very few had got past that 'famous barrier', no more than you could count on your fingers. He had asked Primo Levi to give his opinion on the reasons why this gang of pioneers was so small. His answer was:

> It's not surprising. For men of my generation the split between the 'two cultures' was dramatic. My teacher of Italian, a very good teacher, would repeat that only literature is genuinely formative, whereas the exact sciences are informative and no more. It made my hair stand on end, but in the Gentilean and Crocean school[72] such statements were common. Now, nobody who is cultivated can be ignorant, for example, of the connections of the genetic code with semiology: there's a whole kind of language that revolves around it.

In the case of Primo Levi it was his family environment that righted the 'historic wrong' committed by his school.

> My grandfather and my father were both engineers and our house was full of technical and scientific books. It was my father who pushed me in that direction, imperceptibly, without abusing his authority. At the age of eleven I moved mountains and seas to have an etymological dictionary. I got it, it was my *livre de chevet*[73] for many years and it still is now. Even then I was interested in understanding the reasons for words. Then I rationalized that interest. Knowing what's behind a word that's been historically formed seems important to me.

It certainly was not unrelated, that old *livre de chevet*, to another of the tests, perhaps the most surprising one, that Primo Levi made himself undergo in writing *The Wrench*. This was Faussone's way of speaking, which the dialectologist and philologist Gianluigi Beccaria called 'a newer and more important innovation than the idea of the book itself',[74] observing: 'Pavese and Fenoglio have given lofty performances of cultured Piedmontese. Levi on the other hand offers us an urban and extremely concrete popular Italian, based on plots which are not invented but real.' Having revealed how 'rich and appetizing the language of the protagonist' is, 'with its continual insertion of metaphors taken from professional language', and how the language of these working men flows 'smooth and clear without being condescendingly mimicked', Beccaria affirms: 'In a bold and successful experiment Primo Levi gives us, not a translation from dialect into Italian, nor an Italian infected with dialecticisms[...] but rather an Italian thought in dialect, whose dialectal character is played out in the syntax more than in the vocabulary and idiom.'

In all the interviews there are questions about Faussone's language. The answers are thick with meaning, reflecting a stylistic and lexical project developed over a long time. They bear the mark of a firm loyalty to Piedmont and Turin, the homeland of 'our roots, not powerful but deep, extensive and fantastically intertwined', and to the mountains of that homeland, which 'had taught us hard work, endurance and a certain wisdom'.[75] The mountains from which Faussone had come, with his store of freedom carried in his hands and in his name.

Giorgio De Rienzo:

> *There's a noticeable innovation in this book, which is the language used, spotted with Piedmontese dialecticisms and terms from technical jargon [...] which gives the impression of being transcribed from real life, recorded with curiosity and satisfaction by the writer, almost as if he had known Faussone. Who nevertheless does not exist. Is Faussone's language also a fake?'*
>
> It's a literary operation to be sure, but it has a basis in truth. This is in fact the language that the educated Piedmontese labourer uses when he speaks. I wouldn't say that it's a fake or a fraud. If anything, it's a restoration. Popular language has exceptional resources. It uses delightful metaphors, and I felt the need to put them down in writing.

Radio commentator: 'Will Faussone continue to live, after *The Wrench*?'

> I don't know yet. I fear he won't. I'm afraid he'll become tiresome for readers also because I'm not sure that the language Faussone uses is pleasant to ears with little experience of it. The Italian reader is used to beautiful style, and this book of mine, unlike my previous ones, isn't written in a beautiful style; it's written in an ugly style, sometimes even a repetitive and I won't say irritating one, but certainly a sloppy one, because I've tried to depict a human type who speaks like that, who doesn't pay attention to the elegance of what he says, but to its clarity.

Guido Davico Bonino:

> *This book of yours, besides taking on an unusual character and theme, is also unusual stylistically, because you (rightly in my opinion) wanted to remake the speech of the character, choosing a precise linguistic mélange. Can you describe this?*

I deliberately abandoned the kind of writing I have maintained up to now in my other books, which is an accurate kind, a studied, meditated, carefully chosen Italian, and I made my character speak as high level technicians would (and in fact do) speak, still in Italian, but a humble Italian; often repetitive, yet rich in images drawn from the world of work. I didn't invent them, almost none of them. They're common expressions and figures of speech strangely parallel to those that were once drawn from the ancient arts. The language we use is studded with metaphors derived from the trades, from the arts. Even now we continue to use (though we don't notice them, and few would be able to indicate their origin) phrases drawn from arts that no longer exist. My character, on the other hand, draws on the trade he practises now and speaks as a 'mechanical', even when he describes other things, from outside his world.[76]

Silvia Giacomoni:

Faussone speaks an extremely particular language, a very amusing Italo-Piedmontese. Why?

It seemed to me that if Pasolini could make his *Street Kids*[77] speak in Romanesco, and Eduardo De Filippo could make his characters speak in Neapolitan, it would be fair for the Piedmontese to do something similar. It exists, that Italian of Faussone's, as a demotic language, perhaps a degraded one, which is the Italian of the factories. I had a lot of fun writing Faussone's language: I've never written with such ease [...] Faussone's stories are very difficult to tell in normal Italian because their language is this one. There are technical terms in this Italian which nobody else uses or even understands. Man the maker speaks the language of makers. Try saying *scodimento*[78] in proper Italian. Probably you'd need some circumlocution that goes on for two lines. Try making Giovannin Bongee[79] speak in proper Italian. It isn't on a whim that Porta makes him speak in Milanese. I don't know if '*el mestée*'[80] has come off for me, but I don't believe the attempt was wrong.

Francesco Poli:

But isn't there the risk that the language used by your hero, which is very funny and easy to understand for a Piedmontese, loses its bite for a non-Piedmontese reader?

There is that risk. I was aware of it myself: if the delivery, from that point of view, is 100 per cent for a Piedmontese, for others it's 70 per cent. Still, that doesn't count for very much. When I read for example

> *The Street Kids* or *A Violent Life*[81] by Pasolini, something of the Romanesco speech may have escaped me, but I still learned how a kid lives in the Roman slums. I chose to make Faussone speak according to his dialect jargon (which I Italianized, trying to change as little as possible) because that's what he uses every day, that's how he tells me about everyday things.

It came naturally to Primo Levi to use the expression 'he tells me'. And it really was like that for him when he was writing *The Wrench*. The character 'told him' things and he transcribed them, obediently. Thinking back to that time, he said:

> [...] I wrote *The Wrench* with extreme ease. I still have the manuscript: typed directly on the machine and almost without corrections. It seemed very easy to me to write in this way, almost freeing myself from the obligations of the literary writer. And it really seemed to me that I was recording with a tape recorder what someone was telling me.[82]

The rigger and his jargon, it was perspicaciously observed, 'have a long history'.[83] And here we see that consistency we've talked about, to which the author referred to in his almost didactic answer to Professor Giuseppe Grassano's question:

> *In* The Wrench *we observe a very original linguistic undertaking: but wasn't the main project in this book already sketched out in the previous ones?*
>
> If all characters spoke the same kind of language, they would be flattened like figures cut out of cardboard [...] In *The Truce*, Cesare speaks his own kind of language, and I too speak it when I speak of Cesare. When there's indirect speech that refers to him, there's a slide towards his language. I'd say there can't not be one, if the discourse is to maintain a certain concreteness. When one introduces a character, he must be whole: he must have a life of his own and so also a language of his own [...] One of the main difficulties for anyone who writes in Italian is direct speech, because Italian is little spoken and spoken Italian is quite a poor language.[84] Dialect is often richer than Italian, and so is jargon. For that reason, it came naturally to me to make Faussone speak in that particular way of his, which is not an invention of mine: it really is the way one speaks in the workshop, at least in Piedmont. In other workshops, in Lombardy or in Campania, people would speak differently, but here they speak like this. It came spontaneously to me to let Faussone speak in that style of his which is syntactically quite poor, yet extremely precise when referring to

> technical things: things that he knows and has a name for. His competence extends even to language.[85]

In this 'lesson', Primo Levi refers only to the precedent of Cesare, but Giovanni Tesio observes in his careful account of the writer that 'homages to dialect' are already present, both in the theatre version of *If This is a Man* whenever Lorenzo, the bricklayer from Fossano, appears; and in the speech and etymological insertions of *The Periodic Table*, where the shoemaker in 'Arsenic' anticipates the realism of Faussone.

Words. Work. Morality. And also environment. The author lets the mysterious fascination the city holds for him filter into the rugged mind of his character. Levi says:

> [...] the Mole Antonelliana, the piazzas of Castello and San Carlo, the via Roma are his terms of comparison.[86]

At the beginning of *The Wrench* there is a revealing passage on the deep bond that unites Faussone with Turin. We read that in his monastic room in the Togliattigrad guest house the rigger had 'put up on the wall a view of Turin taken from an airplane and a grainy photo of the local football team covered with autographs. As far as household goods go it wasn't much, but then again I didn't even have that, and I felt more at home in his room than in mine.'[87] Primo Levi declared that he had a 'natural relationship' with Turin: he had always lived in the same house, thus being 'an extreme case of sedentary life'.[88] Moreover:

> [...] apart from the odd journey, apart from a year in Auschwitz and another in Milan, I have always been here, in this city. I have made myself at home here: I have a long settling-in behind me in this city, which doesn't leave me any alternatives or comparisons. My adherence to Turin is total: by all means say that I am integrated.

'What do you like about Turin?' Professor Giorgio De Rienzo pressed him.

> The things I didn't choose; the habits that took root in me; the routes I've had to use. Here I was born, got married, wrote my first book: these are all things that stay with you, that create a connection to a city. And then it'll sound like a cliché, but the seriousness of Turin, its tenacity, its capacity to take on problems in a concrete way is remarkable. It may seem strange to you, but I find Turin a friendly city, in the relationships between people too: it's not a cold city.

He explores it every day with renewed curiosity; he studies it in its most humble and neglected particulars (take 'Signs on Stone':[89] never before had a famous Biblical verse been recalled in such a singular way). He scans its skyline to see Superga[90] on a clear day, or to seize the moment to climb (he and Faussone know where) to collect the dust that comes from the stars.

But surely there's *something* that doesn't suit him. In fact there is, and he admits it with an excuse, a justification and a claim to ownership.

> *What don't you like about this city?*
>
> The outskirts, which are badly built: but one can look elsewhere, towards the hills, or further still towards the mountains. Outskirts, like violence, are the ills of every industrial city, they are the inevitable downsides: they aren't specific to Turin. They say that Turin doesn't have a cultural life: but what there is seems enough to me.

Giovanni Tesio asked Primo Levi other questions on his link with Turin, in an interview *Nuova Società*[91] published together with an article on the writer's roots.

> *How did Turin appear to you after the hell of the Lager and the odyssey of the return?*
>
> I'll tell you something that's not in my books. I was deported from Aosta to Fossoli,[92] before the final deportation to Auschwitz. When the train arrived in Chivasso,[93] there was a February sunset. The sky was cloudy, but from the station I could make out the Mole.[94] That was the wrenching moment, the farewell that ripped through me. The return was in the morning. The train dropped us off at Porta Nuova.[95] A friend was with me. From the train he saw an apartment block on Corso Sommelier,[96] where relatives of his lived, and it was intact. He told me that, if the worst came to the worst, we could find a place for the night there. The city was seriously damaged by the bombing raids and by the insurrection, but I remember that I was astonished by the extreme vitality of my friends. They were all victorious; I wasn't.
>
> *What are the places in the city you feel most connected to?*
>
> Those that appear here and there in my books: the area around my house, my school – that is, the d'Azeglio – the University. A bit to the Valentino Park, a bit to via Po where among other things my paternal grandfather used to live. Also to the old via Roma,[97] though I remember it only vaguely. One of my legendary grandfathers had a textile shop on the old via Roma where it was possible at Carnival time to go up on the mezzanine balcony and watch the parade. On the list

> I'd also put the route I took for twenty years from Turin to Settimo and from Settimo to Turin.
>
> *Has coming from Turin had an influence on your formation as a writer?*
>
> I don't know how to answer that question, as I don't know how to answer when people ask if I'd have been the same writer if I hadn't been in the Lager. The fact that I'm Turinese certainly hasn't had an influence on my decision to become a writer. On my style of writing, yes. Today the city is changing very rapidly. It seems to me worth the effort to contribute towards conveying its image before it disappears altogether.

He contributed strongly to that with *The Wrench*, the only book of his, Lorenzo Mondo said, that was 'carefree and happy';[98] the only one over which the Lager does not cast its shadow. He was invited to examine this by a question from Mario Miccinesi, editor of the literary periodical *Uomini e libri*:

> The Wrench *undoubtedly presents an unusual narrative model. Would you like to explain to your readers what goal you set yourself with this new book of yours?*
>
> If the question refers to the structure of the book, that is to the narration delegated to a character, I must say that the narrative model isn't as unusual as all that. I could cite at least four predecessors, all of whom I hold dear: Carlo Porta with Giovannin Bongee; G.G. Belli[99] with infinite storytellers, one for each sonnet; Conrad with Marlow; Sholem Aleichem with Tevye the Milkman. All these writers have felt the need to construct another self to impersonate: an entirely different character to entrust with a different language, so that he can tell the story of a different life. If I'd told the exploits of my rigger myself, I would have abused him, by attributing to him, together with my 'literary' language, a sensibility and an experience that are mine and not his. The subject of the book, however, a collection of work adventures, is quite unusual. The main goal I set myself in choosing it is this: I wanted to confer literary dignity on a way of life which, as far as I know, today's literature has overlooked, not only in Italy; that is, on a man who fights to preserve his own freedom and creativity in the alienating maze of industrial society. I wanted to show that this enterprise is possible, or at least that it isn't mad to undertake it.
>
> All the same, I don't believe that a book can or should aim towards a single end; if that happens it's a polemical book, and that wasn't my intention. I certainly didn't want to set myself up as a moralist. If a

> moral emerges from this book it's a fall-out, a by-product. I hoped that the book would contain other things: I wanted to demonstrate, as Giovanni Raboni put it in his *Tuttolibri* article, that 'it's possible to create suspense from building a crane'.[100] I wanted to put myself to the test and create a three-dimensional character in the flesh; one credible enough to deceive the reader and make him think that Tino Faussone really exists and really dined and walked along the Volga with me. In a word, I wanted to 'assemble' him whole with his virtues, vices, tics, neuroses, prejudices, ambitions, defeats, victories and language, something that I'd never attempted in my previous books. I wanted finally to demonstrate to the reader and to myself that one can build a book without running it through the usual channels (which are a bit clogged up now) of sociology, of escapism, of sex and violence, of private life. I wanted to write a modern book about modern adventures, which are not invented, not difficult to follow and not too sad. In writing, I realized that the enterprise wasn't as difficult as all that: I didn't have to go far to find my man to do the storytelling. It was enough for me to revisit the experience of technical work which I myself had lived for nearly thirty years, and which is lived by innumerable men-the-makers of our time; and then to extract my typical and essential one from them.

****

Primo Levi was very tidy. As the reviews came out he catalogued them on a sheet of paper: author's name, title of the publication, date; then two columns filled with points from one to five, so many for the level of the criticism, so many for a fair appraisal of the book. Raboni, for example, had five points in both columns. But there was one account, singing the praises of *The Wrench*, which he couldn't put together with the others, despite its being particularly dear to him. It was included in a letter, of which he gave us a copy, and which was signed Vincenzo Consolo. It said, among other things: 'In this book there's Turin, a "Turinese" culture and morality, but at the same time there's the world, seen from the top of cranes in a broad and gliding movement that reminded me of another such movement across destroyed Europe in *The Truce*.'

According to Vincenzo Consolo, the book's thesis 'is of great relevance: that with the crisis of history and ideologies, with the triumph of impostors, with the confusion and reversal of roles [...] for the man and the writer there is only one path left: faith in the structure and morality of work.' The letter then took a bitter, pessimistic turn; but it pleased Primo Levi to know that Consolo regarded himself 'as an ordinary and affectionate reader of yours, who has been following you and who has learned a lot from you since the time of *If This is a Man*.'

On Wednesday 16 May 1979, at the home of Maria Bellonci, the titles of the seventeen long-listed candidates for the 33rd Strega Prize are announced, and there are many people, Elio Pecora reports in *Tuttolibri*,[101] who are saying that *The Wrench* has already won. In competition with Primo Levi, who has withdrawn his entry for the Viareggio Prize, are Ferruccio Ulivi with *Le mani pure* [The Pure Hands], Carlo Sgorlon with *La carrozza di rame* [The Copper Carriage], Laudomia Bonnani with *Il bambino di pietra* [The Stone Baby], Stanislao Nievo with *Aurora* [Dawn], and Gian Luigi Piccioli with *Sveva*. In the same issue of *Tuttolibri* Rosanna Ombres, who on 15 June will be among the 440 jurors voting for the famous shortlist of five, writes that she has already put *The Wrench* at the top of her list. In a mischievous article in *La Stampa* Giovanni Arpino announces that 'an almost easy victory for Primo Levi is emerging at the Strega'.[102] Still in *La Stampa*, gathering together the first leaks about the candidates, Giulia Massari reports the protests from Einaudi's rival publishers: 'If Primo Levi is there the die is cast. The mournful note cannot be resisted.' The journalist points out that the book is not about the concentration camps, but 'with little respect for justice', the others retort 'Yes, yes, but it's the same thing.'[103]

As the days pass the same forecasts are repeated. Antonio Debenedetti from *Corriere della Sera* spends the eve of the announcement hovering around the expert 'prizologists', who rule out any possible surprise: 'Either Levi or Ulivi.' Better to bet on the most probable winner and interview the writer from Turin. What do they ask him about if not the 'double register' of *The Wrench*, which fuses humanistic with scientific culture. The question has been put to him a hundred times, but he does not miss the opportunity to stress its absurdity:

> It's a cliché to be rejected, the idea that there are two mutually exclusive cultures: there weren't for Galileo, or for Einstein. It seems to me that it's a distortion typical of the European continent to maintain the barricade between humanistic culture and scientific, technical culture. This book of mine, and for that matter its predecessor, *The Periodic Table*, are both attempts to lower and eliminate that barricade. In particular, in *The Wrench* I've struggled to show that even the work of 'rude mechanicals' can be a source of inspiration and therefore of storytelling [...] In this sense, even *The Wrench* can be considered a testimony.[104]

And finally, at the start of July, in the nymphaeum of Villa Giulia, between the silks and the tulles Faussone enters cultural high society. And where is the author? There he is.

> Primo Levi, with his clear, innocent eyes, and the face of a kind country doctor or retired Alpine soldier [...] kept to the side as the count was pronounced in the stentorian voice of Giorgio Bassani, and

> noted down on a bit of paper the way the vote was going. As a practical man, he didn't report every ballot, only the gap between himself and his closest pursuer.[105]

Paolo Granzotto, the correspondent for *Il Giornale*, is thrilled by the contest:

> At first it was very beautiful. It seemed like the duel between Villeneuve and Arnoux, with Primo Levi as the Ferrari driver and Ferruccio Ulivi in the Renault. When the ballots counted reached 50, Ulivi was in the lead with 22 votes, followed by Levi with 19. At a hundred, Levi took the lead, with 35 votes to Ulivi's 34: by a hair's breadth, as they say. At 150 the suspense was nearly over. Levi was gaining a considerable lead over his opponent; and the 33rd Strega Prize has gone as everyone knew it would. Primo Levi has won.

With 153 votes against 110 for Ulivi, 'an authoritative scholar and academic, who became a novelist two years ago'.[106] Carlo Sgorlon, one of the five finalists, remarks chivalrously: 'This book by Primo Levi is certainly his best. And then there's this invention, the *Thousand and One Nights* told by a worker, a character it's impossible not to love...'[107]

At a certain point in the count, Primo Levi had set paper and pencil aside, patiently enduring the glare of the spotlight focusing in on him. The first to congratulate him, with thirty votes still to go, was Giovanni Spadolini, minister for Public Education. Then Maria Bellonci and the tide of others arrived. Receiving the prize, he was moved; he even seemed happy, and the photo published by the news agencies confirmed it. He announced:

> I think that the Strega Prize was not given to me so much for *The Wrench* as for my books as a whole, all of which I love equally. And I'm happy to receive the Strega because it's one of the few prizes to have kept pace with inflation.

Describing 'the emotional declaration', Girolamo Mangano for the *Gazzetta del Popolo* has no qualms about saying: 'Yes, of course, it's never just one book they give a prize to, but also the man, his previous works, what he says and does; but [...] *The Wrench* would have won the prize without that.'

There followed the ritual of adding his name to the ballot box signed by the winners, the receptions and gala lunches. Primo Levi returned to Turin bewildered but pleased and cheerful; he came to *La Stampa* to show us the cartoon of him, glasses on his forehead, tie blowing in the wind and a wrench in his pocket, flying on the wings of a hook-nosed witch riding a broomstick.[108] He said of the evening:

People applauded, and it seemed to me that it wasn't just politeness. They seemed really convinced. There were many writers in particular. And Maria Bellonci was stunning in her blue dress embroidered with lilies-of-the-valley. 'Imagine!' she said to me, with a hug. 'It was sixteen years ago, when you competed with *The Truce*: you should already have won then.'

Notes

1. The 'years of lead' were the period of Italian history between 1968 and 1982, marked by left-wing and right-wing political terrorism.
2. Giorgio Manzini, 'Elogio del libero lavoro'[In praise of free work] *Paese Sera*, 11 December 1978.
3. An ironic reference to the nineteenth-century poem, 'Il sabato del villaggio' [The village Saturday] by Giacomo Leopardi. While Leopardi celebrates Saturday as a day of relief from toil, Levi reclaims it as something which gives life meaning and purpose.
4. He left the management of the Siva factory in 1975, but only in 1977 did he decisively bid farewell to this 'piece of his life'. He registered at the Goethe Institute in Turin in that period to brush up his German.
5. Gabriella Poli, 'L'alfabeto della chimica' [The alphabet of chemistry], *Tuttolibri (La Stampa)*, 6 December 1976.
6. 'With Malice Aforethought', the first chapter in P. Levi trans. N. Rich, *The Wrench* in A. Goldstein (ed.), *Complete Works of Primo Levi* (New York: Liveright, 2015) Vol. II, pp. 953-9.
7. On 11 March 1977, violent clashes broke out at the University of Bologna between an extreme left-wing student group, who had been trying to break up a meeting of Catholic students, and the police. One student in the left-wing group was killed, leading to more riots the following day, which resulted in army tanks being sent in.
8. 'The Bevel Gear' in P. Levi trans. N. Rich, *The Wrench*, pp.1077-82.
9. Giorgio De Rienzo, 'In un alambicco quanta poesia' [So much poetry in a still], *Famiglia Cristiana*, No.29, 20 July 1975.
10. P. Levi trans. N. Rich, *The Wrench*, p.1005.
11. Ibid, p.1039.
12. P. Levi, *La chiave a stella, Letture per le scuole medie n.65* [*The Wrench*. Books for middle schools no.65] (Turin: Einaudi, 1983), p.232. See also J. Conrad, 'Note to Typhoon', quoted in P. Levi trans. N. Rich, *The Wrench*, p.1165, and available in full at: https://ebooks.adelaide.edu.au/c/conrad/joseph/c75ty/preface.html [Accessed 13 June 2016].
13. From the programme 'Personalmente', RAI Radio 3, 23 December 1978.
14. Giorgio De Rienzo, 'Come il mio Faussone io celebro la religione del lavoro' [Like my Faussone I celebrate the religion of work], *Stampa Sera*, 29 December 1978; and 'All'eroe dell'ultimo romanzo di Primo Levi lavorare piace' [The hero of Primo Levi's last novel likes working], *Famiglia Cristiana*, January 1978.
15. A well-known historian, writer and magistrate who fought in the Resistance, friend of Primo Levi.
16. P. Levi trans. A. Shugaar, *Other People's Trades*, in A. Goldstein (ed.), *Complete Works of Primo Levi*, Vol. III p.2, 281 ('A Long Duel', pp. 2, 275-81). The story was originally published as 'Polvere olimpica' [Olympic dust], *La Stampa*, 14 August 1984.
17. Enrico Boeri,'Quattro chiacchiere con Primo Levi' [A chat with Primo Levi], *Tecnologie chimiche* [Chemical Technologies: scientific journal], December 1983.

18. G. Grassano, *Primo Levi* (Florence: Il Castoro/La Nuova Italia, 1981), p.12.
19. F. Camon, *Autoritratto di Primo Levi* [Self-portrait of Primo Levi], (Padua: Edizioni Nord Est, 1987), p.8.
20. P. Levi trans A. Goldstein, *The Truce,* in *Complete Works of Primo Levi*, Vol. II, p.397.
21. Francesco Poli, 'Intervista a Primo Levi' [Interview with Primo Levi], *Il Quotidiano dei lavoratori* [The Workers' Daily], 28 February 1979.
22. Ibid.
23. Silvia Giacomoni, 'Il mago Merlino e l'uomo fabbro' [Merlin the Mage and man the maker], *La Repubblica,* 24 January 1979.
24. Gianluigi Beccaria, Foreword to the middle school edition of *La chiave a stella* (Einaudi: Turin,1983), p.viii.
25. Francesco Poli, 'Intervista a Primo Levi'.
26. From the feature 'Segnalibro' on RAI 3 presented by Guido Davico Bonino, 3 January 1979.
27. Enrico Boeri,'Quattro chiacchiere con Primo Levi'.
28. P. Levi trans. N. Rich, *The Wrench*, p.1135.
29. Guido Davico Bonino, 'Segnalibro'.
30. Roth (see Notes on the Translation and Note to Chapter I).
31. Ferdinando Camon, 'Se il Lager oltre la vita spezza la dignità' [If as well as life the Lager destroys dignity], *Il Giorno*, 5 June 1986. The interview is included in his *Autoritratto di Primo Levi* [Self-portrait of Primo Levi], pp.56-7. The book referred to is A. Solzhenitsyn, trans. R. Parker, *One Day in the Life of Ivan Denisovich* (New York: Dutton, 1963).
32. Grassano, *Primo Levi,* p.4.
33. A term of abuse used throughout Alessandro Manzoni's novel *I promessi sposi* (Milan: Guglielmini' e Redaelli, 1842), *passim*. It means literally 'vile mechanic', as it is rendered in the English translation of the novel: A. Manzoni trans. B. Penman, *The Betrothed* (St Ives: Penguin, 1983), *passim*. The book is so famous in Italy that *vile meccanico* has become a common phrase, close to Shakespeare's 'rude mechanical' (*Midsummer Night's Dream,* III.2.10), which will be used to translate subsequent instances.
34. P. Levi trans. N. Rich, *The Wrench* ('Tiresias', pp.983-90).
35. Ibid ('Metalwork', pp.999-1018).
36. Ibid ('The Bevel Gear', pp.1077-82).
37. De Rienzo, 'All'eroe dell'ultimo romanzo di Primo Levi lavorare piace'.
38. From the programme 'Amico libero' [Free friend] on RAI Radio 3, February 1979.
39. Silvia Giacomoni, 'Il mago Merlino e l'uomo fabbro'.
40. Giovanni Tesio, 'Le radici di Primo Levi' [Primo Levi's roots], *Nuova Società*, 22 March 1980.
41. Stefano Reggiani, 'Diventa sfida il lavoro ben fatto' [Work done well becomes a challenge], *La Stampa*, 14 January 1979.
42. Italo Calvino uses the expression in the 1978 Italian edition jacket flap.
43. Confederazione Italiana Sindacati Lavoratori [Confederation of Italian Workers' Unions], pro-government and associated with Catholic socialism, as opposed to the more radical Confederazione Generale Italiana del Lavoro [General Italian Confederation of Work] or Cgil.
44. Unione Italiana del Lavoro [Italian Union of Work], a social-democratic and reformist union confederation, which was also pro-government and allied to the Cisl.
45. Carniti was secretary of the Cisl-affiliated union Federazione Italiana Metalmeccanici [Italian Federation of Metalworkers], known as Fim-Cisl.
46. Guido Davico Bonino, 'Segnalibro'.
47. Guido J. Paglia, 'Ma davvero un Faussone cammina ancora tra noi?' [But does a real Faussone still exist?], *La Stampa*, 6 July 1979.
48. 'Amico libero', February 1979.

49. Francesco Poli, 'Intervista a Primo Levi'.
50. Massimo d'Azeglio was a Piedmontese-Italian Risorgimento statesman, who was Prime Minister of Sardinia from 1849-52. The classical *liceo* or secondary school Levi attended was named after him. He was the author of a book of memoirs relating his experiences of the Risorgimento wars, translated into English by Count Andrea Maffei as *Recollections* (London: Forgotten Books, 2012).
51. 'Continuous Struggle', a newspaper published from 1969 to 1982. It was set up by the far-left extra-parliamentary group of the same name, but continued after the group was disbanded in 1976.
52. The IPCA was an artificial dyestuffs factory outside Turin, where numerous workers died of bladder cancer in the late 1960s. The factory owners were jailed in 1982.
53. Grassano, *Primo Levi,* p.105.
54. 'Amico libero', February 1979.
55. Guido J. Paglia, 'Ma davvero un Faussone cammina ancora tra noi?'
56. Francesco Poli, 'Intervista a Primo Levi'.
57. The humanities building of the University of Turin.
58. From the shorthand notes of the news team of *La Stampa*. Primo Levi expressed himself in similar terms on the subject of this 'message' in his preface to *Terza pagina: Racconti e saggi* [Third page: Stories and Essays] (Turin: *La Stampa*, 1 January 1986), a collection of stories and essays published in October 1986 as part of *La Stampa*'s series 'Terza pagina' [Third page], which collected the work of the paper's most distinguished contributors. In the *Complete Works* the preface does not appear, although the pieces themselves are translated, as *Collected Stories and Essays*, by Alessandra and Francesco Bastagli (Vol. III, pp.2257-2404).
59. Francesco Poli, 'Intervista a Primo Levi'.
60. The unskilled labourer who is the main character in I. Calvino trans. W. Weaver, *Marcovaldo: Or the Seasons in the City* (London: Secker & Warburg, 1983).
61. Francesco Poli, 'Intervista a Primo Levi'. Edmondo De Amicis was a famous nineteenth-century author of sentimental children's books.
62. Grassano, *Primo Levi,* p.13.
63. Francesco Poli, 'Intervista a Primo Levi'.
64. Guido Davico Bonino, 'Segnalibro'.
65. Enrico Boeri, 'Quattro chiacchiere con Primo Levi'.
66. From the proverb 'Piemontese falso e cortese, italiano falso e villano' [The Piedmontese are false and polite, the Italians false and rude]. *Commedia dell'arte* was Italy's popular theatre tradition of travelling players, which revolved heavily around such stereotypical characters.
67. Guido J. Paglia, 'Ma davvero un Faussone cammina ancora tra noi?'
68. Primo Levi, 'Le parole esportate' [Exported words], *La Stampa*, 17 February 1988. A review of G. Elliot, *Parliamo Itangliano*[We speak Itangliano] (Milan: Rizzoli, 1977). *Itangliano* is a neologism modelled on 'franglais'; the book is a study of anglicized Italian, subtitled 'Ovvero le 400 parole inglese che deve sapere chi vuole fare carriera' [Or the 400 English words which anyone who wants to be successful must know].
69. Grassano, *Primo Levi*, pp.8-9.
70. Mario Miccinesi, 'Intervista a Primo Levi' [Interview with Primo Levi], *Uomini e Libri*, Milan, January-February 1979, No. 72, p. 39.
71. Ernesto Ferrero, 'Se lo scrittore sapesse che la scienza è anche fantasia' [If the writer knew that science is also imagination], *Tuttolibri (La Stampa)*, 21 January 1984.
72. The education system in fascist Italy was extremely traditional, prioritising Latin, Ancient Greek and rote learning of passages from Italian literature. It was strongly influenced by the ideas of Benedetto Croce (1866-1952), and Giovanni Gentile (1875-

1944), 'the philosopher of fascism'. Both philosophers were idealists: they believed that reality is fundamentally mental and immaterial.

73. 'Favourite book'.
74. Giovanni Beccaria, foreword to *La chiave a stella* (middle school edition cited), p.x.
75. P. Levi trans. A. Goldstein, *The Periodic Table* in *Complete Works of Primo Levi*, Vol. II, p.795.
76. Guido Davico Bonino, 'Segnalibro'.
77. P.P. Pasolini, trans. A. Goldstein, *The Street Kids* (New York: Europa Editions, 2016).
78. In the Italian edition of *The Wrench*, Faussone explains to Levi that a stretched-out object lacks *scodimento* when it can fit into a tube as long as it's straight, but on getting to a bend or a corner stops, and no longer *scode* [moves].
79. A comic character, representing regional stereotypes, in the Milanese language. *Desgrazzi de Giovannin Bongee* [*The Misadventures of Giovannin Bongee*], written in 1812, and *Olter desgrazzi de Giovannin Bongee* [*Other Misadventures of Giovannin Bongee*], written in 1814, were considered the masterworks of the most famous Milanese-language writer Carlo Porta.
80. Task, profession or dialect in Milanese, used here by Levi in the first sense.
81. P.P. Pasolini, trans. W. Weaver, *A Violent Life* (Carcanet: Manchester, 2007).
82. Grassano, *Primo Levi*, p.16.
83. Giovanni Tesio, 'Ritratti di contemporanei: Primo Levi' [Portraits of contemporaries: Primo Levi], *Belfagor*(literary journal), Florence, 30 November 1979, p.657.
84. Dialects are still widely spoken at home in Italy, by about 41% of the population, according to official statistics (whether on their own, or alongside standard Italian), and this was even more the case in the 1970s and 80s. Standard Italian tends to be used for most purposes outside the home.
85. Grassano, *Primo Levi*, p.8.
86. Guido J. Paglia, 'Ma davvero un Faussone cammina ancora tra noi?'
87. P. Levi trans. N. Rich, *The Wrench*, p.976 ('The Helper', pp. 975-82).
88. P. Levi trans. A.Shugaar, *Other People's Trades*, p. 2015 ('My House', pp. 2015-8).
89. Ibid, title of chapter, pp. 2070-4.
90. A basilica on a hill outside the city.
91. Giovanni Tesio, 'Le radici di Primo Levi'.
92. A concentration camp within Italy.
93. A town outside Turin.
94. The Mole Antonelliana, Turin's landmark domed building. Originally built as a synagogue, it was owned by the local government and undergoing reconstruction at the time. Today it houses Italy's national cinema museum.
95. A station in central Turin.
96. A street in the centre of the city.
97. Via Roma, the main street in Turin, was substantially renovated by Mussolini between 1931 and 1938 and resurfaced in 1944 following damage during the war. Via Po is another main street in Turin, leading down to the Po river.
98. Primo Levi International Study Days, Piedmont Regional Council, 28-9 March 1988.
99. Nineteenth century writer of sonnets in Romanesco.
100. Giovanni Raboni, 'Riesce a creare suspense col montaggio di una gru' [He creates suspense in the building of a crane], *Tuttolibri (La Stampa)*, 23 December 1978.
101. Elio Pecora, 'Parliamone male ma concorriamo tutti' [We speak ill of them but we all compete], *Tuttolibri (La Stampa)*, 26 March 1979.
102. Giovanni Arpino, 'Non lamentiamoci dei premi letterari' [Let's not complain about literary prizes], *La Stampa*, 17June 1979.
103. Giulia Massari, 'È già stagione di premi, ma chi vincerà la corsa?' [It's already prize season, but who will win the race?], *La Stampa*, 1 May 1979.

104. Antonio Debenedetti, 'Vincitore il romanzo' [The novel's the winner], *Corriere della Sera*, 6 July 1979.
105. Paolo Granzotto, 'Una chiave d'oro per Levi' [A golden key for Levi], *Il Giornale*, 6 July 1979.
106. Mario Guidotti, 'Senza sorprese lo Strega a Primo Levi' [No surprises as the Strega goes to Primo Levi], *L'Avvenire*, 6 July 1979.
107. Girolamo Mangano,'Primo Levi ha vinto lo Strega' [Primo Levi has won the Strega], *Gazzetta del Popolo*, 6July 1979.
108. 'Strega' is the Italian word for witch. The prize's sponsor, Guido Alberti, a friend of Maria Bellonci, was the owner of a liqueur company named after a legend about witches in Benevento, his home town.

VIII

'If We Keep Silent, Who Will Speak?'

A prophet, an intellectual, a scientist? Sent by *La Repubblica* to interview Primo Levi just after *The Wrench* came out, Silvia Giacomoni had felt overwhelmed in the company of this man 'of whom so many different images coexist' and she had told him so. The writer had laughed:

> But did you want me to live my whole life as a survivor? I am a survivor, but I don't want to write only about Auschwitz. I also want to speak to the younger generation. I've been to talk about *If This is a Man* in at least a hundred and thirty schools, but I won't accept these invitations any more. For some time now I've been asking myself if the things I've told are really true. And I've become convinced that, looking at it from another angle, the subject of the Lager will continue to be shocking, but that it's not topical any more. The risk of that universe returning, in Europe at least, isn't there now. Or it's in second or third place compared to other threats, other fears, other uncertainties.[1]

It was the end of January 1979 and for some time Primo Levi had been saying that he thought his dialogue with school students had slowed down. He wanted to end it, or at least to reduce it – or better still, to take advantage of *The Wrench* to change the subject and talk about work (and aspirations) with young people, who were growing up worried and discouraged. But something obscene was happening to end the witness's time of truce. There were those beyond the Alps who persisted in denying that the Jewish genocide ever happened, 'maybe trusting', Levi wrote in *La Stampa*, 'to the blurring of memories after 35 years; maybe hoping that, in the meantime, the survivors and witnesses, few but troublesome, would have disappeared from the scene'.[2] The guilty themselves who had been brought to justice had never denied the reality of the mass slaughters, neither the defendants of Nuremberg and Frankfurt, nor Eichmann in Jerusalem. 'This audacity has however been achieved by two Frenchmen', Louis Darquier de Pellepoix, responsible as Commissioner for Jewish Affairs under the Vichy Régime for the deportation of 70,000 Jews, and Robert Faurisson, a professor at the University of Lyon. The latter 'has cultivated a most innocent obsession: for eighteen years he has set himself the goal of showing that in the Nazi Lagers the gas chambers never existed'.

Darquier, according to Levi, was not worth spending many words on. Interviewed by *L'Express* 'he denies everything: the photos of piles of bodies are fakes; the statistics of millions of dead have been fabricated by the Jews, always greedy for publicity and sympathy; the deportations happened, but he did not know where to or with what result; in Auschwitz, yes, there were gas chambers, but they were only used to kill lice'. Almost eighty-five years old and 'blatantly senile', Darquier was typical of anyone who has built himself 'a convenient truth that allows him to live in peace'.

The Faurisson case was less clear. It was true that the rector of his university had suspended him from teaching, expressing doubts about his mental balance. But it was also true that, bombarded for four years by letters from a man who must surely have appeared to the editors as 'affected by a monomania that borders on paranoia', *Le Monde* had ended up by giving in, and had agreed to publish, on 29 December 1978, some brazen pages of his on 'Le rumeur d'Auschwitz', in which he maintained that the Jewish genocide was a myth. What is worse, the authoritative daily had preceded the piece with an editorial comment that Levi, with much restraint, called 'curious': 'As aberrant as this thesis may appear, it has created some confusion, particularly among the younger generations, who are little inclined to accept existing ideas without examination.' There is no rage in the refutation of the survivor who opposes the sordid ideas of Faurisson with the reality of lived experience. He should know, that *maître de conférences*,[3] that yes, it was possible to savagely compress two thousand and more people into the 210 square metres of a gas chamber: he is hearing it from a Häftling who, while waiting for his selection for death by gas, had been crammed with 250 companions into a room of seven by four metres. He should also know that hydrogen cyanide was used for the slaughter; but that there was no danger (as he would fear, with paternal concern) that too slow a release of the gas would kill the German operators as well: first of all because the operators were not Germans, but prisoners; and secondly because the poison, in the conditions in which it was used (that is to say, in the chambers packed with human beings, with temperatures above 37 degrees) was extremely volatile, since it boils at 26 degrees. It's a chemist who's speaking.

In quite a different tone is the passionate declaration by Levi fifteen days before to *Corriere della Sera,* who had questioned him on the spur of the moment:

> So, the operation has succeeded.The ravings of Darquier de Pellepoix in *L'Express* last November weren't enough. It wasn't enough to grant the murderers of that time space and voice in respectable magazines, so they could detail their truth with impunity: that the millions of dead in the Lagers never died; that the Holocaust is a fairy tale; that only lice were killed with gas in Auschwitz. All this wasn't enough. Obviously the hour is ripe, and from his university position Professor Robert Faurisson comes to set the world's mind to rest: fascism and Nazism have been denigrated, polluted, defamed. Let people talk no more of Auschwitz, it was all a set-up: let them talk about the lie of Auschwitz. The Jews are

cunning, they've always been cunning, so cunning as to fabricate a massacre that never happened, to slander the innocent Nazis; to construct themselves, *après coup*, the gas chambers and crematoria of the Lager. I don't know who Professor Faurisson is. It could be that he's just a madman, there are some of those even in universities, but another hypothesis is more likely: that he is one of those responsible for the events of that time,[4] as Darquier was; or that he is the son, friend or supporter of someone responsible and that he is struggling to exorcise a past which, despite today's permissiveness, is weighing down on him. We know certain mental processes well. Guilt is bothersome or at least inconvenient; in a time now long past in Italy or in France, it was also dangerous. One starts by denying it in court. One denies it for years, in public and in private, and finally to oneself. And there we are, the spell has succeeded: black has become white, wrong right; the dead aren't dead; there is no murderer; there's no more guilt, in fact there never was any. Not only did I not commit the act, the act itself didn't exist.

No, Professor, that is not the path. The dead existed, including women and children, tens of thousands in Italy and France, millions in Poland and the Soviet Union: they're not so easy to get rid of. Ask the survivors, there are some in France too. Hear from them what it meant to see their companions die around them, one by one; to feel themselves dying, day by day, for one year or two; to have lived without hope in the shadow of the crematoria chimneys; to return (those who returned) and find their families destroyed. This is not the way to cleanse oneself of guilt, Professor: even for those who speak from university Chairs, facts remain stubborn adversaries. If you deny the massacre carried out by your friends of that time, you must explain to us why the seventeen million Jews of 1939 were reduced to eleven million in 1945. You must refute hundreds of thousands of widows and orphans. You must refute every one of us who has survived. Come, Professor, to discuss with every one of us, you'll find it more difficult than preaching lies to your gullible students. Are they all gullible to the point of accepting them? Has not one of them put up a hand to protest? And what have they done in France, the academic and legal authorities? Have they tolerated that, by denying the dead, you should kill them a second time?[5]

Desperate questions, which in the next piece Levi writes became a tirade. What were *Le Monde*'s motives? 'Maybe to spread confusion among the young?' If that was the aim, Levi comments bitterly, the result is certain: by its very enormity, 'genocide drives people to disbelief, to cancellation, to denial'. He had often quoted the mocking forecast of the Nazis to their victims: 'Even if you survive and tell, no-one will believe you.' That a serious newspaper had opened its pages to a sinister madness suggested to him that 'the other soul of France, the one that sent Dreyfus to Guiana, that accepted Hitler, that followed Pétain' was now emerging . As if to say that the leaden cloud of anti-Semitism is re-appearing, an ancient and inexorable plague which infects the world, dragging it into the abyss of instinct, and every now and then exploding furiously, it doesn't matter where.

This reaction to the 'audacity of the two Frenchmen' must have been in the mind of the interviewer from *La Repubblica* who provocatively objected to the writer who wanted to change the subject of his conversations with young people: 'But while you're talking to them about work, others are casting doubt on the truth about the Nazi Lagers. People will end up forgetting them, just as the slaughters of the Cathars and Albigensians[6] were forgotten.' Levi's reply reclaimed his identity as a witness and his inalienable freedom as a 'centaur'. At the same time it was the occasion for an advance announcement from the writer of memory:

> I've stopped writing as a survivor, but I continue to be one. Next week, I'll be with Nelo Risi[7] and Ludovico Belgiojoso[8] to organize an Italian memorial to Auschwitz. But in the past thirty-five years I've accumulated different experiences, and it seemed useful to me to speak about them. And Giovanni Raboni[9] has picked up a continuity between *If This is a Man* and *The Wrench,* which both defend the dignity of man. My next book will be a delicate discussion of the ambiguous condition of the prisoner, of the difficulty of judging him. It's a big problem because the typical prisoner of the Lager died. If someone survived it's because he benefited from some privilege: I was a chemist, for example. It's difficult to judge the limits of compromise. There's a whole scale, which starts when one agrees to survive, when one agrees to work for the enemy. As I've told you, it's a delicate discussion, especially because there have been false discussions, false films like the one by Cavani, on the identification of the victim with the jailer. Of course, everything happened in the Lager, really everything, but the women weren't sexual objects. They were ugly, they lost their hair, they seemed old.[10]

He will conduct the 'delicate discussion' himself, in his last book, *The Drowned and the Saved*, a synthesis of all the whys, a reply to all his questionings of himself from as far back as 1955, when he wrote:

> Today it's indelicate to speak of the Lagers. One is at risk of being accused of victimism, or of gratuitous love for the macabre, or even of an outrage to decency. Is this silence justified? Must we tolerate it, we survivors? Must we consider it finished, this task of bearing witness which, in the view of our enemies themselves, history seems to have reserved for us? There can only be one answer. It isn't permissible to

> forget; it isn't permissible to be silent. If we keep silent, who will speak? Certainly not the guilty and their accomplices. If our testimony is missing, in a not too distant future the feats of Nazi bestiality, by their very enormity, could be relegated among the myths. Speaking out, therefore, is necessary.[11]

He spoke out. He always spoke out. With his voice, with his pen, until the end, without rest; in his stories, poems and essays, even in his only real novel *If Not Now, When?*, so that not even a crumb of this experience would be lost. He entered battle regularly, spurred on by memory, by duty, by emotion, by pity. But also by disgust in his arguments against the producers of films like *The Night Porter* and, descending even one step further, *Salon Kitty* and similar Nazi porn flicks:

> Please, my dear cinema producers, leave the women's Lagers alone [...] they weren't theatres for sex shows. People suffered there, yes, but in silence. And the women weren't beautiful, on the contrary they aroused infinite pity, as defenceless animals do. As for the SS, for the most part they weren't monsters, nor idiotic lechers, nor perverted dandies: they were state officials, more pedantic than brutal, insensitive to the daily horror they were living in and which they soon seemed to get used to.[12]

He debated with detached toughness when, for example, before falling silent for ever, he wrote about the revisionist historians.[13] He was haunted by the thought that the witnesses would fall silent, one by one; and at the same time he was tormented by the feeling that their words would not find sufficient hearing:

> We have never been many[...]Now we are reduced to a few dozen: maybe we are too few to be listened to, and besides we often have the impression of annoying people with our stories. Sometimes, even, a curiously symbolic dream that haunted our nights of imprisonment comes to life before us: the person we are speaking to doesn't listen to us, doesn't understand, lets their mind wander, goes off and leaves us alone. Yet tell we must: it's a duty towards the comrades who have not come back; and it's a task that gives a meaning to our survival.[14]

In the context of a television interview he added:

> Memory is a duty. It is so for all human beings as such; and it is so especially for us, who have suffered the ordeal, and in a way also had the opportunity of living through fundamental experiences. It would

> be more than a denial of duty not to pass on what we have lived through.[15]

At the start of the 1970s, in the *Galleria d'arte moderna* in Rome, plans had been displayed for a monument to the Italian prisoners in Auschwitz. 'It doesn't matter if it's beautiful', wrote Primo Levi in *La Stampa*, 'it doesn't matter if it verges on the rhetorical, even if it falls into it. It mustn't be used for partisan ends. It must be a warning-monument, which humanity dedicates to itself, which can bear witness and repeat a message that is not new to history, but is too often forgotten: that human beings are, and must be, sacred to human beings, everywhere and always.'[16] It must rise up on the site of the greatest massacre in human history. 'In this camp around 400 thousand prisoners were registered, only a few thousand of whom survived. Almost four million other innocents were swallowed up by its extermination machinery', its colossal gas chambers and crematoria 'the size of cathedrals', 'built for the purpose by the honest firm Topf & Sons of Erfurt, who had been commissioned to supply ovens able to incinerate 24,000 people a day.' Not enemies, but whole families of Jews, elderly people, children, pregnant or breastfeeding women: all those in a word judged unfit to swell the ranks of 'a giant army of slaves forced to work until they die'.[17] Even if it is impossible to answer the questions about these foul and terrible events ('Why? How did they happen? Will they be repeated?'), even if it is impossible to trace the paths of the leaders responsible ('their actions, their words, remain for us shrouded in obscurity'), nobody knows the reality of Auschwitz better than those who have dedicated their lives to exploring it. So that when the moment came to prepare the text for the inside of the Italian Block in Auschwitz, the task was assigned to the author of *If This is a Man*, who prepared a draft in which he laid bare the roots of the massacre. There were eight paragraphs, each of which, he explained, should guide the comprehension of the documentary material. Technical demands got in the way, changing the entire project; on the Italian Memorial in Auschwitz only the last few words of Levi's text survive. Here it is in its entirety:

> 1)The history of the deportations and the extermination camps cannot be separated from the history of the fascist tyrannies of Europe: from the first fires in the Camere del Lavoro in Italy in 1921,[18] to the book burnings in the squares of German towns in 1933, to the infamous flames of the Birkenau crematoria, there is an unbroken connection. It is old knowledge, and Heine, a Jew and a German, had already warned of it: 'Where they burn books, they will end by burning human beings'. Violence is a seed which does not extinguish itself.
>
> 2)It is sad but necessary to remind ourselves and others of this: the first European experiment in crushing the workers' movement and

sabotaging democracy emerged in Italy. It was fascism, sparked by the crisis of the interwar period and the myth of 'mutilated victory,'[19] and fed by ancient miseries and guilts. And fascism gave birth to a delirium that would spread: the cult of the man of destiny, of organized and imposed enthusiasm, with every decision entrusted to the judgement of a single man.

3)But not all Italians were fascists: we, the Italians who died here, testify to that. Together with fascism, another movement was born in Italy: anti-fascism. Alongside us testify all those who fought against fascism and who suffered because of it: the workers martyred in Turin in 1923;[20] those sent to prison, to internal and external exile; and our brothers of every political faith who died to resist the fascism restored by the National Socialist invader.

4)And alongside us testify still other Italians, those who fell on all the fronts of the Second World War, fighting unwillingly and desperately against an enemy who was not their enemy, and realizing the deception too late. They too are victims of fascism: unconscious victims.

5)We were not unconscious. Some among us were partisans and political fighters: they were captured and deported in the last months of the war, and while the Third Reich tottered, they died here, tormented by the thought of how close the liberation was.

6)The majority among us were Jews: Jews who came from all the Italian cities; and also foreign Jews, Poles, Hungarians, Yugoslavs, Czechs, Germans, who – in fascist Italy, a country forced to be anti-Semitic by Mussolini's racist laws – had encountered the benevolence and civilized hospitality of the Italian people. They were rich and poor, men and women, healthy and sick.

7)There were children among us, many of them, and there were old people on the brink of death, but we were all loaded like goods onto wagons, and our fate, the fate of whoever crossed the gate of Auschwitz, was the same for everyone. It had never happened before, not even in the darkest centuries, that human beings were exterminated in their millions, like noxious insects; that children and the dying were sent to their deaths. We, children of Christians and Jews (but we do not like those distinctions), from a country that had been civilized, and that became civilized again after the war, testify to that here.

8)In this place, where we innocents were killed, the pit of barbarism was reached. *Visitor, observe the remains of this camp and consider:*

> *whatever your nationality, you are not a foreigner here. Ensure that your journey was not in vain, that our death has not been in vain. For you and for your children, may the ashes of Auschwitz serve as a warning: act so that the dreadful fruit of hatred, whose traces you have seen here, does not yield new seed, not tomorrow, not ever.*[21]

'Visitor, observe…'. Primo Levi listened again to the warning in June 1982, returning to Auschwitz for the second time after the Liberation, with a group of students, their families and teachers, ex-deportees and members of the Jewish Community of Florence. Travelling with him was a crew from the television programme 'Sorgente di vita' [Source of life], led by its presenter Daniel Toaff. They were anxious to gather the survivor's impressions in this place of extreme suffering and to learn, filtered through his experience, pointers to the German enigma. The interview with him[22] took place mostly on the bus, as they approached the Lager and as they left it. 'Do you recognize these places? What emotion does it arouse in you?'

> It's all different, almost forty years have passed. Apart from anything else, Poland was emerging then from five years of terrible war: it was probably the country that had suffered most in Europe. […] I experienced this place in winter, and the difference is total because the Polish winter was, and still is, a harsh one: not like what we in Italy are used to. The snow persists for three, four months, and we were unfit, incapable in fact of holding out against the Polish winter, either during our imprisonment or afterwards. I crossed this land in a state of abandonment, without bearings, searching for a centre to hold on to, for someone to welcome me. And it was a truly desolate landscape.
>
> *And these railway tracks, these goods trains we see going past, what effect do they have on you?*
>
> That's it – I would say that it's precisely the goods trains that trigger the responses, that make the most impression on me: because even now seeing a goods train, or still more entering a goods train, has a violent […] in fact a re-enacting effect on me. Much more, I would say, than seeing these villages and places again, than seeing Auschwitz itself. Having travelled for five days in a sealed goods wagon is an experience one doesn't forget.
>
> *What feeling does the Polish language arouse in you?*
>
> That too is a conditioned reflex, anyway for me. I'm a man who speaks and listens: I'm very struck by other people's languages and I try to make

good use of my own Italian language. Now, Polish was the incomprehensible language that greeted us at the end of the journey. And it wasn't the civilized Polish we hear now, in our hotels, from our guides. It was a rough Polish, made of swearwords, of curses we didn't understand [...] it was an unknown language, the language of nothingness. It made a big impression on me, yesterday evening, meeting two drunk Poles in the lift who were speaking as they did back then, not like the others here: they spoke in curses; they spoke that language that seemed to us to be made only of consonants. A truly hellish language.

You told me that the smell of coal gives you a similar feeling.

Yes, that too, perhaps because I'm a chemist: a chemist is trained to identify substances by their smell. Now as then the entry into Poland, into Polish cities at least, is marked by two specific smells that don't exist in Italy: the smell of roasted malt and the acid smell of burning coal. This is a mining country, coal is everywhere, even a lot of private heating systems operate on coal, which in winter fills the air with a smell that isn't even that bad [...] but for us, for me at least, that's the smell of the Lager. It's the smell of Lager Poland.

And do the people seem like those back then?

No, the people are no longer the same. We didn't see the people then, only the tyrants and their collaborators in the Lager. Many of them were Poles, Jews or Christians; but the Poles of the streets, the Poles who lived in their own houses, we didn't see them, or we saw them far away, outside the barbed wire. There was a country road running around the Lager, but very few people passed along it. We learned later that the local peasants had been moved away. Yet the buses taking the Polish labourers to work went past, and I remember that on one of these buses there were adverts. They said *Beste Suppe Knorr Suppe*, 'the best soup is Knorr soup', and it had a very strange effect on us seeing a soup being advertised. As if one could choose between a good and a less good soup.

What impression did it make on you to return to the camp, starting from a luxury hotel for foreigners?

The impression of a dislocation, I would almost say a chasm opening up: something impossible that nevertheless happens. Because the difference is too great. It's something that we would never have hoped for, then, to return to these places as tourists in a luxury or almost luxury hotel. And this contrast is like all contrasts: in one way it's gratifying, in another it's alarming.Things can return [...]

When you left Italy did you know what your destination was?

We knew practically nothing: we'd seen the destination 'Auschwitz' scribbled on the wagons in Fossoli station, but we didn't know where that was and we thought it was Austerlitz. We thought: who knows, it'll be some place in Bohemia. At that time in Italy I don't think anyone, not even the best informed people, knew what 'Auschwitz' meant.

How was it, then, that journey? What do you remember about those five days?

I remember them very well. There were 45 of us in a very small wagon. There was just space for us all to sit down, but we couldn't all lie down. There was a young mother who was breast-feeding her baby boy [...] We'd been told to take supplies with us. Stupidly, we hadn't brought water, or not much water: nobody had told us, we thought there'd be water on the train. So we suffered, even though it was winter, from a terrifying thirst; it really was the first tormenting experience, those five days of thirst. I remember that our breath froze on the bolts of the wagon, and we would all compete, scraping off the frost, which on top of everything was full of rust, to have a few drops to wet our throats with. And the baby screamed from morning to night and all through the night because his mother had no milk left.

What was it like when you first came into contact with Auschwitz?

It was at night, after five days of a disastrous journey, in which people died in every wagon, arriving in a place where we didn't understand the language, where we didn't understand what it was for. There were senseless notices: a shower [...] the dirty side, the clean side [...] And no one explained anything, or they spoke to us in Yiddish, or Polish, and we didn't understand. It was a truly alienating experience: everyone had the impression they were completely mad, that they'd left behind their capacity to reason[...] Against this cruel backdrop, at night, with floodlights, with people who were screaming. They screamed as I'd never heard anyone scream before, they screamed orders we didn't understand. We got off the wagons and they made us line up. In front of us there was a non-commissioned SS officer, or an officer, I learned later that he was a doctor, who asked everyone: can you work or can't you work? I consulted with the person next to me: he was a friend of mine, from Padua, older than me and not in good health. I told him: I'm going to declare myself fit for work. And he replied: Do as you like, it's all the same to me. He'd already given up all hope: in fact, he declared himself unfit and he didn't enter the camp. I never saw him again, nor any of the others, for that matter.

What happened to young children and their mothers?

They were killed immediately. Of the 650 of us who were on that train, four-fifths died the same night, or the following night. They were [...] sent immediately to the gas chamber.

How was work in the camp?

I must say first that there wasn't just one camp at Auschwitz, there were many, and some of these had been built on a labour plan, attached to a factory or a mine. The Birkenau factory, for example, was sub-divided into lots of different teams who worked for different factories, even arms factories. My camp, Monowitz, with 10,000 prisoners, was part of a factory belonging to I.G. Farben, a huge German chemicals conglomerate that has now been split into several parts. The plan was to build a new factory for chemical products on something like six square kilometres of land. It was in an advanced state, that construction site, and everyone worked there: English, French and Russian prisoners of war worked there; also Germans of course, and free Polish and Italian workers. In total, forty thousand individuals of whom we ten thousand were the last rung, the lowest rung. The Monowitz Lager, made up almost entirely of Jewish prisoners, was to provide the unqualified workforce. Despite everything, since specialized workers were very scarce in Germany at that time, with all the men who were away on the front, from a certain point onwards they looked for specialists even among us, who were in theory unskilled workers and slaves. From the very first day, from the entry into the Lager there was a kind of research into our personal data: they asked everyone how old they were, what qualifications they had and what trade they had. And that was one of my pieces of good luck, because I said I was a chemist, without knowing that we were assigned to a factory for chemical products. And much later that brought me some advantages, because I worked for the last two months in a laboratory.

And how was the food?

Food was the number one problem. I don't agree with those who describe the soup and bread of Auschwitz as disgusting. As far as I'm concerned, I was so hungry that I found them good, and never found the food disgusting. Not even the first day. It was meagre, they gave us a minimal portion, equivalent to around 1,600 or 1,700 calories a day. In theory, because food got stolen halfway, so what got to us was even less than in theory. But that was, let's say, the official allocation. Now, with 1,600 calories a day a man who doesn't weigh much can live, provided he doesn't work and stays lying down. But we had to work, and to work in the cold, in very heavy jobs; so that ration of 1,600 calories was a slow death by malnutrition. Afterwards, I read about the calculations made by the Germans. They calculated that a prisoner in these conditions, on that food and using up his personal reserves from before, could last for two to three months.

Did people adapt to everything in the concentration camps?

It's a curious question. Those who survived adapted to everything; but the majority didn't adapt, and died. They died from not knowing how to adapt even to things which now seem banal to us: to the shoes, for example. They tossed each of us one pair of shoes, no, not even a pair, two unmatched shoes, one with a heel and one without. A man almost needed to be an athlete to learn to walk this way. One was too small and one was too big. You had to make complicated swaps, and if you were lucky, you found a way to match up two shoes that went together. Even then they injured your feet. Anyone who had sensitive skin ended up having foot infections. I had them too, and I still have the marks. Miraculously, mine healed on their own although I never stopped work for a day. But anyone who was sensitive to infections died from those shoes, from foot wounds that infected and wouldn't heal. Your feet swelled up and rubbed against the shoes; you ended up going to hospital. But in the hospital 'swollen feet' were not admitted as an illness; they were too common. So anyone with swollen feet went to the gas chamber.

How was it when you'd left Auschwitz, what was your first contact with the population?

The Polish people were distrustful. They'd gone from a savage occupation by the Germans, to a less savage but perhaps more primitive one by the Russians, and they were distrustful towards everyone. Even towards us. We were foreigners, essentially, and they didn't understand us. We had a uniform, that forced labourers' outfit which terrified them.They didn't want to speak to us; only a few of them took pity on us, those with whom we managed to make ourselves understood. Understanding each other is very important. Between the man who can make himself understood and the man who can't there's a difference the size of an abyss. One escapes and the other doesn't.

> That was also a Lager experience, the fundamental importance of understanding and being understood. For Italians, not understanding was a cause of their death rate, which was higher than for all the other groups – for the Italians and also for the Greeks. Most of the Italians who were with me died in the first days from not understanding. They didn't understand the orders, and there was no tolerance for anyone who didn't understand an order. It had to be understood; it was yelled, repeated once, then that was it, the blows came. They didn't understand when it was announced that we could change our shoes; they didn't understand when we were called to come for a shave, once a week. They were always the last; they always came late. When they had a need, even if that need might have been satisfied, they couldn't express it, and they were mocked. Morally too that meant an immediate collapse: in my view among the many causes of shipwreck in the Lager, language is one of the first.

Not just the language, not just the smells. There was also a piece of music that had the power to bring back to the survivor what Poland had been like then: '[…]Everywhere ruins, skeletons of concrete, beams of blackened wood, people in rags, with a savage and starving look'.[23] It was the *1812 Overture* by Tchaikovsky. He mentioned it a few months after his second return to Auschwitz, to Dina Luce, who interviewed him on the radio programme 'Il suono e la mente' [Sound and mind]. She started by asking him if music was important in his life. He had replied:

> Sometimes yes, sometimes no […] I can say that the *New World Symphony* by Dvořák has had its importance for me; but if you ask me why, as you're about to do, I'll have to answer that I don't know, that it remained in me somewhere, I don't know whether in my heart or mind or some other organ. But when I hear it, it echoes inside me like a sound box. Maybe because it's a kind of theft; maybe because it's a symphony from the 'New World', where I've never been.

Reasons just as mysterious made him particularly like Mussorgsky's *Pictures at an Exhibition,* or Gershwin's *An American in Paris* ('maybe because it's happy music, because it's gentle, it's not bossy, it's not romantic and it stays in the air like a tethered balloon'). But the *1812 Overture* was for him a place of memory:

> And that's for a particular reason: because when I was liberated from Auschwitz, I roamed around with my companions until I landed in Kraków, at Kraków railway station, in February 1945. And in this corner of Poland that had just been liberated, the Russians broadcast from all the loud-speakers that symphony by Tchaikovsky, which

> celebrated the victory of the Russians over Napoleon; in particular, the bit that quotes the Marseillaise. I was in tatters, but there was this glorious march in the air, which made a lasting impression on me.

On his return to Turin from his journey with the Florentine school party, he told how the young people and their parents had besieged him every time the cameramen left them a chance. With what questions? The usual ones, those he heard repeatedly in schools, after lectures and from every journalist who interviewed him. They aimed at understanding his feelings, at delving into the inner world of the man and the writer. We have no record of the replies he gave the students, horrified by the strange, impersonal voice that guided them through the testimonies to the massacre ('[...] around 7,000 kilograms of women's hair were found in paper bags, ready to be sent off [...] there are records of a company in Bavaria that paid fifty pfennigs per kilo of hair [...]'). But we can learn a great deal from other interviews, or from meetings before or after. From his answers on key themes a singularly detailed and vivid portrait of the Lager comes to life, as well as portraits of the Nazi system and of the problems connected with the difficult reintegration of the ex-prisoner.

An audience member asked him, after a lecture at the Carignano theatre in Turin: 'What did you prisoners talk about among yourselves? About fear of death? About the crematorium?'

> We talked obsessively about eating. Even though it upset us to hear talk of succulent meats, of rich sauces, of fine flavours, we all did it, and we even invented dishes that had never been eaten. But nobody talked about the crematorium, or about death. It was there, death, a step away from us, but it wasn't immediate. We had more urgent problems. And then the crematorium was in another camp, at Birkenau: we didn't see the smoke, we didn't notice the smell, speaking of it was forbidden. Besides, even in normal life, it doesn't do to talk about cancer or death. We know that we're all going to die, but we don't willingly talk about it.[24]

The journalist Renato Romanelli: 'You write that to survive in the Lager one must renounce a part of one's own moral world, unless one is made of the stuff of martyrs and saints.'

> And that's how it was. I also tried to explain and exemplify this in some stories in *If This is a Man*. Dying was simple: it was enough to content yourself with what they gave you to eat and to obey all the orders. Living was more complicated: it was necessary to disobey, to evade, to harden oneself, not to strike back. Above all to realize that you lived

> in a world where the ordinary moral law no longer applied, a world divided by an abyss: on one side us, the oppressed, on the other them, the enemies, who often came from within our ranks, and who felt themselves more separate from us the greater the privilege they'd gained.[25]

Where the moral law is not in force, corruption thrives. On this point, touched on by many, Primo Levi said to Anna Bravo, a lecturer in social history at the University of Turin:

> Corruption prevailed in the Lager, something which greatly astonished us all, because we – at least we Italian Jews who had contact with the Germans very late – had made ourselves an image of Germans as cruel but incorruptible people. In fact, they were extremely corruptible. We learned it more or less quickly, from experience: not just the Germans, who were quite external figures, who were inaccessible gods, but all the hierarchy of the camp from the Germans down was corruptible. Indeed, one learned that Polish word, *protekcja*, straight away.[26]

Critic and writer Beniamino Placido: 'What type of fear did one feel in a concentration camp?'

> [...]I would say one of the most regular, most constant experiences in the Lager is that of losing the sense of past and future. The past disappears and the future too: one deals with the present and one has problems for every hour and minute – protecting oneself from the cold and the blows, defending oneself from hunger, enduring the fatigue. What will happen tomorrow fades away and what happened yesterday is immediately forgotten; one lives in the present. And since fear is relative, it's linked with the future, like hope. Hope and fear are symmetrical; they are desire and flight, flight from future danger and desire for future happiness: so both fade away. To put it in a single phrase, there wasn't time to be fearful: almost never. It reappeared, the time to be fearful and therefore the fear, in the few moments of truce, for example in the infirmary, when one had a few days of illness. For me it came when, at the end of my imprisonment, I worked for two months in a chemical laboratory: it saved my life, but there, there was fear. Because back came the awareness which otherwise was snuffed out in the face of immediate, daily cares; in fact not daily cares, only immediate ones. Of surviving instant by instant. Hour by hour.

'What helps', asked Placido, 'in overcoming a situation like the one you have lived through?'

> Two things, I would say, which once again are opposites: unawareness and faith. Unawareness in most cases: the majority of my comrades, and I too, lost consciousness. Besides, it corresponds to what I said before, about losing the notion of past and future: we lived in the moment, in quite an animal-like way. In the other, rarer, case, it was faith: not necessarily religious faith, but any kind, political faith too; also any kind of transcendental faith, regardless of denomination. But this was observed: people who had been intensely politically active or people who were deeply religious didn't give in either to unawareness or to despair, and so had a greater probability of surviving. Not a total probability, because there was no single key to survival.[27]

A student in Settimo: 'Did friendship, solidarity in the Lager help people to survive?'

> Some friendships were decisive for me: that of Alberto, who was a brave man and capable of making other people brave; and that of Lorenzo, the civilian worker who risked his own life to bring me soup in secret. I've spoken about both of them in my books many times. Solidarity [...] is something else. It wasn't there for the new arrival, who was mocked because he was incompetent, because he didn't understand anything, because he believed everything they told him and tried to do everything they ordered him to. I wrote about that too. But solidarity wasn't born even with the passing of time; one always saw a competitor in the other person. The dullness, the no doubt healthy incapacity for emotion which we all acquired, left us concerned only with the immediate satisfaction of primal needs. What mattered was to get to the end of the day alive.[28]

The journalist and writer Enzo Biagi: 'You have told how in the Lager few suicides took place: despair only rarely got to the point of leading to self-destruction.'

> Yes, I saw that, and afterwards it was studied by specialists, by sociologists, by physiologists. Suicide was rare. The reasons given by the scientists are many: personally, I propose one and it's this [...]: animals don't kill themselves. And we were more animals than men.

Virgilio Lo Presti for *Lotta Continua*: '[...] the structure and the dynamics of the Lager seem to develop and exacerbate some aspects of the society of work. Is the Lager the opposite of society or is its extreme expression?'

> I would say that it's more its expression than its opposite, because at least in the last period almost all the concentration camps were labour

> camps [...], a compromise between slaughter and exploitation, in which exploitation gradually prevailed, until the end [...] Of course, in these conditions, besides the exploitation imposed from on high, many features of the society we live in developed spontaneously from the bottom, in a form I would describe as a caricature. For example, the division into classes. There was a stratification: proletariat, lumpenproletariat,[29] bourgeoisie, let's say, and then the bosses [...] And that happened outside of and beyond any deliberate will of the Nazis. The men and women who had just entered the camp joined the 'lumpenproletariat': they were kept to the margins; they did useless jobs. As soon as they found a regular job they entered the 'proletariat' – these terms are always between inverted commas, of course. In the camp where I was, as I've described in detail in *If This is a Man*, there was the phenomenon of the rise of commerce – it was a characteristic element, as if the Lager were part of any human society – and that too was a caricature. There was, for example, a 'market' in bread, in shoes, in combs and so on [...] A network of commercial relationships was immediately established. I would say that one can indeed conclude that the camp was the expression of society, I'm not saying of industrial society, but of society *tout court* [...] Privileges were immediately established: naturally uncorrected by laws [...] The privileges were strength, cunning, protection and so on. There was no corrective, far from it. Anyone who had a minimum of privilege continued to climb up without limits. In the camp there were no laws, which put limitations on privilege.[30]

With Nicola Tranfaglia, who questions him in the context of a television report on work, Primo Levi goes into more depth on the subject, illustrating a further stratification of the Lager, this time explicitly among the oppressors. The journalist asks: 'You said that you perceived the sign over the Lager, "Work sets you free", as savagely ironic, but it seems that it wasn't, for those who had written it. It what sense wasn't it?'

> In the sense that official Nazi ideology really believed that work was liberating, in the sense that it integrates you with the Vaterland, with the country you live in: it's the only way in which the citizen who isn't a warrior can contribute to the country's strength.
>
> *Except that this ideology concerned the German working class, but showed a very different face to other people who came into contact with the citizens of the Third Reich.*
>
> Of course, from our point of view we were witnessing an extremely refined and clearly deliberate stratification, with five or six levels.

The German worker was inaccessible for us, was almost unseen: the majority of German workers were at the front [...] The top level was that of the volunteer workers: French, also Italians. Then came the Allied prisoners of war, then the Slavic, Russian and Polish prisoners of war. And then the last level, that of the pariahs, was the Jews.

What do you think of the hypothesis put forward by some historians and scholars that Nazism, with that organization of labour (both the internal organization and the organization of the Lagers themselves), has prefigured inevitable aspects of the mass society of the twentieth century?

[...] I didn't know that hypothesis; I can say though that it's plausible. I don't like the idea – in fact I'm profoundly irritated by it – that the factories of today are Lagers. Having tried both, I can say that it makes quite a difference to go home in the evening, or not; to have a secure job, or on the contrary not even to have a secure life. Yet it's indubitable that some common elements exist. The Lager is useful as a metaphor, in my view, but not as a claim to identity.

It has also been said that there's a fundamental contradiction between the conception of work in Nazi society, which aimed at efficiency, at productivity, and the organization of labour in the Lager, where the prisoners were not treated in a way which produced maximum productivity. It seems on the contrary that productivity in the Lager was minimal. What do you think of that contradiction?

I think that it exists [...] Nazi society wasn't a monolith. We saw it, day by day, as a form of diarchy. There was an authority which oversaw the Lager, which was the SS; and another authority, the factory, which oversaw production, especially war production. And they didn't agree. From the point of view of the Lager, that is of the SS, we were people to destroy, in an exemplary way: that is, to be made to suffer first, to vilify first, to make abject first, with the aim of showing how abject we were, and then to destroy. Our use as a workforce was secondary for the SS. From the point of view of the factory things were different: it was a question of exploiting us in the way that was most rational, which doesn't mean most inhuman. Often the two didn't coincide: sometimes yes, sometimes no. It was a case of extracting the most possible from the enormous and endless mass of workers that was provided, not exactly free but certainly cheaply, by the concentration camps.

> *So there was a contradiction, and it depended on the racial madness that oversaw the organization of the Lagers and that won out against the German factories' demands.*
>
> Without doubt, but who won depended on the moment. We witnessed that competition, that arm-wrestling match, for example when the SS forced us to steal four bricks each from the building site, forty thousand bricks a day. This was both a theft by the SS from I.G. Farben and a way of persecuting us, because carrying bricks for two kilometres is very heavy work. It was also a way of worsening our condition, using us as the vehicle for a theft.[31]

Leonardo Vergani, correspondent from *Corriere della Sera*: 'But did the Germans know?'

> It's a question to which one can only give two answers. The majority of Germans didn't know because they didn't want to know, because it was better to close their eyes and put their hands over their ears. I don't say these words with hatred. Hundreds of thousands of Germans were shut up in the Lagers from the first months of Nazism – Communists, Social Democrats, Protestants, Catholics – and the whole country knew it, and knew that in the Lagers people suffered and died. There wasn't a German family that hadn't had a relative or a friend imprisoned. Yet, despite that, it's also true that the great mass of Germans was not aware of the most appalling details of what happened later in the Lagers: the methodical and industrialized slaughter; the gas chambers; the crematoria; the vile exploitation of the corpses. All this wasn't meant to be known and in fact, until the end of the war, few did know about it. To keep the secret, among other precautions, cautious euphemisms were used in official language: one didn't write 'extermination' but 'Final Solution', not 'deportation' but 'resettlement', not 'killing by gas' but 'special treatment'.
>
> But the Germans *didn't want* to know. Whoever knew didn't tell, whoever didn't know didn't ask questions, whoever asked questions didn't get an answer. All had been witnesses to anti-Semitic barbarism, from the burning of the synagogues to the Jews forced to kneel in the mud. The trains carrying deportees crossed Germany. Magistrates, lawyers, police officers, businessmen who asked for slave labour, army officers, those who lived near the camps – none of these could be unaware of what was happening. The German citizen looked the other way, respected the secret that was imposed on him. Maybe he couldn't measure the extent of the extermination programme. He had imposed

> not believing on himself. Besides we deportees did not believe either. Or rather, we pretended not to believe. It's a bit like what happens to cancer sufferers who should know they're condemned, but who think they don't have cancer. I arrived at Auschwitz together with 650 others. They chose 29 women and 96 men, the youngest and strongest. We had to work. The others disappeared. They were immediately gassed. Our group was used as unskilled labour in a chemical factory, the I.G. Farben factory. Every now and then someone, weakened by illness and starvation, disappeared. The Kapos told us: 'If you don't work well you'll go to the gas chamber.' But the idea of extermination, of such a terrifying slaughter, was so monstrous that we, despite knowing it, didn't believe in it. It was a kind of desperate defence, an unfathomable defence which every man carries inside him. Some of us said: 'It isn't true.' Others, when they didn't see a friend anymore, insisted: 'He's been sent to another camp.' A young man, who'd been chosen to work together with his father, one day couldn't find him anymore. He knew too, but he confided in me: 'They've sent him to a convalescence camp.' How could one accept such horror?

Vergani's second question: 'The managers of the factories in which the slave labourers worked, were they in the dark about their fate?'

> How could they not have known? Every now and again one of us disappeared into nothingness and was replaced. Where did he go? At the I.G. Farben plant we were ten thousand slaves.The turnover was continuous: anyone who couldn't cope was eliminated. But the managers closed their eyes. A certain Dr Müller, one of the bosses, wrote to me after the war. He wasn't an evil man, but he was very frightened. He wanted me to forgive him. Did he know? Almost certainly he did. But in the letter he sent me that was vague, nebulous.[32]

The director Daniel Toaff: 'Can one destroy, in your view, the humanity of man?'

> Unfortunately, yes. I would say that that is precisely what characterizes the Nazi Lager (I don't know about the others because I'm not familiar with them, maybe in the Russian one it happens just as much). That is, the extinction of personality both externally and internally, and not only the prisoner's personality. The Lager guard also loses his humanity: these are two different routes which lead to the same result. I would say that few had the luck of being able to keep themselves aware during their imprisonment [...] it happened to everyone, essentially: a profound change in personality, a lessening of sensitivity

> most of all, in which the memories of home and family fall into second place in face of the urgent need to fend off starvation, to take refuge from the cold, to defend oneself from blows, to hold out against fatigue. All this led to conditions which could be called animal-like, like those of working animals. It's curious how that condition of animality was reflected in the Lager. In German, there are two verbs to eat: one is '*essen*', which is the eating of human beings, and the other is '*fressen*', which is the eating of beasts. One says that a horse '*frisst*', not '*isst*' – a horse or a cat devours, in fact – and in the Lager, without anyone having decided to make it so, the verb to eat was '*fressen*' and not '*essen*', as though the animal-like regression had spread through everyone.[33]

Journalist Dina Luce: 'Ten months in a Lager, when you were 24, do they mark a person for life?'

> I must say that it's been like that for me, but there are no rules: I know comrades, men and women I was deported with, who have cancelled out everything or have done their best to cancel out everything. Some have succeeded, they have suppressed the memory that disturbed them; others have suppressed it in the daytime hours but dream of it at night; others still live inside it, and I have chosen that path. I couldn't say why, but if it doesn't sound cynical to you, I have the impression that that adventure has enriched me, that it's provided me with a huge amount of experience of which I have poured a part (a substantial part) into my books. But I have the impression that the job isn't over, that it's still worthwhile thinking about it, reflecting on it: considering which elements of that experience are repeating themselves in the world around us today, which ones I think can never repeat themselves again, which ones are already repeating themselves. It's a theme I set myself. I wanted to write a book of essays, in fact I have already written some.[34]

'Ten months in a Lager', Dina Luce persists, 'do they stop people being happy for the rest of their lives?'

> No, I haven't said that. I must say that on the contrary I have had happy years afterwards, because I've had many pieces of good luck. My adventure in the Lager hasn't destroyed me either physically or mentally, as has happened to others; it hasn't destroyed my family; it hasn't deprived me of a country; it hasn't deprived me of a house. Not only has it not deprived me of a job, it has given me a second one, because I would probably never have written if I hadn't had those things to write about. So next to my day job, which I already had

> before, the job of a chemist, I gained a sort of spare job, that of writing, which I hope still carries on now.

The Lager also marked the flesh. He said this at the end of a brief account of his 'adventure' there for *Gli altri* [The others], the periodical run by Rosanna Benzi, the young woman trapped for more than twenty years in an iron lung.

> [...]This is the experience I have come out of and been deeply marked by. The tattoo I still wear on my arm is a symbol of it: my name when I didn't have a name, the number 174517. It marked me, but it didn't take away my desire to live; in fact it increased it, because it gave my life a purpose, that of bearing witness so that nothing similar will ever happen again. And that's the purpose of my books.[35]

Unable to understand how one can overcome the devastating trauma of the Lager, a man asked him one evening in Cuneo: 'But how is it possible for someone who has escaped Auschwitz to become a normal man again? To live like everyone else, to joke, to love, to meet friends?'

> Every one of us experienced re-integration in a different way. There are those, as I've said at other times, who see the chimneys at night, even now; those who haven't re-integrated at all. Many are neurotic; some even killed themselves later, after freedom had come. If I had to say why none of this happened to me, I'd be a bit embarrassed, because, as it's said, '*De individuo non fit scientia*': the science of the individual does not exist. I think that if I've 'saved' myself – and I say 'saved' in the widest sense of the word – it's because I've written *If This is a Man*. That is, without knowing it, in a more intuitive than calculated way, I've freed myself by writing things that were weighing me down. And in fact, as I wrote them, I felt ever lighter. Clearly, there can't be a general rule. For me it went that way, because I'm a man who needs to tell, who takes pleasure in telling; and that pleasure is liberating. I wouldn't know what else to say. It could be that I have particularly steady nerves [...] but I don't think that's true, because they've given in in other circumstances, afterwards. I've found myself much closer to neurosis on certain days in the factory than I did on coming out of the concentration camp. Who knows what else has played a role: perhaps the fact of being, despite appearances, more or less physically strong; maybe even the mountain training I had. All factors I wouldn't know how to define. But, as I say, I'm not the only case; there are others I know of, who've overcome the experience of the Lager fairly easily.They've swallowed it; they've digested it; they've metabolized it, if I can allow myself the technical term. As for me, I must also add practical details: I've got

> my family, home, health and work back. I'm full of gratitude for my work: it has helped me not just during my imprisonment but also afterwards, when having a trade has been without doubt a reason for my salvation.

Immediately afterwards another member of the audience re-opened the question of forgiveness, a constant of Primo Levi's interviews: 'I've read quite a lot of books by ex-deportees and I've always noticed hatred, bitterness in them. Not in you. Speaking to you, reading *If This is a Man*, one has the impression that you've overcome this experience and that perhaps you've forgiven.'

> That I wrote *If This is a Man* without any intention of revenge is true. It wasn't a calculation; it was a choice on an intuitive level. It seemed to me that the things I'd seen absolutely had to be written down: to free myself from them and to bear witness [...]. And I wrote in that state of mind: it seemed to me that I would spoil the things I was telling if I underlined their enormity, case by case. For exactly the same reason, *If This is a Man* is historically insufficient. For example, it doesn't include anything on the numerical data, the terrifying reality of the four and a half million dead of Auschwitz [this was the current but incorrect thinking on numbers] and of the two million victims of Nazism in other Lagers. I didn't put this in because at that moment I didn't know it. It's something I've learned later, from other documents. Essentially, it was a case of writing a testimony, and that's what I did. For that reason, there's no bitterness, because a witness can feel bitterness in private, but he can't include it in his statements. Still less did I want to play the victim. I was a victim. Yet it seemed to me to be harmful to the goal I had set myself, that is to the diffusion of what I had seen and lived through, to adopt the state of mind of the lamenting victim. Because a lamenting victim arouses more pity than belief, and I wanted to be believed more than pitied. That, let's be clear, has nothing to do with forgiveness of the guilty. I don't agree at all with forgiving everyone. Especially not with forgiving those who persist. And they are out there. There are neo-fascists; paleo-fascists who are still fascists; there are neo-Nazis; there are Nazis who haven't been punished. I ask myself why, really, I should forgive them; I ask myself what justice it would be to forgive them [...] a subject that could be discussed at length. But I want it to be understood that my lack of a thirst for vengeance, that thirst that isn't in my book, doesn't correspond at all to abstention from justice.[36]

A reader of the *Gazzetta del Popolo* asks via the reporter Michele Florio: 'My son and I would like to know from Primo Levi what he feels, even so many years later, when he unexpectedly hears the hard German tongue spoken. Has he managed to forgive?'

> No, hearing German spoken I don't feel repulsion or distress: that happened to me, just after the Liberation, but I forced myself to stifle those feelings, and I've succeeded. I know that other ex-deportees feel them: I understand them, but I don't approve of them. In my view, these are only conditioned reflexes. I consider it unfair to see only the language of Nazism in German. It was also the language of Goethe and Heine and (why not?) of Freud, Marx, Kafka and Einstein. I learned it in the Lager. Why should I forget it, thus depriving myself of a hard-won treasure and of a cultural tool, a tool for awareness? The question of forgiveness is difficult. I haven't forgiven any of the truly guilty, nor am I prepared to forgive any of them now or in the future, unless they have demonstrated (with deeds not words, and not too late) that they have become aware of the faults and errors of Italian and foreign fascism, and that they have renounced them, instead of denying them, as many do, in these very months. In that case, yes, I who am not a Christian am prepared to follow the Jewish and Christian precept of forgiving my enemy. But an enemy who mends his ways has stopped being an enemy.[37]

Dina Luce again: 'What is forgiveness for Primo Levi?'

> I've been asked that many times and I must admit that I don't have a precise idea of what the word means. Not that I'm *not* a forgiver, either. I've even been reminded that I am: '*Du bist ein Verzeiher*', German friends have told me, 'you're a forgiver'. I don't feel like one. Faced with wrongdoing, and in particular with that wrong committed against the Jews of Europe, I feel an urgent need for justice, not for revenge. That is, the thought of killing a German, even a guilty German, would never enter my mind, but it seems to me that our Western, and Christian and Jewish, tradition consists precisely in rejecting personal and individual revenge and in accepting and supporting what is called justice, that is the legal code: a law that precedes the crime, not one that is constructed afterwards. So, my forgiveness consists in this: in wanting the guilty to pay. I was satisfied when Eichmann was captured, I was satisfied by the Nuremberg trials and I must confess that in these cases even the death penalty has not offended me, even though I am generally against the death penalty. But forgiveness just like that, out of thin air, forgiving the guilty person who doesn't repent, or who doesn't give certain signs that he's repented, I don't accept. It doesn't seem to me to be included in the things which are just...[38]

Journalist and writer Stefano Jesurum: 'The deportee Primo Levi has a thirst for justice?'

> Yes, for what has been done to us and for the evil that is done to others. I feel the same thirst for justice as I do towards a murderer in the Red Brigades.[39] I say almost equally, because towards certain historical events, as a Jew I've an additional component. The torturer has paid badly and late. Some even too late; others have died scandalously in their beds.[40]

And then came that senseless yell, chanted by a crowd of youths on the terraces of the stadium of Varese[41] at the Israeli basketball team: '*ten, a hundred, a thousand Mauthausens*'. Sorrow and indignation, and some concern among Italian Jews, who wondered whether there was a connection to the French events and what attitude to adopt. The Jewish Youth Federation [Federazione Giovanile Ebraica] organized a national conference: guests included Senator Umberto Terracini, Primo Levi and a large group of ex-deportees 'with still open wounds', among them the Hungarian writer and director Edith Bruck, and the author of *Le donne di Ravensbrück* [The Women of Ravensbrück], Lidia Rolfi, 'who isn't Jewish, but as a woman and as a political prisoner was "twice guilty" in the eyes of the fascists'. In a succinct report of the event, Levi underlined in *La Stampa* that in Terracini's view 'a return of anti-Semitism is possible, especially because of the equating of Zionism with Judaism, which comes out of ignorance or bad faith', and that according to other participants the episodes in France and Varese 'must be seen in a much wider framework of the denial of history and the rejection of reality'. Improvising the role of the reporter, Levi writes of his own and Lidia Rolfi's contributions: 'In agreement due to our parallel paths in life, we affirmed that essentially pessimistic opinions can and must be accompanied by optimistic actions, that is, in one's daily conduct'. He explained to the somewhat dumbfounded public:

> Wishing (as was done in Varese) '*ten, a hundred, a thousand Mauthausens*' on Israeli athletes confirms a fact that is consoling in itself: that today's neo-Nazism, or neo-anti-Semitism, for reasons difficult to clarify, now seems inclined to seek its new recruits among the ignorant.

What was to be done? Faced with the risk, pointed to by some, of a rejection of written testimonies, and with the consequent question of what would happen when there were no longer any eyewitnesses left, the Auschwitz survivors offered the only guarantee available to them:

> We said that we feel re-affirmed in the duty we have chosen for ourselves, that of repeating our testimony across decades and generations, for as long as we have a voice to do so.[42]

On his return from Rome, Primo Levi finds a novel on his desk sent by *Tuttolibri*, asking for his appraisal. *Holocaust* is a book of more than five hundred pages on the genocide of the Jews by the American Gerald Green. It comes out just before the television series of the same name which, after its huge success in the US and across Europe, is destined to be just as successful in Italy. Levi writes in his review:

> The facts that the book describes are all true. If sometimes they don't seem true [...] it's the fault of the enormity of the facts themselves, which has been so great as to make them unbelievable, and that unbelievability, even now, some ignorant people and cynics try to take advantage of [...] Yet the millions of dead happened, and even today weigh upon the world [...] It's a terrible task to remember that in Europe, only forty years ago, a people and a civilization were killed, but that is what occurred, and its having occurred places the horrendous event among possible events, among the facts that are still possible.[43]

He told readers that despite naivety, inaccuracies, oversights and anachronisms, both the book and the television series would serve 'to reawaken the curiosity of those who don't know and have a good conscience, and maybe also (but this is less likely) to persuade those who don't have a good conscience'. For that he described Green's novel as an 'ally': 'we would have preferred one that was less talkative, of greater historical sensibility, in better proportion to its aim: but it remains an ally all the same'. The day after the first episode of *Holocaust* was broadcast on Italian television, he expressed in *La Stampa*'s editorial his pleasure that it had been seen by millions of people, thanks to the 'huge power of penetration' of two associated media, the novel and television (though he regarded the latter's intrinsic danger with a shudder). Not one of the hundreds of books and documentaries on Hitler's genocide, he observed, had won the global attention of this story. For *Holocaust,* then, a vote of approval, since it served to spread awareness of 'a tragedy unique until now, and we hope for ever, in the bloody history of humanity'; and also an acquittal from one who had sat down to watch it with the distrust of all witnesses, too often hurt and disappointed at seeing their experience, which was 'so singular, so beyond human measure', 'made use of'.[44]

Introducing a small volume based on the RAI 1 programme, and exploring the 'Images of *Holocaust*',[45] Primo Levi told how he had been gripped by unease at the news of the work being prepared in the USA, not so much for the utilitarian premises of the operation as out of fear 'that the cynicism would be too heavy and the pity marginal'. Fortunately, he stated, even in its crudeness and inadequacy 'the film doesn't abuse the red-hot material it is built on; the authors understood the limits and did not give in to the demands of the macabre, the base, the hideous'. This was an honest ally, who could be talked about positively, if not enthusiastically, with students in their schools. Students who, in this period, are calling ever more frequently for the man who has lived through events of such significance to come to speak to them. He had to say a lot of yesses, and spoke to large audiences (in Lanzo Torinese, Valenza, Cuneo, Asti, Trieste and Milan) who wanted to meet the author of *The Wrench*, alongside the noisy student halls that were showing renewed interest in *If This is a Man*. To one school, especially, he went willingly: the Rosselli middle school in Turin, where the pupils in Mario Barrera's first year class had dedicated the year to studying the Nazi-fascist phenomenon, had read Levi's books and put on a production of Peter Weiss' *The Investigation*. Primo Levi, fifty young people and their teachers. 'A debate? Something more', writes Piero Bianucci in *Gazzetta del Popolo*, 'these kids want to know, want to understand'.[46] And Renato Rizza for *La Stampa*: '[...] onto the stage he comes, the witness: he subjects himself to a barrage of questions; he recalls now with the detachment of the historian, now with the engagement of the protagonist, the incidents of that year spent in the Lager'.[47] No trace of the tiredness complained of a few months before, nothing vague about this dialogue, which abolishes the distance from the events described :

> *What relations were there between the prisoner and his persecutors?*
>
> The odd blow, the odd kick, not more than twenty words in a year.
>
> *What are the thoughts of a deportee?*
>
> Not many and not very poetic. The day started early and your first thoughts were of getting yourself a decent pair of shoes, being assigned a job that wasn't too painful, holding out until the evening. The fight for survival doesn't leave much room for thought.
>
> *What would you do if you met an ex-SS man and you recognized him?*
>
> I'd bring him before an objective court of law. It would be difficult to find one, both in Italy and in Germany, but not impossible.
>
> *Is your condemnation of the SS all-encompassing?*

> They were volunteers, they freely chose the trade of torturer. From that it is difficult to absolve them. Yet some have realized what they did and have ended up suicidal.
>
> *Did you ever try to rebel during that year of imprisonment?*
>
> A rag doesn't rebel and we were like rags: escapes and escape attempts can only be made by those who still have the privilege of physical strength, or weapons, or uncompromised will.
>
> *Where does anti-Semitism come from?*
>
> From contempt for minorities: the pseudo-political source of the massacre lies in intolerance.
>
> *In West Germany there's talk of a statute of limitations for Nazi crimes: what feeling does this news arouse in an ex-deportee?*

On this question Primo Levi has already stated his position on TV, 'with his usual calm civility, but also with deep emotion in his voice,' as the *La Stampa* critic observed.[48] Opposed to wiping the slate clean over the liability of the criminals, he expressed stern disapproval for a part of the German judiciary now bereft of all decency:

> [...] they haven't taken much care of their honour up to now – I don't mean all German judges, but many, in the not very many cases in which a Nazi criminal was judged, and where they've used kid gloves. I don't say that they've behaved iniquitously, not usually, but they've had a light touch. I would say that they lost their honour then.

To the young of the Rosselli school he replied:

> To me it would be monstrous if certain people who have been guilty of the crime of genocide should be happy in the knowledge that they can't be tried anymore.
>
> *What do you feel now, when you hear Auschwitz being named?*
>
> It may seem strange, but I don't feel anything any more. I haven't forgotten, but the emotions have been overcome. I've overcome them by telling, as I started doing straight away with friends, as I'm still doing now with you. And writing [...] first of all to free myself, and then to bear witness.

'How does one avoid', their teacher Mr Barrera asks, 'the risk of reducing Nazism to the level of a simple story of monsters? How can we train young people's minds towards freedom?'

> One must insist, first of all, on an upbringing which doesn't incite violence. And then Nazism and fascism were born because everyone believed everything. In those years, the right to criticize wasn't extinguished, but the ability to criticize was. The engagement must be that of distrusting the 'prophets', so as not to fall under the enormous spell that appeals to the emotions but not to reason.
>
> *Is there a relationship between Nazism and the terrorism of today in Italy?*
>
> I distrust certain connections. Certainly, they have violence in common. But I don't think terrorism here will ever become a political force.
>
> *What do you think of* Holocaust, *the TV film the RAI is screening and which is said to have had a devastating effect on the Germans?*
>
> I regard it as quite a bad piece of work, though it's done with a certain diligence. It seems to me a kind of superficially romanticized Western.
>
> *Is it worthless to screen it then?*
>
> No, it's an ally anyway, not an enemy. Even if it's historically debatable, it constitutes a stimulus to analyse the problem better [...] it can serve to remind people; it's better to see it than not to see it.

He did not tell the students of the Rosselli that he disliked the word Holocaust for what it suggested of the sacrificial, of the expiatory, of mythical ritual. He did say it though, as an aside, to Daniel Toaff, who after the return visit to Auschwitz asked him: 'What did the Holocaust represent for the Jewish people?'

> It wasn't a new thing, there had been others (incidentally, I've never liked that term, Holocaust, it seems to me inappropriate, it seems rhetorical, above all wrong). But the Hitlerite slaughter represented a turning point in form and scale. Because perhaps it was the first time, in recent times, that anti-Semitism has been planned, designed, organized by the State; not just tacitly agreed to, as in Tsarist Russia, but intended. There was no escape here: the whole of Europe had become an enormous trap. That was the thing that was new and that

> brought about a profound turning point, not only among the Jews of Europe: also among the Jews of America, among Jews all over the world.

'In your view', the director inquired, 'could another massacre like that of forty years ago ever happen again?' It's one of those cyclical questions, and the essence of Primo Levi's answer does not change over the years, despite gradually darkening with troubled forebodings.

> In Europe no, in my view, it can't happen [...] There's a sort of immunization that makes it unlikely that, in the course of this decade, in fifty years, in a hundred years, Nazism will be reborn in Germany or fascism in Italy. I think that in Europe this can't occur, but the world is much bigger than Europe. I think there are countries in which the wish could be there to build an Auschwitz and only the tools are missing.[49]

He had already referred to Europe's acquired immunity with the correspondent from *La Repubblica.* And he had been even more explicit with the one from *Lotta Continua,* who, quoting the poem that introduces *The Truce,* asked what was, for him, in Italy in 1979, the truce before the return to barbarism.

> [...] I wrote that poem at a very difficult moment for me, the moment straight after my return, when I really was still struggling with trauma and I dreamed at night (and sometimes also during the day) of being back in the camp. It was a recurring dream, now it's over. But I have a theoretical fear of the return to barbarism today. That is: since that other barbarism was also quite unexpected, quite unpredictable, and yet it came, attention and vigilance are needed even today so that it doesn't repeat itself. But I don't feel fearful of a return to that barbarism. Not in Europe. On the other hand, if we look a bit further, we have to say that the danger exists: not on that scale, not in that way [...] But that the danger's there, one can't deny. The examples range from Chile to Vietnam, to the Soviet Union.[50]

However, there is a distinction to be made as far as the Stalinist Lagers were concerned, based on the texts of famous dissidents:

> I've studied Solzhenitsyn's book, to see the affinities and differences between the Russian Lagers and the German ones, and I can say one thing: in the Russian Lagers death is a by-product, it's not the aim. And that makes quite a difference.[51]

And again:

> I read Shalamov's book about Kolyma. It's shocking and at the same time surprising: because people's ruin is not so total; they do have the hope of being able to get out; they do even have a semblance of legal existence, which means they can make collective protests. And they're cured when they get ill.[52]

Doubtlessly an odious and cruel system, he will observe in his last writings, but completely different in its substance from that *unicum* that was the Nazi Lager system. The goal of Auschwitz was the annihilation of a people. That of the Gulags was the elimination, *coûte que coûte*,[53] of an ideological resistance. Primo Levi refused to believe in the rebirth of Auschwitz. He re-affirmed that refusal much later, on two occasions a short time apart, when he revealed that as well as horror for a tragic past, he also felt anxiety for a future threat. The first occasion was in reply to *Tuttolibri*, who saw in *The Drowned and the Saved* the return of the Lager casting its shadow over our world, and here and there establishing worrying connections. 'Is this book concerned with the historicity of that experience or with fear of its current relevance?' they asked.

> One of my wishes would be to make it current. The decisive question for me is: will we go back there or won't we? I'm not a prophet. I don't believe that we'll go back there in Europe, at least not at any time that is foreseeable now. But it's obvious that the threat exists. The little we know about Cambodia reminds us dreadfully of what happened in Germany.[54]

He took the second opportunity five months later with 'Focus', the last of his television interviews:

> I don't believe in a resurgence of Nazism, not in that form. In similar forms, perhaps: we observed, or rather we refused to observe, what happened in Cambodia, and it's terrifying. We barricaded ourselves behind the geographical distance, behind the scarcity of information, though that was our fault: we didn't send anyone to see what was happening. Or only sporadically, and at great risk. Still, it's a warning, what happened in Cambodia, where out of pure ideological fanaticism a people destroyed half of itself, amid the silence of the world. In the same way as silence had shrouded Hitler's genocide.[55]

It was the stubborn memories of the survivors of the Nazi Lagers that tore through that shroud. But will that be enough? 'Don't you believe', asks Daniel Toaff, 'that others, today, want to forget Auschwitz as quickly as possible?'

> There are signals that that is happening. Forgetting. Or even denying: that is significant. Anyone who denies Auschwitz would be ready to remake it.[56]

There are those who deny, who fall silent, who forget. 'Survivors apart', another journalist asks him, 'how do people remember the fact of the Lager?'

> In general, they don't remember it at all, because many years have passed. What they remember is a false memory, which comes from the most disparate sources, from various waves of commemorations, all more or less to be treated with care. An image has spread of life in the Lager which is stereotypical, I notice this myself because I continue to be invited to talk in schools [...] They see above all the single horrendous event: that is, torture and things like that. Those things were there too, but they were absolutely marginal. What must be remembered and what isn't remembered is the mass event: hundreds of thousands of people lived in the Lager, perhaps without ever being tortured (I was never tortured, nor were my companions) and 95 per cent of them died. Without torture. Died from exhaustion, from hunger, from dysentery, cold, frostbite, overwork [...] If people have surprised and disappointed me? No, not surprised. Given the circumstances, nothing other than this could emerge. Disappointed [...] Yes, it's disappointing that [...] a distorted image comes out of an experience which in my view has been fundamental.[57]

Some distortions offended him. After the visit to Poland he confided in the director of 'Sorgente di vita':

> [...] it upsets me a bit that the Polish government has appropriated Auschwitz; has made it the place of the Polish nation's martyrdom. It was that, in the early years, from 1941 to 1942. But afterwards, with the establishment of the Birkenau camp, and most importantly with the installation of the gas chambers and the crematoria, it became above all the instrument of the destruction of the Jewish people. It's not that that's denied (we've seen it – there's the Museum Block for the Jews, as there are those for the Italians, the French, the Dutch and so on). But the resounding fact that at Auschwitz the largest number, the huge majority of the victims, were Jews, and only partly Polish Jews, is not exactly denied, but at least glossed over.[58]

He also felt hurt by the sometimes inappropriate use of words, in particular of the word 'Lager', which had entered into the language of protest as a convenient substitute for any term that was more accurate: a mental hospital was the Lager; a prison was the Lager; a factory, hospital, or school was the Lager. Asked what effect this constant misuse had on him, he said:

> [...] certainly, the asylum system isn't nice. But when I hear it said that the Fiat factory is a Lager, well, that offends me.[59]

He completed the thought with one of his biographers, Professor Grassano:

> Recently, I received some poems by Sante Notarnicola. They're quite good, but there's a dedication that disturbed me. He had dedicated them to me, saying: 'As you see, the Lagers are being reborn in today's world.' I replied to him that his poems are good, but that in Auschwitz ten thousand people died every day, and that today if a political prisoner or an ordinary prisoner dies in a state prison it's a scandal. And rightly a scandal: he shouldn't die. But one. And that makes a difference. And in Auschwitz no books of poetry were published.[60]

Also (but not only) to make the image of the concentration camp less stereotypical, Primo Levi wrote the twelve Lager stories that open *Lilith*, published by Einaudi in November 1981. Some of these stories were born in previous years, others from 1979 onwards, despite his many commitments, which became more and more frequent after that year. These were not only to newspaper and television interviews (and not only in Italy, as he did one for German TV, who wanted to question Jean Samuel, the unforgettable 'Pikolo' of *If This is a Man*, alongside him), but also to lectures, conferences and occasional immersions, together with Calvino, in the *Petite cosmogonie portative* of Queneau.[61] Also to debates and literary prizes (he received several besides the Strega, for example at Bergamo, Treviso and Faenza), and to seminars and journeys in Italy and abroad. He had happy memories of the one to Vienna:

> At the Casa Italiana della Cultura an engineer came up to me. He told me: 'I'm the boy who was sleeping on the floor of the Krakòw barracks when you arrived there with your Greek.' They had told me, that night, that among the prisoners there was a 'sprog', a sixteen-year-old partisan; the Germans had captured him, weapon in hand, in the mountains.

And finally, between avid readings and careful re-readings, he studied and wrote. He was studying Yiddish, and conducting rigorous inquiries into the 'happy and ferocious Partisanka'[partisan resistance] that had taken place behind German lines: that research was preparing the ground for the novel that he started writing in January 1981. He also put together *The Search for Roots*, an anthology of the essential books in his life; he worked painfully

('I can't manage to write more than a page a day') on the essays of *The Drowned and the Saved*; and increased the frequency of his contributions to *La Stampa* in both prose and poetry. In the meantime, there were new successes. His works were published in Braille; the two books on the Lager appeared simultaneously in Tel Aviv in Hebrew and in London in the Penguin Modern Classics edition; in Italy the print runs increased. He took stock of sales one evening, together with the editor of *La Stampa,* Giorgio Fattori: at the end of October 1979, 600,000 copies of *If This is a Man* and *The Truce*; 70,000 of *The Periodic Table*; 114,000 of *The Wrench*. Not counting the unexpected take-off of *Natural Histories* – with the author's real name. So goodbye Damiano Malabaila, that unfortunate pseudonym.

Lilith (the title, he told us, was chosen by Giulio Einaudi) was given a final push by the wave of stories brought to him by an unexpected visitor, the protagonist of 'The Story of Avrom'. He had come from a kibbutz,[62] where he lived with his sons, daughters-in-law and many grandchildren. 'Strong, beautiful, tall and blond, with sky-blue eyes and strong peasant hands, though now he has stopped working the earth and makes condensers' was how Levi described him to his friends. He was Mark Herman, a small Polish Jew, son of a poor hat maker from L'viv, driven out by the Germans from all the hiding places of Europe and ending up as a partisan in the mountains of Gran Paradiso, where he had had a 'revelation of a splendid and new world'. In one of the liveliest chapters of *Lilith*, Primo Levi relates 'The undertaking of the eighteen-year-old Avrom, an innocent soldier of fortune, who, like many distant Nordic travellers, discovered Italy with a virgin eye and, like many heroes of the Risorgimento, fought for the freedom of all in a country that wasn't his.'[63]

But there were two other impulses behind the birth of *Lilith*, one practical and the other moral. First of all, the friend he'd called Cesare in *The Truce* finally gave him permission to tell the story of his adventurous return home. And second, many years had now passed since the death of Lorenzo, the author of Levi's survival in the Lager, and he felt released, as he put it, from the bond that stopped him from transforming a living person into a character. On the contrary, he thought it was now right to reconstruct Lorenzo's image 'in these stories… which bring together what was left out of my first two books'.[64] Why they were left out was clarified in his Preface to the North American edition:

> With the passing of the years […] I realized that my experience of Auschwitz was far from exhausted. I had described its fundamental features, which today have historical importance, in my first two books, but a host of details continued to surface in my memory, and the idea of letting them fade away distressed me. A great number of human figures, especially, stood out against that tragic background: friends, people I'd travelled with, even adversaries, begging me one

> after another to help them survive and enjoy the ambiguous existence of literary characters. This was no longer about the anonymous, faceless, voiceless mass of the shipwrecked, but about the few, the different, the ones in whom (if only for a moment) I had seen the will and capacity to react, and hence a rudimentary virtue.

These, then, were men. No longer persecuted, prostrate, knowing no peace, no longer beings about whom the question 'if this is a man' was legitimate. And set in minor scenes, the author notes, even bizarre ones: 'moments of reprieve, in which the compressed personality can for a moment reacquire its lineaments'. The American publisher seized that aspect of *Lilith,* took from it only the stories of the Lager, and entitled the book *Moments of Reprieve,* enriching it with three other stories absent from the Italian edition.[65]

Soon after the publication of *Lilith*, in the literature faculty of the University of Turin, Primo Levi meets a group of students who have chosen his books for a course. Among their questions is this: 'Why do the three sections of the book refer to the tenses of verbs: present perfect, future perfect and present indicative?'

> Because the first group draws, once again, on memories of deportation, whereas the second supposes a future, but not too distant, world, and the third describes situations that are current and 'indicative' of our time.
>
> *Is it all true, what you've written in your books, or has the truth sometimes been obscured by literary demands? Is it indelible, the experience of the Lager that constantly re-emerges in your work?*
>
> It's all absolutely true, I've been able to verify it by talking with companions from that time. Of course, with the passing years, memory erases some things and emphasizes others. Perhaps some incidents didn't happen in the same order as in the story, but they did happen. As for the rest, after the first two books I was convinced that I'd said everything I needed to, but then memory brings back certain incidents, time interprets them in different ways, and one realizes that there's still so much to say.[66]

So much to say decades later? Yes, and for a specific reason, which he outlined in an interview he gave a year and a few months after the birth of *Lilith*, to Anna Bravo and Federico Cereja:

> In *If This is a Man* I tried to write the things that were largest, heaviest, most important. It seemed to me that the theme of indignation must

> prevail. The book was almost a piece of legal evidence; I intended it to be an act of accusation – not with the aim of provoking reprisal, revenge or punishment, but bearing witness all the same. So some subjects seemed to me to be marginal, on a different level: and I wrote about them much later.[67]

Primo Levi had sifted rigorously through his memories from the very beginning. He gave further confirmation of this in 1976, explaining animatedly in public why the story titled 'Cerium' had ended up in *The Periodic Table* and not in *If This is a Man*. He had already done it in a practical way years earlier. Between the 1947 edition of *If This Is a Man* and the 1958 one, he had made substantial changes and additions to the book, adding not only a whole new chapter, 'The Journey', but also a series of new characters. These range from the poignant little figure of Emilia to the child Schlome, '[…] welcoming me on the threshold of the house of the dead'; and from Flesch the interpreter to Chaim, the pious watchmaker and student of the Law, who is '[…]among the few who are able to preserve the dignity and self-assurance that comes from practising a trade one has been trained for'. And finally, Alberto: 'my best friend […] Alberto entered the Lager head high, and lives in the Lager unscathed and uncorrupted'.[68]

None of these insertions has a literary aim: as Giovanni Tesio rightly noted in a careful study, 'every detail added is always founded on a solid consciousness as a witness'.[69] Each of the new characters belongs to the group whom the witness-writer significantly called 'heading downwards'.[70] The survivor-writer kept everything in his memory, a quite 'pathological' memory, as he defined it. He wrote: '[…] as far as Auschwitz is concerned, I feel like a brother of Irenio Funes 'the memorious' described by Borges, the man who remembered every leaf of every tree he had ever seen, and who said, "I have more memories in myself alone than all men have had since the world began."'[71]

His mind is crowded with incidents, characters and interludes from life in the Lager, which emerge from the depths (as when he happens to see a face from that time in a photograph) to produce a kind of 'dazzling' effect on him. Why throw back into the dark Bandi, the peasant woodcutter who 'had a unique talent for happiness', and who when he first arrived in the camp did not want to steal or lie? With bitter realism Primo Levi had taught him that ordinary morality, in the Lager, was a currency that no longer functioned, and the disciple had learned. Or why not give voice to the 'unusual, fascinating and sinister' history of Chaim Rumkowski, the king of the Łódź ghetto, a renegade and collaborator, yet convinced that he was a saviour of his people? And Rappoport, and Eddy, and Wolf, and Vladek who never washed, and Ezra, a mixture of piety and madness? Primo Levi, freed from the duty of testimony and the irrefutability that must characterize it, gave independent life to each of them because, as he had said to the literature students, 'time interprets incidents in different ways'.

But *Lilith* does not just contain stories of the Lager: its three sections correspond to the three strands Levi identified in his work. The author declared as much to Anna Maria Rebaudengo, who asked him for Piedmontese TV how the themes of *Lilith* connected with his previous work.

> I would say that *Lilith* follows those strands. It's divided in fact into three sections, of which the first relates openly to *If This is a Man* and *The Truce*; the second to *Natural Histories* and *Flaw of Form*; and the third, more vaguely, to *The Wrench* and *The Periodic Table.*

The story that had struck the interviewer most is the one the book is named after: 'Lilith'. Is it taken from eastern Judaism?

> In fact, it has much more distant roots, because eastern Judaism took it in its turn from Babylonian legend. It's the extraordinary story of Adam's first wife, who wasn't Eve; she was a rival, who immediately comes into conflict with man because she wants to be equal to him; who argues with God, because God is also a man, and finding herself not listened to, comes down to Earth in a spirit of spite and retaliation, and becomes a she-devil.
>
> *Almost forty years separate the younger generation from Hitler's Lagers. What attention do they pay to the subject?*
>
> Young people's attention is naturally diminishing with time. Ten or twenty years ago they didn't hesitate to accept what we survivors told them as real; now they still accept it, but they have to make an effort. They see it as far away, like the incidents of the Risorgimento.

Or even, he sometimes said, 'like the Punic Wars'. Was it with this in mind that he wrote in a copy of the book he signed for a friend that it was 'mildly fané' [faded]?[72] It was possible, even if in the tripartite division of *Lilith* all his souls were there; the souls he talked about with Giovanni Pacchioni from *Il Globo*.

> As for the discussion on multiple souls, my inner being is profoundly hybrid, and it's not by chance that hybridism comes out so profoundly in my stories. I've talked of centaurs, of splits between rational and emotional; in *Lilith* the story 'Disphylaxis' is all about such hybridism.

> I'm Jewish and also Italian, or Italian and also Jewish; I'm a chemist and also a writer; I tend to be rational, or at least I would like to be rational, yet I too have a shred of 'Id': so it's a bit of a constant of mine, to feel that I'm hybrid and moulded from different materials [...] Yes, I'm sure that I've wanted that too – that I've wished, without success, to be a whole man; and I believe that that's desirable in general, maybe because the general is better than the particular, because that way more readers will see themselves in one's writing. I notice in fact that some readers are touched by the moral aspects of what I write, others just by the adventure or technical side. I was happy that *The Wrench* was read even by 'non-readers' – and that happened, I've written proof, from the ex-labourers, specialist labourers and pensioners who've written dozens of letters to me, saying: 'Finally I read in a book what I've done in my life!'[73]

When Primo Levi read the review in *Tuttolibri* by G. Bàrberi Squarotti, who saw in *Lilith* a quiet discussion of the problems of life and history, he replied with the bilingual palindrome of Ettore, protagonist of his story 'Dizzying Heat': 'In arts it is repose to life: è filo teso per siti strani. (It's a thread stretched through strange sites.)'[74] Which seemed to us an enigmatic and playful way of evading Squarotti's high praise, and the question of whether, in gathering together these documents of scattered memory, he had carried out a 'mild and patient inquiry into the often mysterious manifestation of good and evil in the world'.[75]

Notes

1. Silvia Giacomoni, 'Il mago Merlino e l'uomo fabbro' [Merlin the Mage and man the maker], *La Repubblica*, 24 January 1979.
2. Primo Levi, 'Un Lager alle porte d'Italia' [A Lager at the gates of Italy], *La Stampa*, 19 January 1979.
3. Senior lecturer.
4. In the *La Stampa* article on 19 January Levi, who in the meantime had learned Faurisson's age and other details about him, wrote: 'Faurisson doesn't have personal guilt: who stands behind him and encourages his fixations?'
5. Primo Levi, 'Ma noi c'eravamo' [But we were there], *Corriere della Sera*, 3 January 1979. The declaration appeared on the first page coupled with a scathing article by Leonardo Sciascia, 'A chi giova l'atroce bugia che vuole cancellare le stragi nelle camere a gas del regime nazista' [To anyone pleased by the atrocious lie which seeks to erase the massacres in the gas chambers of the Nazi regime].
6. Medieval heretics.
7. Writer interned in Switzerland during the Second World War.
8. An architect and designer imprisoned in Mauthausen 1944-5.
9. In his article published in *Tuttolibri, (La Stampa)*, 23 December 1978.
10. Giacomoni. The film referred to is Liliana Cavani's *The Night Porter*, a highly controversial 1974 film about the sadomasochistic relationship between an SS officer and a Holocaust survivor.

11. Primo Levi, 'Anniversario' [Anniversary], *L'Eco dell'educazione ebraica* [Jewish educational echo], special edition for the tenth anniversary of the Liberation, ninth year of publication, April 1955, p.14. An English translation is available in the chapter 'Deportees. Anniversary' in Belpoliti, M. (ed.), trans. Sharon Wood, *The Black Hole of Auschwitz* (Cambridge: Polity Press, 2005), pp.3-4.
12. Primo Levi, 'Film e svastiche' [Films and swastikas], *La Stampa*,12 February 1977. An English version exists under the title 'Films and Swastikas' in Belpoliti, p.38.
13. Primo Levi, 'Buco nero di Auschwitz' [Black hole of Auschwitz], *La Stampa*, 22 January 1987. An English version exists under the title 'The Black Hole of Auschwitz' in Belpoliti, pp.90-2.
14. Primo Levi, 'Così fu Auschwitz' [This is how Auschwitz was], *La Stampa*, 9 February 1975.
15. From the television programme 'Rifarsi una vita' [Making a new life], presented by Lucia Borgia, broadcast by RAI 3 on 3 February 1985.
16. Primo Levi, 'Monumento ad Auschwitz' [Monument at Auschwitz], *La Stampa*, 19 July 1959. An English version is available under the title 'The Monument at Auschwitz' in Belpoliti, *The Black Hole of Auschwitz*, pp. 5-7.
17. Primo Levi, 'Così fu Auschwitz'.
18. The Camere del Lavoro [Chambers of Work] was the organization of Italian trade unions preceding the present-day CGIL. On the night of 25 April 1921, its Turin office was set on fire by local fascists, none of whom was arrested. Mussolini came to power the next year, 1922, and the Camere were closed in 1927 to be replaced with a fascist trade union organization.
19. Fascist rhetoric often referred to the outcome of the First World War as a 'mutilated victory' for Italy. The term was coined by the poet Gabriele D'Annunzio to refer to the fact that, after the war was over, the London Pact of 1915 was not honoured. This Pact was a secret agreement made just before Italy entered the war, which promised that Italy would be awarded Austrian territories in return for fighting Germany.
20. A reference to the massacre of trade unionists and anti-fascists by fascist militia on 18 to 20 December 1922. Levi seems to have confused the dates.
21. The writer delivered the draft to *La Stampa*, in the event that the paper would want to use it at the time of the inauguration. The (photocopied) typescript is from 8 November 1978. The capitalized letterhead reads: 'Bozza di testo per l'interno del Block italiano ad Auschwitz' [Draft of a text for the Italian Block in Auschwitz]. The numbers in the margin are the author's. Our italics correspond to the passage that survived.
22. With the title 'Ritorno ad Auschwitz' [Return to Auschwitz], the interview was broadcast on RAI 2 for the Jewish cultural programme 'Sorgente di vita' [Source of life] on 25 April 1983, the 38th anniversary of Italian liberation. Here we reproduce the questions and answers word for word, though not in order. The attendees of the Primo Levi International Study Days organized by the Regional Council of Piedmont on the occasion of the first anniversary of the writer's death were able to listen again to the interview on 28 March 1988, in the Council's headquarters in Palazzo Lascaris, Turin.
23. *The Truce* in *Complete Works of Primo Levi*, Vol. I, p.326.
24. Shorthand notes provided by *La Stampa*.
25. Trino Vercellese (Piedmont), 30 January 1982, Mostra della Deportazione [Deportation Exhibition].
26. A. Bravo & D. Jalla (eds), *La vita offesa* [The wounded life] (Milan: Franco Angeli, 1987), p.170. The declaration is taken from the interview given by Primo Levi to Anna Bravo and Federico Cereja on 27 January 1983. *Protekcja* means protection, which in the camps has been paid for.
27. From the programme 'Film Dossier' presented by Beniamino Placido, broadcast on RAI 1 and recorded at the studios in the Milan fairground area, 27 October 1983.

28. Shorthand notes by Renato Romanelli for *La Stampa*, Mostra della Deportazione, Settimo, April 1982.
29. The lowest stratum of the proletariat. A term in Marxist theory.
30. Virgilio Lo Presti, 'Tornare, mangiare, raccontare...'[Returning; eating; telling...], *Lotta Continua*, 18 June 1979.
31. The television interview recorded with Nicola Tranfaglia in the surroundings of old and new Turin factories was broadcast on RAI 3 on 22 March 1981, for a series dedicated to a report on work entitled 'Col sudore della fronte' [By the sweat of one's brow].
32. Leonardo Vergani, 'Parla Primo Levi, il numero 174517' [Primo Levi, number 174517, speaks], *Corriere della Sera*, 20 March 1979. The Müller whom the writer refers to is the protagonist of the story 'Vanadium', included in *The Periodic Table* in *Complete Works of Primo Levi*, Vol. II, pp. 927-38.
33. 'Ritorno ad Auschwitz', 'Sorgente di vita'. *Essen* and *fressen* mean 'to eat', *isst* and *frisst* 'eats'.
34. Conversation between Primo Levi and Dina Luce, 'Il suono e la mente' [Sound and mind], RAI Radio 2, 4 October 19824 October 1982. The essays were published with the title *The Drowned and the Saved*.
35. Rosanna Benzi, 'Quel treno per Auschwitz' [That train for Auschwitz], *Gli Altri*, second quarter of 1979.
36. From the 'Incontro con Primo Levi' [Meeting with Primo Levi] organized by the Leo Club of Cuneo in Autumn 1975, recording by Franca Veglia Grosso.
37. *Gazzetta del Popolo*, 21 January 1979.
38. 'Il suono e la mente' [Sound and mind], RAI Radio 2, 4 October 1982.
39. An extreme left-wing terrorist group, active from 1970 to 1988 and responsible for a large number of kidnaps and assassinations, most notoriously of former Christian Democrat Prime Minister Aldo Moro in 1978.
40. Jesurum, *Essere ebrei in Italia* (Longanesi: Milan, 1987) p.101.
41. A town in Lombardy known for basketball.
42. Primo Levi, 'Chi vuole l'odio antisemita' [Those who want anti-Semitic hatred], *La Stampa*, 13 March 1979. In those few days the writer was in Rome to take part, together with the editor of *Il Ponte*, Enzo Enriques Agnoletti, and some other eminent contributors to the review, in a meeting with Italy's President Alessandro Pertini. This was on the occasion of the special issue *Il Ponte* had dedicated to the fortieth anniversary of the fascist laws '*Per la Difesa della Razza*' [for the Defence of the Race].
43. Primo Levi, 'Un olocausto che pesa ancora sulla coscienza del mondo' [A Holocaust that still weighs on the world's conscience], *Tuttolibri (La Stampa)*, 28 April 1970. Translated as 'A Holocaust That Still Weighs on the World's Conscience' in *Uncollected Stories and Essays: 1949-1980*, in *Complete Works of Primo Levi*, Vol. II, pp.1278-81. The article is a review of Green, G., *Holocaust* (Ealing: Transworld Publishers, 1978).
44. 'Perché non ritornino gli Olocausto di ieri' [So that yesterday's Holocausts do not return], *La Stampa*, 20 May 1979. Translated as 'So That Yesterday's Holocausts May Never Return', *Uncollected Stories and Essays: 1949-1980* in *Complete Works of Primo Levi*, Vol. II, pp.1282-5.
45. Foreword to *Le immagini di Olocausto - dalla realtà alla tv* [Images of *Holocaust*—from reality to the TV], (Turin: Eri, May 1979), pp.2-5. A special edition of the RAI's listing magazine, edited by P. Giorgio Martinelli, and published by the RAI's publishing arm Eri. Translated as 'Images from Holocaust' in *Uncollected Stories and Essays: 1949-1980*, *Complete Works of Primo Levi*, Vol. II, pp.1286-9.
46. Piero Bianucci, 'Olocausto è brutto ma può servire' [*Holocaust* is bad but it can be useful], *Gazzetta del Popolo*, 25 May 1979.
47. Renato Rizzo, 'Olocausto? Come un western, romanzato e superficiale' [*Holocaust*? Like a Western, romanticized and superficial], *La Stampa*, 25 May 1979.

48. Ugo Buzzolan, 'La voce di chi conobbe i crimini nazisti' [The voice of those who knew the Nazi crimes], *La Stampa*, 15 May 1979.
49. 'Ritorno ad Auschwitz', 'Sorgente di vita'.
50. From the interview with Silvia Giacomoni for *Lotta Continua* on 18 June 1979.
51. From the interview with Virgilio Lo Presti for *La Repubblica* on 24 June 1979. The book referred to is A. Solzhenitsyn, trans. T.P. Whitney, *The Gulag Archipelago* (place unknown: Harper & Row, 1974).
52. Lo Presti, 'Tornare, mangiare, raccontare…'. The book referred to is Shalamov, V., trans. Glad, J., *Kolyma Tales* (St Ives: Penguin, 1994). Kolyma is a region in which many Gulags were located.
53. 'Whatever it costs'.
54. Giorgio Calcagno, 'Primo Levi: capire non è perdonare' [Primo Levi: understanding is not forgiving], *Tuttolibri* (*La Stampa*), 26 July 1986. On the same subject see also Camon, *Autoritratto di Primo Levi*, p.57.
55. The opening episode of the programme 'Focus', presented by Ennio Mastrostefano and Paolo Meucci, was broadcast by RAI 2 on 22 December 1986.
56. 'Ritorno ad Auschwitz', 'Sorgente di vita'.
57. Lo Presti, 'Tornare, mangiare, raccontare…'.
58. 'Ritorno ad Auschwitz', 'Sorgente di vita'.
59. Silvia Giacomoni, *Lotta Continua* interview.
60. Grassano, p.11. (Sante Notarnicola was serving a life sentence for crimes connected with left-wing terrorism.)
61. 'Small Portable Cosmogony' (Paris: Gallimard, 1950), a French poem translated into Italian as *Piccola cosmogonia portatile* [Small portable cosmogony] by Sergio Solmi and revised by Calvino with help from Primo Levi for the part concerning chemistry (Turin: Einaudi, 1982).
62. Communal farm in Israel.
63. *Lilith and Other Stories* in *Complete Works of Primo Levi*, Vol. II, p.1389.
64. Ibid, p.1401.
65. From the introduction, dated 6 June 1985, that Primo Levi wrote for *Moments of Reprieve*, translated by Ruth Feldman (New York: Summit Books, 1986), pp.9-10. The stories in this edition that are not included in the Italian edition or in *Lilith and Other Stories* in the *Complete Works* are 'Last Christmas of the War' (included in *Uncollected Stories and Essays:1981-1987*), 'The Quiet City'and 'Small Causes' (included in *Stories and Essays* with the titles 'Wartime Pipette' and 'That Quiet Town of Auschwitz'): the first was the title story in *L'Ultimo Natale di Guerra* [The last Christmas of War] printed privately in Lugano by Levi's friend Sergio Grandini for Christmas 1984; the other two appeared in *La Stampa* on 8 March 1984 and 23 May 1985 respectively.
66. Tiziano Longo, 'La Lilìt di Primo Levi' [Primo Levi's Lilith], *La Stampa*, 20 January 1982.
67. Bravo and Jalla (1987), from the interview given by Primo Levi to Anna Bravo and Federico Cereja on 27 January 1983.
68. *If This is a Man* in *Complete Works of Primo Levi*, Vol. I, *passim*. The changes Levi made are reflected in the differences between that edition and Woolf's 1959 translation. All the changes and additions which Giovanni Tesio studied carefully for his critical work were signed by the author and filed under the title 'Per Einaudi' [For Einaudi].
69. Giovanni Tesio, 'Su alcune giunte e varianti di *Se questo è un uomo*' [On some additions and variants of *If This is a Man*], *Studi Piemontesi*, November 1977, vol. IV, issue 2, p.273.
70. Levi referred to prisoners who move 'upwards' towards being saved (surviving), or 'downwards' towards being drowned (death).

71. 'A "Mystery" in the Lager' in *Stories and Essays*, in *Complete Works of Primo Levi*, Vol. III, p.2313. The Borges quote is from 'Funes the Memorious' (1942) in *Ficciones* (New York: Grove Press, 1962), p.113.
73. Giovanni Pacchioni, 'Segrete avventure di eroi involontari' [Secret adventures of accidental heroes], *Il Globo*, 13-14 June 1982.
74. *Lilith and Other Stories* in *Complete Works of Primo Levi*, Vol. II, p.1445.
75. Giorgio Bàrberi Squarotti, 'Dio creò il male e lo chiamò Lilìt' [God created evil and called it Lilith], *La Stampa*, 5 December 1981.

IX

Giving and Having

It is the programme 'Prima pagina' on Canale 5 TV,[1] presented by a famous journalist who is no stranger to controversy, Giorgio Bocca. In front of him is the keen face of Primo Levi. The first part of the interview has passed pleasantly, almost casually, in the play between two minds. Bocca says:

> *You are a writer who stands out in Italy, in large part because of your talent, but also because you've been a chemist and you say yourself in your books that you write as a chemist. That is, if not as a scientist at least as a technician. That poses two problems in our literary landscape and the first seems to me to be this: you say that a writer must be clear, but I have sometimes struggled a bit to read you because you use technical terms so precisely that at a certain point one would need a glossary…*

Primo Levi laughs in amusement:

> It's a price to pay. It seems to me that it's a lesser price, because it only takes a good dictionary, compared to so many other texts that are obscure not for reasons of lexis, but for reasons of syntax or for hidden reasons, texts that are truly indecipherable and insoluble.
>
> *But isn't there at certain moments a touch of smugness in you? Of the kind that says: look how much I know?*
>
> Yes, of course; of course there is. But it comes naturally. I don't know if you have ever happened to read the texts of doctors. A doctor can't avoid using medical terminology, which is very useful because he has an arsenal of metaphors that the layman lacks. And the same thing happens to us chemists. I find myself, not as a trick or affectation, but naturally being induced to draw on that reserve of terms and also of metaphors which aren't at the public's disposal. I don't think that I've committed such a serious crime; and precisely it only takes a good dictionary…
>
> *The other problem is one which leaves your readers puzzled. Probably it's our own fault for not familiarising ourselves with your kind of writing.*

> *We're used to the idea that the writer must be sentimental, introspective, whereas you [...] For example, I very much enjoyed a chapter of yours devoted to the pavements of Turin*[2] *in which in a certain sense you are an archaeologist. One always expects emotion, memory etcetera to come out; but instead it's an exercise, very elegant, but that's it.*

An observation intended to sound out the writer on his 'feelings'. The reply is evasive and ironic:

> There is a division of labour in certain things. There are already so many who deal with feeling; world literature is saturated with feeling. Why not try to beat a different path? To me it comes naturally. Feeling? Very well, I admit it, I too experience feeling, but it seems to me a bit threadbare.

After that the conversation moves on to other subjects. Feeling had only been nodded at. The introspective theme generally falls outside Primo Levi's interviews, except in one case where he lets himself be introspective for a moment: perhaps due to the lightness with which Dina Luce put the question, or because it was on the radio and not television, which always embarrassed him a bit; perhaps due to his state of mind after his second Campiello Prize, which he had just received for *If Not Now, When?* exactly twenty years after the first, which had been awarded to *The Truce*.

> *Tell me a quality that you know you have, that you like having?*

The writer hesitates, then says doubtfully:

> A quality that I know I have [...] let's say fairness, being impartial, not letting myself be carried away by feelings. perhaps this [...] which can also be a fault [...]
>
> *Not letting yourself be carried away by feelings: never? Are feelings always negative?*
>
> No, they're not always negative, sometimes they are positive. But I am incapable of letting myself be carried away by feelings, so that I'm seen, rightly enough, as someone who isn't very emotional, isn't very warm, is very reserved. Or at least quite reserved.
>
> *Would you ever like to write a love story?*
>
> I would like to very much, but I fear I'm not capable of it. Because there are things that I experience very privately, very intimately, and I

think that if I wrote a love story, even about other people, I'd expose too much of myself.

You're a very discreet person?

Yes, yes. I really think I am.

And also a bit protective of yourself?

Also a bit protective of myself.

What moves you?

I'm a hardened person, I'm almost never moved. I'm moved by the things that affect more or less everyone, children who suffer, elderly people who suffer, defenceless people [...] but perhaps because of my experiences I am quite hardened, I'm not moved easily.

And what are you afraid of?

Of physical pain. Mine and other people's.

And your roots? You've written a book called The Search for Roots. *Are your roots inside your family?*

The title of the book you've cited alludes to another kind of roots: it's an anthology of books I've read. My roots are my family, they're in Turin, they're in the mountains around Turin, they're also in the books I've read. And they're naturally in my previous trade, which hasn't disappeared; I've still preserved a good part of the chemist's reflexes.[3]

A reply which covers both identifications (his family, his trade) and origins (his city, his mountains, his reading). All roots, but separate ones, as taught by Genesis. Plus chemistry. In the Preface to *The Search for Roots* Primo Levi wrote: 'At a certain point in the journey, it is natural to draw up one's accounts. Everything should be included: what you have received and what you have given.'[4]

He drew up his accounts as a writer in public, according to the ethical code he had adopted. To this he remained rigorously faithful, never, for instance, turning a living person into a character, 'because such a task, even when it's carried out with the best intentions and in the case of a loved and respected person, verges on private violence and is never painless for the one who is the object of it'.[5] Thus to his first root, his family, he dedicated various stories on his long-dead ancestors, from 'Argon' in *The Periodic Table* to 'My

Grandfather's Shop' in *Other People's Trades*; and dwelt with a certain expansiveness, in speech and in writing, only on his father, whom he had lost many years before. Levi was in his father's debt for the books he had precociously read, as well as for the imperceptible nudges that had led him towards his life choices. In his *Dialogo* with Tullio Regge[6] he described him thus:

> [...] He too was a bibliophile, he bought books at random, and he had the passions of a self-taught man. He'd studied lots of things on his own, and he continued to study until the end. He filled the house with strange books, some of which I still have. He'd specialized as an engineer in Liège and he'd found a job in Budapest, where he'd learned German [...] He bought me the Mondadori popular science series, *Microbe Hunters, Concerning the Nature of Things*, an early book on genetics which was still in its infancy – this is the beginning of the thirties – *Man, The Unknown* by Carrel and *A Short Introduction to the History of Human Stupidity*, by Wilkins, I think.[7]
>
> My father hated nature, he had a savage hatred for the countryside, which for him meant staying shut up indoors without ever putting his nose outside, because there were ants, because it was dusty, because it was hot. The few times we managed to make him go for a walk he took two books with him in his pocket, and as soon as we'd reached our destination, instead of looking at the view, the mountains or the sea, he sat on the ground, on a newspaper so as not to get his suit dirty, and pulled his books out [...] My father was in love with the centre of Turin. He took me there, even when I didn't want to go, and he didn't understand the fact that I went into the mountains to go skiing. Tennis yes, because it wasn't dangerous, and it was done within a confined area. But the mountains were incomprehensible to him. Drink, smoke, go with girls, he told me. Now I didn't smoke, I didn't drink, I didn't have girlfriends. There wasn't a huge amount of comprehension between me and my father. I was a romantic, I hoped to reach very far, to find the key to the universe, to understand the reason for things. Now I know that there isn't one, at least I don't think there is, but then I thought there was. Still I wasn't religious, religion didn't say anything to me, and deep down even classical culture didn't give me much, I endured it with a certain impatience, though I was a good student. I had a curious sensation: that there was a conspiracy against me, that family and school were keeping something secret from me, which I went looking for in the places that were reserved for me: for example chemistry, or astronomy. My father, who was very liberal, had bought a whole cellar full of books from an old man in Bardonecchia, in which there was everything, from Voltaire to Camille Flammarion.

Among the works by Flammarion were *Astronomie populaire* and *Les étoiles*:[8] one of the 'cautious pressures' which the engineer Cesare Levi applied to direct his son towards the scientific side, helping him to escape from the 'Gentilean plot' for which the writer didn't forgive his school. It was, he explained to Regge, an insistent discouragement. As if they constantly said:

> You young fascist, you young Crocean, you young man who's grown up in this Italy, don't go near the sources of scientific knowledge, because they're dangerous.

He added:

> I've never read Croce on this subject, but it seems that he considered the sciences pseudo-sciences, mere technical matters, useful for life but not for an understanding of the world.

This was made up for in his father's library, where he found everything the *liceo* was hiding from him, even the non-marmoreal Latin of his beloved Lucretius.[9] Since he had been a good student, in the long run he had to recognize that having 'digested Gieek and Latin diligently, willingly even, because they amused us linguistically, for philological reasons' proved useful to him at the right moment, when he read among others Vitruvius and Celsus:

> Celsus is very interesting. He explains to you how the tonsil operations of his time were carried out. Reading him you realize, as I realized only ten years ago, that Latin was a spoken language, and not just a language for orators.

Did his father influence him in his search, if not for the ultimate then at least (to use the expression of the *Dialogo*) for the penultimate reasons for things?

> My father went to the synagogue at Yom Kippur because he was a bit superstitious, but he frequented Lombroso,[10] and the positivist physiologists of Turin; he took part in séances not because he believed in spiritualism, but to understand what was behind it. He never bought me a telescope, but he did buy me a microscope with a magnification of 250, with which I organized shows, with an alum solution to see the crystals [...] I had a little Pathé Baby movie projector. I invited my friends, and when I put the slide in the slot where the film passes through, we saw the crystals growing...

In his conversation with Stefano Jesurum the writer recalled his father with a mischievous smile:

> [...] he was a secular man essentially, but attached to certain customs. Out of a kind of superstitious fear, I think, he didn't eat pork. But he was mad about Parma ham and so, every now and then, he gave in. Then he would taste it, with a guilty expression, looking at us children as if to say: I sin because the flesh is weak, but don't you give in, behave yourselves.[11]

With that rough man who was not very communicative ('between me and him there was too great an age gap, and there wasn't much conversation') Primo Levi almost never discussed political questions, nor the Jewish tradition. One reads in a passage of Ferdinando Camon's *Autoritratto*:

> My family was bourgeois. In my early years no one talked about ostracizing the Jews, at least not in Italy. My father, who had worked for a long time in Hungary and France, had had some experiences. He knew what anti-Semitism meant in those places. He'd watched Bela Kun's revolution in Budapest and had a traumatic memory of it, but he told me little about it, extremely little. As a bourgeois he'd been frightened by Bela Kun's attempt, doubly frightened because Bela Kun was a Jew and known in Hungary as such. And in 1919 he'd enacted a Soviet constitution. My father was afraid of Communism, and afraid of the reaction to a Jewish Communist. As for the founding of the *fasci di combattimento*[12] in Italy, all in all it wasn't talked about much. I was born and grew up in a fascist climate, even though my father wasn't a fascist. He was hostile to fascism for superficial reasons; he didn't care for the mummery, the parading, the lack of seriousness. [...] As for predictions and presentiments, in our house, I'd really have to say no, there weren't any. I was too young, and my father had a tendency to criticize everything. He died in 1942 [...] fortunately for him, and for us, since he wouldn't have survived what happened later.[13]

When he died in the big house on Corso Re Umberto, the engineer Cesare Levi was sixty-four. He left his books, bought without method, but with insatiable excitement, and the affectionate memory of his son:

> My father was always reading three books simultaneously; he read 'when he sat in his house, when he walked by the way, when he lay down and when he rose' (Deuteronomy 6.7); he ordered from his tailor jackets with large and deep pockets, each one of which could hold a book. He had two brothers just as interested as he was in indiscriminate reading; the three (an engineer, a physician and a stockbroker) were very fond of each other but stole books from one another's bookcases on every possible occasion.[14]

Giorgio Bocca joked: 'However hard I search my memory, I can only come up with two grandmothers and four aunts, whereas you seem to have hundreds of ancestors [...] all very ordinary and very peculiar characters at the same time'. Levi corrected him, catching the humour behind his hyperbole:

> I have dozens – and then others have lent me theirs. I often meet friends who say, 'It's strange, your grandfather said exactly the same things as mine did'. To write 'Argon', the chapter you're alluding to, the first in *The Periodic Table*, I drew on memories not just of my own family but also of other families [. . .] They were bourgeois of the last century, and as such were by definition always engaged with economic questions. For the most part they were tradespeople. They aren't such ordinary characters, though. Naturally there were dull, drab, pale ones among them, but I put those to one side. They left no trace. However some peculiar types *have* left a trace; some curious types have passed into private history, into family history, perhaps for a single saying. For example that great-grandfather of mine (or maybe not a great-grandfather, I'm not sure) who had flat feet and struggled to walk on the cobblestones of Casale Monferrato. One morning he wakes up and finds the street paved – and *toto corde*, with all his heart, he says in Judaeo-Piedmontese slang 'naabrakhà a coi gojim c'a l'an fait I losi'; that is, a blessing on those unbelievers who made the flagstones![15]

His second root is his trade. This was a complex account, which Primo Levi settled over time, because if chemistry was a system of thought for him, an intellectual and ethical choice, work in chemistry was an existential parable, a ground for confronting and measuring oneself against things. He explained this many times in his public meetings, and he was never miserly in his explanations to his interviewers should they ask, and they often did, for his reasons for continuing to be a chemist after his literary successes, or for clarifications on the debt the man and the writer owed to his previous trade:

> [. . .] a trade of remarkable usefulness also on the level of style, because it teaches you to keep an eye on what's essential, and like a police academy shows you how to follow tracks, how to distinguish the true ones from the false ones so as not to get lost in dead ends.[16]

In the *Dialogo* with Tullio Regge, he emphasised his relationship with chemistry. Indeed it was on this occasion that he went into it in the greatest depth, starting from his youthful memories:

> I still remember the first lesson with Professor Ponzio, in which I received clear, precise, verifiable pieces of information, without useless words, expressed in a language I liked beyond measure, from a literary

> point of view as well: a clear-cut, essential language. And then the laboratory: every year had its laboratory; we spent five hours a day there, it was quite a commitment. An extraordinary experience. First of all because you touched your material with your own hands, literally. It was the first time that happened to me, no matter if perhaps you burned your hands or cut them. It was a return to the origins. The hand is a noble organ, but school, all taken up with the brain, had passed it over. And then the laboratory was a collegial space, a centre of socialization where we truly became friends. In fact, I have remained friends with all my laboratory colleagues. Such teamwork had been unknown at school (but I don't know whether it was as intense outside the chemistry course). Being wrong together is a fundamental experience. We played a great part in each other's victories and defeats. [...] We gave one another advice, we sympathized with one another. It was also a school of patience, of objectivity, of ingenuity, because the methods they suggested to you for doing an analysis could be perfected; it was up to you to take a step forward yourself, to simplify.[17]

The passion that had inspired the boy, accompanied the man and never died out. To Ferdinando Camon, who asked him 'What is it in chemistry you're interested in?,' he replied:

> I'm interested in contact with matter, in understanding the world around me; I'm interested in the chemistry of the human body, in biochemistry. In science, in short: but the science of particles doesn't say much to me, whereas the discovery of genetic mechanisms fascinates me, the way in which the individual is coded, the minuscule chain whose alphabet is made up of molecules. There's a bridge between linguists and geneticists. These new linguistic concepts of 'pregnancy', of 'redundancy', of 'ambiguity', apply very well to genetics; thus genetic failures are due to the lack of redundancy, because it takes only the slightest error and the reading is broken. But the reasons that brought me to chemistry were different then, because chemistry then was a different science. I chose chemistry when I was a boy of fourteen or fifteen: because I was thrilled by the parallelism between the formula written on paper and what happens in the test tube. Chemistry already seemed something magical to me then, the main key to open the secrets of heaven and earth. And when I read that a spectroscope allows you to know the chemical composition of a star, it seemed to me one of man's greatest powers.[18]

That was his last statement on the subject, but he had addressed it as soon as he was given the chance, with hints or with broad brushstrokes according to the question and who asked it.

'What is a chemist?' a television journalist asked him in front of the science faculty in the Valentino area. He replied:

> According to the classical specification, a chemist is a transmuter of matter; he's a descendant of the alchemists who thought they could turn lead into gold. The chemist of today still does that: if he's a nuclear chemist he effectively transmutes one element in another. More modestly he transmutes anything, cellulose into paper, beet into sugar, pigments into varnish and so on. But I must say that in chemistry today, as in many other careers, nine times out of ten science gives way to technology and technology gives way to bureaucracy. I would say therefore that nine times out of ten the chemist is a civil servant, if not a bureaucrat plain and simple, and one time out of ten he's a researcher and remains one all his life.[19]

And did he, Primo Levi, recognize himself in this kind of chemist? In his interview with Philip Roth he admitted, with some regret:

> I am not a scientist [...] wanted to become one, but war and the camp prevented me. I had to limit myself to being a technician throughout my professional life.

Roth pointed out to him that he had lived through the Lager experience as a scientist:

> *The description and analysis of your atrocious memories of the Germans' 'gigantic biological and social experiment' is governed, very precisely, by a quantitative concern for the ways in which a man can be transformed or broken down and, like a substance decomposing in a chemical reaction, lose his characteristic properties.* If This Is a Man *reads like the memoirs of a theoretician of moral biochemistry who has himself been forcibly enlisted as the specimen organism to undergo laboratory experimentation of the most sinister kind. The creature caught in the laboratory of the mad scientist is himself the very epitome of the rational scientist.*
>
> *In* The Monkey's Wrench*[...]you tell Faussone, your blue-collar Scheherazade, that 'being a chemist in the world's eyes, and feeling . . . a writer's blood in my veins', you consequently have 'two souls in my body, and that's too many'. I'd say there's one soul, capacious and seamless; I'd say that not only are the survivor and the scientist inseparable but the writer and the scientist as well.*

Levi liked the diagnosis and found it useful in crediting his writing style to his intellectual training once again:

> I lived my camp life as rationally as I could, and I wrote *If This Is a Man* struggling to explain to others and to myself the events I had been involved in. But with no definite literary intention. My model (or, if you prefer, my style) was that of the 'weekly report' commonly used in factories: it must be precise, concise, and written in a language comprehensible to everybody in the industrial hierarchy. And certainly not written in scientific jargon. [...]
>
> I agree with you on there being only 'one soul [. . .] and seamless', and once more I feel grateful to you. My statement that 'two souls [. . .] is too many' is half a joke, but half serious. I worked in a factory for almost thirty years, and I must say that there is no incompatibility between being a chemist and being a writer: in fact, there is a mutual reinforcement. But factory life, and particularly factory managing, involves many other matters, far from chemistry: hiring and firing workers; quarrelling with the boss, customers and suppliers; coping with accidents; being called to the telephone, even at night or when you're at a party; dealing with bureaucracy; and many more soul-destroying tasks. All this business is brutally incompatible with writing, which requires a fair amount of peace of mind. Consequently I felt hugely relieved when I reached retirement age and could resign, and so renounce my soul number one.

It is tiring to be a 'centaur' all one's life, but also extremely fruitful for someone in Primo Levi's situation. Roth continues:

> *To my knowledge, only two writers of importance have ever been managers of a paint factory, you in Turin, Italy, and Sherwood Anderson in Elyria, Ohio. Anderson had to flee the paint factory (and his family) to become a writer; you seem to have become the writer you are by staying and pursuing your career there. I wonder if you think of yourself as actually more fortunate – even better equipped to write – than those of us who are without a paint factory and all that's implied by that kind of connection.*
>
> I entered the paint industry by chance, but I never had very much to do with the general run of paints, varnishes, and lacquers. Our company, immediately after it began, specialized in the production of wire enamels, insulating coatings for copper electrical conductors. At the peak of my career, I numbered among the thirty or forty specialists in the world in this branch. The animals hanging here on the wall are made out of scrap enameled wire.
>
> Honestly, I knew nothing of Sherwood Anderson till you spoke of him. I read a brief biography of him yesterday. No, it would never have

> occurred to me to quit family and factory for full-time writing, as he did. I'd have feared the jump into the dark, and apart from anything else I would have lost any right to a pension.
>
> However, to your list of writer/paint manufacturers I must add a third name, Italo Svevo, a converted Jew of Trieste, the author of *The Confessions of Zeno* who lived from 1861 to 1928. For a long time Svevo was the commercial manager of a paint company in Trieste, the Società Veneziani, that belonged to his father-in-law, and that dissolved a few years ago. Until 1918 Trieste belonged to Austria, and this company was famous because it supplied the Austrian Navy with an excellent antifouling paint, preventing shellfish incrustation, for the keels of warships. After 1918 Trieste became Italian, and the paint was delivered to the Italian and British Navies. To be able to deal with the Admiralty, Svevo took lessons in English from James Joyce, at the time a teacher in Trieste. They became friends and Joyce assisted Svevo in finding a publisher for his works.
>
> The trade name of the antifouling paint was Moravia. That it is the same as the nom de plume of the noted Italian novelist is not fortuitous: both the Triestine businessman and the Roman writer derived it from the family name of a mutual relative on the mother's side. Forgive me for this hardly pertinent gossip. No, no, as I've hinted already, I have no regrets. I don't believe I wasted my time in the factory. [...] In managing it I acquired more valuable experiences, which have been added and combined with those of Auschwitz.[20]

And still less did he regret not having changed course when success smiled on him. In 1982, for the volume dedicated by *Il Gazzettino*[21] to the twentieth anniversary of the Campiello Prize, he had dictated this announcement:

> The idea of leaving my job and dedicating myself to writing was far from my mind. I sometimes thought about it, on the bad days that happen in all trades, but without seriousness, like dreaming of archipelagos. It wasn't a plan but a daydream; the Turinese don't leave certainty for uncertainty, the devil they know for the devil they don't.

With a few others, like Tullio Regge, he found himself at ease exchanging opinions: 'I will never stop talking to him', he said, 'above all listening to him'. It was thus that during the *Dialogo* he asked the physicist the same question that journalists had often addressed to him: 'what have you been given by non-scientific culture, that is art, literature, music?' Regge cited his love for the piano, for Bach and Mozart, for Mann, Musil and Carroll. In return Levi traced the outlines of his own inexhaustible debt, summing up what he had said in lectures, or on television and radio:

> Regarding my experience, I must say that my chemistry, which was a 'low' chemistry, almost cookery, has provided me first of all with a vast assortment of metaphors. I find myself richer than my fellow writers because for me terms like 'bright', 'dark', 'heavy', 'light' and 'blue' have a broader and more concrete range of meanings. For me blue isn't just the blue of the sky, I've got five or six blues at my disposal [...] I've had materials in my hands that are outside common use, with properties outside the ordinary, which have served to expand my language. So I dispose of a catalogue of raw materials, of 'tesserae' for writing, a little broader than someone without my technical training does. Plus, I've developed the habit of writing compactly, of avoiding the superfluous. Precision and concision, which I'm told are my way of writing, came to me from my trade as a chemist. As does the habit of objectivity too, of not letting oneself be easily taken in by appearances. As in the story of potassium, which I've told in *The Periodic Table*: sodium looks very like potassium, but when you come near it you realize that there's a difference [...] Also the habit of weighing words, of not trusting in words that are approximate – these are all cookery rules, nothing abstract about them: using a word only after investigating its significance and linguistic field. Then one can draw on the great reservoir of artisanal languages, which allow the rediscovery of old linguistic mechanisms [...] In this kind of operation my previous trade is useful: for me as an ex-chemist 'filter' means something more than it does to the layman. There's a wealth of concepts that have a precise meaning, and that can easily be put to good use, with effects that may be different to the ones I'm expecting, but which have an effect all the same. Everyone uses the word 'crystallize' incorrectly, because the concept has been lost, at least partly.[22]

He borrows hundreds of words and comparisons from his trade, conscious of the inexhaustible richness of a 'personal or almost personal store', of a repertoire which made him feel 'as if I enjoyed an unfair advantage over my new writer colleagues':[23]

> [...] because everyone knows roughly what 'filter' means, but what 'sublimate' means only a few people know. It's not by chance that this operation has such a beautiful name and that only chemists know its essence. The word 'essence', which I've just used, comes from chemistry too. Essence is the *ousia* of the Greeks, the inner being of things: the chemist must really know the essence of manganese or of potassium alum.[24]

Thus he gives a demonstration in reverse of the harm caused by the traditional and very Italian split of scientific from humanist culture; which he did not fail to lament once again, adding:

> It would be very important, in my view, for this historic barrier to be dismantled, that is for the person with a scientific and technical education to have a humanist culture and vice versa.

The mental habit of concreteness, he often recognized, came to him from the 'habit of delving into matter, the yearning to probe its composition and structure, to predict its properties and behaviour'[25] slowly and carefully, exercising patience, another quality he had been taught by his trade:

> Naturally it was no pleasure to spend a week analysing a mineral, but it allowed us to develop other qualities, those of perseverance, of not being discouraged, of assiduously applying oneself. Today [...] the question arises in chemistry whether it's worth teaching the manual method of analysis any more, so-called systematic analysis, which requires a lot of time and perseverance. Now you just take a tenth of a milligram and put it in the machine, a bit like what happens in clinical analysis, which is capable of giving an electrophoresis in the space of a few minutes. Before, separating proteins was very hard work. It's clear that for practical results it's better to have a machine analysis, yet manual analysis, like all manual jobs, has its formative value, it's too close to our animal origins to be neglected. We must not forget how to use our hands, our eyes and our noses. I am very happy to have trained my nose, I can still identify certain functional groups with my nose faster than infrared spectroscopes and gas chromatographs can. In this way the trade of the chemist integrates you as a complete person who doesn't neglect any of his faculties. Both as a student and as a varnish technician I've always tried to exploit to the full the help that my eyes, fingers and nose can provide.

In concluding the discussion with Tullio Regge on the debt he owes to his profession, Primo Levi does not overlook the other side of the coin. He says:

> Despite all this, after describing how much I owe to my old trade and my gratitude for what it has given me (including a pension and the opportunity to travel halfway around Europe on business), I must add that the day I left was a day of liberation for me. It felt as though I were walking on clouds, as you said about passing your school-leaving exam. A purer, less contaminated liberation than the one that brought an end to the Lager and took place against a

> backdrop of massacre and death. The day after I resigned I spent walking around Turin on a weekday: a weekday, you understand? No more timetable, no more crossing the city at rush hour every day, no night-time calls because a fuse had broken or a downpour had flooded the cable shaft.[26]

All the anxiety was over too. 'It seems to me', Giorgio Bocca suggested to him, 'that one of your worries was fire'.

> I was afraid of accidents in general, but fire was a nightmare of every night. I am at peace with myself for managing to come out of it with clean hands, without fatal incidents.

Bocca remembers in particular two stories of fire from *Other People's Trades:* the one about the nest of embers in a drum of sawdust: 'the other about how terrified he'd been when a solvent became electrified and ignited.'[27]

> Yes, it happened because I made a mistake, which fortunately didn't result in a disaster. I learned later that the operation was wrong, that using carbon dioxide fire extinguishers to prevent a solvents fire was a mistake; to extinguish one it's OK, but to prevent one it's very bad indeed, it can start a fire instead. But these are things that don't get taught. I graduated in chemistry with the highest grades, but they didn't teach me anything as far as preventing accidents was concerned. I wonder if they do even now. I think that technicians should pass an exam on the prevention of accidents before anything else. on the prevention of accidents first of all.[28]

He identified some incidents in his professional life as the only real mistakes he had ever committed, when Dina Luce asked him point blank: 'Are there any mistakes that have stayed with you and that you regret?' He searched his memories and said:

> It really seems conceited to me to say no, but no really big mistakes come to mind […] But yes, I committed many in the factory, when I was the manager: I've taken wrong initiatives, I've let things be done that shouldn't have been done, taken on people I shouldn't have taken on, dismissed people I shouldn't have dismissed. And yes, I was guilty of two fires, which didn't cause serious damage, however. I'd say that my mistakes almost all happened during my active life – as they would....[29]

He derived morals from this, delicately expressed. For example, that mankind today is 'condemned and accustomed to living in a world where everything seems stable but in fact isn't, in which terrifying powers (and I'm not just talking about nuclear arsenals) sleep but only lightly'; that learning to do something is different from learning something; that in today's ever more complicated world 'each of us needs am increasingly refined and up-to-date expertise'.[30]

One journalist, worried by the years of lead, wanted the writer's opinion as the chemist he had been. He asked: 'You're a chemist, do you want to talk a bit about chemistry? Let's consider mankind as a chemical system: is it reaching an optimum stage or is it becoming corrupted?' Primo Levi replied with initial hesitation, then went on ever more confidently:

> The question is difficult; it's taken me by surprise. To say that progress is happening today is clearly controversial. It certainly exists in some fields: life is getting longer in almost all countries, especially in those where it is still very short. It's getting longer despite everything, despite epidemics and hunger. This can be called pure progress: the overall suffering of mankind has diminished, if only because there are no longer so many infectious diseases. But certainly in other fields there's no progress: for example, there's no moral progress, we're no more moral than we were a hundred or a thousand years ago [...] What else? I wouldn't deny that there's been very rapid progress in knowledge: the things we now know about particles and the cosmos are fundamental, we have learned more in the last ten years than we've done since Plato. And it seems to me that this is a common asset, maybe one still to be exploited, but it exists; it's likely that in twenty years, when the nuclear quarrel has been overcome, we'll arrive at the indefinite production of low cost energy. That could be a great liberation of mankind from suffering. I'm not sure of any of this, but I can see a goal to aim for, and for that reason I am not an outright pessimist.
>
> *The progress of mankind is on the rise, then. Yet we have diseases that seem incurable by progress, I'll name just three: cancer, terrorism and heroin. Isn't progress rather an original sin, the desire to bend nature to our evil instinct for power?*
>
> It's likely that it is, but we started down that road thirty million years ago, when humanity began. For as long as human beings have existed they've raped the nature around them [...] in short we're born that way, it's part of our nature, we wouldn't be what we are otherwise. As for the three incurable illnesses, I wonder if it's legitimate to call cancer

> incurable today. Fifty years ago diphtheria was incurable and now it's almost disappeared. I wonder if it's not part of our experience, our common sense, our logical ability, to work it out; I think it is [...] How many, as a percentage, are struck down by heroin or terrorism? It's true, they're loathsome things both of them, but how many people die from terrorism? Much fewer than from road accidents. So it's a bogeyman, a Medusa, but in fact it's a very marginal phenomenon.
>
> *So, your conclusion on the system 'mankind' is positive?*
>
> It's a tangle of positive and negative data. Which side should we choose? The sum of pain a man feels in his life? The years he lives for? Both? I wouldn't know which to choose. I would say both. I still remain quite optimistic. There have been fluctuations, wars [...] But I think that the net balance today is probably still positive. Certainly a mother suffers less now than she did a hundred years ago. Today the number of hours worked in a factory is eight, tending towards seven. People used to work for fourteen, and in worse conditions.

Primo Levi had the reserved character, the seriousness and the tenacity typical of what he identified as his third root: the city in which he was born and grew up. He spoke about it, during a lecture tour in Switzerland, when he hadn't yet conceived of Libertino Faussone, the Turinese protagonist of *The Wrench*, his alter ego. He told a lecturer from Bern who asked him if being Piedmontese, and in particular from Turin, had marked the man and the writer:

> I am very fond of my small homeland. I was born in Turin, my ancestors were all Piedmontese. I discovered my vocation in Turin. Here, I've studied; I've worked; I've lived all my life; I've started a family; I've written and published my books with a publisher from here, who is internationally famous. I love the city: its dialects, its streets, cobblestones and boulevards; its hills, the mountains that surround it and that I climbed as a young lad. I like the rural and mountain origins of its people, the conscientiousness of its labourers, the flair of its artisans, the rigour of its technicians. Now that I've been catalogued as a 'writer', when someone asks me if being Turinese has influenced the choice of my second trade I reply that no, it had nothing to do with my becoming a writer. On the other hand it certainly does have something to do with my way of writing, which is influenced in large part by my trade as a chemist, but also by having grown up in a sober, down-to-earth and symmetrical city, a city of technology where I have dug a niche for myself.[31]

He affirmed elsewhere that his adherence to Turin was total, that between him and the city a 'rhythm of correspondence' had been created. This was also true stylistically, as he implied in his last interview.[32] Discussing *The Wrench,* the journalist Roberto Di Caro asks him: 'Faussone's work is building, polishing, a bit of *bombé*.[33] Is it the same for you?' He replies:

> There isn't much difference between building a laboratory device and building a good story. Both need symmetry. Both need fitness to the goal. What's superfluous needs to be removed. What's indispensable needs not to be left out. And in the end it all needs to work.
>
> *Writing is a technical problem too?*
>
> For me it is. Besides, I've always dealt with technical problems: planning, production, sales. For twenty years, even when I was already the company manager, I spent my time in the laboratory, the brain of the factory. I did some building work there with my hands, small scale, of course. I miss that work, which is so precise, so focussed on a goal, the results of which are seen the same day or a few days later, and not after five or six years, as with the big projects.
>
> *Is writing a less precise job?*
>
> On the contrary, for me it's a very precise job [...] It seems to me that the decisive element in narrative must be a well-calculated balance between the necessary and the superfluous. I read a bit of everything, but I prefer the writers who don't indulge too much in the superfluous. Well, I very much like Sterne's *Tristram Shandy*, too which is full of digressions, or Stefano d'Arrigo's overflowing *Horcynus Orca*.[34] But I'd never write like that. My books – I think I can boast of this – don't contain anything that's superfluous. It comes naturally to me to refrain from adornment, from additions put there just to make the page look nice.

This is the 'rhythm of correspondence'. The interviewer grasps it and observes: 'A very Piedmontese trait, that.' The writer agrees:

> Probably, yes: the object is an object, there's no need for flourishes and circumlocutions. Certainly, we too had the Baroque, but it came from outside, and in Piedmont we cut down on its affectations and frills. The fact is that while the rhythm of poetry makes it a close relative of music, the literary text is in a way a relative of manual labour. One makes, at least mentally, a plan, a design, and then one tries to carry out the work as much as possible in keeping with the plan. Naturally, as I've made

> Faussone say, it's much less dangerous to write a book than to build a bridge: if a bridge collapses it can cause a lot of damage, including to people. If a book collapses it only causes damage to its author.

From which we see that Primo Levi, who aims to be a writer who sticks to essentials, already is one. And when Giorgio Bocca asks him, 'How have you experienced living in a city where big companies and intellectuals live side by side? In other words, how do you, as a Turinese intellectual, feel about Fiat?' his reply starts from his personal experience in the factory, then moves to a general judgement, more as a citizen than an intellectual.

> I must say that I've avoided any relationship with Fiat, as has my boss; we've managed to run the company for thirty years without ever being either friends or enemies, clients or suppliers. We remain neutral. I realize that some of Fiat's choices are harmful for the city; others have been useful to it, there's no doubt about that. One can't make a straight choice, I at any rate don't feel able to write either Long live Fiat or Down with Fiat on the wall. There's a for and an against. That Turin owes some things to Fiat is beyond dispute; that it owes some of its greatest defects to Fiat is equally beyond dispute.

'As for Einaudi', Bocca reflects, 'there's a typical case of non-communication. For so many years company and town have gone their separate ways.' Now it is the intellectual who replies:

> Yes, that too is quite a typical case. Maybe one of the links that still bind me to Einaudi is precisely that.

This conversation touches on another of the recurring themes in Primo Levi's writing: the study of the Piedmontese dialect, which he loved because 'it is mine, the dialect of my childhood, the language that my father used with my mother and my mother with shopkeepers',[35] which he was sorry to see decline, and dedicated not only *The Wrench* to saving, but also, with loving attention, several of his stories. Bocca recalls the incident mentioned in 'The Squirrel', in which the author introduces his aunts to a gentleman by the name of Perrone, which they immediately transform into Prùn. Primo Levi admits:

> Language is an unrequited love of mine. I would have liked to have been a philologist and studied it seriously. But things didn't go that way, and I've had a completely different trade. Still, I've picked up a few languages, I speak French, English and German more or less well, and I've always been very interested in why words are used the

> way they are. So yes, 'Prùn' means lots of things in Piedmontese: squirrel, rabbit, sometimes even guinea pig. It seems to correspond to the Latin *pronus,* and the whole thing fascinated me: squirrels are always more or less prone, when they're on their haunches or when they're on all fours, as their forepaws are shorter than their hind paws, so they always lean towards the ground. In any case I was struck by the fact that those old aunts of mine – deaf, uneducated and provincial – had immediately reconstructed the real name of Signor Perrone: Perrone was a false name, his real one was 'Prùn'.[36]

Primo Levi's two debts, to chemistry and to Piedmont, combine when he expresses his dedication to writing clearly and economically ('my literary model is neither Petrarch nor Goethe'), and his conception of writing as public service, as work well done:

> I'm not sure if my plan and aim are reflected in what I write, but my intention is this: I see the trade of writing as a public service which must work. The reader must understand what I write. Not all readers, because some are almost illiterate, but the majority of readers, even if they're not very well prepared, must have access to, must receive my communication – not message, that's too lofty a word – but my communication. It must be a working telephone, the written book, and I think that chemistry taught me those two qualities: concision and clarity.[37]

There aren't many pages Primo Levi gives to mountains, but they're among his best and best known. His story of climbing the Sbarüa peak with Sandro Delmastro still hangs on the wall of the mountain hut at the foot of that terrifying ascent. Together with a nerveless account of mountaineering, it contains the extraordinary portrait of a friend, and friendship was like a seal for the writer: 'Each of us carries the imprint/Of the friend met along the way,' as he said in a poem. In November 1982 writers and mountaineers met at the Museo della Montagna in Turin, to discuss the rift between mountain culture and the written word. During the meeting *Tuttolibri* carried out a survey on the theme: how important are mountains for a writer? Primo Levi replied:

> My mountain years coincided with the years of my youth, and therefore with years of danger and suffering. That experience was precious to me, because I learned some fundamental virtues in the mountains: patience, doggedness, endurance; and other things which are not virtues, but equally providential: how to cope with fatigue, hunger, thirst and hardship. And finally: when people are roped together they form a bond that lasts their whole lives.[38]

In a television conversation with the musicologist Massimo Mila, a famous mountaineer and partisan, he recalled the formative influence of the mountains on his generation. To open the programme, an actor read the passage from 'Iron' in *The Periodic Table*, in which Levi describes his youthful climb with Sandro and their bivouac in the freezing night, writing nostalgically of the taste of 'bear meat', 'which is the taste of being strong and free, free even to make mistakes, and to be master of one's destiny.' He was quiet for a moment, then commented:

> [...] seen from many years' distance now, those training grounds were real ones. Not just those, of course. Also serious mountaineering, which I've practised too to some extent, though certainly much less than Massimo Mila. I think that without that preparation, without that unintentional, unconscious preparation in the mountains, my generation wouldn't have lived through the war and the resistance as well as it did. Maybe it wouldn't have lived through it at all, maybe it wouldn't have survived. I think that we learned some of the fundamental virtues there; those of enduring, of holding out, of not losing faith, of preparing for danger and the unexpected. I don't know if Massimo Mila agrees...

Mila: 'I agree. And in the mountains even the least well-suited people learn to use their hands, and to straighten themselves out, as was necessary during the resistance.' Levi agrees with him:

> Yes, very true. In fact for most of us, entering the resistance was called 'going into the mountains': they were synonyms, although there was also an urban resistance, and ones in the plains and hills. But the expression that took root immediately after 8 September[39] then: let's go into the mountains.

And on the wave of memories shared with the warm and gentle 'Commissar Mila', he lets himself be carried away into talking about a period of his life which he generally did not like to linger on, because he suffered from its inadequacy. This time he does so, with a kind of melancholy self-pity.

> My partisan experience was very brief and unsuccessful, even clueless: because I didn't get to it in time. None of us, in the tiny brigade I belonged to, had any military experience, which can't be improvised or inherited; like any other trade it needs to be learned. None of us possessed weapons, and if we had possessed them we would have been incapable of using them. I can tell you my only exploit in the month and a half or so of my partisan experience. I was in the Aosta Valley, in the area of Col de Joux; we were unarmed and looking for arms

> wherever they could be found, since they weren't yet being parachuted in by the Allies, that contact hadn't begun yet, at least not for us. Well: word had reached us that in a side valley above Nus there was an old socialist who had a barn two hundred metres up, and in this barn, under all the hay, there were sub-machine guns. and we needed to go and get them. We left, on foot naturally, at night, we walked all those kilometres from Col de Joux to Nus and then from Nus up to the barn, we emptied the barn (which was hard labour) in the middle of the snow, and we found one magazine of wooden bullets, of the kind that are used for practice. One. And being civilized people, we put all the hay back in place before climbing back down the valley.[40]

The way mountaineering and resistance had been seen as one also emerges in the interview with Giorgio Bocca, who had been a famous partisan commander and who in recalling the writer's friendship with Sandro Delmastro said to him: 'The figure of Delmastro is an introduction to Piedmontese anti-fascism. It seems that at first that anti-fascism was based around mountaineering. To conspire you went into the mountains.' Levi confirmed:

> Indeed. It seemed at that time that the world had been reduced to forty people: they were those who were in the mountain refuges, clinging to rock-faces, at concerts, and sometimes in via Roma. It seemed that the world had been reduced to a very few.

Bocca: 'It was also a minority, elite world of a few Protestants, a few Jews…'

> Yes, it's true: the marginalized. The marginalized tend to come together. And to recognize each other.[41]

The journalist Alberto Papuzzi centred his whole interview with Primo Levi[42] on the mountains, rightly convinced that if the mountaineering feats of this famous writer (it was March 1984) were not extraordinary, they were still part of his story. He went to meet him at the Einaudi publishing house and was greeted with 'a kind smile with just a touch of irony'. Levi recounted:

> I started going into the mountains when I was thirteen or fourteen. My family belonged to a tradition that believed the mountains are healthy, a bit like the background Natalia Ginzburg describes in *Family Sayings*[43]. It wasn't mountaineering strictly speaking, not rock-climbing [...] You just went into the mountains for the contact with nature.

His first encounter was a dramatic and humiliating shock, which showed the necessity of making the means fit the ends you were seeking to achieve:

> I was in Bardonecchia and we'd decided to go on an outing – I, who was fourteen, another boy of the same age, and a sixteen-year-old who was our self-appointed guide. The idea was to reach the Valle Stretta across the Magi range. Except that we left in the afternoon, without eating and without backpacks. By the time we reached the top it was almost dark; we could see a treacherous drop below, and at the bottom the dim light of a refuge, I no longer remember its name. We started yelling, and a team of mountaineers came up to rescue us. They shouted down: '*Son mac dei gagno brodos*' ('They're just a bunch of little pests'...). Then they tied us together like salamis and lowered us down by lantern-light.

He did real climbs, without a guide, around the age of eighteen or nineteen: 'out of a desire for adventure', notes the interviewer, 'but also for independence, for having a stab at it, for going it alone'.

> *What did it mean to go climbing, alone, for a young Jew at the end of the thirties, in the climate of the racial laws?*
>
> It was an absurd form of rebellion. You fascists discriminate against me, isolate me, say that I'm someone who's inferior, *unterer*: well, I'm going to show you you're wrong. I promoted myself to lead climber, without experience and without training: rashness was part of the game. My first time alone was on the east ridge of the Herbétet. Our group didn't even have any contact with the Cai. It was a fascist institution and we were against all institutions: the mountains, precisely, represented freedom. Maybe there was also an obscure need to prepare ourselves for the future.

The figure of Sandro Delmastro is once again in the forefront, in this conversation: his lessons merge with those of the mountains, equally rugged and clear. What were they? No conveniences; no concessions to fashion; suffering, sweat, confrontation with risk. Was it an unconscious training for the future? Primo Levi is certain: Sandro knew that he would end up defeated, and he prepared himself.

> We never went up the Sestriere because there were cable cars, and cable cars were worse than the devil! No padded jacket, no new shoes, and the Cai guide was useful only for doing the opposite of what it advised. Our equipment was minimal: my sister had given me a hammer, a couple of karabiners and three pitons. That was all the gear I had. Our strength, both physical and technical, had to be pushed to the limit every time. I remember one Easter, when Daladier[44] had just replied 'Jamais' to Mussolini. It meant war, but we didn't think about

> that. Sandro Delmastro, Alberto Salmoni and I set off on foot one night from Bard to Champorcher; the next day, on skis and with thirty kilos each in our backpacks, we had to cross as far as the so-called Finestra di Champorcher, then descend, go back up the Valeille, reach Piantonetto, and aim for the Gran Paradiso...It was an idea of Delmastro's; the harder the task, the happier he was. I didn't make it past Cogne...But I'd read the great mountain writers too – Lammer, *Fontana di giovinezza*[45], and Whymper and Mummery. Their ideas had come down to us through their pages – that one should measure one's strength against extreme conditions, and that it's essential always to do one's utmost.

This romantic vision of the mountain, with the two young chemistry students in plus-fours and old boots, has as its constant counterpoint the mountain as scientific object and discovery, an instrument for escapism and freedom, fascination and research:

> I thought I'd found in chemistry the answer to the questions philosophy leaves unsolved. I was looking for an image of the world more than a trade. Now, the passion for the mountains was a partner of the passion for chemistry, in the sense of finding in the mountains the elements of the periodic table, trapped in the rocks and ice, and trying to decipher through them the nature of the mountains, their structure, the reason for the shape of a gully or the architecture of a serac [...] Once, at the Picchi del Pagliaio, Sandro grabbed onto a crystalline handhold, which broke off in his hands. He showed it to me without losing his composure, remarking that this kind of crystal starts to crumble 'on the 001 plane', which is stereographic terminology [...] So the mountains for us were also exploration, a substitute for the voyages of discovery of the world and ourselves that we couldn't go on; the voyages recounted in the books we read – Melville, Conrad, Kipling, London. Our homespun equivalent of those voyages was the Herbétet.

He continued his mountaineering for many years after Auschwitz, climbing extremely strenuous stretches of the Testa Grigia alone: 'I wanted to show myself that I was still capable, although I was over forty.' And since friendship and mountaineering were synonymous to him, when he abandoned the peaks for long Saturday and Sunday walks he always went with old friends: with Norberto Bobbio and his wife; with Bianca Guidetti Serra and Nicoletta Neri; with Silvio Ortona, who was his cousin and with whom he had shared the failed climb of Monte Disgrazia in the true story 'Weekend', four delicious pages of *Lilith*. He had first tried to write a mountain story in his youth:

> I never finished it, it's unpublished and will remain so, because it's really no good. It contains the whole epic of the mountains, and the metaphysics of mountaineering, the mountain as key to everything. I wanted to represent the sensation you feel when you're climbing, with the line of the mountain above you closing off the horizon: you climb, you don't see anything but that line, nothing else – then unexpectedly you cross it, you find yourself on the other side, and in a few seconds you see a new world, you're in a new world. That's, that's what I'd tried to express: the crossing. Then I'd read the story to my friends: it wasn't worth much.

Papuzzi: 'After 8 September 1943 Primo Levi went looking for his "crossing" in the mountains again, and it wasn't about metaphysics this time, but about taking sides and fighting.' And from that moment on, having 'eaten bear meat' was doubly useful for him: because the unforgettable taste of freedom remained within him all his life; and because having tasted it was one of the factors in his escape from the slaughter of his people.

It was in 1980 that Einaudi's Giorgio Bollati had the idea of asking certain writers to settle their accounts with the books they had read over the years that had proved fundamental to them. Primo Levi accepted the proposal willingly and rapidly fulfilled it, spurred on by his primary impulse of curiosity, 'because', he noted, 'it is agreeable to experiment and to observe the effects'. *The Search for Roots* however, which came out at the end of February 1981, remained the first and only text of the planned series. But according to Geno Pampaloni in *Il Giornale*, if any other authors *had* attempted the challenge, the results would never have 'the clearness of Levi's confession', which in listing the books that had been important to him, and explaining the reasons why, constitutes 'a sort of indirect autobiography, a taking stock of his life'.[46]

A self-portrait, then, and the most complete one the writer has given to us. He was perfectly aware of this, admitting in the preface the high cost of the enterprise, and which was 'not empty, or superficial, or gratuitous'. He expanded on this: '[...] I felt more exposed to the public, more as though I were giving everything away, when I was making these choices than when I was writing my own books. Halfway through the journey I felt naked.'[47]

Perhaps it was this revealing of himself, so unusual for him, which meant that after the broadside of reviews there were no interviews on this collection of texts annotated with brief, pithy comments. Primo Levi called *The Search for Roots*, jokingly, 'half a book'; but he did not think it was a secondary work, he had found writing it rewarding and he was particularly fond of it. When it came to answering a question on the subject (the journalist Giovanni Pacchioni from *Il Globo* had mentioned that literature comes out of the contact with great books), he declared:

> I really liked the idea of *The Search for Roots,* but in the context that Bollati had planned: a small series in which others were meant to appear, especially Calvino, Sciascia, Volponi etcetera. I liked it first of all for narcissistic reasons: opening up your stomach and showing your innards is an exhibitionist act that tickled me; also, next to my non-literary roots, there are my literary roots; indeed deliberately, even controversially, I included both literary and non-literary pieces: in deference to the truth of the facts. Truly I carry that Preface to Gatterman's *Organic Chemistry* within me to this day, and in its time it was far more than the preface to a technical book for me – it was the voice of a father, giving you instructions and prohibitions: *you shall do this, you shall not do that.*[48]

Beyond the anthology, he expressed himself sporadically in his letters, which were many, but irregular and erratic. Once was in reply to the same journalist from *Il Globo,* who had asked his opinion:

> I can't say much, because I'm a bad reader: I read very little fiction, I prefer non-fiction. But it's true, Italian writers tend to work on their own nests, their own regions: everyone chooses his own area and works within it, vertically more than horizontally.

In an interview done a few years before for *Il Ragguaglio Librario*, the journalist Claudio Toscani had asked Primo Levi: 'Who are your ancestors? Pushkin, Gogol, Tolstoy have been suggested.' He had replied:

> Thank you for the illustrious company, which astonishes me, because I have read little Tolstoy or Gogol and no Pushkin. [...] I couldn't say what authors have had a decisive influence on my way of writing; in different times I've felt attracted to different models: Thomas Mann, Manzoni, the Bible, Aldous Huxley, Hemingway, Conrad. I don't know whether I owe anything to some or all of them.

Speaking of the title 'mon maître' he'd awarded to Rabelais, he affirmed:

> I like Rabelais and often read him, but only rarely have I felt capable of feeling and writing in his wonderful way: I think that the only vaguely Rabelaisian pages of mine are those devoted to the centaur, in *Natural Histories*. I like Rabelais as one can like a friend, who isn't necessarily a model, but can be stimulating as a contrast, or as the occasion for an intellectual holiday. I called him 'mon maître' out of irony.[49]

He spoke of famous authors in September 1979 with Professor Grassano who – citing Conrad, Dante, Mann and Rabelais – asked which books had left a mark on him.

> Those by the writers you've cited, first of all. And a myriad of others. I'm an odd reader. I'm reading Proust now, for example, which is a bit late. Then I've read a lot of professional things that have been as useful to me as the greats you've cited. To write *The Wrench* I read a beautiful book on bridges, which seemed almost as fundamental to me as *The Divine Comedy*. But maybe now I've gone off the subject a bit, because these are not books in your sense of the word, they're documents. In general their writers pay little attention to style, and more to the things they write about. But that doesn't bother me, it doesn't disturb me, on the contrary I'd say that often an extremely lively and concrete style is born from the simple need to communicate. I've recently read a book by Spallanzani which I liked very much. He describes putting trousers on frogs to see what happens to fertilization [...] Now I'm reading the *Relazione sulla Cina* by Magalotti.[50] It's a little book of a hundred pages, but it's beautiful. *The Travels of Marco Polo* are just as beautiful too.[51]

Italo Calvino was of the view that *The Search for Roots* was more an encyclopaedia than an anthology and recognized the graphic at the beginning suggesting 'four possible routes through some of the authors in view' as the most important page of the book. It's in this graphic that Primo Levi reveals the four roads of his intellectual and human journey. There are two poles: black holes and Job. '[B]etween these two poles', wrote Calvino, 'which both represent a challenge to man's strength (most of all to the strength of his mind) from a universe which cares little for us, Levi lays out four meridians, four lines of resistance against despair; four answers which define his stoicism.' They are the salvation of laughter; the salvation of knowledge; and in the middle two lines, 'more than solutions or salvations, the moral stances that can be their basis'. On the one hand, awareness that 'mankind suffers unjustly', on the other, awareness of the 'nobility of mankind'. Between the four lines, Calvino also notes, 'there's a rapid succession of links, proof, if any were needed, of a consistency excluding all eclecticism'.[52]

It was the journalist and writer Rosellina Balbi who noticed that the eloquent page at the beginning of *The Search for Roots* foreshadowed to some extent the journey taken by the characters of the next book, *If Not Now, When?* It too sets out 'from oppression and injustice, and by coming to awareness, arrives at salvation'.[53]

Notes

1. The interview was broadcast as part of the programme 'Prima Pagina' on Mediaset Canale 5, 13 June 1985.
2. The story to which Giorgio Bocca is referring is 'Signs on Stone' included in *Other People's Trades* (trans A. Shugaar), in *Complete Works of Primo Levi* (New York: Liveright, 2015), Vol. II, pp. 2070-74.

3. From the interview cited on the programme 'Il suono e la mente', broadcast on 4 October 1982 on RAI Radio 2.
4. P. Levi, trans P. Forbes, *The Search for Roots: A Personal Anthology* (London: Allen Lane, 2001), pp.1-3.
5. *Lilith and Other Stories* (trans. A. Goldstein), in *Complete Works of Primo Levi*, Vol. II, p.1401.
6. P. Levi and T. Regge, *Dialogo* (Milan: Edizioni di Comunità, 1984), p.11 *passim*. Our translation; the book is available in English as *Dialogo* [Dialogue], translated by Raymond Rosenthal (Princeton, NJ: Princeton University Press, 1989).
7. Levi was reading the Italian translations (in a series published by Mondadori) of popular science books: P. De Kruif, *Microbe Hunters* (New York: Blue Ribbon Books, 1926); W. Bragg, *Concerning the Nature of Things* (London: Bell & Sons, 1925); A. Carrel, *Man, The Unknown* (New York: Doubleday, 1935); W.B. Pitkin, *A Short Introduction to the History of Human Stupidity* (New York: Simon and Schuster, 1932).
8. 'Popular Astronomy' and 'The Stars', books by the French astronomer Camille Flammarion, which Levi read in the original.
9. Lucretius wrote his poem *De rerum natura* [On the Nature of Things] in a style which Levi enjoyed, unlike the Latin texts taught in schools, which could be dry and stilted.
10. Cesare Lombroso, a criminologist and physician based in Turin in the late 19th and early 20th centuries.
11. S. Jesurum, *Essere ebrei in Italia* [Being Jewish in Italy] (Longanesi: Milan, 1987), p.96.
12. 'Leagues of combatants', the organization led by Mussolini, which gave fascism its name.
13. F. Camon, *Autoritratto di Primo Levi* [Self-portrait of Primo Levi] (Padua: Edizioni Nord Est, 1987), pp.13-4.
14. *The Search for Roots,* preface, p.4.
15. 'Prima pagina', Canale 5.
16. Gianni Milani, 'Al chimico va stretta la memoria del Lager' [Lager memory constricts the chemist] *PiemonteVip*, March 1986.
17. Levi and Regge, *Dialogo*, pp.17-18.
18. Camon, *Autoritratto di Primo Levi*, pp.17-18.
19. The interview was broadcast on the Piedmont regional edition of RAI 3 on 25 September 1984.
20. Roth (see Notes on the Translation and Note to Chapter One).
21. The main regional newspaper of Northeast Italy.
22. Levi and Regge, *Dialogo*, pp.48-50 *passim.*
23. *Other People's Trades*, in *Complete Works of Primo Levi*, Vol. II, p.2025 (from the essay 'Ex-Chemist').
24. RAI 3 regional edition interview.
25. *Other People's Trades* in *Complete Works of Primo Levi,* Vol. II, p.2024.
26. Levi and Regge, *Dialogo*, p.51.
27. *Other People's Trades*, in *Complete Works of Primo Levi*, Vol. II. See the stories 'Stable/Unstable', pp.2172-5 and 'The Force of Amber', pp.2149-53.
28. 'Prima Pagina', Canale 5.
29. Interview on 4 October 1982.
30. *Other People's Trades*, in *Complete Works of Primo Levi*, Vol. II, *passim*.
31. Swiss lecture tour, 8 to 12 November 1976. Primo Levi's books were published by Einaudi, Turin's famous publishing house.
32. Roberto Di Caro, 'Il necessario e il superfluo' [The Necessary and the Superfluous], *Piemonte Vivo*, No.1, 1987, p.53 and 'La fatica di scrivere' [The Struggle of Writing], *L'Espresso*, 26 April 1987. *Piemonte Vivo* is a periodical on Piedmontese economics, art and culture, published by the Cassa di Risparmio di Torino. The *L'Espresso* article was published with an introduction that expalined: 'Shortly before his death, in an as yet

unpublished interview, the writer spoke of his intellectual tiredness, convinced now that he had said everything. It is the most intimate confession of a just man in civilized despair.'

33. A French adjective meaning rounded or convex, from the resemblance to the common shape of a bomb. Here it means smoothing something, rounding it off.
34. An epic novel of more than 1000 pages, not divided into chapters, whose Latin title means 'Killer Whale' (Milan: Mondadori, 1975).
35. *Stories and Essays* (trans. A. M. Appel) in *Complete Works of Primo Levi*, Vol. III, p.2392 (from the story 'Fair as a Flower').
36. 'The Squirrel' is included in *Other People's Trades*, in *Complete Works of Primo Levi*, Vol. II, pp.2104-7. The interview with Bocca is the one broadcast on Canale 5.
37. 'Il suono e la mente', 4 October 1982.
38. Giorgio Calcagno, 'Per i nostri scrittori la montagna non è incantata' [For our writers the mountain isn't magic], *Tuttolibri* (*La Stampa*), 27 November 1982.
39. 1943, when the Armistice between the Italian Government and the Allies led the army to split into those who joined the Resistance and those who remained loyal to fascism and the German occupiers.
40. From the programme 'Bric-à-brac' broadcast by RAI 3 on 29 November 1983.
41. 'Prima Pagina', Canale 5.
42. Alberto Papuzzi, 'L'Alpinismo? È la libertà di sbagliare' [Mountaineering? It's the freedom to make mistakes], *Rivista della montagna,* year 16, no.61, March-April 1984, pp.106-9.
43. A semi-autobiographical book by the Jewish Piedmontese writer. Trans. D.M. Low (New York: Arcade Publishing, 1989).
44. An anti-fascist Prime Minister of France.
45. 'The Fountain of Youth' (Milan: L'Eroica, 1932), Italian translation by Raffaelo Prati of *Jungborn* [an archaic form of *Jungbrunnen*, fountain of youth], the autobiography of the Austrian mountaineer Eugen Guido Lammer, which became a cult classic in Italy and encouraged mountaineers to take risks. The Englishmen Whymper and Mummery wrote similar works.
46. Geno Pampaloni, 'Padri e figli' [Fathers and Sons], *Il Giornale*, 29 December 1981.
47. *The Search for Roots*, p.5.
48. Giovanni Pacchioni, interview cited. Gattermann is cited in *The Search for Roots*, pp. 74-6.
49. Claudio Toscani,'Incontro con Primo Levi' [Meeting with Primo Levi], *Il Ragguaglio Librario*, No.3, 1972.
50. 'Account of China', Count Lorenzo Magalotti's 1676 book on Fr. Johann Gruebel's three-year journey to the country (Adelphi: Milan, 1974).
51. G. Grassano, *Primo Levi* (Florence: Il Castoro/La Nuova Italia, 1981), p.10.
52. Italo Calvino, 'Le quattro strade di Primo Levi' [The Four Roads of Primo Levi], *La Repubblica,* 11 June 1981.
53. Rosellina Balbi, 'Mendel il consolatore' [Mendel the consoler], *La Repubblica*, 14 April 1982.

X

A Happy Creature

Giulio Einaudi discarded dozens of proposals for the cover image (there was a flight of birds; there was a Chagall violinist) and chose, on his own and with extreme care, the cover for *If Not Now, When?* Primo Levi confided in some of the publisher's friends:

> It's an oil painting by a Russian artist of the nineteenth century: a big field covered in snow on which is projected the blue shadow of an invisible tree. In the background there's a peasant woman, dressed in the costume of a century ago, walking along a barely verdant path carrying two buckets of water. At first sight I was left a bit perplexed by it, then I almost succumbed: it's an allusive image, chaste, clean. I would still prefer, if possible, that they cut out the peasant woman; that only the segment of snow with the long shadow of the bare tree remained.

But Einaudi prevailed and the woman with the buckets remained. The posters of the cover picture reached the bookshops at the start of April 1982, when the novel was published. It recounts the odyssey of a band of Jewish partisans travelling from the snowy wastes of Russia to Milan, the city from which they could reach the Promised Land. The book was an immediate success: because it was the only fully-fledged novel the Auschwitz witness had written; and because it was an adventure and war novel, a picaresque story built around historical events, a western whose characters were Jews with weapons in their hands. Nobody expected that from Primo Levi, despite his having written *The Truce,* which undoubtedly has its basis in the picaresque. The rush from the top of the bestseller ratings to the classic prizes was inevitable: *If Not Now, When?* won the Viareggio Prize in June and the Campiello in September. The author shed light on the matrix from which it was born, and why, at an international conference on Jewish writing, organized at the end of November 1982 by the Rockefeller Foundation in Bellagio, and then on a lecture tour of various American universities in September 1985:

> It's a novel, and its origin goes very far back in time. It developed essentially from two seeds. The most distant is my almost photographic memory of an incident on our return from deportation.

In October 1945, near the Italian border, we realized that the very long goods train that was taking us back to Italy had not sixty cars, but sixty-one. This is how I described it in *The Truce*:

'At the tail end of the train, travelling with us towards Italy, was a new car, crowded with young Jews, boys and girls, from all the countries of Eastern Europe. None of them looked more than twenty, but they were extremely determined and confident: they were going to Israel, taking any route they could and by any means they could. A ship awaited them in Bari. They had bought the train car and to hook it up to our train had been the simplest thing in the world, they hadn't asked permission from anyone – they had simply hooked it up. I was amazed, but they laughed at my amazement. "Is Hitler not dead?" their leader asked me, with the intense gaze of a hawk. They felt immensely free and strong, masters of the world and of their destiny.'

The more recent seed is the story that a friend, Emilio Vita Finzi, told me in 1971. In the summer of 1945, Finzi, who had himself been a refugee in Switzerland, volunteered to help the Jewish refugees who were pouring into Italy from devastated Central and Eastern Europe. They were pitiable, traumatized people who had lost everything: relatives, home, money, health. Everything except the hope of building a future for themselves elsewhere. Yet at the refugee centre in Via Unione, Milan, he'd seen a small number of refugees who belonged to a different group. They were young men and women who were sure of themselves, who refused the label of 'Displaced Persons': they insisted on being identified as partisans and told of how they had led guerrilla and sabotage operations against the retreating Nazi troops.

The two seeds remained dormant for a long time, but they were reawakened by the intergenerational debate that flared up a few years ago (around 1979) in Israel and elsewhere about how Jews had behaved when faced with the Nazi massacre: had they really let themselves be led to the slaughter without resisting? If so, why? If not, how many, when, where, and how had they resisted? In my view, it's a discussion that is deeply unhistorical and polluted by prejudices: as an ex-deportee and an ex-partisan, I know well that there are political conditions in which one can resist and others in which one can't. So it wasn't my intention to enter the debate, but I felt that there was a story worthy of being told: clearly, an historical novel; maybe also, in a more subtle way, a novel with a message; but primarily a very wide-ranging action novel. I wanted, moreover, to pay tribute to those Jews, however many or few they were, who in desperation had found the strength to

> oppose the Nazis, and who in that unequal fight had testified to their love of freedom and to the dignity of their people.[1]

There was another homage he wanted to pay, to:

> [...]the importance that Italy had for all Eastern Judaism, as a point of reference and as a hospitable country where there was no longer to be feared what was (and still is) to be feared in Poland and Russia.[2]

The first of the many interviews on *If Not Now, When?* was Rosanna Balbi's in *La Repubblica*:

> *I feel that, for the first time since* If This is a Man, *you've sensed a pressing, irresistible need to write. What's more, the period in which the action of* If Not Now, When? *takes place is more or less the same as the one in which the events of* If This is a Man *and* The Truce *unfold. Is there a reason for this return? Is it due perhaps to the rising tide of anti-Semitism?*
>
> No, I wouldn't say so. At least, if such a motivation was there I wasn't aware of it. What I did want to do was to show how false the accusation was – one that even came from Jews themselves – that the Jews remained inert and passive, letting themselves be led to the slaughter like sheep.

He acknowledges (he always will, to express his gratitude) the core of the novel: the story told to him by his friend of those proud Jewish partisans, strange migrating birds in the in the chaos of newly-liberated Italy. He went on:

> You will wonder why, after hearing that story, I waited ten years before setting to work. The fact is that at that time I was busy with other things, for example with my trade as a chemist. So I just jotted down a few notes. Then one day, when I was clearing out my drawer of unused ideas, I found this little bit of paper and decided to make a novel out of it. Except that Vita Finzi could no longer remember clearly how things had happened [...] So I had to read and research a lot of things, and almost a year went by between finding the bit of paper and writing the book. How did my research help me? To establish that there *was* a Jewish resistance movement, much more substantial in numbers but also in moral importance than it's thought to be. And it wasn't just a case of bands made up exclusively of Jews, but also of Soviet bands led by Jewish officers or soldiers. It's well documented in Soviet sources. Not that they speak explicitly about Jews: but names can tell you a lot.[3]

There was enough evidence , in other words, to take this position. Though it hadn't been possible – except for a few heroic exceptions – to fight back in the extreme physical and psychic debilitation of the camp, there were those outside the barbed wire who *had* fought. Even in the desperation of a wiped-out family, of a burned house, of a destroyed village, even in the anguished awareness that their homeland had become an enemy. Just like the characters of *If Not Now, When?* To the radio journalist Ennio Cavalli, who the morning after the Campiello Prize asks him if the novel returns to an ancient suffering, Primo Levi retorts:

> It seemed to me that it was worth developing a theme that isn't very well known in Italy. In Italy, knowledge of the participation of the Jews of Eastern Europe, as Jews, in the resistance of the Second World War is limited to the episode of the Warsaw Ghetto, glorious but unique. In reality, Jews resisted not only in other ghettos, especially in the Soviet zone occupied by the Germans, but also in the open field. They faced many difficulties, because the advancing Soviets didn't like either resistance movement, Polish or Jewish.[4]

If Not Now, When? thus takes sides. Its purpose, states the author:

> [...] can be linked to the controversy that has raged and is still raging between the younger generation and my own, which is accused of not resisting. Young Israelis feel bewildered when they consider their own extremist behaviour and the behaviour of their fathers and grandfathers, who let themselves be killed in their millions without reacting, according to the current historiography.[5]
>
> *Who are the protagonists of the story of a Jewish band, which is invented but true to the facts?*
>
> The characters of *If Not Now, When?*, about thirty of them, men and women, are Russian and Polish Jews: deserters from the Red Army, survivors of the ghettos and of the massacres of the Einsatzkommandos.[6] They don't have any definite political or ideological training. Only one woman professes herself a Communist and a Zionist. The others are moved primarily by the need to defend themselves, and by a vague desire for revenge, rehabilitation and freedom. They meet and join together 'like drops of mercury', individually or in groups, in the woods of White Russia and the marshes of Polesia,[7] sometimes accepted, sometimes rejected by the Soviet partisan formations. [...]
>
> Obeying Moscow's orders, they move to the west in order to stay behind the German lines, but also because they no longer have a

> country, a home or a family – and they hope to be able to start again in that Land of Israel, of which they have built themselves a mythical, thousand-year-old image. The hard life they've suffered – the endless marches, fights, round-ups and escapes, the daily hardships – has made them primitive and wild, like the other partisans they meet. But they haven't lost some traits that make them different: creative imagination; the old Jewish self-mockery that makes them immune from rhetoric; the taste for dialectical discussion; the conflict between their traditional mildness and the necessity of killing.[8]

Mario Miccinesi of *Uomini e Libri* thought he discerned, not just in this inner conflict but in the whole novel, a clear inclination to the value of non-violence. Does the author agree with this?

> There are no moralistic or edifying intentions behind this novel of mine. It's not a novel with a thesis: it's not aimed specifically at supporting any thesis, not even that of non-violence. All the same, every page of it contains disgust for violence, because I myself contain that and I've transmitted it by underground routes to many of my characters. Not to all of them, obviously, because every thesis requires its antithesis, as light requires shadow. Nor would it be right to depict as completely meek and resigned characters like mine, who have been overwhelmed not only by a pitiless war but also by the horror of the Nazi manhunts. In the times and places I've described (and unfortunately not only in those: one need only open a newspaper) human nature was under attack and in disarray. It swung tormentingly between the rejection of violence and the compulsion to exercise it, a wretched need people felt emerging from the depths of our animal heredity. My protagonist Mendel, after taking part (reluctantly) in a bloody reprisal action against the Germans, admits uneasily 'I feel better': he's ashamed of it, but he recognizes it.[9]

There is, observes the writer Roberto Vacca, more than a good story in the novel: 'there are important thoughts, moral teachings [...] the characters explain themselves, teach, show how one should live'. Again Primo Levi shields himself from the well-meant accusation:

> I didn't want to write a moral book at all. If it is one, that's a by-product. I wanted to write an adventure story, a western. And at the same time, I wanted to show the contribution of Jewish fighters [...] without making my characters saints or swashbuckling heroes. I read so many books on the subject. Then I wove together the facts I found. Almost all the things I tell really happened. Partisans did build a false drop-field and put out the signal fires of the real one, in order to steal

> the supplies dropped by the Germans. They did steal a railway carriage and hang pumpkins on the railway line to make the Germans think it was mine-strewn. And the relationships between the Jewish, Polish and Russian partisans – sometimes of tolerance, sometimes of mutual aggression – are historically accurate. On the other hand, the characters are invented: except the pilot of the Po-2 partisan plane, she was real.[10]

She was called Polina. The author explained elsewhere:

> [...] she was a Russian girl, the daughter of a rabbi, who really existed and perhaps still exists. She was the champion pilot on those extraordinary wooden planes that maintained the links between the partisan bands. Polina Gelman – I read this in a reliable, that is a Soviet, record – had done 860 missions. I stopped the story at her seven-hundredth.[11]

We know what Mendel, the watchmaker from Strelka (who is now with his wife and all the other peasants, Jews and Christians, in the grave they had to dig themselves) did and what he thought, but we do not know what he looks like because there is nothing about his face that distinguishes it from the others. He is the protagonist: he reflects, ponders and assesses; and we are always told what he is thinking, not what others are thinking about him. He is the first to speak and to appear. In front of him stands Leonid, with the restless eyes of one who feels he deserves better.

'Why does Leonid die?' *L'Unità* correspondent Laura Mancinelli asks.

> Leonid is born dead: he has too much death inside him. He tries to escape his destiny by falling in love with Line; when he can't have Line he desires and finds death. He too is based on a real person I knew [...] Line is the demonic woman, who makes men fall in love and doesn't fall in love with them, an almost biblical figure: it is not by chance that Mendel goes through the great seductress figures of the Bible in his mind when he thinks about her.
>
> *And Gedale, the partisan violinist?*
>
> Gedale is youth, adventure. But he too is modelled on a real person.
>
> *Near the border with Italy, Mendel begins to think more about philosophical questions. (Is killing so as not to be killed, or killing to avenge those who have been killed, any use in settling accounts? And doesn't violence add to violence, increasing its injustice?) And Gedale reawakens everyone's love of life with his violin, and they all sing and*

> *dance on the goods train bringing them south. Just then, the violin suddenly caves in the bottom of the violin falls out unexpectedly. The silence that follows is heavy with significance.*
>
> Yes, it's the realization of the new reality that awaits them the reality they must now confront, torn from their roots, without country, home, family, identity. The Palestine they seek is far away and problematic. The Gedalists have a long and difficult road ahead of them.[12]

The band's journey west is threatened by hostility, by prejudice, by ill-will. Roberto Vacca inquires:

> *But what is this racism that pushes Russian partisans to leave Russia? Do even the Russians, and at least some Poles, approve of the extermination camps built by the Germans? What was their racism – an unfair generalization that classifies all Jews as enemies?*
>
> No, that explanation would be too reductive, like Italian generalizations about the meanness of the Genoese.[13] There's no equivalent in Italy. It passed me by. Being an Italian Jew, I wasn't recognized in Poland and Russia. They were astonished. They said: 'But how can you be Jewish? Are there Jews in Italy? And what kind of Jew are you, if you don't speak Yiddish and you don't have sidelocks?' You see: what arouses hostility is the difference, of someone who should be the same as you: It's perceived as a betrayal. 'You're Russian, but you speak Russian badly.' With German it's even worse, because the German language and Yiddish resemble each other like man and monkey. For Jews, the monkey is the German. For the German, Yiddish is an offensive caricature. The same happens with physical traits. Animals use scent to pick out strangers; for humans there are other subtle indicators – dress, gesture, accent.

Difference as a source of intolerance. According to Guido Lopez, from the television programme 'Sorgente di vita', one of the keys to understanding the novel lies in the dialogue between the Jewish band leader Gedale and his Polish counterpart Edek. The author agrees:

> [...] when he is asked 'But why have you Poles persecuted the Jews?' Edek, who feels personally innocent, replies that Poland is a sad country: it's a besieged country, always crushed between powerful enemies, and so it lives on hatred. 'We Poles', says this man who doesn't hate anyone, 'are enemies of the Lithuanians, of the Czechs, of the Hungarians, of the Germans, of the Russians. And also of you Jews, because you haven't blended in with us.'

The other key to *If Not Now, When?*, thinks the interviewer, is a Hebrew word, quite difficult to pronounce, which literally means 'they will give'. Is that right?

> It's *V'natnu*: 'and they will give', 'and they will return'. It's introduced in a reprisal episode. The group of Jewish partisans liberate a Lager and kill the SS who were commanding it. Later, there's a brief discussion between the characters about whether or not they should claim responsibility for the killing. One cuts off the discussion and says 'I'll see to it'. He writes this word on the wall with coal: *V'natnu*, 'and they will give back'. It's a quotation, I think, from a psalm [...] And it's a palindrome. They're five Hebrew consonants, VNTNV, which can be read from right to left and from left to right: 'what you've done', it means, 'I can do too'.
>
> *And the title: is it true that it comes from a Hebrew song?*
>
> There's another story behind the title. It begins with the legendary Rabbi Hillel, quoted in the *Pirkei Avoth*, the sayings of the fathers, as the author of the maxim: 'If I am not for myself, who is for me? If not like this, then how? And if not now, when?', which probably had a very different meaning for Hillel than the one attributed to it afterwards. For example, the maxim – I'd call it a slogan – was one of the propaganda lines of early Zionism in Italy. 'If not like this, then how? – that is, 'If not with our own means, then how? 'If I am not for myself, who is for me?' – that is, if I don't help myself, who will help me? And finally 'If not now, when?' – in the very precise, very current sense that now was the time for the re-founding of the Jewish nation.[14]

That is as an allusion to a dreamed-of future. During a radio broadcast, Primo Levi pointed to the political and psychological dimension of his novel, expressed in the question of the title:

> The distant saying of Rabbi Hillel, interpreted simplistically, had been included in some Zionist songs of the last century. It seemed suitable to me as a title for this book, in which a certain aspect of Eastern European Zionism is the subject, that is Zionism as national redemption and as recovery of identity. And so I constructed a song which is attributed to a Jewish folk song composer and where the refrain is precisely: 'If not like this, then how? And if not now, when?'[15]

'But the title phrase', the presenter Luciano Luisi asks on the evening of the Campiello, 'can also mean: if not now, when will we be able to operate in a way that will leave behind a lasting memory of us? Is that the inner reason behind the book?'

> Without doubt. This is a book about the search for identity. Against the background of the Second World War and the complex story of European resistance, it is most of all about the search of these displaced and outcast people for themselves as they come together and start their march through the remains of Europe.[16]

'Why', Lopez asks, 'does the fighters' path finish precisely in Milan, in this courtyard of Palazzzo Odescalchi where we find ourselves now?'

> It finishes here because that makes an arc in space and time [...] They were steered in that direction, because it was known that in Italy, and particularly here in Milan, and more particularly still in via Unione, there was a junction, a necessary transit point. So they aimed confusedly for the Brenner Pass, for Verona, for Milan, for via Unione.[17]

An infinite journey, which for Roberto Bertacchini from *La Notte*, evokes the biblical exodus towards the land of milk and honey. 'Is that impression correct?' he asks.

> It's correct, also because it's typical of Judaism to look for its reflection in the past.

The journalist is thinking of the novel by Bassani, *The Garden of the Finzi-Continis*, and compares its protagonists, who try unsuccessfully to maintain a normal life in fascist Italy, with the pride of the Jewish brigade that has replaced 'Thou shalt not kill' with 'They will give back'. 'Can the themes driving the two novels', he inquires, 'be considered in that sense as alternatives?'

> They reflect two different aspects of the same reality. No people has just one side. Within each civilization one can distinguish different strands. In Judaism, there's a strand of mildness, of resignation; but there's also a resistance movement.[18]

Introducing the book to a Turin audience, the critic Lorenzo Mondo says: '*If Not Now, When?* marks a great innovation in Levi's fiction. It is the first time that he moves away from the habit, or the familiarity, or the friendship, of his own experience.'[19] Only the route taken by the band retraces the labyrinthine journey of *The Truce*. The rest is imagination, even when the author is mirrored in the protagonist:

Deep down, I identified with Mendel. I mean that he does what I would have done, or rather what I should have done if I'd been able to.[20]

Giulio Goria, from *Paese Sera*:

The exploits take place in remote, almost legendary places. Did you know them?

[…] when I was liberated by the Red Army I was transferred to White Russia. They were clearly keeping us hostage; waiting to see how it was all going to end. Finally, in October 1945 they put us on the craziest train in the world, which after 35 days, with tortuous detours across Russia, Poland, Romania, Hungary, Germany and Austria, finally landed us in Italy.[21]

Lea Canducci from *Avanti!*, on the occasion of the 53rd Viareggio Prize:

How much in your book is autobiographical?

Not much. Only the background: countries I've been in, but in very different conditions to my characters. In fact, I haven't lived through the exploits I recount: they're precisely the ones I haven't lived through. My partisan career ended with capture after only a few weeks. In a way I've transferred onto my characters the experience of active resistance, which in my own life I've only partly experienced.[22]

Guido Gola for the television programme 'Tuttilibri':

How did you manage to return to a narrative so close to that of your first books?

It was a bit of an account to settle and also a revenge. I told of a way of living through the tragedy of the Second World War that wasn't mine, and that I would have preferred to that of a prisoner, which I had to suffer in reality. Without meaning to write an exemplary novel, I tried to tell how not all Jews were like the Auschwitz prisoners, like us. Some had the courage and also the luck to be able to find a different path; they had the means to build their own future with their own hands.[23]

Ennio Cavalli for the RAI 1 News:

The novelist prevails, from the beginning, over the survivor. What guided that unprecedented transformation?

> It seemed to me and it still seems to me that I had used up the essential part of my autobiographical memories, both as an ex-resistance fighter and ex-Auschwitz prisoner, and also as an ex-chemist. So the only way to continue to write was to move lock, stock and barrel into the field of creation, of invention.[24]

Mario Miccinesi for *Uomini e Libri* wants an in-depth analysis. In his view, *If Not Now, When?* is not Levi's first invented novel, as the author himself and many critics maintain, though in it 'he has certainly given the most mature proof of himself as a writer'. The answer is thorough:

> The question seems to me mainly one of definition. Certainly, invention (in all senses of the term, including the classical one) is intrinsic to writing: one can't write anything valid without '*invenire*',[25] without finding something new, which wasn't there before—so there is no book without invention. What I've said in some interviews, and various critics have repeated, is only that in this last book of mine the level of invention is higher than in all my previous books (with the exception perhaps of *Natural Histories* and *Flaw of Form*: but those stories, which have nothing to do with reality, are a different thing altogether.) In *If This is a Man* and *The Truce*, there is no conscious invention: there may be some transfiguring, some interpreting or reorganizing of the facts, but no invention; I remember rigorously rejecting precisely that temptation. The things I told of were too burning and too recent: I didn't want to contaminate them; I didn't want the reader to have the merest suspicion that I had given any space to adornment, to exaggeration, to 'beautiful writing'. I allowed myself a bit more freedom in *The Periodic Table*, but above all in the two stories in the middle, which are *admittedly*[26] invented, but the book still has a documentary and autobiographical framework. With *The Wrench*, my journey towards invention takes another step. It's a book of its genre, in which I deliberately pushed my imitation of the protagonist's spoken language to an extreme, so much so that many readers mistook him for a person of flesh and blood. He isn't one, he is indeed 'invented'; but I constructed him from various people I knew and worked with when I was a chemist, people who had on real building sites the adventures I attributed to him.
>
> With *If Not Now, When?*, I burned the bridges, as far as that was possible for me. I resolved to write a novel in no uncertain terms: a historical novel, based on classical models. I admit that I began it without paying much attention to theories of historical fiction. It's a naturally hybrid literary genre, in which truth and fiction are merged.

> I tried (in the text, and above all in the final note) to be honest with the reader. That is, to ensure that no page could give rise to doubts, to confusions between the real and the fictional. The facts I narrate can be documented, so too can the historical background: but the characters are mainly invented. Indeed, my subjective impression during the act of writing was that invention dominated, proliferated. The characters coincide only in small part with ones I have met personally on my voluntary and involuntary journeys. For this reason, and also so as not to mislead my readers, who for the most part have learned to know me as the author of strictly documentary works, I've been careful to define this book as a novel.[27]

Anna Maria Rebaudengo for the RAI 3 television news:

> *How does one move from books of testimony to a real novel?*
>
> With a feeling of great freedom. A writer is always free; but a writer of memoirs is constrained if nothing else by his own memories and by historical rigour. Writing a novel – because this is a novel – on a historical foundation is different: it feels like flying.[28]

Piero Bianucci, correspondent for *La Stampa,* at the Carriello Prize:

> *What does* If Not Now, When? *represent for your writing career?*
>
> A beginning. It's my ninth book, but my first novel. It's been a pleasure, it's been fun. For eight months, I studied the Yiddish language and worked in archives, then I wrote for a year. The story and characters are fictional, but in essence it's all true [...] This book, like all my others, I wrote joyfully: I hope that comes across. I wanted to write a book on a rising note, a book of redemption if not exactly of liberation. But its optimism isn't simplistic: on the last page, there's the birth of a baby conceived during the tortuous wanderings of that band of Jewish partisans, but there's also the news of the atomic bomb falling on Hiroshima.[29]

The ending intrigues TV journalist Luciano Luisi:

> *What do those two signs point to?*
>
> They are two opposite signs, because I didn't want to finish the book on the purely optimistic note of the birth. I preferred to set it against the events in Hiroshima, out of a sense of honesty, of fairness. Our world today isn't made of optimism: it can't be. If there's optimism,

> there's also pessimism. I wanted to close with those two opposing signs to evoke the ambiguity we are living in.[30]

A few days after *If Not Now, When?* appeared, Einaudi had to rush out a 50,000 copy reprint. Primo Levi's book, fought over by the main literary prizes, was the bestseller of the season. Levi's cheerfulness in adversity involved the reader; and the incredible odyssey of those Russian Jews towards an uncertain promised land seemed to answer the expectations of the audience, who found in an adventure of forty years ago something which resonated with contemporary concerns. The critic for *Tuttolibri* asks:

> *For readers it's a return to a classical story, a traditional novel. Was that your intention?*
>
> It was my cynical intention. In the middle of this vapid discussion of whether the novel is alive or dead, I thought that it was better just to write one. The novel is always alive and always dead: it depends what people write. There can be a period in which experimenting with forms prevails over content; but then one needs to go back to storytelling, because there's need for it, a demand for it. It was my 'Columbus's egg'[31] to write a readable book: it's more difficult to write a book that's readable when it's also something else.

The 'something else' is linguistic experimentation: 'That prose, with its biblical cadences, which seems to come almost naturally off the page, must instead be one of the things you worked most carefully to attain. How did you do it?' Levi points to the works on the bookshelf next to his desk:

> Before writing the book I did eight months of preparation and total immersion. I stopped reading anything else; I read Yiddish history, Yiddish grammar, novels, to immerse myself in that Eastern European atmosphere that is full of biblical echoes. People of my generation still received a religious education and bore the imprint of the Bible within them. Having the characters talk in a biblical way is intentional. Their vocabulary and their proverbs are inspired by the Bible.
>
> *They also speak a vernacular language, your characters. There's a continual correspondence between biblical and Italian folk vocabulary. Is that calculated too?*
>
> Perhaps it is. There are common traits among all vernaculars, because they are concrete and proverbial. It's characteristic of them to lean on the support of proverbs, to seek ancient knowledge to support them.

> And then I was forced to reproduce a language that isn't mine: it came naturally to me to resort to Italian dialectal expressions.[32]

He goes into more detail with the correspondent from *Il Globo*, who is struck by the dual tension of both imagination and language.

> I tried in *If Not Now, When?* to write an adventure story, but also to stick to my linguistic interests. I'm Italian, and know a bit of German. My knowledge of Yiddish is very poor. I heard it spoken in the Lager without understanding it; so when I resolved to start this book, I felt the need and the duty to get some practice. I studied, I read, I found myself a grammar and a dictionary; also for practical reasons, because there's a Yiddish document I had to read: it's by a band who went through Rome, and wrote a kind of collective memoir in two different editions. I found it in Paris, in the National Library, and I laboriously translated it for myself: with the aim, as well, of seeing how one reasons, how one thinks and how one writes in Yiddish. In the process I absorbed certain expressions, which I then tried to transfer to my characters. I don't vouch for their accuracy because my knowledge is too superficial: it wouldn't astonish me if a genuine Yiddish speaker told me that mine is a reader's Yiddish. But I'll be happy if the Italian reader is satisfied.[33]

It happened as he had predicted. To Philip Roth, four years later, he reported:

> In Italy the book was very successful, in every respect. The same can be said for Britain and Germany, at least judging by the first reactions of the public and the critics. In the US, as you know, it was only moderately successful. Its *Yiddishkeit* [Jewishness] was judged to be superficial and based on common knowledge. In other words, American readers realized something that was true, that this is a Yiddish book written by an author who isn't Yiddish, but who has tried to become so studying texts and listening to stories.[34]

How successful the linguistic experimentation had been was something he always had doubts about, and he didn't hide them. He had run the risk quite deliberately:

> [...] but I wanted people to sense, in Italian, the flavour and the aroma of a language that isn't Italian. Though in the text the characters speak Italian, we understand that they're actually speaking Yiddish. So I had to master a bit of that language, which I didn't know and which I still know only a little.[35]

> [...] and which I pretend here to translate into Italian: this may result in a flavourless mixture, although I've tried to liven it up by drawing on proverbial and biblical sources. I realized, after all this, that the effort to construct dialogues in simple language even led to Piedmontisms – perhaps a legacy of *The Wrench*.[36]

Giulio Nascimbeni, *Corriere della Sera*'s correspondent for the Campiello Prize, is curious:

> *After the last line of the book there's a date: Turin, 11 January-20 December 1981. Why that precision?*
>
> Because it seemed right to give the dates of what had been a happy year for me. It felt like discovering a new trade: I was learning to create something from nothing. A new trade for me, since I'd always stuck to autobiography when I tackled certain themes.
>
> *What was your main feeling during your work? Liberation from autobiography?*
>
> The main thing was the pleasure of story-telling. At the beginning it was surprise at things I didn't know, which friends helped me to discover, I know people may laugh at this, but it really was total immersion. In the sense that for a year I did nothing and read nothing that wasn't relevant to this job.[37]

It was the longest planning stage in his life, then everything came by itself, with a kind of dizzying and intoxicating joy he spoke of many times, with rare spiritedness:

> When I began writing, I was fascinated by the fact that I was testing myself as a novelist, for the first time. I had to create an adventure out of nothing; I had to invent characters, with complete freedom. And I invented a whole herd of them – characters capable of roguish tricks, capable of dancing and shooting, of courage and fear. [...] Especially during the first part of the writing process, I had the strange sensation I'd put children into the world. But once they were born, they grabbed the lead, they rebelled, they stirred up union trouble, so to speak. They demanded the right to choose. And in fact they decided: especially in the stories about their relationships with women. I had a plan, which I then completely disregarded. I wanted to make Racinian heroes out of them, but instead they preferred ordinary, average roles, containing more toil than spectacular feats.[38]

In the message he wrote in Roberto Vacca's copy of the book, Primo Levi called his novel 'a transgression'. To the friend who asked him why, he answered:

> Because *The Wrench*, for example, had a simple plot, with a single character who tells concrete, contemporary stories. Whereas this is a real novel. It's a transgression also in a positive sense. Writing my first novel, it felt as though I'd removed a barrier. I spent a happy year writing this book. I've never felt so free to do whatever I like on the page: to give birth not to one but to fifteen children at the same time, and to direct them, make them fight, make them die. I'd never tasted such creative freedom before, though I later realized that these creatures, however disembodied, still share many properties with human beings. The idea of Pirandello's six characters taking on a life of their own is one I fully understood well only after writing this book.[39]

He'd referred to the comparison with Pirandello and with the ' great story' of Pygmalion in the very first interview about *If Not Now, When?*[40] And he had concluded:

> Of course, a character in a novel is a very strange creature. He's made of paper; he's drawn in black and white; he lives on a page. Yet one can fall in love with him, one can hate him: in short, one is emotionally involved. That happens even with characters created by other people. When one has brought a character to life one establishes with him – at least that's what happened to me – that singular relationship I was talking about, a reciprocal, collaborative relationship ...[41]

Sometimes even a relationship of conflict – as when, he confessed to the correspondent Giovanni Pacchioni, he should have killed off the tormented Leonid. But with one of the group's best loved characters, this was something he could not do:

> Dov died too, and I had to bring him back to life because I felt guilty. Killing off a character is criminal: I mustn't exaggerate, it's not like killing a person, but it feels a bit the same. There are traces of this obsession I have with characters in the two stories in *Flaw of Form* about the National Park for fictional characters. Because characters are nothings of ink and white paper, but in their own way they have bodies. It's difficult to give a philosophical definition of them: they're certainly not mammals, because they have their own way of reproducing, which we have complete control over. You, the author,

find yourself bestowed with unlimited powers. You can do what you will with a character: you can kill him; you can make him beautiful, omnipotent, perverse; you can make him suffer or be happy – and that has been a quite new experience, for me a feeling of childlike omnipotence.It's true: children build themselves worlds where they can do what they want. From that viewpoint, writing a novel is a regression.

Your heroes are humble people.

Heroes *are* humble: if they're not, they're not heroes, it's too easy for them. It seems to me that only those who find the strength inside themselves to make themselves heroes can really be called heroes. Those who are born heroes, like Siegfried or Achilles,[42] are invulnerable, and so less deserving .

Still, your characters want to enter into that other history, the history of the greats. In battle Dov invites Mendel to shoot, so as to win three lines in the history books.

That phrase is a quotation from the historian of the Warsaw Ghetto, Emanuel Ringelblum, and I imagined that Dov knew he was quoting him. In fact the revolt in the Warsaw ghetto really did echo through all the ghettos of Eastern Europe, arousing awareness and the will to resist.

Does your interest in the humble derive from Tolstoy?

I'm a bad reader of Tolstoy, but I can't deny that there's something Tolstoyan about my book, for reasons closely linked to its background. Russia is a country I know quite badly; so I had to build myself an image of it, partly on things I'd seen and lived through and partly on things I'd read. I admit that some of my landscapes are Turgenev's and some are Tolstoy's. But the fact that my characters are Tolstoyan is a lucky coincidence. Maybe it's because we write about the same things: about war and peace and Russia. My characters are Jewish, but they're also Russian, and I've known many Russian Jews: they are singular hybrids. Gedale, for example, is Polish, but he is from Białystok, which is on the border, and his father is Russian. In Gedale, I've tried to convey the most sympathetic and amusing aspects of the Russian character: the imprecision, the tendency to improvise, the daydreaming to the detriment of plan, rigour and reason.

You say yourself that Russians are either crazy or boring.

That too is a quotation, but I don't know from whom. It was said to me once when I went to Russia on business: 'Remember that Russians are either crazy or boring and three quarters of them are boring.' I verified this: three quarters are civil servants, who are boring by definition; their job is to be boring bureaucrats, that's what they're there for. The other quarter are mad people.[43]

Among the cultural influences Levi acknowledged in his book, the *Tuttolibri* journalist is struck by the reference to Chagall's painting. He rereads the passage to the author : 'a dark and snowy sky, in which perhaps a large silvery fish is swimming, along with a bride dressed in white and a green ram, its head down'.

Is this a casual reference?

No, it's a precise homage. Chagall was born in Vitebsk. He left his country early, but Russian Jewish culture remained inside him. The skies of the book, those low skies which one's head touches, are Chagallian. The character of Gedale, the partisan with the violin, is Chagallian. In Chagall, one finds an intersection between the Jewish spirit and the Russian spirit: a dazed, topsy-turvy poetics.

Do the contradictions of certain characters also belong to that dazed poetics? For example, the prayer of Mendel, the protagonist: 'Let the war end, Lord God in whom I do not believe'?

Mendel was educated by a rabbi; later he worked in the kolkhozes;[44] then he entered the Red Army, and presumably also the party. So he's in conflict, and he can even pray to a God whom he believes he doesn't believe in. Let's bear in mind that he finds himself in an extreme situation: and in that situation, even a secular man can pray, or feel the wish to.

But the question about God occurs on so many pages of the book. Is it legitimate to draw a sense of religiousness from it?

I'm not religious, I never have been, not even in conditions like Mendel's. I was at peace with myself for not having felt even in Auschwitz the need to pray. I said to myself 'Well done: if you prayed now you'd be a coward.' But writing about characters like these I took on another personality: an author gets infected by his characters.

And he takes on their hopes, and he is spurred on by their desperate awareness of having nothing left. He can only lead them onward, on the road to Aliyah, the going up towards the land the Lord promised Abraham. Yet only one character in the novel is openly Zionist.

> *What is your attitude towards Zionism?*
>
> It isn't stated, but I think it can be guessed at. I considered Zionism a guiding idea and a political necessity, then. Those people could only follow words that had a biblical form. Today the question has become complicated, because Palestine is a geographical centre of frightening tensions, forced into wearing and extremely costly defence measures, which also encourage reckless and politically misguided actions. Zionists imagined a farming country then. Today Israel has become a military and industrial country.[45]

Some people would have liked Primo Levi to categorise his book. People such as Giulio Nascimbeni, who asked him:

> *Did you want to write an epic novel?*
>
> I would say that the term epic goes a bit beyond what I intended, and I'm not sure the book deserves it. Of course, it's a story with a lot of characters, which concerns one of the great tragedies of this century, the Second World War[...]but I've deliberately tried to deglamorize it, to avoid everything that could smack of hagiography and the classics. I've created average characters, full of defects: some are vulgar, others are violent, others are uncertain; and the protagonist himself is very doubtful.[46]

He expressed similar uncertainties to the correspondent from *Avanti!* who tried to persuade him to define *If Not Now, When?* as an epic adventure rather than a novel:

> I wanted to write a novel. If you asked me to define what that is, though, I'd be embarrassed. Still, the theme I chose led me instinctively to use a structure that has something in common with the epic story. Long distances in space and time; common action; great tension; and in the background, the two great oppositions of life and death,victory and defeat [...]Other interests and wishes of mine, apart from those which I consciously intended, may have flowed into this book, which I wrote with extreme freedom. For example: love and nature; wanderlust; language; technical and geographical matters.[47]

During the book's Milan launch an audience member asked: 'Can *If Not Now, When?* be classified as a picaresque novel?' Levi rejected the pigeonholing, but admitted:

> Essentially my Jews are picaresques, because I like the non-standard, slightly deviant kind of character, and I've deliberately accentuated the irregularity of mine: they are all irregular in one way or another. And then, if you think about it, one inevitably ends up in the picaresque genre when one deals with a minor history set within a universal framework. From that point of view who would deny that there are picaresque elements in *War and Peace*, or indeed in *The Betrothed*, as my presenter remarked earlier? My novel unfolds on two levels. There's Big History which strides over everything, and there's the minute history of those poor devils who are the protagonists. Little people, in short, trapped in the tangles of history.[48]

The writer had come across the little people of *If Not Now, When?* during his interminable return from the Lager. He told his American audience:

> The journey of repatriation wasn't pleasant, but it was a wonderful opportunity to observe many realities that were hard to access for a Westerner. Among these, I should include the direct contact with Eastern European Judaism. In the Lager I'd had a distorted (everything in the Lager was distorted) and above all schematic idea of it: there were millions of Jews in Russia and Poland, and the Nazis had sent them to Auschwitz and exterminated them. That picture, in the course of the very long journey imposed on us by the Russians, acquired details and chiaroscuro: the countries we went through were very different from Italy, they were desolate and wild, primitive and violent. Hostility to the Jews went back a long way before the German invasion: it was endemic, constant. Jews had lived here for centuries in a condition of separation, including linguistic separation. [...] In our peregrinations in Ukraine, then in White Russia, we'd come across Jewish soldiers in the Red Army; young men who'd served among the partisans; families who'd fled the Einsatzkommandos taking refuge in distant areas, and who were now going back to their villages by any and every makeshift means; villages lost in the middle of the woods that had housed Yeshivas,[49] once flourishing, now destroyed: in short, fragments of an exploded, mortally wounded Jewish world now looking for a new equilibrium. A few years later I extracted a brief poem from it, which I will reread here:
>
> 'Our fathers of this earth,
>
> Merchants of many gifts,

Shrewd wise men whose fertile progeny

God sowed across the world

As mad Ulysses sowed salt in the furrows

I have found you everywhere,

As many as the sands of the sea,

You stiff-necked people,

Poor tenacious human seed.'[50]

How does Primo Levi's image of Eastern Judaism differ from that of Isaac Bashevis Singer, its greatest bard? There were many questions on this subject. He answered on TV:

> [...]between the shtetl[51] Jews Singer describes in his novels and the Jews of *If Not Now, When?* many years have passed; among other things, the October Revolution destroyed those already enfeebled small communities, creating new problems and giving a new face to Yiddish-speaking Judaism, very different to the one we in Italy know through literature.[52]

He adds, to the correspondent for *Paese Sera*:

> Singer's books are a generation back. He tells the stories of the fathers of my characters, and after that time a lot of things happened [...]. When I came into contact with that culture, I discovered with amazement that they were full-time Jews, whereas as a Jew, I was barely registered. Anti-Semitism left a different mark on my coreligionists here in Italy than it did there. In Italy, there have been no pogroms, nor have language differences ever constituted a barrier. Our nineteenth-century ghettos, however painful, were laughable compared to the apartheid system that still existed in Russia and Poland in the twentieth century; which gave birth to a secondary civilization, stuck like the tessera of a mosaic in the middle of that other civilization. That is the world explored by Singer. Quite simply, I met that world thirty years later.[53]

When he met it, it was unrecognizable and in pieces, as if Hitler's rage had fallen upon it with destructive fury. One of the aims of *If Not Now, When?*, he says on the radio, is to read in that fabric that is forever torn:

> Jewish culture was flourishing in Eastern Europe at the time when the Second World War broke out; and one of the reasons I wrote this book was to learn myself, and to show Italian readers, some of the less well known aspects of that culture. For example, its habit of self-mockery; its extraordinary desire for joy despite misery, persecution and massacre.[54]

In the Lager he had started to learn and to understand. This is how he explained his learning process to Stefano Jesurum:

> Yiddish wasn't just a dialect, or a language. It was a civilization, a world that we didn't even know existed, that we knew nothing about. I just had my father's few superficial stories. Then I saw the few remaining shreds of what had been an immense civilization. Afterwards, after my return, I began to be curious about that civilization. I read Joseph Roth, Saul Bellow, Bernard Malamud, the Singer brothers. I started to take an interest from an anthropological point of view. Just think: a whole world had disappeared from Europe in a few years: it had been razed to the ground, obliterated. Nothing is left of it now, except in America.[55]

The members of Gedale's band, according to Vacca, reflect a complex inheritance: the continuity of Talmudic forms of reasoning. Primo Levi denies this: his Gedale is not a great reasoner; his Ashkenazim are not the children of Talmudists. But he takes advantage of the remark to linger over a people whose communities, all extremely poor, were hotbeds of culture.

> It's something simpler. A cultural tradition can have its basis in reading. Very few Jews don't know how to read. A Jew who doesn't know how to read gets little respect. He's almost a criminal. The duty to read the Bible, the Torah first of all, is a constant in all the varieties of Jewish civilization: Western, Eastern, and dispersed communities like the Italian one. The book is the cornerstone of Jewish culture. This comes from the fact that the written word is sacred. Every single letter of the Torah was sacred. If a scribe got a single letter wrong, the whole scroll was destroyed. So every written word has a theological dignity. Memory was also important.[56]

He will return to the theme of the centrality of education in Judaism during his conversation with Giorgio Bocca, in reply to a reflection from the journalist:

> *I've a great many Jewish friends: in my view the only thing that distinguishes them from others is the importance they give to culture – what you call the best merchandise.*

> It's a Yiddish saying, I learned it travelling in those parts. Culture doesn't obstruct you, it doesn't pay customs duties; you carry it with you in any migration, from any country from which you're expelled. [...]I really think this is a constant in Judaism, in all times and places [...] I'd call this Darwinian; it's the way an organ develops. The terrible history of the Jewish people, a history of expulsions and persecutions, has obliged it to take refuge in the only moveable good that can't be confiscated.[57]

There was a time when, as well as winning prizes, the novel's title became in certain circles and in the newspapers, almost an idiomatic expression. 'If not now, when?' was the reply to questions that deserved a proper answer. Primo Levi was amused. He said in a radio broadcast:

> I think the title works precisely because it's polysemantic, as they say. It has many meanings, everyone can experience it in his own way. It's like saying – don't waste your time, use it as well as you can, carpe diem; how beautiful youth is, although it flees.[58]

However, to the question 'And for Primo Levi, now in the autumn of 1982, if not now, then what?' he replied by referring to the real meaning of the title:

> For me personally it doesn't have a precise sense: because I've never lost my identity, I feel much more Italian than Jewish, I've never been a Zionist even though this book is about a Zionist adventure; and so, I don't perceive the question as a warning said to me or a warning to me or by me.[69]

Despite the public and critical success of *If Not Now, When?* there was nonetheless a shadow. The author spoke of it with sad irony:

> The coincidence of its publication with the war in Lebanon has increased its publishing success, and at the same time distorted its meaning among some critics and readers, who have mistaken it for an 'instant book'. In fact, the idea that in certain circumstances even Jews can fight does not seem to need demonstration just now.[60]

Notes

1. From an earlier draft of the text, which became 'Itinerario di uno scrittore ebreo' [Itinerary of a Jewish writer], *La Rassegna Mensile di Israel* [Monthly Israel Review; in fact published quarterly], nos. 5-8, 50th year of publication, 1984. This text is based on a

lecture given at a conference organized by the Rockefeller Foundation and held at Bellagio, near Lake Como, from 29 November to 2 December 1982. An English translation by Gail Soffer, *Beyond Survival*, Prooftexts, Vol. 4 (Baltimore: Johns Hopkins University Press, 1984) was used by Levi on his lecture tour of the United States. The quotation is from P. Levi trans. A. Goldstein, *The Truce* in A. Goldstein (ed.) *Complete Works of Primo Levi* (New York: Liveright, 2015), p.395.

2. From the interview Primo Levi gave to Guido Lopez, broadcast by 'Sorgente di vita' [Source of life], a television programme on Jewish culture, on 17 March 1982. The interview took place in the courtyard of Palazzo Odescalchi, in Milan, which after the Liberation was Italy's main centre offering assistance to Jewish refugees.
3. Rosellina Balbi, 'Mendel il consolatore' [Mendel the consoler], *La Repubblica,* 14 April 1982.
4. Interview Primo Levi gave to Ennio Cavalli on the RAI Radio 1 news, 5September 1982.
5. Giovanni Pacchioni, 'Segrete avventure di eroi involontari' [Secret adventures of accidental heroes], *Il Globo,* 13-14 June 1982.
6. SS killing squads.
7. A large area of swamp and forest, covering parts of Poland, Belarus, Ukraine and Russia.
8. Primo Levi, text based on the Bellagio lecture.
9. Mario Miccinesi, 'Un romanzo storico costruito secondo i modelli classici' [A historical novel built according to the classical models], *Uomini e Libri*, November-December 1982, p.40.
10. Roberto Vacca, 'Un western dalla Russia a Milano' [A western from Russia to Milan], *Il Giorno*, 18 May 1982.
11. Interview Levi gave to Lopez.
12. Laura Mancinelli, 'Così ho inventato Gedale, il partigiano che amava il violino' [This is how I invented Gedale, the partisan who loved the violin], *L'Unità*, 8 July 1982.
13. A common stereotype for centuries, due to Genoa's history as a banking centre. Mentioned as a distinctive Genoese trait in Montesquieu's travel writings, it is still jokingly alluded to today.
14. Interview Levi gave to Lopez. The Rabbi Hillel quotation is cited here as it appears in Levi's book. In fact, Levi has adapted it. The second question in the *Pirkei Avot* is 'And if I am only for myself, what am I?' See Chabad, *Ethics of the Fathers (Pirkei Avot)*, 1.14, available at: http://www.chabad.org/library/article_cdo/aid/682498/jewish/English-Text.htm [Accessed 13 September 2016].
15. Conversation between Primo Levi and Dina Luce, 'Il suono e la mente' [Sound and Mind], RAI Radio 2, 4 October 1982.
16. From the Campiello prize-giving ceremony, 4 September 1982.
17. Interview Levi gave to Lopez.
18. Roberto Bertacchini, 'Quando le "pecore" colpiscono' [When the 'sheep' strike], *La Notte*, 26 May 1982.
19. Incontro con Primo Levi [Meeting with Primo Levi], Libreria Campus di Torino, via Ratazzi, Turin, 20 May 1982.
20. Rosellina Balbi, 'Mendel il consolatore'.
21. Giulio Goria, 'Sono diventato ebreo quasi per forza' [I became a Jew almost by force], *Paese Sera,* 3 May 1982.
22. Lea Canducci, 'La cinquantatreesima edizione del Premio Viareggio; parlano alcuni dei protagonisti' [The fifty-third edition of the Viareggio Prize: some of the contestants speak], *Avanti!* 30 June 1982.
23. 'Tuttolibri', weekly educational book programme presented by Giulio Nascimbeni and Guido Gola, RAI1, 24 May 1982.
24. Interview Levi gave to Cavalli.
25. To find or discover in both Italian and Latin.

26. In English in the Italian text.
27. Miccinesi, 'Un romanzo storico costruito secondo i modelli classici'.
28. The interview was broadcast as a special feature at the end of the regional news on RAI 3, 17 April 1982.
29. Piero Bianucci, 'Sì, anche la mia cultura può essere considerata yiddish' [Yes, my culture can be considered Yiddish too], interview with Primo Levi after he won the twentieth Campiello Prize, *La Stampa*, 6 September 1982.
30. Campiello prize-giving ceremony.
31. A brilliant discovery that seems simple or easy after the fact. From an apocryphal story that Christopher Columbus, when he was told that discovering the Americas was inevitable and no great accomplishment, challenged his critics to make an egg stand on its tip, and, after they gave up, succeeded by tapping the egg on the table to flatten it.
32. Giorgio Calcagno, 'La Terra Promessa dei miei ebrei non è una potenza militare' [The Promised Land of my Jews isn't a military power], *Tuttolibri*(*La Stampa*), 12 June 1982.
33. Giovanni Pacchioni, 'Segrete avventure di eroi involontari'.
34. Roth (see Notes on the Translation and note to Chapter 1).
35. Campiello prize-giving ceremony.
36. Paola Cacianti, 'Primo Levi vince il nuovo Campiello' [Primo Levi wins the new Campiello], *Avanti!*, 8 September 1982.
37. Giulio Nascimbeni, 'Campiello '82: dopo vent'anni ancora premiato Primo Levi' [Campiello' 82: Primo Levi awarded the prize again after twenty years], *Corriere della Sera*, 6 September 1982.
38. Balbi, 'Mendel il consolatore'.
39. Vacca, 'Un western dalla Russia a Milano'.
40. Pygmalion is a legendary figure from Cyprus, included in Ovid's *Metamorphoses*. He carved a woman out of ivory and found the statue so beautiful he prayed to Aphrodite to have it changed into a woman; his wish was granted and they married. In Pirandello's play *Diana and Tuda*, out of print in Marta Abba's English translation (New York: Samuel French, 1934), the dramatist presented an ironic parody of the artist in love with his statue.
41. Balbi, 'Mendel il consolatore'.
42. Mythological characters whose noble birth destines them to be heroes: Achilles is the son of the nymph Thetis and the king Peleus; Siegfried, hero of Wagner's *Götterdämmerung* [Twilight of the Gods] is a German prince.
43. Pacchioni, 'Segrete avventure di eroi involontari'.
44. Collective farms in the Soviet Union.
45. Calcagno, 'La Terra Promessa dei miei ebrei non è una potenza militare'.
46. Nascimbeni, 'Campiello' 82: dopo vent'anni ancora premiato Primo Levi'.
47. Canducci,'La cinquantatreesima edizione del Premio Viareggio; parlano alcuni dei protagonisti'.
48. The launch, organized by the journalist Paolo Pacchioni, with Guido Lopez, and Waldo Aldovrandi representing the publisher, took place in the Einaudi bookshop in Milan on the evening of 4 May 1982.
49. Rabbinical schools teaching scriptural texts such as the Talmud and Torah.
50. Bellagio text. The poem, 'Ostjuden', appears in P. Levi trans. J. Galassi, *Collected Poems*, in *Complete Works of Primo Levi*, Vol.III, p.1894.
51. Village or small town.
52. Interview given by Primo Levi to Anna Maria Rebaudengo, RAI 3 Piedmont Regional Television News, 17 April 1982.
53. Goria, 'Sono diventato ebreo quasi per forza'.
54. Conversation between Levi and Luce.
55. S.Jesurum, *Essere ebrei in Italia* [Being Jewish in Italy], (Longanesi: Milan, 1987), p.98.

56. Vacca, 'Un western dalla Russia a Milano'.
57. Interview given by Primo Levi to Giorgio Bocca, 'Prima pagina' [First page], Mediaset Canale 5, 13 June 1985.'The Best Merchandise' is the title of an essay in P. Levi trans A. Shugaar, *Other People's Trades* in *Complete Works of Primo Levi*, pp.2009-12.
58. 'Quant'è bella giovinezza che si fugge tuttavia', an Italian proverb derived from Lorenzo de Medici's *Canzona di Bacco* [Song of Bacchus],ll.1-2.
59. Conversation between Levi and Luce.
60. Bellagio text: 'instant book' in English in the Italian text.

XI

Jewishness

Being Jewish had never mattered much to the young Primo Levi, either within himself or in contact with his Christian friends. He considered his origin 'a small, cheerful anomaly, like having a crooked nose or freckles'. He became suddenly aware of it when the antisemitic journal *La Difesa della Razza* [The Defence of the Race], founded in August 1938, began talking about racial purity; and the Jewish student began to feel proud of being 'the impurity that causes the reaction, the mustard seed that fertilizes the ground'. The story 'Zinc' in *The Periodic Table* introduces, in the context of a delicate love story, 'the hostile years that were coming on'.[1] In the fullness of time, some interviewers began to question him about how Jewish he felt. Once he said:

> I became a Jew in Auschwitz, before I didn't feel like one. The awareness of feeling *different* was imposed on me. Someone, without the slightest reason in the world, decided that I was different and inferior; as a natural reaction, I saw myself in those years as different and superior. Now that doesn't count any more. Yet, in that sense Auschwitz gave me something, which has endured. Being forced to feel Jewish spurred me on to recover, later, a cultural heritage I didn't have before.[2]

In a radio interview he was asked:

> *Are you Jewish in religion as well?*
>
> I'm Jewish as a name on the register, that is to say that I'm on the records of the Jewish Community of Turin, but I'm not practising or even a believer. Yet I'm aware of being part of a tradition and a culture. I tend to say that I feel, depending on the moment, either three quarters or four fifths Italian, but the fraction that remains is quite important to me.[3]

He also said:

> My Judaism is entirely culturally determined. If there hadn't been the racial laws and the Lager, I probably wouldn't be Jewish anymore,

> except for my surname. Yet those two experiences, the racial laws and the Lager, moulded me. Now I am a Jew: they sewed the star of David on me, and not just on my clothes.

He is intimately Jewish; an integral part of his people. With the high morality of his writings he became and has remained a point of reference in Jewish consciousness, even though he has repeated on many occasions, often with a kind of regret, that he was agnostic.

> I'm not a believer. I never have been; I'd like to be, but I can't manage it. [...] There's Auschwitz, so there can't be God. I can't find a solution to that dilemma. I look for one, but I can't find one.[4]

And he ends by repeating a conviction expressed many years earlier:

> I'm not religious. I wasn't before Auschwitz, the experience of the Lager reconfirmed this lack of religiousness in me; even though I noticed then that anyone who had any kind of faith, whether Jewish or Catholic, had a much greater chance of survival, because in the end they had answers that we who were secular did not.[5]

Primo Levi expanded on his own Jewishness on two occasions: first when the Rockefeller Foundation asked him to give a brief account of his life and work at the Jewish writers' conference in Bellagio; and then in 1986 in a long interview on the subject with the journalist Stefano Jesurum, who was gathering material for a book to be called *Essere ebrei in Italia* [Being Jewish in Italy], published by Longanesi. Levi used the account at Bellagio as a basis for what he would say to American audiences in April 1985. Looking at his life and work specifically from the perspective of the history and culture he belonged to, he said this:

> By my readers and critics, in Italy and abroad, I am thought of as a 'Jewish writer'. I accepted that definition with a good grace, but not immediately and not without resistance: in fact I only accepted it in its entirety quite late in life and in my itinerary as a writer. I became a Jew only as an effect of the racial laws, promulgated in Italy in 1938 when I was 19; and of my deportation to Auschwitz, which happened in 1944. I became a writer even later, after the age of 45, when I'd already had two books published, and when the trade of writing (which I still never thought of as a real trade) started to prevail over my 'official' trade as a chemist. For both these steps, it was much more an intervention of fate than a deliberate and conscious decision. [...]

> Like most Jews of ancient Italian stock, my parents and grandparents belonged to the middle class and were deeply integrated in terms of language, customs and moral outlook. In my family, religion counted for little: which is explained by the fact that equal civil rights, obtained only around the middle of the last century by non-Catholic Italians, had been the fruit of the predominantly secular character of the Italian Risorgimento,[6] which, precisely, had recognized the civil equality 'of all subjects'. Fighting in the Risorgimento's struggles involved, if not an obligation, at least a strong inducement to secularism.
>
> Nonetheless, neither in my family nor in Italian Jews in general had the awareness of their Judaism been extinguished. It was manifested in the preservation of some family rituals (especially the feasts of Rosh Hashanah, Pesach and Purim); in the importance given to study and education; and in a small but interesting linguistic differentiation. In parallel with the well-known hybrid structure of Yiddish, in the Jewish families of the various Italian provinces curious variants of the local dialects were spoken, with Hebrew insertions more or less distorted to conform to local phonetics. Ever since childhood I'd been intrigued, and also moved, by that poignant survival of biblical language in family and dialect speech. I took from it, many years after my literary debut, the subject for the first chapter of *The Periodic Table*.[7]

Essentially, he said, that book was the writer's way of thanking the chemist who had opened the way for him. But not only that:

> [...] it contains the story of a generation, and filtering out from many of its pages is the traumatic experience of the segregation of Jews in fascist and Nazi Europe, and of the blind rush towards war and massacre; and also the renewed pride that accompanies every separation and discrimination.

Among the twenty-one incidents described in *The Periodic Table*, he pointed to three that encapsulated key elements of his Jewishness: 'Argon', which Alberto Cavaglion, a scholar of nineteenth and twentieth-century Judaism, saw as the pivot around which the whole ethical and civic discourse of Levi's most famous books revolved;[8] followed by 'Zinc' and 'Gold'. He explained:

> Argon is a gas that does not react with other gases [...] In the chapter of that name, I offered a humorous analogy between that rare gas,

> which is present in minute quantities in the air we breathe, and our ancestors from the little rural Jewish communities of Piedmont—isolated in small groups, sometimes individual families on their own; secluded, still mindful of distant persecutions, neither much loved nor much hated, sometimes the targets of scorn or mistrust. Of these bizarre and remote characters no trace remains, apart from the occasional playful anecdote, some sayings handed down, almost in parody of the famous rabbinical sayings collected in the Talmud. I've tried to bring them back to life in these pages, with ironic affection: for example, the story of a legendary uncle in Chieri near Turin, who, fell in love with the family's Christian maid. Because his parents were opposed to the marriage, this uncle went to bed and stayed there for twenty-two years, until his parents died and he could marry the girl. In bringing back these strange and comic family legends, I've also tried to document the hybrid language I referred to earlier: which is a minor, Mediterranean version of Yiddish, more local and less illustrious, in which I nonetheless recognized my domestic roots.
>
> In 'Zinc', the still subtly ironic chemical analogy has shifted. We are in 1937: the racial laws in Italy have not yet been announced, but you can feel them in the air. Newspapers and magazines orchestrated by the totalitarian regime talk persistently of the Jews as different, as potential (or actual) enemies of fascism, as harmful 'impurities' in pure Italian blood. They cite the Nuremberg Laws[9] as a model. They take up the themes of Goebbels' fanatical propaganda: the Jew, portrayed in caricatures with traditional semitic features, is at one and the same time the capitalist who starves the Aryan peoples and the bloodthirsty Bolshevist whose hands drip with blood. [...] I should note that zinc is capable of reacting with acids only if certain impurities are present: if it's perfectly pure it doesn't react. The young self whom I describe here is vaguely proud of being an impurity [...]
>
> In 'Gold', things have come to a head. The Second World War is raging. In 1943 the Allies landed in Italy, fascism fell, and the German army invaded Northern Italy. Despite being both politically and militarily unprepared, it seemed to me that the only decent choice was to join the anti-German resistance. Most of my friends and contemporaries, Jews and Christians, did the same. In fact Jewish participation was relatively conspicuous, both in numerical terms and as a contribution to the ideology and direction of the movement. But my partisan career was destined to be short-lived.

Three hundred militiamen went looking for his partisan band, on the hills white with the first snow; and found eleven of them, almost defenceless.

Locked up in prison, next to the gold-bearing stream, Primo Levi asserted his identity and took the first fateful steps towards the Lager:

> In the interrogation I was subjected to by the fascists, I admitted to being Jewish: partly out of tiredness; but partly too out of the irrational pride I mentioned earlier, a pride that is the fruit of persecution, and the intensity of which is proportional to that persecution.

Talking later to Ferdinando Camon (who included this part of the discussion in his *Autoritratto*), Levi further justified that surge of pride:

> [...] I was a very bad partisan. I hadn't done military service, I didn't even know how a gun worked. I had one but I didn't know how to use it. I only fired one shot; any more would have been a waste of bullets. Nonetheless I was a partisan. And I would have been very sorry if it hadn't come to light that I was a Jew: that therefore even Jews can resolve to fight.'[10]

From Aosta prison to Fossoli, a transit camp, and from there to Auschwitz in February 1944:

> I was well aware that my hopes of being saved were minute, but I also knew that if I were to survive I would have to tell, I wouldn't be able not to: and not only that, but that telling, bearing witness, was an aim it was worth preserving oneself for. So much so that even today, to anyone who asks me how I survived, I reply after luck, this resolution of mine must have played a part. Not just living and telling, then, but living in order to tell. I was aware in Auschwitz that it was the essential experience of my life.

If This is a Man is born from the survivor's needs:

> It's not a book of pure testimony. Rereading it a long time later, and looking at the many reviews in Italy and abroad, I recognize many interlaced themes: the effort to understand how it could have happened; the almost scientific study of human behaviour (my own and other people's) in those extreme conditions; the painful everyday confrontation with the the freedom we saw around us; the resurfacing (sometimes intentional, sometimes unconscious and spontaneous) of literary references to Dante's *Inferno*. But I'd like to draw attention to one of those themes here, and that's the way the book refers to the Bible.
>
> Right at the beginning, in the Italian transit camp in Fossoli, I found myself, for the first time in my life separated from the everyday world

> and immersed by force in an exclusively Jewish environment. It was a brutal confirmation of my Jewishness: almost a condemnation, a relapse, a reliving of the biblical stories of exile and migration. A tragic return in which, nevertheless, hope and pride in having found my identity again coexisted with despair.

Reading brief passages from *If This is a Man* to the audience,[11] Primo Levi, pointed out that biblical themes and a biblical tone can be found throughout. In the description of the night in Fossoli, before the departure for Auschwitz (the poignant scene of the group gathered around the Gattegnos, whose yearning lament exemplifies 'the grief without hope of the exodus, renewed in every century'); and also in the account of the months of imprisonment. In the sense that destiny is decided outside the human world, by the incomprehensible and vengeful God of the Prophets; and in the sense that of the confusion of languages is a punishment inflicted by God on mankind's hubris. ('Here, however…the hubris is that of Hitler's Germany, forcing its slaves to build its towers of Babel.') Finally, at the moment of liberation, biblical scenes of salvation are remembered, 'but with utter ambivalence'.

The Truce, written long after and in a profoundly different political and economic climate, is the story of a new diaspora: in the days after the flood, driven on by an unknowable will, Jews meet on the roads of exile, amid deep swamps and boundless plains. In the deserted spaces and terrifying forests of *The Truce,* we can already see the uprooted Jewish world of *If Not Now, When?*, the story of strangers in their own land, obsessed by memory. Yet in the stories he wrote next, in *Natural Histories* and *Flaw of Form*, which often border on science fiction, the author says that the Jewish theme appears only briefly:

> Though some connect (perhaps unconsciously) to the Midrashic tradition of the moral tale. For example, in 'Angelic Butterfly', a Nazi scientist discovers that human beings are the larval state of another animal, as the caterpillar is to the butterfly, but never reach the stage of transformation, because they die too soon. Perhaps they would become angels, or supermen! The scientist gives a medicine capable of accelerating the change to a group of mysterious characters (in fact they are prisoners from a concentration camp): but instead of angels they are transformed into monstrous birds of prey unable to fly, who are devoured by starving citizens during the final Battle of Berlin. More closely linked to Jewish themes is 'The Servant', a Gothic reworking of the Golem legend, in which it is imagined' that Rabbi Loew of Prague[12] knew the secrets of genetics and information technology, and that therefore his creature, the Golem, was in fact a robot. Another story imagines that on the sixth day of Creation a

> committee of technicians and scientists meets to discuss, in strictly company terms, 'project humanity'. They decide to create a bird-human, but God the Father intervenes. In an instant, He creates a mammal man, vaguely monkey-like, and carves a woman from his rib.

The only book from which any reference to Judaism is absent is *The Wrench*:

> I deliberately excluded it, since the central idea of the novel is the dignity of work, especially artisan work, as a modern-day substitute for adventure and creative research, and that is a theme I consider valid in every time or place or social structure. Still, in writing it, the many references to the dignity and necessity of work spread throughout the Talmud were no strangers to me. Indeed, several readers have pointed out to me that the protagonist of the book, Tino Faussone, a mechanical rigger from Turin, knows the Bible a bit too well to be a Gentile.

The characters of the first twelve stories of *Lilith*, to whom critics have given most attention, are for the most part Jews:

> From a distance of thirty years, it seemed to me that the memories I'd inherited from the Lager had not all been used up and that they were worth going back to. Naturally, the point of view had changed: I no longer felt the urgency of testimony and of inner liberation. It seemed to me that I had said everything about the sociological situation of the Lager, about its essential horror, about its appearance as a distorted mirror of today's world, about its rules. But I still felt a relatively serene wish to look at again and study more closely some figures from that time, victims, perpetrators and survivors, who had remained clearly in my memory against the grey, collective, impersonal background of the 'drowned'. [...]They included an honest and gentle fellow-prisoner, whom I had to teach that he needed to steal from the Germans in order to survive; another, an observant Jew, who on the evening of Yom Kippur had refused to eat his soup; and a third who told me the provocative story of Lilith, first wife of Adam and concubine of God.

Levi emphasized the importance of one story in Lilith for the study of power:

> I summarize in a few pages the story of Chaim Rumkowski, president of the Judenrat in the Łódź ghetto. It's well known that Rumkowski stooped to every compromise to acquire and keep the miserable power that the Germans had given him. He adopted, without hesitation or

> any sense of absurdity, all the external, 'regal' symbols of power, and defended that power bravely against the Germans themselves. According to a rumour in Poland at that time, when the Ghetto was dissolved and he himself was condemned like everyone else to die in the Lager, he asked for and obtained the right to make his last journey in a special wagon. In this last act of his, with its Shakespearian flavour, tragic and grotesque at the same time, I recognized a metaphor for our western civilization: especially for the huge imbalance, which we're so used to we hardly notice, between the huge amount of time and effort we expend to gain power and prestige, and the essential futility of these goals.

If Not Now, When? is based entirely on a ruined Jewish universe, on its tradition and culture, destined to be transplanted and become extinct. Primo Levi affirmed that in preparing the book he had studied not just texts and documents in archives, but the unifying idiom of the Jewish world, the 'mother tongue' as Yiddish was affectionately called:

> I wanted to write a novel, yes, but I absolutely didn't want to find myself at odds with historical facts, or anyway to distance myself from reality [...] and since Yiddish civilization, like all patriarchal and pre-industrial civilizations, is strongly impregnated with popular wisdom and proverbs, I didn't ignore the collections of Yiddish sayings and proverbs, or the collections of '*Yiddische Witze*' [Jewish jokes]. It's no coincidence that the title of the book itself is derived from a famous verse in the *Sayings of the Fathers (Pirkei Avoth).*
>
> This was perhaps the only time I found myself confronting a real, but unusual, linguistic problem: I had to give my readers the impression that the dialogue between my characters, which is obviously in Italian, had been translated from Yiddish, a language I know badly and Italian readers don't know at all. Whether the problem has been solved or not I don't know: that is for those readers who really know Yiddish to judge.

Jewish subjects also emerge, tenderly, ironically and with nostalgic fascination, in the works written after *If Not Now, When?* In *The Drowned and the Saved*, for instance; in essays like 'The Best Merchandise' and 'Ritual and Laughter', a celebration of *subtilitas* and the disinterested playfulness of intelligence; and in stories like 'My Grandfather's Shop', an appendix to 'Argon', or 'Fossil Words', which suggests a parallel between the most ancient language in the world and the dialects spoken at the foot of the Alps. To the journalist Stefano Jesurum, who asks him to what extent he feels Jewish, Primo Levi replies first of all that he is the son of a positivist father and an inherently secular mother; that he has never been religious, although he has had a bar mitzvah like all good little middle class Jewish boys, worn the phylacteries for two years, eaten unleavened bread at Pesach, and celebrated Purim.[13] It is clear that this youthful observance meant paying homage to a tradition more than recognizing a transcendent presence:

> I'm a typical example of someone who has gone back to being a Jew. What I was before is easy to imagine from the portrait I painted of my family. And so I remained until I was captured. It was in Auschwitz that I had a sharp and brutal revelation of what being a *Jude* really meant. The welcome we Italians were given was certainly not pleasant. We were double strangers and double enemies. For the Germans, we were enemies as Jews and enemies as Italians, that is traitors. For our fellow-sufferers, as Italians we were fascists [...] And we had a terrible handicap, together with the Greeks. We were very obviously of another ethnicity and language. A minority within a minority.
>
> *And what has changed between 'before' and 'after' from a religious point of view?*
>
> Nothing. I think I was vaccinated. I watched many people losing their religion. A lot of pious men lost it, because it was incompatible with our surroundings. Those who hadn't already lost it earlier [...] You know, we knew evil there: the same evil that is the basic problem for all religious thought.
>
> *Why do you feel Jewish?*
>
> It's difficult to tear off a label they've sewn onto you: *Jude*, and a registration number. It's very difficult to say 'I'm not one, it doesn't interest me anymore.' Also, I've studied it now, I've worked in it, lived in it; I now possess a Jewish culture that differentiates me from Christian Italians that's enough for me. You know, I've maintained relationships with some of my fellow-prisoners. They live in Germany now, in Israel, in France. It would seem a betrayal of them not to call myself, not to be, Jewish. It's difficult to explain what I mean. I'm thinking of a Czechoslovakian rabbi who was in the Lager with me. I see him sometimes; he's still a rabbi; he lives in Dortmund. I'd feel guilty towards him, towards the survivors, towards the many who didn't survive.
>
> *Not far from your house, there's a wall: it has 'Juventini[14]=Jews' written on it. [...] Everywhere, even now, people discriminate, humiliate, kill, over a surname, over membership of a group. What is this?*

> It's anti-Semitism. And of the rawest, the most ignorant kind, in that it makes an absolutely arbitrary identification of the state of Israel with a fellow-citizen whose culture, or religion, or simply whose origins, are Jewish.

Primo Levi, as he said many times, was never a Zionist. However, he did say:

> My relationship with that land isn't just any relationship. For emotional and personal reasons. [...] This is a state founded by those who were with me in the Lager. A country of fellow-soldiers, of comrades, of people dear to me. In material terms, they may be only twenty out of three million, but those twenty were in Auschwitz with me; and later they found a homeland, a land of their own. I'll tell you, for me it's a horrifying idea that Israel could one day be swept away, annihilated.[15]

'Have you ever thought about moving there?' Lucia Borgia asked him for the television program 'Rifarsi una vita' [Remaking a Life for Oneself].

> No. Unlike many of my comrades who were Polish or Hungarian and knew that there'd be nothing left for them on their return, my relatives and friends were and are in Italy. I had a clear reason to go home.[16]

In Israel, he had friends, relations, fellow-prisoners. He kept up with them by letter; his door was always open to unexpected visits from people coming from 'home'. He listened sympathetically and anxiously to what they told him. But when the time came, he took sides publicly with painful determination. When Israel invaded Lebanon in Operation 'Peace for Galilee' he was among the first to put his name to a letter signed by hundreds of democrats, calling 'for the Israeli government to withdraw its troops immediately'. This document, published in *La Repubblica* on 16 June 1982, stated the necessity of a solution to the conflict 'in which the right to national sovereignty of all peoples in the region is recognized'. It asked Israel to have the courage to oppose the policy of Prime Minister Menachem Begin, not only in order to support the self-determination of the Palestinian people, but in order 'to fight against the potential seeds of a new anti-Semitism that would add to the old anti-Jewish tendencies that have never disappeared from the heart of civic society'.

A few days later, when this prophecy was beginning to be fulfilled, and at the same time incredulous or angry letters from Israel were starting to reach the organizers of the appeal, Primo Levi wrote an editorial in *La Stampa*:

> I'm not ashamed to admit to feeling agonized. My link with that country remains; I feel that it is in a way my second homeland; I would

> like it to be different from all other countries, but precisely for that reason I feel shame and distress at this engagement. [...] I fear that this initiative, which is extremely costly in terms of blood, will inflict a wound on Judaism which will be difficult to cure and will pollute its image. I sense in myself, not without surprise, a deep emotional bond with Israel, but not with this Israel.[17]

The authoritativeness of the signatories gave wide resonance to the appeal. Debates and press campaigns were started; bitter disagreements emerged and extremist attitudes broke cover. In a survey of the deeply divided feelings of the country's Jewish community, Alberto Stabile of *La Repubblica* asked:

> *Why do some Jews identify the Palestinian tragedy with the persecutions they suffered forty years ago?*
>
> It's not only Jews, many non-Jews do so too. Something of an analogy does exist. I don't want to push things too far, but the analogy seems to me to be this. It's about a 'nation' – let's call it that between inverted commas, because in the Arab world things are always difficult to define – that has found itself without a country. And that is a point of contact with the Jews. There is a recent Palestinian diaspora that has something in common with the Jewish diaspora of two thousand years ago...
>
> *Two victim peoples...*
>
> Victims of neighbours with too much power. Still, I refuse to equate what Hitler called the final solution with the things the Israelis do today, violent and terrible as they are. There isn't a plan to exterminate the Palestinian people. That is going too far.
>
> *What do Jews (and non-Jews) feel most upset by today, seeing what is happening in Lebanon?*
>
> For me and my friends it's the gulf between our image of the state of Israel, based on our hopes and what events had promised – that it would be an oasis on which the Jewish nation could be rebuilt – and its evolution in a militarist and latently fascist direction. Back then it was about restoring not just a geographical but also a cultural centre to world Judaism. Now we're seeing nationalist demands, in the aggressive sense, prevail, while international Judaism takes second place.
>
> *What impression does this leave in European Jews?*

> [...] that Israel has overstepped the mark. It's in the nature of things for Israel to have hot borders. It was like that from the beginning, from 1948. But this initiative seems excessive and unmotivated to me. The reaction to the provocations of the PLO has been disproportionate. It seems to me that even from the standpoint of the crudest realpolitik, this time the Israelis have been excessive.
>
> *How do you think the appeal has been received?*
>
> Maybe more than half the Jews of Italy have approved, but certainly not all. Many others are bound at an emotional and visceral level to whatever Israel's policy may be. But what proportion I couldn't tell you.
>
> *Are there those who refuse to sign because it would mean dissociating themselves from Israel?*
>
> Yes, it's felt by some as a desertion, a betrayal.
>
> *And what can you reply?*
>
> That everyone must face up to his own conscience and to his own feelings, and that if we are democrats we must be democrats first, and Jews or Italians or anything else only secondly.[18]

These were hellish months for Israel, for the world, for the Jews and their friends and adversaries. Two names are enough: Sabra and Chatila, massacres for which Israel was held responsible. If Israelis had not actually carried them out, they had not held back the ferocity of the Phalangist militias. These events shook even the most powerful Jewish organizations to the core: organizations from the American Jewish Congress to the World Jewish Congress backed an inquiry into the killings, which Begin refused to conduct, bringing hundreds of thousands of protestors onto the streets of Tel Aviv. Primo Levi signed the call for a similar protest to take place in Italy and added his name to the telegram that communicated this initiative to Israeli democrats. The first words were: 'Dismayed by the infamy that stains the entire country and worried about its future...'

On 24 September 1982, the same day that *La Repubblica* published the telegram, it also published a long interview the writer had given to Giampaolo Pansa. Why had he hesitated to grant it?

> For two reasons. One is an inner reason of mine: civil war is very close to the bone for me. The other is that in these last few days I've received

many letters, a terrifying pile of letters, about what I've recently said and written about Israel's most recent war.

There were letters of agreement and of disagreement: some accused him of being too Zionist, some of not being Zionist enough.

Do you feel afraid at this moment?

In what sense? Personally, or as a Jew?

In both senses.

Personally, no, I'm not afraid. Fear is an deep, instinctive thing, and personally I don't feel it. But I don't feel fear as a Jew either. No, I don't sense another Holocaust coming, for us Jews nor an imminent massacre of the Hitler stamp. If anything, I feel pain. This Israeli war, this Beirut massacre, are polluting the image of Jews around the world.

Is there the risk of a new anti-Semitism?

Yes, to a certain extent there is that risk. But for the moment it's limited to occasional incidents. It's not by chance that this danger is felt above all in Paris and Brussels. Anti-Semitism has never died in France, from the Dreyfus case onwards: it's linked to the underlying xenophobia of the French. [...] But in any case: yes, anti-Semitism is a beast that is raising its head. But that's not an argument we Jews of the diaspora can put to Begin. It doesn't make sense to say to him 'Don't do what you're doing because you're harmng us.' The arguments are quite different [...] One is moral and the other political. The moral argument is this: not even a war justifies the bloodthirsty arrogance Begin and those around him have demonstrated. The political argument is just as clear: Israel is rapidly falling into total isolation. This is terrible, something which has never happened before. It's clear that not even the national interest, which Begin and Sharon invoke, can justify the latest decisions of the government of Israel.

But Begin isn't an isolated leader. His government has majority support. [...] What does that suggest to you?

Something obvious. Begin is kept in office mainly by the votes of the young and of recent immigrants: that is, not of refugees from Eastern Europe, but of Jews who come from Middle Eastern countries, or who

> are born in Israel. They're all people who harbour a strong resentment towards neighbouring states, which they often come from; and that, to a certain extent, explains this war and what has happened during it. Still, I condemn it totally. I say so clearly. And I also have a hope, the same hope that pushed me to accept this interview. I'm not interested in my words having an effect on Italian readers, I'm interested in their having an effect in Israel, on its leaders, on its electorate, on Israeli journalists.
>
> *What do you have to say to Israel's rulers?*
>
> That they should resign. I have no other message, seeing that it's impossible to change how they think. Of course, I know very well that in a moment like this even asking them to resign is unrealistic. Still, if he's got a sliver of reason left, Sharon must resign. [...] Begin, Sharon, in short the whole group that now rules Israel very much resemble the ruling classes of other Middle Eastern countries. Paradoxically, Begin and those around him are realising an ancient Zionist dream: to become a Middle Eastern country. But they're realising it in the worst possible way. That is, they're conforming to the demagogy, to the instability, to the scant faith in promises and treaties which distinguish too many Middle Eastern leaders.

Levi does not hesitate to call Begin, who had been a disciple of Jabotinsky and a member of his youth group,[20] a 'fascist'. He says of Sharon that he is a 'hard and unscrupulous' soldier. Pansa presses him:

> *Might Israel become a totalitarian state?*
>
> It could happen, but only through a civil war. Today the opposition to Begin is a minority, but it's a big minority. No, I don't think what happened in Chile could happen in Israel. I can't see that risk. Israel is an extremely viable country from the democratic point of view. [...] And the people of my age there have had direct experience of the horrors of fascism in Europe, which they pass on to their children and grandchildren.

In the general excitement, the newspapers wrote that the state of Israel was in danger of becoming the Jews' own worst enemy. Primo Levi measures the accusation and says:

> It seems to me a bit harsh, and also too general as an observation. It can at the most be valid for this moment, for today. [...] The correct appraisal seems to me to be the following: the current behaviour of

the current government of Israel is in danger of becoming the Jews' worst enemy. Still, not even that is an argument to put to Begin. [...] The real arguments are the two I have mentioned before. And on the basis of those arguments, we have the right to say to Israel: for as long as things stay as they are now, you can't ask for economic or moral support from the Jews of the diaspora any more.

He does not believe in the 'olive branch' of Arafat, whom he says Begin has given 'political victory, and also the accolade of leader of all Palestinians, which he didn't have before'. He watched with suspicion how Arafat was welcomed when he visited Rome in September 1982. It was Begin, Levi repeated, who had given Arafat the glory of defeat.

Yet, after the defeat, there was the massacre of the Palestinians in the two camps in Beirut. What was your instinctive reaction?

I don't have instinctive reactions. If I do, I repress them. At first, I was doubtful it had really happened. Then I understood that it was all true. Now, the massacre in those two camps reminded me very much of what the Russians did in Warsaw in August 1944: they sat back on the Vistula, while the Nazis slaughtered the Polish partisans. Of course, like all historical parallels, this one too is unsound. But like the Soviets then, Israel could have intervened; it had the strength to stop the militias that were massacring those people, and it didn't do so. Why, I don't know. Maybe there's some truth even in Begin's hypocrisies. This massacre isn't in the Israeli style. He could have lost control of the situation. Then again, it might be that someone deliberately took their time to defend those women and children [...] What more can I say? I still have a certain loyalty to Israel, an emotional bond. I'm not so pessimistic as to say that Israel will always be like this.

But what can you Jews and we non-Jews do so that Israel will not always be like this?

You say 'we' and 'you' [...] That's wrong. There's no difference. God willing, for once being Jewish or not doesn't matter. There's a single valid response for everyone. And it's not, as some think, breaking off diplomatic and economic relations [...] Those are senseless reactions, which will only entrench Begin's position [...] We must all do two or three things. Recognize the situation. Stifle our impulse of emotional solidarity with Israel and think coolly about the errors of the current Israeli ruling class. Topple that ruling class. Help Israel to find its way back to its European origins, or to the wisdom of its founding fathers, of Ben-Gurion, of Golda Meir. Not that they all had clean hands, but

> who has clean hands? Abba Eban, for example, seems to me a reliable option for the future of Israel; he isn't even that old. But today is terrible. I get agonizing letters from friends there. They've fought in all Israel's wars and have children who have died in them. They write to me 'You are blind, because you don't see all the Israeli blood, all the Jewish blood shed in these years'.
>
> *And what do you reply?*
>
> I reply that that blood gives me pain, like any other blood that is shed. But they are agonizing letters all the same. And I feel agonized, because I know that Israel was founded by people like me, but not as lucky as me. Men with the Auschwitz number tattooed on their arm, without a home or a homeland, having escaped from the horrors of the Second World War, who found a home and homeland there. I know all that. But I also know that that is Begin's favourite argument. And I deny validity to such an argument.
>
> *I see that you are capable of very cool reasoning...*
>
> I do my best, though this is a tragic time for us. There's an old comedy, written in the last century by Sholem Aleichem. Do you know what the title is? *It's Hard to be a Jew*. Now more so than ever. Yes, now it's harder than ever.[21]

The pressure from the democrats forced the Israeli leaders to set up a commission of inquiry led by Yitzhak Kahan, President of the Supreme Court. But in February 1983, when it came to learning the lessons from the experts' report, political tension in the country reached boiling point. Ariel Sharon refused to go, the streets exploded, and the opposition leader and former prime minister Shimon Peres warned the government that the country's democratic structures could collapse. Seeing the danger of separating power from responsibility, Primo Levi spoke out again:

> Sharon should go immediately and Begin should also resign. Refusing to accept the responsibility that the verdict of the three experts has laid on them seems to me an extremely arrogant attitude.

There was a positive side though, which restored the trust of even the most severe and impartial Jews:

> First of all, the conclusions of the commission's judges have shown that in few other countries in the world is there as great a sense of justice. The three experts have worked with unexceptionable moral

> rigour: which also shows that Israel has developed a strong democratic consciousness. Another aspect to underline is that the images of Sharon and Begin come out of this affair in tatters, but the image of the country in world public opinion comes out very much strengthened, especially on a moral level.

Nonetheless Levi recognized that though the internal opposition to Begin was strong, there was still a large part of the nation, made up essentially of young soldiers, which continued to regard the massacres of Sabra and Chatila as just 'what happens':

> I don't like this military image of Israel. I understand that Israel needs an efficient army. But the need to defend oneself is one thing; militarism is another.[22]

After that statement, Primo Levi was quiet for a long time. When he decided to make his thoughts public again, he did so with a carefully thought out interview granted to *L'Espresso* and published by Gad Lerner. It was at the time when the right-wing leader Ariel Sharon had returned to the cabinet in a dubious government of national unity with Labour, despite their previously strong opposition to him, and the time too of the racist proclamations of Rabbi Meir Kahane. Levi declared straight away, as though to get a weight off his mind:

> I've become convinced that Israel's role as the unifying centre of Judaism is now (I stress *now*) in a phase of eclipse. So it's necessary then for the centre of gravity in Judaism to be turned around, to return to us Jews of the diaspora, who have the task of reminding our Israeli friends of the role of tolerance in Judaism.

Not that he considered Israel's regression, or its blurring of ideals (which, he observed, it shared with the whole world) as irreversible. Nor did he see the return of the hawk Sharon, or even the ravings of Rabbi Kahane on driving out the whole Arab population, as reasons for rupture:

> Kahane is just a loose cannon [...] for a country to become racist it needs to be close-knit, to be able to form a solid, uniform, manoeuvrable block. Hitler's Germany managed it, but Italy for example didn't, because of the simple fact that the difference between a Piedmontese and a Calabrian is too great. It could hardly happen in a community fragmented by a three-thousand-year history, characterized by a mosaic of ethnicities and traditions, like Israel. That said, I know that there's a racist strand in the Torah. You can find everything and the opposite of everything in it.

To the ravings of Kahane, who is convinced that in the twentieth century the Arabs will become the majority, and that therefore Israel must stop being a democracy in order to safeguard its Jewish identity, Primo Levi counters that it is senseless to make demographic projections more than five years ahead. Not to mention that the Arab Israeli birth rate is decreasing while the Jewish one is increasing; and that in the hospitals and universities the two groups are becoming profoundly integrated. However:

> It's a different question for the million and a half Palestinians in the occupied West Bank, [...]which should lead the Israeli rulers to withdraw quickly from the territories. I think that if it weren't dragging that heavy load of the West Bank and Gaza, Israel's Palestinian problem would already be solved.

'What do you mean', Gad Lerner asks, 'when you talk about the degradation of Israeli political life?' Primo Levi cites the paralysing agreement which led to the 'grand coalition'; the 'disgusting' compromises made in order to win votes.

> That doesn't happen only in Israel, but maybe we're not so used to its happening there. We think of Israel as a country of miracles – the Israel of 1948, a Zionism that includes. Now we're seeing a decline that's actually a normalization. Israel, unfortunately, is becoming a normal country. And being a Middle Eastern country, it's tending to become more or less similar to the other nations of that region. For example, we might well fear a contagion between Islamic Khomeinism and the spread of religious fundamentalism in Israel. Though looking at it in perspective, I don't see the Israeli masses prostrating themselves before a new ayatollah, whether Kahane or Sharon himself.

But in normalizing themselves, aren't Israelis changing their identity? asks the journalist, thinking of European Jews shaped by their diversity; of the Jews in Levi's books, tragically attached to the fragile value of tolerance. In his reply, Levi energetically reasserts his harsh initial position:

> One can foresee that in the future. I think that it is up to us, Jews of the diaspora, to fight. To remind our Israeli friends that being Jewish means something else. [...] Of course, I realize that I am touching on a crucial point here, which is the question: where is the centre of gravity of Judaism today? I have thought long and hard about this: the centre of gravity is returning to the diaspora. As a diasporic Jew, much more Italian than Jewish, I would rather the centre of gravity remained outside Israel.

That could sound as though you are taking leave of the Israeli nation, of what it has turned into.

Nothing of the kind. It's the development of a deep and passionate relationship. I just think that the main current of Judaism is better preserved elsewhere than in Israel. Jewish culture itself, especially Ashkenazi culture, is more vibrant in the United States, for example, where indeed it could be said to play a decisive role.

Isn't that tantamount to saying that, in order for Jewish identity to be preserved, Jews must remain minority communities?

I would say exactly that. I would say that the best of Jewish culture is linked to its being dispersed and polycentric.

But wasn't it the opposite? Wasn't it Israel that infused strength and confidence in Jews around the world?

Sadly, there's been a reversal. From the source where the Jews of the diaspora once drew their strength they now draw reflection and disquiet. That is why I speak of an eclipse, I hope a temporary one, in Israel's role as the unifying centre of Judaism. We must support Israel as its embassies ask us to; but we must also make it feel the numerical, cultural and even economic weight of the diaspora. We have the power and also the duty to bring some influence to bear on Israeli politics. First of all, I think we must demand a withdrawal from Lebanon. Equally urgent is halting the new Jewish settlements in the occupied territories. After that, as I've said, a withdrawal [...] Maybe the moment will come when an Israeli government will be able to negotiate with the PLO, but not now. Both parties are too unsettled at the moment.

The journalist comes from Israel and is Jewish. He well remembers the protest the writer initiated against the Israeli government and asks:

Is indignation the incentive that can unite the Jews of the diaspora?

Let's say, more calmly, disapproval. Yes, that is an incentive, though I can hear what Israelis will say – 'What do you know, you armchair Jew over there in Italy?' Yet I insist. The history of the diaspora has been a history of persecutions, but it's also been a history of inter-ethnic exchanges and relationships, and therefore a school of tolerance. Especially in Italy. If I were less tired, if I had more strength, I'd work in the Italian Jewish community to make it become a model. Because I'm happy with the integration of the Jews in Italy; but not with their

> assimilation, their disappearance, the dissolution of their culture. Right here in Turin, there's the positive example of a Jewish community integrated into the life and culture of the city, but not assimilated.

It cost Primo Levi a great deal to say what he did to Gad Lerner. So at the end he becomes less peremptory.

> *Are relations with Jewish institutions difficult, for someone who thinks as you do?*
>
> I'd say we have an affectionate and argumentative relationship. Certainly, a profound one. Because I'm convinced that Israel must be defended: I believe in the painful necessity of an efficient army. But I'm also convinced that it's good for the Israeli government that our support should be conditional.[23]

It fell to Primo Levi to give a lead to another of Einaudi's publishing ideas, as had already happened with *The Search for Roots*, which had been intended as the first in a series about writers' influences. Now, it was Levi's translation of Kafka's *The Trial* that opened the series STS, Scrittori tradotti da scrittori [Writers translated by writers]. According to the editors, the idea was to write through another writer, to make another writer's work one's own, because translating is examining a book through a microscope, penetrating it, merging with it. Levi's *Trial* entered the bookshops at the end of April 1983. He told Luciano Genta from *Tuttolibri*:

> Kafka is a maelstrom, a vortex that draws you into the evil of the world. His agitation affects you. I felt myself becoming ill, put on trial like him. I came out of this translation as you come out of an illness. *The Trial*, like all Kafka's work, is an unhealthy book, outside the norm. Its disturbance is transmitted to the translator, in amplified form because translating is to reading what ploughing the soil is to touching it. You have to examine, digest, every single word.[25]

Ills, illness, falling ill. He hammered away at the concept, at the word and its derivatives and synonyms, in his translator's note and in the interviews he gave on this book, which he called in a signed copy he gave to a friend 'this son-in-law who makes me suffer'.

'Where did the idea of offering a new version of Kafka's text come from?', Giuseppe Bernardi of *Il Giorno* asks. 'From a personal need of yours?'

> No, it was a proposal from Giulio Einaudi, who was obviously thinking of Kafka's centenary and the other Kafka events going on at that time. I accepted willingly. I'd just finished *If Not Now, When?* and found

> myself out of ideas [...] But it's a text one doesn't emerge from unscathed.[26]

He'd also accepted the assumption behind the publisher's suggestion, he told Fabrizio Dentice of *L'Espresso,* but had not been able to keep to it:

> It was assumed that the writer-translator would leave traces of himself in the work. But in doing the job I tried to strip myself of my identity as much as I could: out of respect, out of humility, most of all out of dazzlement before such an extraordinary work. We've all read it; but translating it means weighing it, idea by idea, word by word, undergoing its full effect.

Between the fluent, uninhibited translation of Alberto Spaini and the rigorous, philological one of Giorgio Zampa, he had kept to the middle road:

> [...] I tried most of all to pass on what *The Trial* was for me, in my personal and private reading. Kafka set off unconscious defences in me: I hadn't even included him in the anthology of my 'roots', because I feared him, he's so threatening. Those defences collapsed as I translated him, and I felt as though I'd fallen into the character of Joseph K. I felt that I was being tried together with him.[27]

'Someone must have slandered Joseph K, because one morning, without having done anything wrong, he was arrested.' This is how Primo Levi's translation begins. The correspondent for *Il Giorno* would like him to explain 'anything wrong'. What does it mean? Isn't it enigmatic?

> It is indeed, because the book itself is enigmatic. We could complete the phrase by saying: without having *consciously* committed any wrong. Unconsciously carrying a burden of guilt is part of many spiritual traditions. Catholics are born into the world with original sin, and I think there's something similar in the Jewish tradition. Without transcendent meaning, birth itself is an addition to the burden of the world: an intervention on the world around one, like physically occupying a space. Joseph K is thirty, and how many things can you do wrong in thirty years without knowing it? [...] He becomes convinced that he is guilty of something. When a person is marked out as guilty, the suspicion that he is guilty slowly grows in him. It's one of the beautiful and terrible things about this book.
>
> *And at the end he's ashamed. Of what?*

> Perhaps he's ashamed of his guilt, or of defending himself, or of not defending himself enough, or of all those things at the same time. It seems to me a mistake to ask Kafka for consistency, especially within this book. People aren't consistent, even within a single moment.[28]

'You've written in the afterword, that you don't feel akin to Kafka', Luciano Genta observes. 'In what sense?'

> I'm Italian and much less Jewish than him. Most of all, I force myself to have a rational view of the world: in my books I've tried, as far as possible, to overcome my anguish, to resolve it, not to remain trapped in the distorted world of the Lager. Kafka follows the opposite path. He plunges into the depths and never comes out of them. For example, despite being a contemporary of Freud, he stays away from psychoanalysis: because he's not interested in a scientific, positivistic study of the human soul, in the search for the rules that drive our behaviour. His denunciation of reality in never explicit, but it's always there in the way he tells the story. In his writing, he sought his own personal liberation he didn't believe in literature as a vehicle for communication, as a dialogue between writer and reader.

The exact opposite of this writer-translator, for whom the experiment of pouring himself into someone else, of entering someone else's skin, had been a risk that was not without its consequences:

> I had to strip myself of my own way of writing and seeing the world – because his writing is the mirror of the way an author sees the world. [If it had been up to me] I would have chosen Conrad or Thomas Mann, whom I feel closer to; I would have preferred an author who taught me the serenity that comes from overcoming things.

The journalist would like to know whether Kafka's Jewish roots were a motive for translating him:

> No, at least not consciously. Of course, I sense in Kafka a man nourished on the Bible and the Talmud. The Jewish component in him is always present, but underground, buried, never openly declared; I don't think he ever used the word 'Jew'.
>
> *The term 'Kafkaesque' encapsulates a philosophy of life; it's used politically to refer to the alienation of capitalist society, or to the Soviet gulag. Are they inaccurate, these parallels that bring him up to date?*

> We can't not bring Kafka up to date. I don't want to attribute prophetic qualities to him, but he was sensitive to what what was brewing in the Europe he lived in. He must have had a sensibility like the kind animals have for earthquakes. Of course, seeing a prophet in Kafka is limiting, because there's everything in him. Every reader recognizes himself in Kafka so the interpretations are infinite, as many as there are readers.
>
> *His friend Max Brod claims that he loved life, loved jokes; that he possessed humour and irony. Is that a paradox?*
>
> The split between the man and the writer is often considerable; in Kafka it's enormous. It doesn't seem to me that laughter as such is found in his work. Sometimes there's a laugh, but it's never a happy one: it's grotesque, twisted; it arises from surreal events; it's impregnated with the anguish of nightmares.

On his relationship with Kafka's language, Levi said:

> I learned German in the Lager, out of necessity, so that I could survive, and I brought back with me a deep and unsatisfied curiosity about German language and culture. Kafka's German seemed fluid and clean, to me; I didn't have big technical difficulties. The aim of my translation is to make Italian readers feel the same emotions as German ones. I tried to soften out the rough patches; to attain, while still remaining faithful to the original, a fluidity of language. When I'd finished, I felt dizzy that I'd had that audacity. I await my readers' judgement with fear and trepidation.[29]

The reactions were for the most part flattering. Some of them (Oreste Del Buono in *La Stampa*, for instance, called him 'a mediator [...] between Kafka and himself the Auschwitz survivor') led him to rethink the criteria he'd used in the translation, and most of all his claims that he was not akin to the author of the *Trial*.[30] It was true – he was fascinated by Kafka's style of writing, which was totally precluded to him, the high priest of clarity and balance. He felt at the same time attracted and repelled, terrified and seduced, wounded and dazzled, so much so as to come away with 'the feeling of a collision, of a conflict' as he said in his Translator's Note. 'It was', he observes acutely to del Buono, 'a real battle between two writers, between the German Jew from Prague who had foreseen something and the Italian Jew from Turin who had seen it, between the prophet and the witness'.[31] The two combatants arrive at agreement on the last page, about the essence of Joseph K's shame at his journey's end: it is shame at being human, because of what humans can do. The same 'shame' pervades the Auschwitz survivors, is discussed at the beginning of *The Truce* and has a whole chapter dedicated to it in *The Drowned and the Saved*.

Translating Kafka took up the summer of 1982, which was useful for getting out of every public engagement until the Campiello prize-giving ceremony, the crowning moment in the success of *If Not Now, When?* He kept on saying no after that to all invitations to take part in debates on Israel and anti-Semitism. 'I collect refusals', he said. 'There are already more than forty of them, but I don't feel up to these things'. He had started by refusing an interview to Antonio Baglivo of *Corriere della Sera*, who was investigating how Jewish communities were reacting to the Israeli invasion of Lebanon: 'I don't want my name to be linked to that war any more.'[32]

He was disturbed by the demonization of Israel; he was irritated by the carelessness with which words like 'racism', 'genocide' and 'extermination' were used in the reports of Middle Eastern events. He had taken the position he had, but he could not tolerate Jews being put on trial as Jews, and would not lend himself to the blame game that was developing before his eyes. On the day of the Rome synagogue attack he declared to *L'Unità*:

> I do not think that this savage form of anti-Semitism has any particular meaning. These events are a pretext for giving vent to old envies and resentments. The political errors made across the Mediterranean do not in any way justify these actions, which are pure criminality.[33]

He immersed himself in the anthropology of Claude Lévi-Strauss and translated, between long breaks, *The Way of the Masks* and *The View from Afar*. As a result he enjoyed a correspondence with their author, who had read *The Wrench*, and despite the unsatisfactory French translation declared himself a fan, 'because I like stories about trades'. At the start of 1983, Levi tried to go back to talking in schools, but stopped almost immediately. Emerging from one exhausting exchange with students he told a journalist:

> Language has become difficult. I don't know them anymore. They ask me what I think of them, they ask me questions about the future and about God, and I don't know how to reply. They're nice, I like them, but they're strangers to me now.

He signed many contracts for translations of his works. The American publisher told him that work on *The Periodic Table* was going well and that *If Not Now, When?* would be entrusted to William Weaver, the prince of American translators. His friend, the Italianist Stuart Woolf, had come to see him, and they'd reminisced about their meticulous work together to translate *If This is a Man* into English so many years before. Levi did not grant any interviews in this period, apart from those on Kafka. Between one piece for

La Stampa and another, he gave free rein to a new 'outbreak' of poetry; and he read a lot, especially Pliny.

He received a shock in July, after *If Not Now, When?* had sold more than 150,000 copies, by the visit of two young men of the new Right, and what he later called the 'wicked and sacrilegious' discussion he had with them. Sceptical about the existence of the gas chambers, they nonetheless nurtured an unhealthy curiosity about the effects of Zyklon B, the gas used for extermination. They insinuated that only typhus had killed people in Auschwitz. He bared his arm, showed his tattooed number and gave them the same explanation that Schmulek had given him in the Lager, before being sent to the gas chambers himself:

> Can you read this? It's a number from February 1944, when there were 10,000 of us in my camp. Where do you think the others ended up? Of 8,000 Italian Jews 600 of us came back. Where do you think the others are?

He came out of isolation with an interview in *La Repubblica* on the current dangers to humanity, and with a piece for *La Stampa* on the crucial choice of 8 September 1943, when Italy had signed an armistice with the Allies and been occupied by the Nazis. In the *Repubblica* interview, he spoke of the serious danger of air pollution, and of the symmetry between the world's moral and material fate:

> Since we've stopped believing in almost everything, it's become as difficult to mobilize people to rescue the Earth as to fight a war or to carry out any other undertaking, good or bad. We don't trust the future. Young people born in a condemned world don't trust the past and think they can sense the end; they suspect the sixty-year-olds are guilty and would prefer not to become guilty themselves. We keep calm by relying on an obsessive unconscious belief that progress is irreversible. But when carbon dioxide in the atmosphere has reached 0.04 per cent, we'll all have to act together. The obsession is worldwide and there's only one world, ever smaller and more fragile. [...] It is contradiction itself that keeps us alive: the eternal contradiction of man, who rationally knows that he is mortal and instinctively feels that he isn't; because a species that had the instinctive awareness that it must die inscribed in its genes would become extinct immediately.[34]

He opened his doors to other interviewers and to students who were doing their dissertations about him; he went to Camerino[35] to receive the prize for mountain literature which he'd won with the story 'Iron' in *The Periodic Table*; he regained his taste for excursions with old friends, rebuilding his ties with them.

In September he met Elie Wiesel, who had been in the Lager at the same time as he had; they were like brothers. He talked about that meeting at the Congresso degli ex deportati di Torino [Congress of ex-deportees of Turin], and again at the conference on Jewish literature in Italy organized by the Jewish Community of Venice two months later. Here, stimulated by the warm words of Guido Lopez ('If not Primo Levi, who?'), he suggested establishing a Decalogue of Jewishness in writers, and testing to what extent each met its requirements.

As for himself, he had already said that he happily accepted the definition of 'Jewish writer' and did not regard it as reductive. It was said of him that 'His books were and are universal, they don't belong to any particular nation or any particular time.'[36] Their rigour, calm and honesty, their morality outside and above any religion, crossed America's ethnic and social divides and reached cultures far away from Judaism. This was confirmed by Furio Colombo, a Turinese-American journalist and writer who, describing to the Jewish Community of Turin the extraordinarily wide appeal of Primo Levi in the United States, aptly defined him as 'the writer dearest to the largest number of non-Jews' in the nation that is home to the largest number of Jews in the world.[37]

Notes

1. P. Levi trans. A. Goldstein, *The Periodic Table*, in A. Goldstein (ed.), *Complete Works of Primo Levi* (New York: Liveright, 2015, p.782).
2. Giorgio De Rienzo,'In un alambicco quanta poesia'[So much poetry in a still], *Famiglia Cristiana*, no.29, 20July 1975.
3. Conversation between Primo Levi and Dina Luce, 'Il suono e la mente' [Sound and mind], RAI Radio 2, 4 October 1982.
4. Ferdinando Camon, 'Ma allora Dio non c'è?' [But then there isn't a God?], *Panorama*, 25 May 1986 and *Autoritratto di Primo Levi* [Self-portrait of Primo Levi] (Padua: Edizioni Nord Est, 1987), p.71 *passim*.
5. Gianni Milani, 'Al chimico va stretta la memoria del Lager' [Lager memory constricts the chemist], *PiemonteVip*, March 1986, p.19.
6. Movement which led to the unification of Italy in 1861.
7. Primo Levi, Bellagio text (see Chapter 10).
8. During the Primo Levi International Study Days (held on 28-29 March 1988 in Turin), Alberto Cavaglion emphasized the significant epigraph Primo Levi had added by hand, next to the title, in his first draft of 'Argon', which dates back to June 1973: '*Quem legis, ut noris*' [So that you may know whom you read], from Ovid's Tristia, IV 10, 1-2, 'Ille ego qui fuerim, tenorum lusor amorum, quem legis, ut noris, accipe posteritas' ['That you may know who I was, I the playful poet of tender love whom you read, hear my words, you future generations.'] The draft was included in an essay by Cavaglion, 'Argon e la cultura ebraica piemontese (con l'abbozzo del racconto)' [Argon and Piedmontese Jewish culture (with the draft of the story)], in a book edited by Cavaglion: *Primo Levi. Il presente del passato* [Primo Levi: the present of the past] (Milan, Franco Angeli, 1991). The draft appears on pp.187-96, Cavaglion's essay on pp. 169-86.
9. Passed in 1935, these laws defined Jews in racial rather than religious terms, deprived them of German citizenship and almost all political and civil rights.

10. Camon, *Autoritratto di Primo Levi*,p.15.
11. In fact, the second two quotations in this paragraph are from P. Levi trans. A and F. Bastagli, 'The Last Christmas of the War', in *Uncollected Stories and Essays: 1981-1987* in *Complete Works of Primo Levi*, Vol. III, pp.2,683-90.
12. There is a legend that the nineteenth-century rabbi created a golem, a clay creature who came to life to defend the Jews from antisemitic attacks. There are many different versions of this legend.
13. Bar mitzvah is the ceremony on the occasion of the boy's thirteenth birthday. From that moment onwards, he is considered an adult and responsible for his own religious conduct. The phylacteries (*tefillin*) are leather boxes containing the precepts of the Torah, the Law: they are tied with leather straps to the head and to the left arm during morning prayers. Unleavened, that is unrisen, bread (in memory of the bread that did not have time to rise on the night of the Jews' flight from Egypt) is consumed on the eight days of Pesach, especially during the Passover feast (Seder), which remembers the solemn days of the 'crossing'. Rosh Hashanah is the Jewish New Year. Purim is the feast on which the Book of Esther is read: it celebrates escape from the extermination decreed by the cruel Persian vizier Haman; it is customary to exchange gifts and give them especially to children and to the poor.
14. Supporters of Juventus, the most successful football team in Turin.
15. S.Jesurum, *Essere ebrei in Italia*[Being Jewish in Italy] (Longanesi: Milan, 1987), p.100.
16. From the interview broadcast on 3 February 1985.
17. Primo Levi, 'Chi ha coraggio a Gerusalemme?' [Who has courage in Jerusalem?], *La Stampa*, 24 June 1982.
18. Alberto Stabile, 'Sì, Israele ha passato il segno, ma non è giusto parlare di nazismo' [Yes, Israel has overstepped the mark but it is not fair to speak of Nazism], *La Repubblica*, 28 June 1982.
19. A miscarriage of justice which deeply divided French politics between supporters and opponents of Alfred Dreyfus, a Jewish army officer falsely convicted, in 1894, of communicating military secrets to Germany. Dreyfus was imprisoned on French Guiana until 1899, when a second trial confirmed his conviction but he was pardoned. He was finally exonerated and reinstated in the Army in 1906.
20. Za'ev Jabotinsky was the leader of a right-wing militant form of Zionism, the ancestor of today's Likud party in Israel. He founded a youth organisation called Betar. Begin was head of Betar Poland before the war and of Betar Palestine after it.
21. Giampaolo Pansa, 'Io Primo Levi chiedo le dimissioni di Begin e Sharon. Begin, gli ebrei dicono basta' [I, Primo Levi, ask for Begin and Sharon to resign. Begin, the Jews say enough], *La Repubblica*, 24 September 1982.
22. Primo Levi, 'Il pericolo viene dal militarismo' [The danger comes from militarism], *La Repubblica*, 11 February 1983.
23. Gad Lerner, 'Se questo è uno stato' [If This is a State], *L'Espresso*, 30 September 1984.
24. F. Kafka trans. P. Levi, *Il processo* [The Trial] (Turin: Einaudi, 1983), Nota del Traduttore [Translator's Note], p.253.
25. Luciano Genta, 'Così ho rivissuto "Il Processo" di Kafka' [This is how I relived Kafka's 'Trial'], *Tuttolibri (La Stampa)*, 9 April 1983.
26. Giuseppe Bernardi, 'Primo Levi traduce Kafka' [Primo Levi translates Kafka], *Il Giornale*, 22 May 1983.
27. Fabrizio Dentice, 'Mi travesto da Kafka' [I dress up as Kafka], *L'Espresso*, 24 April 1983.
28. Bernardi, 'Primo Levi traduce Kafka'.
29. Genta, 'Così ho rivissuto "Il Processo" di Kafka'.
30. Primo Levi, 'Kafka col coltello nel cuore' [Kafka with the knife in his heart], *La Stampa*, 5 June 1983.
31. Oreste Del Buono, 'Primo Levi ritraduce Kafka: il nuovo "Processo"' [Primo Levi retranslates Kafka: the new 'Trial'], *Corriere della Sera*, 7 July 1982.

32. Antonio Baglivo, 'Gli ebrei di Torino: non più Olocausti' [The Jews of Turin: no more Holocausts], *Corriere della Sera*, 7 July 1983.
33. Statement by Primo Levi reported in *L'Unità* (title not known), 10 October 1982.
34. Interview with Edgardo Bartoli, 'Prima che il sole ci ingoi' [Before the sun swallows us up], *La Repubblica*, 16 August 1993.
35. A hilltop town in Marche, in eastern central Italy.
36. Jesurum, *Essere ebrei in Italia*, p.98.
37. Furio Columbo gave the opening speech at the commemorative event organized on the second anniversary of Primo Levi's death at the headquarters of the Jewish Community of Turin [*Comunità israelitica di Torino*, renamed *Comunità ebraica di Torino*, later in 1989], 12 April 1989.

XII

Field Invasions

The year 1984 brought Primo Levi a wave of rejuvenating energy. It came from several happy events: the publication of his second book of poetry; the arrival of a new collaborator, the computer; and last but not least, the unexpected success of *The Periodic Table* in America. This success was displayed in the countless reviews in newspapers, magazines, literary supplements and even scientific reviews; and by the urgent request he received from the across the ocean, inviting him to introduce himself to his new audience.

Even before this new infusion of energy, Levi had been relaxed about growing older. He was just 63 when he answered a question from *Stampa Sera* on the subject:

> Am I old? In objective terms, yes: my documents prove it, as do my long-sightedness, my grey hair, my children who are now adults. Just last week, for the first time people stood up for me on the tram, which had a powerful effect on me. But subjectively I don't feel old, as a rule. I haven't lost my curiosity for the world around me, nor my interest in my fellow humans, and I still want to compete with others and to have a go at solving problems. I still love nature: it gives me great joy to sense it, study it and describe it. My organs, limbs, memory and imagination are all still in good working order. But I'm acutely aware of that ominous word that I've just written three times: 'still'.[1]

His second collection of poetry added another thirty poems – almost all of which readers would have seen first in *La Stampa* – to those already published by Scheiwiller.[2] For this collection too he accepted the offer of a publisher other than Einaudi, which was involved in legal trouble at the time. He signed the contract with Garzanti in March and the book was in the shops in October. Its title, *Ad ora incerta* [At an uncertain hour], was a line from Coleridge's *Rime of the Ancient Mariner,* which Levi had explored many times before. He quoted it in a poem ('The Survivor') and placed it as an epigraph to his last book, *The Drowned and the Saved:* 'Since then, at an uncertain hour/That agony returns'.[3] And – he could have added – if he finds no one to listen to him, the heart within him burns. Quotations, he said, are a rabbinical vice: a vice that he enjoyed, along with the games of intellect, the subtle witticisms and refined humour of his Jewish culture.

Primo Levi counted Giulio Nascimbeni of *Corriere della Sera* among his favourite interviewers. When Nascimbeni came to speak to him about his new poems, Levi showed him the long row of translations of his books, and then the delicate wire sculptures he had made:

> Why do I use this material? I was a chemist for thirty years, and specialized in the glazing of copper wires.

The interviewer starts by asking him to explain the title of his new collection: does poetry come to him 'at an uncertain hour'?

> Yes. It's an observation I made *a posteriori*, when I put the dates in order. My poems cluster around the years 1945 and 1946 and again between 1983 and this year. They seem to have come in two groups. In between came my prose works and my professional life as a chemist. To write after eight hours in the factory I had to find a method, a rule.There was no space for poetry: exactly that 'uncertain hour' was missing.

If This is a Man was first published in 1947, so the first few poems must have been written even before:

> I'd just got back to Italy. It was like finding myself in a bed of mushrooms: you never know why and how a mushroom is born.

'And yet', objects the journalist, 'Adorno had said that after Auschwitz one could no longer write poetry'.[4]

> My experience has been the opposite. It seemed to me then that poetry was more suited than prose for expressing what was weighing inside me. By 'poetry' I don't mean anything lyrical. In those years, if anything I would have reformulated Adorno's words: the only poetry one can write is about Auschwitz.
>
> *And the 1983-84 cluster of poems?*
>
> They were a kind of holiday after the publication of *If Not Now, When?* It was a very challenging moment. The novel came out in the middle of the crisis in Lebanon, which was a crisis for everyone, not just for Jews. It seemed natural to me to find a poetic language to write in again. Not without embarrassment, I admit, because I'm ignorant of poetry: I know little about poetic theory, I don't read

much poetry, and I don't even think these verses of mine are very good.

Isn't the position you find yourself in paradoxical?

Yes, that's true. I'm I don't believe in poetry very much and yet I practice it all the same. There are several reasons. For example, when my poems are published in *La Stampa*, I get letters and telephone calls from readers, both positive and negative. When I publish a story, the correspondence isn't as lively.

The interviewer goes back to the most famous lines, those at the beginning of *If This is a Man*: 'You who live safe/ In your warm houses...' Do they still apply?

You know my story, so you know that the experience of the Lager can't be erased. It can be overcome, made painless, even made useful like all experiences of life, but it can't be erased. In the free time I have, I go on putting the question I put back then: *if this is a man*. It doesn't just refer to the world of Nazism and the Second World War, but also to the world of today, to terrorists, to bad politicians, to anyone who is exploitative or who has let themselves be corrupted. In fact, to all cases in which one wonders whether a human being still retains their humanity, and if not, whether they can get it back.

There is a poem that speaks in Pliny's voice: 'Centuries after the atoms of this old body/Will spin again in the universe's vortices/ Or live again in an eagle, a girl...' Do you believe in reincarnation?

I'm not thinking of anything metaphysical here. It's an idea as old as the world. It's there in Pythagoras, in Lucretius.[5] And the fathers of chemistry in the last century taught us that the oxygen we breathe comes from plants, and that the essence of plants, wood, comes from the carbon dioxide that we and all animals emit during life and after death.

What you call your 'rational half' gave that answer. What is the other half like?

Irrational. It's a mechanism I don't know and which sets itself off unexpectedly, as a result of unexpected stimuli: a spider's web, a germ, a paving stone.[6]

Insisting on the 'continuity of discontinuity in his intermittent and compulsive inspiration', the poet Giovanni Raboni writes of Primo Levi the poet: 'The trigger, the initial impulse of every single poem is always visibly heteronomous: they're born from reason, from the moral reading of reality, from the ability to understand his own suffering and his own indignation as a heritage common to all. The same qualities that make his prose unique and irreplaceable.'[7] Giovanni Tesio looks for a confirmation from the source. In an interview for *Tuttolibri* he asks Levi what causes these intermittent impulses:

> The most unpredictable things. A spider's web, a snail, the devil's bridge in Lanzo,[8] or memory, the return of memory.
>
> *A section of the collection is dedicated to translations: of a Scottish ballad, of Heine and Kipling.*[9] *Did those too come to you at an uncertain hour?*
>
> Yes. I encountered the Scottish ballad a very long time ago, and above all liked its rhythm. It's a bit like that for all of them, they're translations I did for fun. With Heine, I found in him the same irreverence for poetry that I feel myself – also at an uncertain hour. It comes and goes. But I also feel reverence for many poets, and at an uncertain hour, even for myself as a poet.

Despite Levi's dissent, Tesio finds that there is lyricism in the the Lager poems. Whereas in those from the 1970s and 1980s, in his view, there is irony. What does the author say?

> I'm not so sure that irony prevails in the ones between 1982 and 1984. But when it's there, it's there to fill a a void, including a void of inspiration. Besides, the book collects poems written over forty years, and so many things change in forty years, they even change from one hour to the next. And then I think that a a whole collection all in the same tone would be very dull.

Plants and animals often speak in your poems. Is that because of your scientific education?

> It's the fruit of an unsatisfied curiosity. I've often quoted Aldous Huxley, who says that for him a novelist must be a zoologist.[10] For me that love exists, one-sided and only partly satisfied. Love for nature as a whole, and in particular for the *fruschi*, as Carlo Levi called them, using a dialect term – that is, for the poor beasts.[11] In animals there's the great and the small, wisdom and folly, generosity

> and baseness. Each one is a metaphor, a distillation of all human vices and virtues.[12]

Primo Levi fell in love with computers in the summer of 1984 and by September he already had one at home. He approached it slowly, at first just using it for entertainment, doing little drawings and puzzles. The first thing that he wrote on it was a poem. And from that day on it became indispensable to him, for archiving and storing work as well as writing it. Six months later, during an episode of the TV programme 'Italia Sera', he jokingly called his word processor 'my catamite'. For the first anniversary of their cohabitation, he dedicated to this catamite the story 'The Hidden Player', in which he revealed that it was he with whom he played chess.[13]

'But can poetry get along with the computer?' the IT monthly *Genius* asked. He replied:

> [...] the poetic image is born somewhere in our brain, and is then recorded, meeting various obstacles along the way, if not very great ones. Therefore, if you use the computer for writing, it's not incompatible at all. On the contrary, the ease of deleting, correcting, adding and replacing makes ideas flow more easily onto the page. Maybe even too easily – the lack of anything holding you back (writing on a word processor is much less tiring than any other method) can make a writer's work more long-winded and less meaningful. But the opposite is also true: deleting is immediate and doesn't scar the page; stripping away the excess is painless and very easy.

True, the computer can do much more than act as a simple substitute for the typewriter:

> During the creative process properly speaking, it can point out the rhymes, the rhythms, the repetitions, the alliterations, intended or otherwise. Within a text, it can instantly transform a term into its synonym or opposite or correct the spelling. It can act as a store of ideas, a bridge between ideas, and maybe even do other miracles which, novice as I am (I bought a computer a short time ago for word processing), I can't yet imagine. But these are fringe services in my view: they'll never make a non-poet into a poet, nor will they increase a poet's skill – but neither will they destroy it.

He went on listing the prodigious progress of the computer in the forty years since its birth. Pledging to atone for any false predictions, and humorously acknowledging that many famous scientists had made them, he nonetheless declared:

> I know next to nothing about computer theory, nor about poetic theories, so I hope I'm not talking nonsense. But I'll stick my neck out and say that a computer that produces valid, original poetry by itself will never be built. Bad poetry, yes: computers may get as far as [...] correctly composing hendecasyllables with the correct stresses, or maybe even hexameters conforming to the norms of Latin poetry, which will look so like human poetry that they'll amaze us, or make us laugh. But poetry in the strong sense of the term, no.

The machine, if appropriately programmed, will be equally capable of logical operations and random choices. But this is the difference:

> [...] poetry is greater than logic or chance: it can contain both of them within itself, but it is broader than both. It contains other things: associations that are deep or subtle but in any case new; references and archetypes; hard-to-define correspondences between signifier and signified, between music and vision and word; conscious or unconscious quotations of great predecessors. Which one could describe with the French poet Paul Éluard's beautiful phrase 'unbroken poetry' – unbroken across centuries and borders, an essentially unitary poetic heritage that accompanies the human species throughout its history and its sufferings. The computer seems to me an excellent tool for carrying out clear and distinct tasks, but poetry isn't such a task: it's fluid, oblique, continuous, bathed in halos and shadows.[14]

Primo Levi entrusted an important job to his computer: making the cover illustration for *L'Altrui Mestiere* [*Other People's Trades*], published by Einaudi at the start of 1985, 'the product of a decade and more of vagabond and dilettante curiosity'. He described the essays that made it up as 'field invasions' – that is, incursions into other people's areas of expertise; and in its own way, he said, so was that cover. As a guest on the television programme 'Italia sera', he told the presenter, who asked who had done the triplicate drawing of the blue owl:

> My computer did. I work and play on it: but most of all I work on it. I've taken it quite seriously, it's a tool that is very useful to me.[15]

So useful that during his last interview, with Roberto Di Caro, he agreed to compare it to Faussone's hammer, which can repair anything. The journalist had persuaded him to talk about his writing technique. He said:

> Clumsy, poorly written phrases must be removed and replaced. Soon after it's written a text is unreadable, it doesn't make sense, it's like looking in the mirror and always seeing the same face. One needs to leave it to rest, for days or weeks, and only then take it up again. Then a bit of hammering works. Better still: the clippers work. For that, the Macintosh is a wonderful tool, because it cuts everything away without pity, no trace is left of a single deletion.

His curiosity aroused, the interviewer persists: 'Is there much difference between writing a book on the computer and writing it on the typewriter?'

> There's more difference than between writing by hand and using a computer. Using a pen, it's easy to take glue and scissors and make insertions, change and adjust the text. On the computer, that's even easier, it's all done on the screen. Using the typewriter, on the other hand, the tiny effort of taking a page out, or using correction fluid, means that often one gives up, on putting a phrase or a sentence right, out of inertia or laziness. I doubt, though, that any literary scholar[16] will ever be able to establish if a text was written with a pen, a typewriter or a computer.

During the same conversation, the writer explained his process in writing poetry and how it was helped by the computer.

> I'm an occasional poet: all things considered I've written little more than a poem a year across my life, even though there've been periods when it came spontaneously to me to write in verse. But it's an activity that has nothing to do with any other mental activity I know of. It's a completely different thing, it's like a fungus that grows in a night: one wakes up in the morning with a poem in one's mind, or at least the core of one. After that it's an endless task of variations and corrections, for which the computer is the perfect tool – sadly for future literary scholars, who won't find the manuscripts with successive versions that they're looking for. ... Many years ago, in *Natural Histories*, I wrote a story about a poet who'd bought himself a mechanical versifier. All you had to do was to set the theme, the epoch, the metre, the length and the subject and the machine produced the desired work on its own [...] Mine was a commercial machine, paid by the piece: they commissioned him for example, to write an ode to celebrate the victory of A C Milan over Juventus. Of course, it's obvious that *Orlando Furioso* involved a complex assembly job – but that doesn't concern me, since my poems are never longer than my hand.

His American triumph came in the spring, with a glowing tribute from the Nobel prize-winner and undisputed authority Saul Bellow. Having read *The Periodic Table* in Raymond Rosenthal's excellent translation, he had chosen it as his book of the year: 'We are always looking for the book it is necessary to read next [...] There is nothing superfluous here, everything this book contains is essential.' It was a sign that Primo Levi was being rediscovered in the USA (his first two books of memoir, twenty years before, had passed almost unnoticed there). His success was rapidly confirmed by the most prestigious critics reviewing him and publishers fighting over him; by invitations, proposals, and interminable television interviews with the stunned and exhausted author. He ended up going to the RAI studios in Turin to record his answers to eight questions from the *New York Times*: Why a book about a chemical subject? Why so much simplicity, as though he were writing a letter to a friend? What was the situation for Jews between 1938 and 1945 in Italy? Could he go into detail about Müller, the German chemist who is protagonist of the story 'Vanadium'? What was the background to the story of 'Carbon'? What impression did the 'terrific reaction' to his books in America make on him? What had he written after *The Periodic Table*? Did he still practice his profession as a chemist?

In April 1985 he agreed to the request from his American publisher, from the Italian cultural institute in New York, and from the Jewish organization B'nai B'rith, to do a lecture tour of the US, where he spoke to packed audiences in New York, Boston and California. But before then – at the same time as two publishers were arguing over *If Not Now, When?*, Weaver was translating *La chiave a stella* as *The Monkey's Wrench*[17] and Ruth Feldman *Ad ora incerta* as *Collected Poems*[18], and the writer's renown was spreading from the US to Canada – Levi experienced an extraordinary success in Italy. *La Stampa*'s weekly cultural supplement, *Tuttolibri*, organised a survey of its readers' views: which were the most important, most loved and least loved novels of the twentieth century? There were 21,186 replies by the deadline of 16 February. *If This is a Man* was judged the eighth most loved book (*The Leopard* was first). Even better, it was the fifth most important, after works by Svevo, Tomasi di Lampedusa, Pirandello and Carlo Levi. Primo Levi was the only living writer in the top five, who had got more than half the votes between them. He told Nico Orengo, who was gathering the reactions of both winners and losers:

> I'm very pleased; if I were superstitious I'd touch wood. It didn't surprise me that *The Leopard* is the most loved book, it lends itself to many readings. But it's a noble book, which concerns both north and south.[19] The surprise is Svevo. He isn't an easy writer. But he's come to be regarded as an important European writer. A writer of provincial

> Italian who has a European's conception of the world. And Moravia's the least loved? I'm not surprised. He's created his own image as a difficult writer and never pretended to be a cheerful smiling one. He's the writer of the pain of living par excellence.[20]

On television, they remark that he must feel extremely satisfied. He replies simply:

> Of course I do. I wasn't expecting it. I did expect some place on the list, but not such a high one.

'How did you authors experience this kind of contest, which I don't think you're used to?' inquires the presenter Enrica Bonaccorti:

> I can't speak for the others. Personally, I didn't experience it. I was busy with other things, and just waited for the result at the end [...]
>
> *In these last few days you've had great success in America and Levine, the famous cartoonist, has done a drawing of you. Do you recognize yourself in it?*
>
> [...] a bit, yes. Probably Levine used a photograph of me – not a recent one, because I've got more hair in the cartoon than I have in reality [...]
>
> *Still, entering Levine's pantheon is important, isn't it?*
>
> At a small cost to one's image, yes, it's a kind of break-through.
>
> *Why do you think* If This is a Man *won? Why did so many people vote for you?*
>
> I think mainly because it's a long-lived book: it's been on the scene for forty years now, and so it's touched two, almost three, generations. Also I think it can be read on many levels: in an emotional way, for historical interest, by young people who see it almost as an adventure story...[21]

A year after Primo Levi's death, Alexander Stille, the American literary critic, summarized US interest in Levi in these figures: 140 articles in five dailies and the two most authoritative New York weeklies; plus hundreds of others in less popular or more specialized magazines and dozens in provincial dailies; six books published in three years, for a total of 200,000 copies.

> He's been the most interesting cultural phenomenon of recent times, more for how profoundly people have responded to him than for the sales figures. Many of the most important writers and critics, starting with Saul Bellow, have concerned themselves with Levi. But perhaps the most relevant thing has been the depth of feeling and enthusiasm: Levi has become almost an object of worship [...] In an age when literature has been increasingly reduced to pure amusement and escapism, Primo Levi is one of the very few contemporary writers to touch a deep nerve in the American psyche.

The Turinese writer sensed this, moving from city to city, meeting Jews and non-Jews, critics, photographers, reporters, chemists and writers, university lecturers and students, all of whom had questions to ask him, urgent problems to put before him. Stille remembered: 'He was shy, with a plain and simple manner, full of curiosity for everything around him, without even a shadow of narcissism [...] Amused, embarrassed, surprised by his success, he answered even the most banal questions patiently and courteously. [...] But his success made him uneasy, the idea of exploiting the tragedy of the Holocaust appalled him.' They had trouble getting him to attend a reception in his honour at the Jewish Museum of New York: 'On the ground floor there was an exhibition of drawings by an ex-deportee, and they couldn't tear him away.'[22]

Giorgio Bocca interviewed Primo Levi soon after his return from the US on his recently published *Other People's Trades*, but first he wanted to know the secret of Levi's sudden good luck in America.

> *I've read extremely laudatory reviews of* The Periodic Table *in the American newspapers. Why do you think that a writer like you has been discovered now and not before?*
>
> It's a kind of miracle. From what I've been told, it happened in the simplest way possible. An American Italianist, Raymond Rosenthal, came across *The Periodic Table* by chance, I think; he read it and liked it, he suggested it to the publisher, the publisher accepted it and he translated it. And it was immediately, remarkably successful – something I didn't expect, ten and a half years after I'd written it. It appealed in three ways, as an Italian book (Italians are popular in America now), as a Jewish book and as a chemist's book. I was in the US for twenty days and I had to alternate constantly between these three roles, like a Fregoli sufferer in fact[23] transforming myself from a Jew to an Italian, from an Italian to a chemist and vice-versa, to satisfy my various interviewers.
>
> *Is there an interest in European Jews among the Jews of America?*

> There's certainly an interest in anomalous Jews, that is Italian Jews: who don't distinguish themselves from other Italians, who speak Italian, who have largely forgotten their Jewish roots but found them again during the war, and who are an extremely small minority. That certainly aroused American readers' curiosity – plus the fact I was a chemist who wrote.
>
> *What was the main type of curiosity you noticed?*
>
> Curiosity about Europeans in general and Italians in particular. It's remarkable how little is known about Europe in America. It's small and far away, it's reduced essentially to Poland, Italy, Greece and Spain. It's very difficult to compare these elements. Mainly I sensed curiosity about Italy and for that strange subspecies, Italian Jews.[24]

The conversation moves on to *Other People's Trades*, Primo Levi's twelfth book altogether, his tenth of prose. It contains over fifty piquant essays:

> [...] transgressions, we can call them, invasions of other people's fields, outside my own trade as a chemist and a writer: that's why the book's called what it is. They're digressions I granted myself the luxury of making.[25]

In one of these essays Levi suggested nine reasons why people write. 'One reason you don't mention', Bocca says, 'is that it's better to write than to work'. He responds:

> Yes, that's true, but writing is also working. And for my part, having tried both types of work, I can report that writing is much better...

It's the first time he admits that writing is work. A few years before he'd still made a distinction between the two, in an interview with the journalist Nicola Tranfaglia. Tranfaglia asked: 'What is the work of the writer for you?'

> The expression you use, 'the work of the writer', seems a bit contradictory to me, at least as far as I'm concerned. First of all, I've had very few, indeed almost no, relations with other writers; I don't frequent literary circles and I've remained segregated. For me, writing has never been a job. When I was still in the factory, writing was something completely different from what I did all day. I felt free in front of my desk, totally responsible for what I wrote. It also seemed to me that writing was – how can I put it? – more noble, more complete than factory work. Now that I'm retired I still refuse to write

> as a job, as it were. Clearly, sometimes sometimes people have to earn their bread by writing, but it seems to me that, if possible, one should separate writing from one's trade, which can be another and even very different one. If not, one restricts oneself. However, from another point of view I can accept your definition of writing as work. I think that writing is a kind of public service: one writes 'for someone'. And like the products of industrial work, the products of writing have recipients, who must not be overlooked. I don't like writers who write for themselves, or for two or three people: it seems to me that their message is crippled, that it doesn't have a key [...] Even though, for reasons of personal necessity, that's exactly how I wrote my first book.[26]

Four years separate these two statements; and about halfway between them Primo Levi moved closer towards identifying writing with working, in his answer to this question:

> *What trade seems more congenial to you, the chemist's or the writer's?*
>
> They're both very difficult. In industry, an individual's output can vary by twenty percent, more or less. But in writing, there are days when one sits for hours in front of a blank page, without coming up with anything at all: it's absolutely unpredictable how much one will produce. On the other hand, what a chemist produces is rarely acknowledged as his work, if anything it's the work of a team. Managing a factory means depending on a lot of other people: co-workers, clients, the boss, providers, etcetera. The work of the writer on the other hand is dreadfully autonomous: if one writes badly one has only oneself to blame. Of course, the satisfaction is also much greater, for the same reason.[27]

Summer 1985. The faithful computer helped Primo Levi to file the articles that now arrived frequently from America (not all of them enthusiastic: *If Not Now, When?* aroused perplexity in a certain Jewish milieu, which did not consider it sufficiently 'religious'). William Weaver had sent *The Monkey's Wrench,* for him to check the translation ('It's clean, aseptic', said the author, 'with a Faussone who's a bit too much of a gentleman and endowed with a vocabulary with barely a touch of slang'). *Other People's Trades* received the Aquileia prize. The town of Marina di Pietrasanta awarded a prize to *Ad ora incerta.* One surprise was the visit of a student from Beijing, whose name meant 'Splendour of China': he had translated 'Arsenic' and fallen in love with its hero. Now he wanted to translate all of Primo Levi's books. The author gave them to him, saw that he left happy, recorded his name on the computer and went back to his deeply painful task: writing the sixth essay of *The Drowned and the Saved*, about the philosopher and survivor of torture

Jean Améry. In his breaks he turned to the translation of Raymond Queneau's curious poem *Le chant du Styrène*[28] which his friend Italo Calvino had sent him, asking for his help with some chemistry questions. It was while he was working on this that he heard Calvino had suddenly died. Levi commemorated his friend in *La Stampa*; and when he had finished checking the poem, he sent it to his widow. He agreed to share his memories of Calvino four months later, when he took part in a panel discussion at the launch for the translation. His voice was thick with emotion:

> My memories of Italo Calvino go back a very long way, to our joint baptism as writers: that is, to 1947, when Arrigo Cajumi reviewed his first book *The Path to the Spiders' Nests* and my first book *If This is a Man* simultaneously in *La Stampa*, expressing the hope that these young men – as we were then – would go far. There were long breaks in my friendship with Calvino, because he was away a great deal, while I remained more or less permanently in Turin. But his happiest time was during the translation of Raymond Queneau's *Petite cosmogonie portative*. Solmi had translated it and Calvino wasn't completely satisfied. He'd edited it himself, but he wasn't happy with his editing either, because this fantastic poem by Queneau, which starts with the creation of the universe and ends with computers, contains a song about chemistry, and that song contains – as does the whole book – a plethora of problems: it's fair to say that there's not a single line without a hidden trap. Queneau was a master of manipulating words, of squeezing them dry, of drawing sound as well as sense from them: he was a linguistic acrobat. And Calvino was a friend, a disciple and a huge admirer on that account as well.
>
> Now, sifting through the Italian translation, there remained a good many knots in the fabric – some even Queneau himself couldn't undo. When he was questioned about the book, some decades after he'd written it, he'd said, 'Forgive me, I can't remember what I meant any more.' We worked on it very happily together, up in the mountains at Rhêmes-Notre-Dame,[29] Calvino and I (in fact there were three of us, because there was also a kitten on the table, on top of Solmi's manuscript, who helped us as well as he could, trying every now and again to turn the pages with his paw). So it was a game, but a great and beautiful one, the game Calvino was master of: squeezing everything possible out of a word, turning himself into an instrument that could penetrate words.
>
> Just as deep as his love of words was Calvino's love of nature, which had nothing idyllic, sentimental or romantic about it: it was the love

> of the naturalist, which he'd inherited from his parents, which he cultivated to the end and which, to any attentive reader, is clear in every book he wrote. Ever since the title of his first book, in fact: it was Calvino/Pin's discovery that there is a path, unique in the world, where spiders make a nest instead of a web.
>
> I would say that in all Calvino's books the scrupulousness of the scientist emerges: he wasn't academically trained in science, but he was in fact a scientist. Anyone who's read the *Cosmicomics* knows that it's not just an entertainment: it's a book of great depth, a book to reflect on page by page. He really has, at least in his early works, the ability to make people laugh and reflect at the same time. In the *Cosmicomics*, in *t zero*, to a lesser extent in the most famous trilogy but again in *Mr. Palomar*, we see a non-religious awe at the order of creation, at this great clockwork (it's not clear who the clock-maker is), at the passing of time. Time is one of Calvino's obsessive themes, as it is for anyone concerned with cosmology today. The theme of the labyrinth is left open: we can debate whether or not there's a way out of it. But in my view there is a way out of Calvino's labyrinth, at least it's conceivable and to be hoped for that there is, since it's our labyrinth, the labyrinth we live in. It's a complex symbol. In my judgement as a hybrid, half chemist and half writer, a concise definition of Calvino's writing would be that it refuses to follow existing rules, and at the same time has a prodigious ability to create new ones. And therefore I truly believe that of all writers – not just Italian ones – if there's one who will never be imitated because he's inimitable, it's Italo Calvino.[30]

Primo Levi submitted *The Drowned and the Saved* to Einaudi at the end of 1986. Never had a piece of writing cost him such pain. Soon after that an elegantly combined version of his three books of memoir arrived from America; from Germany, an excellent translation of *If Not Now, When?*, from England a good one of *Other People's Trades*, and from France an unfortunate one of *If This is a Man*.[31] To free himself of the weight his last book had left in him, he conceived in these months the plan for an epistolary novel, which he imagined almost as a counterpart to *The Periodic Table*. It would explain the mysteries of organic chemistry and physics, in a fantastical and ironic way, to a lady called Gisella. Perhaps this would be a way of reviving the old idea of *The Double Bond*, which he had never entirely given up. The work started quickly but continued only fitfully: his time was taken up by a demanding journey to England and Sweden, by many meetings in Italy, including numerous interviews with Italians and others, and by a lecture in the Teatro Rossini[32] in Pesaro, where a crowd of very well-prepared young people swamped him with intelligent questions. The TV journalist La Volpe caught up with him in Ancona, on his journey home, to question him about Chernobyl. In Turin his German publisher was waiting for him, together with the translator Barbara Kleiner and some good news. He had decided to reprint all Levi's works, starting with *If This is a Man* in a new translation. 'Language moves fast', he said. 'Riedt's excellent work has now been overtaken'. Levi was happy: he did the sums and found that at that moment twenty-four translations of his books were being prepared .

'How do you experience your fame?' Gianni Milani of *Piemonte Vip* asked him.

> I experience it intermittently, particularly at ten in the morning, when the post arrives. But I don't enjoy applause as I once did.
>
> *And how do you experience your memories of the Lager today?*
>
> That's a very timely question. I've just submitted to Einaudi a collection of nine essays called *The Drowned and the Saved*, in which I return to some of the themes of *If This Is a Man*, and put them under the microscope, so to speak. The importance, for example, of knowing or not knowing the local language in the concentration camps. Shame – the sense of anxiety or distress, tinted with guilt, which paradoxically was felt by the innocent, the ex-deportees, including me; the ambiguity inseparable from that experience of imprisonment. Because there's no doubt that the survivors all enjoyed some privilege, in my case that of being a chemist.
>
> *Have you ever felt a prisoner of your first few books, which came out of the experience of deportation?*
>
> Many times. Even today, when people call *If This Is a Man* 'your book' it annoys me a bit, because I've written other books. But in Italy it almost never happens any more. And since I signed an avalanche of contracts for translations last year, maybe I can soon stop being a one-book author abroad as well.[33]

In his thirteenth book, Primo Levi returned to his origins as a writer, to his central theme, to the great stain on the twentieth century of which he had been a witness, to 'clarify aspects of the concentration camp phenomenon that still appear obscure', and to answer the anguished question, *Can it happen again?* The agony returned and the heart within him burned: but he delivered to the reader another book 'steeped in memory'. When he was about halfway through, the journalist Lucia Borgia put a recurring question to him: 'Is "if this is a man" still a valid question?' Pensively he replied:

> I fear it is, because humanity as a whole is under threat for reasons that are well known; and so is every individual. Each one of us must fight to remain a man today, in ways not so very different from the past.
>
> *Do some drops of the Auschwitz poison still run in your veins?*
>
> No, I really would say not. Many years have passed, and not in vain. I've thought a lot about this subject; it's part of my way of living that I have to refer everything back to that fundamental experience. But the poison has been exorcised, it doesn't run in my veins any more.[34]

The final exorcism was called *The Drowned and the Saved*, the title of one of the chapters of *If This is a Man*. The circle was closing.

Notes

1. Primo Levi, 'Vecchio io?' [Old, me?], *Stampa Sera*, 15 November 1982.
2. See first paragraph of Chapter IV.
3. ll.582-3.
4. Theodor Adorno famously wrote that writing poetry after Auschwitz was barbaric.
5. Pythagoras (c.570-497 BC) taught that human souls could migrate to the bodies of other humans, and also to animals and plants, and that on death and rebirth the soul lost its memory of the past. Lucretius developed this idea, holding that the soul was corporeal and mortal.
6. Giulio Nascimbeni, 'Levi: l'ora incerta della poesia' [Levi: the uncertain hour of poetry], *Corriere della Sera*, 28 October 1984.
7. Giovanni Raboni, 'Primo Levi un poeta vero ad ora incerta' [Primo Levi, a true poet at an uncertain hour], *Tuttolibri* (*La Stampa*), 17 November 1984.
8. 'The Bridge' is included in *Collected Poems* (trans. J. Galassi) in A. Goldstein (ed.), *Complete Works of Primo Levi*, Vol. III (New York: Liveright, 2015). The poem is inspired by a legend that a bridge in Lanzo near Turin was built with the help of the Devil. The villagers are said to have tricked him, saying they would leave a soul in a bag after the work was completed, but in the end they left only a dog.
9. These do not appear in the *Complete Works*. The texts Levi translated are the anonymous ballad 'Sir Patrick Spens', eight poems from Heine's *Buch der Lieder* [Book of Songs] and 'L'envoi' from Kipling's *Barrack-Room Ballads*. See 'Note to the Texts' in *Complete Works of Primo Levi*, Vol. III, p.2685.
10. *Point Counter Point*, a novel first published in 1928.
11. The term is used in the first chapter of *Cristo si è fermato a Eboli*. In Frances Fenaye's translation, *Christ Stopped at Eboli* (New York: Farrar, Strauss and Company, 1947), p.3, it is rendered as 'mere creatures of the wild'.
12. Giovanni Tesio, 'Le occasioni? La memoria, un ponte, una ragnatela' [The causes? Memory, a bridge, a spider's web], *Tuttolibri* (*La Stampa*), 17 November 1983.
13. Enrica Bonaccorti, (presenter), 'Italia Sera', RAI1, broadcast on 11 March 1985. As 'Il giocatore occulto' [The hidden player], the story appeared in *La Stampa* on 19 October

1985. It was then included in the collection *Racconti e saggi*. 'The Hidden Player' is published in English in *Stories and Essays* (trans. A.M. Appel), in *Complete Works of Primo Levi*, Vol. III, pp.2379-82.

14. 'Una domanda a Primo Levi' [A question for Primo Levi], *Genius*, no. 4, 4 January 1985, pp.11-2. *Unbroken Poetry*, trans. G. Bowen (Newcastle: Bloodaxe, 1996).
15. Giorgio Calcagno, editor of *Tuttolibri*, was a guest alongside Levi on this programme, broadcast on RAI 1, 11 March 1985.
16. A practitioner of philology: the study of literary texts and written records, establishing their authenticity and original form, and determining their meaning.
17. *The Wrench* (trans. N. Rich), in the *Complete Works of Primo Levi*, Vol. III, pp. 947-1,116.
18. This was eventually published by Faber and Faber in 1988. In the *Complete Works* (Vol. III, pp.1865-2008). The *Collected Poems* are translated by Jonathan Galassi.
19. *The Leopard* is a historical novel about the effects of Italian unification on Sicily, still one of Italy's poorest regions. It is one of Italy's most famous novels both at home and abroad.
20. Nico Orengo, 'Su Svevo e *Il Gattopardo* niente da dire' [Nothing to say about Svevo and *The Leopard*], *Tuttolibri(La Stampa)*, 9 March 1985.
21. Enrica Bonaccorti, 'Italia Sera', 11 March 1985.
22. Alexander Stille took part in the round table that concluded the Primo Levi International Study Days held on 28 and 29 March 1988 at the Piedmont Regional Council's headquarters in Palazzo Lascaris, Turin, organized by the Region, the Associazione nazionale ex deportati [National Ex-Deportees Association], the Jewish Community of Turin and the publisher Giulio Einaudi. Abridged from the text published in A. Cavaglion (ed.), *Primo Levi: Il presente del passato* [Primo Levi: the present of the past], (Milan: Franco Angeli, 1991), pp.203-11.
23. The Fregoli delusion is a rare disorder in which a person holds a delusional belief that different people are in fact the same person, who changes appearance or is in disguise.
24. Giorgio Bocca, 'Prima Pagina', Mediaset Canale 5, 13 June 1985.
25. Enrica Bonaccorti, 'Italia Sera', 11 March 1985.
26. Nicola Tranfaglia, 'Col sudore della fronte' [With the sweat of one's brow], RAI 3, 22 May 1981.
27. Enrico Boeri, 'Quattro chiacchiere con Primo Levi' [A chat with Primo Levi], *Tecnologie chimiche*, December 1983.
28. 'The Song of Styrene', a poem written by Queneau in 1957 for Alain Resnais' documentary film of the same name (Les Films de la Pléiade/Péchiny, 1958), which Calvino translated into Italian as *La canzone del Polistirene* [The Song of Polystyrene] (Milan: Scheiwiller, 1985).
29. A town in the Aosta Valley.
30. From Primo Levi's speech on 29 January 1986 for the Montedison educational project, published in the company's popular science periodical *Montedison-Progetto Cultura* (Montedison-Educational Project), no.4, 1987. The references for the Calvino works are: A. Colquhoun (trans.), *Path to the Spiders' Nests* (New York: Harper Collins, 2000); W. Weaver (trans.),*Cosmocomics* (New York: Harcourt Brace, 1965); W. Weaver (trans.), *Mr. Palomar* (New York: Harcourt Brace, 1985); W. Weaver (trans.), *t zero* (New York: Harcourt Brace, 1989).
31. Levi was satisfied with the translation by Martine Schruoffeneger, *Si c'est un homme* [If this is a man] (Paris: Julliard, 1987), but not with the earlier one by Michèle Causse, *J'étais un homme* [I was a man] (Paris: Buchet-Chastel, 1961). For full details of the various English translations of Levi's works, see the 'Works of Primo Levi' section at the end of this book. *If This is a Man, The Truce* and *The Drowned and the Saved* were known as *The Auschwitz Trilogy* and were available as a boxed set of three.

32. An opera house in the town on the north-eastern coast.
33. Gianni Milani, 'Al chimico va stretta la memoria del Lager' [Lager memory constricts the chemist] *Piemonte Vip*, March 1986.
34. Lucia Borgia (presenter), 'Rifarsi una vita' [Remaking a life for oneself], RAI 3, 3 February 1985.

XIII

The Circle Closes

Immediately after Levi's death, the writer Ferdinando Camon, who had met him several times, collected their conversations in a slim but important little volume. Camon had already published extracts in *Panorama, Il Giorno* and *Liberation*. In one of these, shortly before *The Drowned and the Saved* came out, he had written: 'The reflections contained in this book constitute an exemplary map of oppression, a description of its Dantean circles of Hell, from the central hierarchy to minor collaborators on the margins'. And: 'This return confirms what some have always maintained: that Levi is the witness not to a temporary 'error' of history [...] but to a problem which returns all too often in it: the difficulty or impossibility of accepting the other, those who are different.'[1] *The Drowned and the Saved* was a genuine, devastating history book: not for nothing did history professor Guido Quazza officially propose that it should be taught in schools. Writing it, extremely slowly and painfully, had left its author feeling drained. Primo Levi admitted as much at the end of May, during a ceremony in which he was awarded the Lion d'Oro prize.[2] And now, for the first time, he reluctantly agreed to go around Italy and present his latest creation.

Levi had intended *The Drowned and the Saved* to be the title of his first book, and it is still there as the title of one its chapters. But Franco Antonicelli, his first publisher in 1947, had been struck by the phrase 'If this is a man' hidden in the epigraphic poem, and had suggested the change to him. 'Thus the original title waited thirty-nine years to be put on a cover', the *Tuttolibri* correspondent noted in his interview. The subtitle to *The Drowned and the Saved*[3] reads: 'The crimes, the punishments, the sentences, the impunities.' The cover picture reproduces the desperate faces of Memling's *Last Judgement*.[4]

'Why did you want to take up these themes again, after so many years?'

> Because of a need for truth, and to resist rhetoric. We ex-deportees are put on the same level as ex-partisans, and rightly so. Nonetheless there are important differences between the experience of victorious struggle and the passive and damaging experience of imprisonment. I wanted to re-establish those points. I'm prepared to tolerate a certain amount of rhetoric: it's indispensable in order to live. We need monuments and celebrations – and etymologically, 'monument'

> means 'warning'. But there needs to be a counter-thesis, a response to the flights of rhetoric. I've tried to make one, knowing that it will hurt some people's feelings. These subjects are quite taboo.

There is a second reason, which goes to the heart of our story and is at the origin of Levi's book:

> I feel the years passing, my own years as well. And with this passing of the years, I thought I noticed a drift in the way these memories are understood. I still meet young people in schools. They have an emotional, even a violent involvement, but not a historical one. When I go into a school hall, I feel a flash of amazement as they see the author of the book they've read: he's still alive, he speaks Italian, not Latin or Greek. I wanted to show them that these things belong to a past that is close, and not just geographically. I don't believe the seed of Auschwitz will sprout again, but violence is close, it's all around us; and that violence has given birth to others. There are underground links between the violence of the two world wars and the violence we have watched in Algeria, in Russia, in the Chinese Cultural Revolution, in Vietnam. Our society, together with our news media (necessary as they are), spreads violence. It has mechanisms that make it multiply.

In *The Drowned and the Saved*, the memory of the Lager casts its shadow over our world; in places it seems to set up worrying reminders.

> *Two verbs recur in your book, to understand and to forgive, the latter sometimes used negatively. Are these the keys to a right reading?*
>
> Yes, understanding is a key. For forty years, I've been trying to understand the Germans. Understanding how it happened is one of the aims of my life. But understanding in a broader sense too, because I want to understand many things. I'm a chemist: I want to understand the world around me.
>
> *And to forgive?*
>
> Forgive isn't my own word. It's inflicted on me, because all the letters I get, especially from young readers and especially from Catholics, have forgiveness as their theme. I ask myself whether I've forgiven. I believe that in my own way I'm a just man. I can forgive some people, but not others. I can only give a case-by-case judgement. If I'd had Eichmann in front of me, I'd have sentenced him to death. General forgiveness, such as I'm asked for, is no good

> to me. Who are the 'Germans'? I'm not a believer, the *absolvo te*[5] has no meaning for me. I don't think that anyone, even a priest, has the power either to bind someone to their crimes forever or to set them free.

He repeats what he has said over the years, in almost the same words and with undiminished conviction:

> Whoever commits a crime must pay for it, unless he repents. But not only in words. I'm not satisfied with verbal repentance. I'm prepared to release anyone who has demonstrated by his actions that he is no longer the man he was. But not too late either.

The *Tuttolibri* journalist has a query. The chapter on the intellectual in Auschwitz stresses the disadvantages for the more educated as compared to the less educated man in the Lager. But the chapter 'Communication' shows the absolute necessity of understanding in order to survive.

> *If language saves us, why should intelligence condemn us?*
>
> I was talking about communication on an ordinary daily level, not the intellectual kind. We're all thinking people. But in Auschwitz we were deprived even of ordinary language, especially us Italians. Of course, understanding was an advantage there. But offset by strong disadvantages, from the very first day. Anyone who said he was a doctor or a teacher or a philosopher was slapped about straight away. The fate of a cobbler or an electrician was better.
>
> *Yet it's intellectuals who've been able to provide the best analyses of Auschwitz.*
>
> But that's afterwards. Afterwards, yes, being an intellectual helps to process the experience. I was educated, but Auschwitz made me an intellectual. I became one because of that experience. I think, for example, of Lidia Rolfi, a primary school teacher from Mondovì[6], who was sent to Ravensbrück at the age of seventeen for sheltering a partisan. She survived because of her determination to understand the system, just as I did. When she came home she realized that this had been her university.
>
> *And how much have the last forty years changed the man who escaped the fate of the drowned?*

He reflects, embarrassed. Then:

> They've been forty years of life, of my profession, most of all of racking my brains to understand.

He picks up his book, pointing to the words he'd quoted from Coleridge:

> 'At an uncertain hour/That agony returns'. It returns every now and then. I don't live inside that world. If I did, I wouldn't have written *The Wrench*, I wouldn't have set up a family, I wouldn't do so many of the things that I enjoy. But it's true that, at an uncertain hour, those memories return. I have relapses.[7]

In the first days of September 1986, Philip Roth arrived from America to interview Primo Levi for the authoritative *New York Times Book Review*. The two writers talked for a long time: in Levi's flat, walking around the ancient centre of Turin, visiting his old factory, sitting down for dinner in the shade of the Palazzo Carignano.[8] Out of these meetings came a profound interview, to which both the New York paper and *La Stampa*, gave ample space. In mid-October, *The Drowned and the Saved* won the Acqui 'Testimone del tempo' [Witness of our time] prize.[9] Towards the end of that month a *TIME* correspondent took about a hundred photos of Levi, to be included in a report [not eventually published] on 'Italians who matter'. Levi agreed reluctantly. He was very tired; and he was struggling with his epistolary novel, with which he was dissatisfied, despite the encouragement of the small panel of friends to whom he had submitted the first chapters. He would have preferred to develop the idea he had sketched in his brief piece 'Hatching the Cobra':[10] the plan for a code of conduct in all university departments, which could warn researchers about the risks of unexpected sinister developments in science. He promised himself he would talk about it again with Norberto Bobbio, with Alessandro Galante Garrone, with Tullio Regge and with Rita Levi Montalcini, who had been a friend since childhood, and who in one of the interviews she granted when she won the Nobel Prize for Medicine had said that Primo Levi's books were her favourite reading.

He appeared in public, and took the floor, on 22 November in Palazzo Lascaris,[11] on the occasion of an important international gathering on the theme of 'Storia vissuta' [Lived history]. It was the last time, and it was to re-affirm once again the duty to which he had remained stubbornly faithful ever since escaping Auschwitz: to give testimony. The conference had been organized by the Piedmont Region, in collaboration with the Associazione nazionale ex deportati [National ex-deportees' association], to present an exceptional work to the public: an anthology of more than two hundred testimonies from Piedmontese ex-deportees who had never spoken before. Primo Levi had partaken in several ways: by offering lessons at the university on the rigour with which memories must be tested; by giving an interview to the editors; and by writing the Foreword. It was published by Franco Angeli in Milan, under the title *La vita offesa* [*The Wounded Life*]. Primo Levi considered it a response 'to the ugly antics of the revisionists [...]who dedicate pages and pages of acrobatic arguments to showing that we haven't seen what we have seen, haven't lived through what we have lived through'.[12] He said:

> Our generation has had the unenviable fate of experiencing events rich in history. I don't mean to say that nothing happened in the world afterwards: natural catastrophes and man-made tragedies have happened everywhere.
>
> But despite the omens, nothing comparable to the Second World War has happened in Europe since then. Every one of us is therefore a witness, whether he or she wants to be or not; and this inquiry into our memories of deportation is right and timely, because that deportation, due to the variety and number of its victims, has been, at least up to now, unique in the history of the human race. I've been called upon to contribute in my dual capacity as a witness and a writer. I'm honoured, and at the same time burdened by the responsibility. People read a book: it can amuse them, it can educate them, it can be remembered and reread. As a writer of the deportation, that isn't enough for me. Since my first book, *If This is a Man*, I've hoped that my writings, even though they bore my name, would be read as collective works, as a voice that represented other voices. And more: that they should be an opening, a bridge between us and our readers, especially the young ones. It's pleasant, for us ex-deportees, to sit around the table in a dining hall and tell each other our long-ago adventures; but it isn't very useful. For as long as we live, it's our task to speak to the others, to those who weren't yet born, so that they know where things can lead. It's no coincidence that a good part of my most recent book is a kind of dialogue with my readers. I get lots of letters full of 'Why's'. They request interviews, most of all, and ask me two essential questions: 'How could the horror of the Lager have happened?' and 'Will it happen again?'
>
> I don't believe there are any prophets, any readers of the future: everyone who's passed themselves off as one so far has failed miserably, often absurdly. Still less do I feel like a prophet myself, or even as an authorized interpreter of recent history. Even so, these two questions were so urgent that I felt obliged to attempt an answer, or rather a set of answers: they've been handed out at this conference. Some are answers to Italian, American and English readers. Others – and they seem to me the most interesting – are the result of letters which for many years brought me into direct contact with *If This is a*

> *Man*'s German readers. They are the voices of the children, the grandchildren of those who committed the deeds, or who let them be committed, or who didn't make the effort to find out about them. Some are the voices of other Germans, who did what much or little they could to oppose the crime their country was committing. It seemed right to me to give both these groups a hearing.
>
> We survivors are witnesses, and every witness is bound (legally as well) to give a complete and truthful reply: but for us it's also about a moral duty, because though we've never been many we are getting fewer now. I've tried to fulfil this duty with a recent book of mine, *The Drowned and the Saved*, which some of you may have read and which will soon be translated into English and German and perhaps other languages. This book, which consists of questions about deportation (not only the Nazi one) and of attempted answers, is another part of what is now a forty-year-long conversation. I sense that it is profoundly in tune with this conference. I hope that, in my readers' judgement, it does justice to the conference's themes: that it makes a modest contribution towards understanding present history, since the violence of today is the child of the violence we were lucky enough to survive.[13]

The audience applauded, especially the many young people among them. Primo Levi let them gather around him in the interval. They wanted his autograph: some asked him to write it on the back of their hands or on their tram tickets. He did. When he returned to the rostrum he said to a fellow-survivor:

> We're their grandparents: two generations have passed, even more. It's not always easy to understand each other, but we must go on speaking.

Before the year's end, *La Stampa* opened its Terza Pagina[14] series with *Racconti e saggi di Primo Levi* [Stories and Essays of Primo Levi]. Lorenzo Mondo wrote in the introduction that the pieces present 'a wide range of all his human and intellectual interests'. His most recent poems were also there. The author added a Preface to this fourteenth book. He asked from his readers 'indulgence for the jumble of topics'; and he begged them above all 'not to go looking for messages', since he was neither prophet, nor oracle, nor seer:

> [...] I am an ordinary man with a good memory who fell into an abyss, who came out of it more by good luck than because of any virtue of his own, and who since that time has had a certain curiosity about abysses, large and small, metaphorical and material.[15]

Three interviews conclude Primo Levi's dialogue with the media: one on television, for the cultural programme 'Focus', about the great questions of the time; one for the periodical *Uomini e libri* [People and books], about peace; and one for *Piemonte Vivo* about narrative. Three important interviews, because taken together they make a rounded portrait of the man. 'Focus' follows Levi as he sits down at his desk after a walk. The journalist gives him the microphone.

It is three days before Christmas: time to do some summing up. Not that long ago, the measure of things was the same for all, the solution to problems familiar and known. Now, with the atom, television, the conquest of space and the successes of genetics, that's not the case any more. Limits that lasted for millennia have broken down, leaving humanity in a new universe, in which it is not yet capable of calculating the potentialities and limits, the risks and changes, which follow each other ever more quickly. What can Primo Levi, witness of our time, writer and poet, survivor of genocide but also rebuilder of his own life, say about all this?

> We find ourselves facing challenges that the human race has never faced before, and so we lack the fundamental data, which is experience. Experience builds up strategies for dealing with the unexpected. We don't have that build-up, so we don't know how to deal with it. This isn't either wholly positive or wholly negative; it's ambiguous, it's double-edged. It involves obvious advantages for a part of the human race, and dangers we have never seen or foreseen.
>
> *Could tough laws control our excesses? Or fear of the worst?*
>
> I don't believe in tough laws: because they would have to be supranational, international, global, in a world in which even the division into two great blocs no longer holds. In this fragmented world, even in the (absurdly unlikely) event that the two great powers were to come to an agreement, it would be disregarded, especially in the third world.
>
> *People are also afraid of genetics now: cloning was an old Hitlerite project.*
>
> Cloning means taking a fragment of an excellent, or not so excellent, man, and making thousands of identical copies of him. It's terrifying, but it's not real. Mengele[16] had thousands of victims, but he belongs to another world, the world of Nazism, and I don't believe in a resurgence of Nazism today.
>
> *Given the changes transforming our lives every day, won't our new culture give us the right tools itself?*

> Yes, there've been signs of that in the last ten years. It seems to me that a reaction – sometimes perhaps too violent a reaction – is spreading among young people. Against the destruction of the environment, for example. The success of the Green parties (first in Germany, but it's spreading here too) and of the ecology movement, the awareness that we're exploiting the planet's resources to excess: all this awareness and practical activity wasn't there thirty years ago. I think, I hope, that there will be more of it, and that we will set a limit to what it is possible to do. Only what doesn't irreparably damage our environment is possible to do. And of course that environment also includes the human race.

Alongside these new problems, there remain old ones that our selfishness has left to fester, such as the intolerable living conditions of large parts of populations, even in the west. The old ideologies are fading. Catastrophes, dilemmas, mysterious and menacing conquests loom. Levi says:

> I believe that humanity has the strength to cross the ford we find ourselves in, and this is without doubt a ford we built ourselves without knowing it.

One day, many years before, he had compared science and technology to Achilles' spear, which wounds or heals depending on the hand that wields it. Faced with the boundless, ambiguous problems of humanity, he has a proposal:

> For a while now I've been mulling over an idea which everyone will probably think is very naïve. We know that doctors have possessed a code of conduct since the time of Hippocrates. Hippocrates realized that a doctor isn't just someone who can cure illnesses and preserve people's health, but someone with some rights and with many duties. He can and must intervene in some cases and abstain from intervening in others. The Hippocratic Oath is a historical miracle: it's 2,400 years old, but it's still essentially valid. Now I wonder if we couldn't, if indeed we shouldn't, impose a similar code on all scientists, and if possible on future scientists [...] Why shouldn't or couldn't we introduce a course, or at least one class, in all science faculties, in which future scientists must take an oath to refuse to engage in activities which are certainly harmful and to accept only those which are certainly good? Well, I see the objection. One doesn't know whether certain activities are bad or good. That, I admit, is a difficulty [...]

The journalist foresees another one: 'It will be said that science is free by definition.' Primo Levi responds:

> I wonder if that's true. I don't agree at all that a scientist is free to study a nerve gas. The neutron bomb was probably commissioned. A politician will have asked a physicist, 'Can you make me a bomb that will destroy only human beings and leave buildings intact?' And the physicist thought about it, and then he said 'Yes, I can.' It's clear that such things can't be stopped. But I would like in some way to morally bind the future scientist, like the doctor, to abstain from them. Maybe he won't abstain, but if he doesn't he'll be a perjurer. And that will make people hesitate. Not everyone obviously, but some at least will say 'No, I can't do that, because I've sworn not to.' I know very well how naïve all this is, but I also know that many naïve ideas have got somewhere.

He will return stubbornly to his 'naïve idea' in more detail. Now, though, the interviewer takes back control of the discussion. He is anxious to know whether Primo Levi believes that any ideology survives, and if so, which one.

> Some ideologies are pretty tired. On the other hand, if you can call democracy an ideology, I continue to believe in that one, because I'm unable to imagine any better system. Currently, there are sclerotic democracies like ours, which still hasn't managed to offer any proper alternatives to choose from. It's a blocked democracy, which if I remember rightly someone defined as incomplete. Maybe it will become complete, maybe there'll be alternatives to choose from. I see no flaws in a well-run democracy. If we can call it an ideology [...] For me it's something above ideologies, because it contains ideologies.
>
> *Is it a religion?*
>
> No, it's a technique, which was invented many centuries ago, of course. It's a value to be preserved.

And now the last question, in the same terms in which it was put ten years earlier, in a public discussion: 'Do you still believe in mankind? Or would you at least place a bet on the human race?' Many things have changed, but his reply is identical:

> Yes, I think so, I think it's still worth placing a bet on mankind. [....] If we didn't have that faith, which is essentially a faith in the young, it wouldn't be worth staying alive.[17]

Mario Miccinesi, editor of *Uomini e Libri* (co-founded with his wife Fiora Vincenti, who'd written a biography of Levi)[18] has for a long time been promoting the idea of establishing a 'Club per le scienze della pace' [Club for peace sciences]. Leading Italian and international writers and thinkers – including Edgar Morin, Giulio Carlo Argan, Franco Fortini, Cesare Segre, Freeman Dyson, Akira Ishida and many others – have already declared their support for a culture of peace against the current culture of war. Now it is the Turinese writer's turn.

The main questions are: Is it possible to help the peace movements in our country and the world to make real progress? What contributions could come from the areas you're involved in? Which lines of research could produce positive results? And here are the interviewee's answers:

> [....] Peace movements are in quite different situations in our country and in the rest of the world. In our country, pacifism is now accepted by almost the entire population. We don't have border problems any more; we don't have aggressive neighbours; we have terrible internal problems to solve, but no hostile minorities or minorities towards whom the majority is hostile. No Italian wants war, though we've joined NATO, unfortunately. Military service is seen as a sad and unnecessary evil. Our armed forces aren't at all belligerent, though our soldiers face a range of dreadful weapons. Still, we do house terrifying arsenals in the hope (I don't know how well founded) of never having to use them. But we live in a world that is preparing for war and which for the moment – a long way from our shores – wages it every day. It's indispensable therefore for a culture of peace to assert itself and prevail; but what we can do in our country isn't much. In my view though that little should be done. Italy should set an example: the culture of peace, or the repudiation of war as a solution to international problems, is part of our Constitution, and that fact is stressed in all our schools, at every level.[19]

Having laid down these principles, Levi brings his 'naïve idea' back into the discussion. This is how he formulates it:

> The armies of the world (especially the quarrelsome third world) would be powerless, if a continuous flow of innovations designed specifically for war didn't emerge from the universities and from a science enslaved to political power. Physicists, chemists and biologists everywhere (but we could start here) need to become aware of the dangerous powers they hold. Science can be neutral, but it can also not be neutral, and to non-neutral science we need to say 'Enough'. It's necessary for a clear moral awareness to spread above all in the science faculties of universities. 'I'll accept this task, but not that one. I'll study a new antibiotic, but not a nerve gas. I'll devote myself to fusion energy, not to the neutron bomb.' In any case, young scientists need to know what use will be made of their work and to have the courage

> to say no when they find that use repugnant. In short, to engage not to work for destruction: if they're believers, to bind themselves with an oath not unlike the Hippocratic one; if they're secular, they pledge their honour.

Not much more than a month ago (it is now January 1987) a vast television audience heard Primo Levi make precisely this suggestion. He repeats again to the audience of *Uomini e libri* the idea he had first expressed in an article in *La Stampa*:

> In all science faculties there should be a course or at least some classes that aim at reawakening the moral conscience we all have. There will of course be cynics and perjurers, but there will still be some conscientious objectors; and it's not impossible that an Italian example won't find imitators elsewhere, especially in the countries where science is most flourishing and at the same time most a slave to power.[20]

It is the chemist's and the moralist's farewell. But in a now distant past Primo Levi had called himself a 'centaur', and had spoken jokingly of his two 'half brains'. The interview he gave to Roberto Di Caro, which was his last, focussed on his other side: the literary one, which was now predominant. Despite brief flashes of inspiration, this interview – unlike all the others – shows the effects of an irreparable tiredness tinged with melancholy. The first question is on the aim of his writing. What is it?

> The book must satisfy the reader. I don't write for myself, or if I do I rip it up, I destroy what I've written. I don't think that it's right to write only for oneself. Naturally, everyone is free to do so, it doesn't cause anyone any harm: but it seems like wasted time to me. My books, in general, were written for an audience, in fact for an Italian audience; they were made for Italian readers. I respect and appreciate those readers. And the letters I get from them confirm that.
>
> *Do you remember any letters in particular?*
>
> There really are so many […] Yes, I remember one, with no name on it. A lady who had read *The Truce* told me that it had solved serious problems for her, though she didn't say what they were. It gives me great pleasure if my books help someone. It's useful to me. I'd be glad if they helped me as much.
>
> *But they don't?*

It depends when. Before, writing was [...] how can I put it? – a need, which assailed me every evening. I wrote more than three books while I was a chemist: *If This is a Man, The Truce, Natural Histories* and a part of *The Periodic Table*. I can't understand how I found the time to do both things. Now I have acres of time but I write less than I did and with less intensity. But it's one thing to be thirty and another to be nearly seventy. Time moves differently. Sometimes I have the impression that I've finished my store of things to say, of stories to write.

Do you know what book you'll write next?

Yes, I'm already writing it. But reluctantly. And I prefer not to talk about it. The truth is that I'm living a neurotic life, with difficult breaks between one book and another. Like this one, after *The Drowned and the Saved*.

Breaks for reflection?

No. Very tiresome breaks, for public relations: you have to present the book, go around talking to people, which isn't my style. It's like when I worked in customer service (because I've done that too, I tell the story in a chapter of *The Periodic Table*) and I had to visit the clients, convince them, get them to buy. I always did it reluctantly.

And now they ask you to do the same thing for your books?

Sometimes, yes. For example, I get strong pressures from America. They want me to come to Brandeis University, where they're awarding me an honorary degree. But I don't think I'll go. Travelling is very difficult for me, both for family reasons and because I've ended up internalizing them, so now it's hard for me to think of moving. Ten years ago it would have been different, I'd have had much more strength and the desire to pursue many more things. Now, I'm tired. And then I ask myself, 'What for?' Once, when the translation of one of my books arrived, it was a cause for celebration: now it has no effect on me any more. Even looking over the translations in the languages I know, English, French and German (that's a clause I've inserted in all my contracts) has become just another boring job. [...], Besides cultural events are extremely random. The great success of my books abroad last year is due to the fact *The Periodic Table* fell into the hands of an Italianist who translated it and made Saul Bellow read it. That's what triggered an explosion of interest: to the point that Summit Books, which is a division of Simon and Schuster, bought all my books, including those yet to be written. Hot on their heels came the English, and then the Germans, though they limited themselves to what was already written.

Is writing a low risk career?

There's only one risk: writing badly.

And uselessly?

Badly and uselessly are the same. At least for me, because it's true that there are books that are badly written but still useful, like certain manuals, or certain kinds of amateur memoirs. I occasionally receive manuscripts, even quite important ones, by people who can't write, but who have something to say. Sometimes I'm tempted to rewrite them.

Have you ever done so?

No. Lots of people have asked me to, though. They offer me their lives, *mon coeur mis à nu*,[21] then say, 'Let's go halves on the royalties' – in short, they want me to be their ghost-writer. I don't deny though that if the right opportunity came along – a life story worthy of being told – I might even accept that kind of contract. Why not? *Papillon*[22] seems to have been written like that, though if you don't know the tricks of the trade you don't realize it.

It seems to Di Caro that the writer is inclined to suspect attempts to analyse the written text. Does he perhaps disapprove of literary critics and think that literary works are mysterious?

No, I don't think that there's any mystery around a written text, unless it comes to us from a very distant time, from an author we know practically nothing about. As for the vast mechanical work which people have been doing for some time now, counting the frequency of certain words and trying to settle their attribution that way, it seems to me very marginal and all things considered pretty useless.

The moment has come for more personal questions, which Primo Levi has rarely allowed during his dozens of meetings with journalists:

Do you suffer much when you write?

Yes, sometimes I do.

From the subject matter or from the writing itself?

From the subject matter. But I do also occasionally feel the inadequacy of my instrument, which is language. Ineffability, that's called, and it's a beautiful word. Our language is human: it's made to describe human things and human proportions. It collapses, it falls apart, it's inadequate (all languages are and always will be) when it's a case of telling people what happens, for example, in a supernova,[23] as I tried to do once, in the story 'A Tranquil Star'.

How much of the writer's character is found in his writings?

Some writers have represented themselves exactly as they are in their books, without any cosmetic adjustments. Henri-Frédéric Amiel,[24] for example. But they are the exceptions. For the most part, when people sit down to write, they instinctively choose a part of themselves: the one they think the best. For instance, I've represented myself in my books at different times as courageous or cowardly, as clear-sighted or naïve. But always, I think, as balanced.

And you're not?

Not very. I go through long periods of imbalance, perhaps linked to my concentration camp experience. I deal with difficulties quite badly. I've never written that. Maybe one day I will. Many of the letters I get admire the strength with which I bore my year of imprisonment: but it was the passive strength with which a rock bears a torrent. I'm not a strong man. At all.

Still, it takes strength to tell about these experiences.

On the contrary. I *need* to tell them. It would take strength not to write about them, not to speak about them. In my first books, and also in *The Drowned and the Saved*, I recognize if anything a great need to reorganize, to put a chaotic world back in order, to explain things to myself and to others. Yet day by day I live a different life, unfortunately a much less methodical and systematic one. Writing is a way of putting things in order. It's the best way I know, though I don't know many.

So there's a split between the flesh-and-blood author and the author as he reconstructs himself on his pages. The way the reader imagines you is different from how you feel yourself to be?

> Very different, judging by the letters I receive. They see me as a kind of guru. Maybe there's a wisdom in my books which I don't feel I have. For me it's just moderation, not biting off more than one can chew. A Piedmontese virtue, perhaps.

He reminds the interviewer of his plea to readers in the Preface to his last book: not to call him a prophet or seer, a type of person he distrusts, or to look for an unlikely message in his work. He had written earlier of the end of prophecy, as certainty became incompatible with the human condition. Now he says:

> They're the plague of our age, prophets. Or maybe they're the plague of every age. Because it's almost impossible to distinguish a true prophet from a false one. They use the same language.

'So', objects the journalist, 'it's language that's deceptive, that is somehow constitutionally misleading? You've said it in the tone of someone who distrusts philosophers. Do you distrust philosophers?' Primo Levi's old irony emerges, as the interview concludes. He says:

> Well, yes. No doubt it's out of ignorance. You know, I manufactured paint; I lived a practical life, in which you either solved a problem or you dumped it. Whereas philosophical problems are still those of the pre-Socratics: people just go round and round them, they keep going back to them [...] And then every philosopher invents his own language, which you have to penetrate before you can understand him. No, that's not for me [...] [25]

He wrote his last poem, 'Almanac', on New Year's Day 1987. In it he spoke of the desert that mankind spreads ever faster 'Into the forests of the Amazon /Into our cities' very hearts/ Into our own'. They were lines without hope. *La Stampa* published them the day after the writer was awarded the Marotta prize in Naples. On 20 January Primo Levi briefly took part in a conference on the anniversary of the Wannsee Conference, which had decreed the Final Solution for the Jewish people. He had not originally agreed to be included among the speakers, but came at the last minute. Professor Maurice Goldstein, president of the International Auschwitz Committee and a prominent figure in the European Resistance, recalled that afternoon in these words:

> I found myself sitting on his right. Although his name didn't appear in the programme, the news of his presence caused a wave of loud applause that seemed to embarrass him. His wonderfully gentle face

> with its questioning expression clouded over, and he looked down. I realized once again how much the representatives of his region and his city, his fellow-prisoners and his friends all loved and respected this son of Turin, whose one great adventure had been his deportation to Auschwitz.[26]

The day after the conference, two articles in *La Stampa* report without comment the theories of neo-revisionist historians like Hillgruber, which have been raging in Germany for about a year. These are no longer the crude blanket denials of Darquier de Pellepoix and Faurisson. They are a much more subtle attempt to make Hitler's massacre seem nothing out of the ordinary, by putting it on the same level as those carried out by the Mongol hordes of the past, with the simple addition of a technological detail: the gas chambers, which the first form of revisionism had denied. Primo Levi does not waste time. In the 22 January edition of the Turinese daily his answer appears, under 'the terrible title', as the historian Enzo Colletti said, 'of "Buco nero di Auschwitz" [Black hole of Auschwitz]: concisely, in one admirably lucid page, all the arguments and counter-arguments are reduced to their essentials.'[27] In this piece Primo Levi repeated what he had been saying for forty years, as 'a witness by right and by duty', in order to demonstrate, as he had in the Preface to *The Drowned and the Saved*, 'that the Nazi concentration-camp system remains unique in both magnitude and quality'. He condensed into a few lines of print his lifelong effort to understand the Germans, without either absolving them or demonizing them. Against those who were ready to normalize the atrocious Nazi barbarism, he ended with the words: 'Germany cannot and must not whitewash its past.' It was his supreme reminder to the world.

Some time before he had written a literary piece, 'Argilla di Adamo' [Adam's Clay], his response to a fascinating book on the origins of life.[28] *La Stampa* published it on 15 February. After that he no longer called in at the newspaper's offices. When his journalist friends rang to ask for his news or to request a new contribution, he replied in a strange, discouraged voice. He did not feel well, he could not concentrate; he did not want to write any more, or even to speak.

> They've invited me to Holland, they want me in Berlin and in America. I'm suffocated by the things they ask of me and by the huge piles of letters. Yesterday's fame is turning against me. I say no to everything. Forgive me.

It wasn't the first time he had closed in on himself. We respected his desire for solitude, not knowing that we would never hear from him again. He decided to die on a gloriously sunny day, 11 April, soon after the arrival of the post. To ask for reasons is to torment ourselves in vain.

A year later, during the International Study Days dedicated to the writer, three friends nonetheless attempted an explanation. Maurice Goldstein said simply: 'Auschwitz finally caught up with him.' The philosopher Norberto Bobbio was faithful to the bond of deep mutual respect which had joined him to Primo Levi. He pointed to that 'uncertain hour' which recurs so often in Levi's work; and he spoke of his friend's 'searching and penetrating reason', which had always been troubled by the dark side of human nature. 'Perhaps we should read that repeated theme as a premonition of the hour that came so unexpectedly, not only for us, but also for him, that 11 April morning.'

The writer Edith Bruck, his 'sister of the Lager', commemorated their long friendship, conducted through phone calls between Rome and Turin, between the Hungarian Jewess who had survived Dachau and the witness of Auschwitz. In her soft and lilting Italian, in words sometimes broken by anguish, she told of a strange conversation that cruel spring:

> Primo was so tired of so many things and said that he had no hope any more. I answered in the stupidest way possible: There isn't any hope? No, no, we can't say that, absolutely not! It was as though he'd said something terrible to me, because he'd always repeated that one can't live without hope, and so I was frightened. But I repressed the thought that it was anything serious; it was just the word that had made me so fearful. Fearful for him, because I'd always had a protective feeling towards him: as though there were something very fragile inside him, a sensitivity so hidden, so terribly fragile that a mere nothing was enough to break it [...] Every time I saw him, such a clear, beautiful, gentle person, I feared for him like a mother for her son, though it was he who was a sort of father for me.

When she learned of his death, she understood:

> It seemed to me that there was no point in going on living; that the world was suddenly empty; that if his voice was no longer heard, ours were useless. [...] If he's gone, what can I say? Though he devoted so many years and such enormous effort to making himself heard.

Edith Bruck continued to search her memory for a reason for that suicide, about which he had said: 'It is a rational act, a choice that is not instinctive'. The life of the man who had survived to testify rose in front of her, in front of the audience, silent and deeply moved.

> The last time we spoke on the phone, he told me that he couldn't remember anything, that he had to consult his own books when people asked about them, that he had no memory any more, and so he was afraid of no longer having anything to say, of no longer being

> able to move on. He said: 'I don't know what to write anymore.' For us, when we no longer know what to write, life is useless; and when we can no longer testify, it's totally useless. Perhaps it's a terrible condemnation of us, after all we've lived through. But the moment we let go, even for an instant, the moment we sense one instant of emptiness inside, we feel we can't go on living.

A desert had spread inside him. His death was a cry that will not allow us to forget.

Notes

1. Ferdinando Camon, 'Ma allora Dio non c'è?' [But then there isn't a God?], *Panorama,* 28 May 1986.
2. The Lion d'Oro [Gold Lion] prize was awarded by the Turin Lions Club to distinguished cultural and scientific figures of the city.
3. Omitted from the English *Complete Works* and the earlier translation by Raymond Rosenthal, but printed on the front cover of the Italian original, *I sommersi e i salvati* (Turin: Einaudi, 1986). The cover pictures used for the English-language editions are also different.
4. A triptych painted between 1467 and 1471, now in the National Museum of Gdańsk, Poland
5. 'I absolve you', from the Latin text for the Catholic Sacrament of Reconciliation.
6. A town in Piedmont.
7. Giorgio Calcagno, 'Primo Levi: capire non è perdonare' [Primo Levi: to understand is not to forgive], *Tuttolibri* (*La Stampa*), 26 July 1986.
8. A seventeenth-century building: once the residence of the Savoy Princes of Carignano, it now houses the Museum of the Risorgimento.
9. A lifetime achievement prize, awarded for witness writing by the town of Acqui Terme, Piedmont.
10. P. Levi, trans. A.M. Appel, *Stories and Essays*, in A. Goldstein (ed.), *Complete Works of Primo Levi* (Liveright: New York, 2015) pp.2,399-402.
11. The headquarters of the Regional Council of Piedmont.
12. A. Bravo and D. Jalla, *La Vita offesa: Storia e memoria dei Lager nazisti nei racconti di 200 sopravissuti* [Wounded life: History and memory of the Nazi Lagers in the stories of 200 survivors] (Milan: Franco Angeli, 1986). The records of the conference are published in the fourth edition (Milan: Franco Angeli, 1988).
13. The text of Primo Levi's speech was given out to the audience at the conference on the theme of 'Storia vissuta – Dal dovere di testimoniare alle testimonianze orali nell'insegnamento della storia della Seconda Guerra Mondiale' [Lived history – From the duty to testify to oral testimonies in the teaching of Second World War history], which took place in Turin on 21-22 November 1986. Together with the speech, the audience were given photocopies of the chapter 'Letters from Germans' in *The Drowned and the Saved* and of Levi's answers to the questions he had been asked by his readers, translated into Italian from what were then the standard American editions of

If This is a Man and *The Truce*: *Survival in Auschwitz* (Orion Press: New York, 1959) and *The Reawakening* (Little, Brown and Company: Boston, 1965), both translated by Stuart Woolf.

14. 'Third page', after the stories and essays published on the third page of the newspaper, which were collected in the anthologies.
15. Preface to A.M. Appel (trans.), *Stories and Essays*, in *Complete Works of Primo Levi*, Vol. III, p.2,261. The Mondo introduction is not included in the English edition.
16. Josef Mengele, one of the most notorious Nazi criminals. An SS officer and physician, he conducted appalling medical experiments on Auschwitz prisoners, most notoriously on twins, and selected arrivals for slave labour or immediate extermination.
17. From the weekly RAI TG2 culture and news programme 'Focus', first episode, presented by Ennio Mastrostefano and Paolo Meucci, 22 December 1986. On the question of faith in humanity, see Chapter V of this book, 'From the laboratory to the writing desk'.
18. Vincenti was the author of *Invito alla lettura di Primo Levi* [Invitation to read Primo Levi], (Milan: Mursia, 1987).
19. Italian secondary schools range from the more practical to the more academic; but the Constitution (especially the first twelve articles, which state the Republic's fundamental principles) is taught to all pupils in citizenship classes. Article 11 deals with peace. Military service was abolished on 31 December 2004.
20. Article (no title given) in *Uomini e Libri*, no.112, 1987, p.13.
21. 'My heart laid bare', the title of a book of poetic fragments by Beaudelaire, published posthumously in *Oeuvres posthumes et corréspondances inédites* [Posthumous works and unpublished correspondence] (Paris: Maison Quantin, 1887).
22. Henri Charrière's 1973 account of his imprisonment and escape on the penal colony of French Guiana, a book whose accuracy has been questioned.
23. The explosion which destroys a star.
24. The Swiss poet and philosopher.
25. Roberto di Caro, 'La fatica di scrivere' [The Struggle of Writing], *L'Espresso*, 26 April 1987, pp.30-3; and *Piemonte Vivo* 'Il necessario e il superfluo' [The Necessary and the Superfluous], number 1, first semester of 1987, p.53.
26. From the speech given in French by Professor Maurice Goldstein at the Primo Levi International Study Days in the Piedmont Regional Council, Palazzo Lascaris, Turin, 28-9 March 1988.
27. From the speech given at the Study Days by Professor Coletti, an Italian scholar of contemporary German history. A translation of the article is available: 'The Black Hole of Auschwitz' in Belpoliti, *The Black Hole of Auschwitz*, pp.90-2.
28. *Seven Clues to the Origins of Life*, by A Graham Cairns-Smith (Cambridge: Cambridge University Press, 1985).

Works of Primo Levi

The following is a list of the works of Primo Levi cited in this book. Where there is no English translation, or the English translation uses a different title from the original, a literal rendering of the Italian title is given. Only the English translations of the books Levi published in his lifetime are quoted in the text. All other translations, including those of essays collected posthumously in the books *Uncollected Stories and Essays 1949-1980* and *Uncollected Stories and Essays 1981-1987*, included in the *Complete Works*, are listed for information purposes only.

Books

Se questo è un uomo (Turin: De Silva 1947 and Turin: Einaudi, 1958).

Translated by Stuart Woolf as *If This Is a Man* for a British edition (1960) and as *Survival in Auschwitz* in an American one (1959).

La tregua (Turin: Einaudi, 1963).

Translated by Stuart Woolf as *The Truce* for a British edition and as *The Reawakening* for an American one, both 1965.

Storie naturali [Natural Histories] (Turin: Einaudi, 1966) (under the pseudonym Damiano Malabaila). Republished in 1979 under the name Primo Levi.

Some stories translated by Raymond Rosenthal for *The Sixth Day and Other Tales* (U.S. and U.K. 1990), and by Ann Goldstein and Alessandro Bastagli for *A Tranquil Star* (New York and London: Norton, 2007).

Vizio di forma [Flaw of Form] (Turin: Einaudi, 1971).

Some stories published in *The Sixth Day and Other Tales* and in *A Tranquil Star.*

Il sistema periodico (Turin: Einaudi, 1975).

Translated by Raymond Rosenthal as *The Periodic Table* (U.S.: Schocken Books, 1984, U.K.: Michael Joseph, 1985).

L'osteria di Brema [The Bremen Beer Hall] (Milan: Scheiwiller, 1975) (poems).

All poems available in *Collected Poems*, translated by Brian Swann and Ruth Feldman (London: Faber & Faber, 1988).

La chiave a stella [The Wrench] (Turin: Einaudi, 1978).

Translated by William Weaver as *The Monkey's Wrench* (U.S.: Summit Books, 1986, U.K.: Michael Joseph, 1987).

La ricerca delle radici [The Search for Roots] (Turin: Einaudi, 1981).

Translated by Peter Forbes as *The Search for Roots: A Personal Anthology* (London: Allen Lane, 2001).

Lilìt e altri racconti [Lilith and Other Stories] (Turin: Einaudi, 1981).

Some stories published in *A Tranquil Star* and in *Moments of Reprieve*, translated by Ruth Feldman (U.S.: Summit Books, 1986, U.K.: Michael Joseph, 1986).

Se non ora, quando? (Turin: Einaudi, 1982).

Translated by William Weaver as *If Not Now, When?* (U.S.: Summit Books, 1985, U.K.: Michael Joseph, 1986).

In 1982 and 1983, Levi translated Kafka's *The Trial*, which was published by Einaudi as *Il processo* in 1983. As well as two volumes by Claude Lévi-Strauss: *The Way of the Masks* [*La via delle maschere*] and *The View from Afar* [*Lo sguardo da lontano*].

In the summer of 1984 he met the physicist Tullio Regge. The product of their conversation was the volume *Dialogo* [Dialogue] (Milan: Edizioni Comunità, 1984), published in English under the Italian title in a translation by Raymond Rosenthal (Princeton: Princeton University Press, 1990).

Ad ora incerta [At an uncertain hour](Milan: Garzanti, 1984) (poems).

Translated in *Collected Poems*.

L'ultimo Natale di Guerra [The Last Christmas of the War], illustrated by Imre Reiner (Lugano: privately printed, 1984).

Translated in *Moments of Reprieve.*

L'Altrui mestiere (Turin: Einaudi, 1985).

Translated by Raymond Rosenthal as *Other People's Trades* (U.S.: Summit Books, 1989, U.K.: Michael Joseph, 1989).

I sommersi e i salvati (Turin: Einaudi, 1986).

Translated by Raymond Rosenthal as *The Drowned and the Saved* (U.S.: Summit Books, 1988, U.K.: Michael Joseph, 1988).

Racconti e saggi [Stories and Essays] (Turin: Editrice La Stampa, 1986). A collection of his contributions to the daily newspaper between 1977 and 1986.

Translated by Raymond Rosenthal as *The Mirror Maker* (U.S.: Schocken Books, 1989, U.K.: Methuen, 1990).

Primo Levi's complete works, edited by Marco Belpoliti, were published in Einaudi's 'Biblioteca dell'Orso' series, starting in 1987.

Volume I, with an introduction by Cesare Cases and chronology compiled by Ernesto Ferrero, comprises *Se questo è un uomo*, *La tregua*, *Il sistema periodico* and *I sommersi e i salvati.*

Volume II (novels and poems), with an introduction by Cesare Segre, comprises *La chiave a stella*, *Se non ora, quando?*, *Ad ora incerta* and *Traduzioni e altre poesie* [Translations and other poems].

Volume III (stories and essays), with an introduction by Pier Vincenzo Mengaldo, comprises *Storie naturali*, *Vizio di forma*, *Lilìt e altri racconti*, *L'altrui mestiere* and *Racconti e saggi.*

There is also a two volume edition, retaining only the first introduction by Cesare Cases, published in 1997.

The English edition of the *Complete Works*, edited by Ann Goldstein, is in three volumes (all New York: Liveright, 2015). The first volume comprises *If This is a Man*, *The Truce*, *Natural Histories* and *Flaw of Form.* Volume II comprises *The Periodic Table*, *The Wrench*, *Uncollected Stories and Essays 1949-1980*, *Lilith and Other Stories* and *If Not Now, When?* The third volume comprises *Collected Poems*, *Other People's Trades*, *Stories and Essays*, *The Drowned and the Saved* and *Uncollected Stories and Essays 1981-1987.* All quotations from Levi's books, poems and stories are from this collection – with two exceptions: *The Search for Roots: A Personal*

Anthology, which is not included in the *Complete Works* and is quoted in Forbes' translation; and Levi's translations of Kafka, which have been translated from his Italian here. Articles published in the two volumes of *Uncollected Stories and Essays*, both translated by Alessandra and Francesco Bastagli, are also in this translation. The translators are credited in the first endnote reference to each book.

2. Forewords

'Foreword to *Auschwitz* by Léon Poliakov' (originally published in *Auschwitz*, Rome: Veutro, 1968), *Uncollected Stories and Essays 1949-1980*, pp.1,186-8.

Foreword to Joel König, *Sfuggito alle reti del nazismo* [Escaped from the nets of Nazism], (Milan: Mursia, 1973).

Translation of and Foreword to Jacques Presser, *La notte dei Girondini* (Milan: Adelphi, 1976).

> Translated as 'Foreword to *The Night of the Girondists* by Jacques Presser' in *Uncollected Stories and Essays 1949-1980*, pp.1,220-3.

Foreword to Yitzhak Katzenelson, *Il canto del popolo ebreo massacrato*, Centro di documentazione ebraica contemporanea (Contemporary Jewish documentation centre), April 1977.

> Translated as 'Foreword to *The Song of the Murdered Jewish People* by Yitzhak Katzenelson' in *Uncollected Stories and Essays 1949-1980*, pp.1,169-71.

Foreword to Luciano Cagliotti, *I due volti della chimica* (Milan: Mondadori, 1979).

> Translated as 'Foreword to *The Two Faces of Chemistry* by Luciano Cagliotti' in *Uncollected Stories and Essays 1949-1980*, pp.1,323-8.

Foreword to *Le immagini di Olocausto: dalla realtà alla tv* [Images of *Holocaust*: from reality to the TV] (Turin: Eri, May 1979), pp.2-5.

> Translated as 'Images from *Holocaust*' in *Uncollected Stories and Essays: 1949-1980* pp.1,286-9.

Foreword to Hermann Langbein, *Uomini ad Auschwitz* [Men in Auschwitz](Milan: Mursia, 1984).

> Translated as 'Foreword to *People in Auschwitz* by Hermann Langbein' in *Uncollected Stories and Essays: 1980-1987*, pp.2,671-4.

Foreword to Rudolf Höss, *Comandante ad Auschwitz*, new edition (Turin: Einaudi, 1985).

> Translated as 'Foreword to *Commandant of Auschwitz* by Rudolf Höss' in *Uncollected Stories and Essays: 1980-1987*, pp.2704-11.

3. Articles and Other Writings

'Anniversario' [Anniversary], *L'Eco dell'educazione ebraica* [Jewish Educational Echo], special edition for the tenth anniversary of the Liberation, ninth year of publication, April 1955, p.14.

> Translated as 'Deportees. Anniversary', in Belpoliti, M. (ed.), trans. S. Wood, *The Black Hole of Auschwitz* (Cambridge: Polity Press, 2005), pp.23-7.

'Monumento ad Auschwitz' [Monument at Auschwitz], *La Stampa*, 19 July 1959.

> Translated as 'The Monument at Auschwitz', in Belpoliti, *The Black Hole of Auschwitz*, pp. 5-7.

'La resistenza nel Lager' [Resistance in the Lager], *Quaderno del Centro studi sulla deportazione e l'internamento* [Copybook of the deportation and internment studies centre], No.3, Rome, 1966.

> Translated as 'Resistance in the Lagers' in *Uncollected Stories and Essays 1949-1980.*

'Un olocausto che pesa ancora sulla coscienza del mondo' [A Holocaust that still weighs on the world's conscience], *Tuttolibri, La Stampa*, 28 April 1970.

'Così fu Auschwitz' [This is how Auschwitz was], *La Stampa*, 9 February 1975.

'Ma perché Auschwitz?' [But why Auschwitz?], *Tuttolibri* (*La Stampa*), No. 8, 28 February 1976.

'Film e svastiche', *La Stampa,* 12 February 1977.

> Translated as 'Films and Swastikas' in Belpoliti, *The Black Hole of Auschwitz*, p.38.

'Meditato con malizia' [Planned with malice], *La Stampa*, 13 March 1977.

> An earlier version of 'With Malice Aforethought', a story in *The Wrench*, trans. N. Rich, *Complete Works of Primo Levi*, Vol.II, pp.953-9.

'Le parole esportate' [Exported words], *La Stampa*, 17 February 1978. A review of *Parliamo Itang'liano* (see 'Other Works Cited' section).

'Il cantore e il veterano', *La Stampa,* July 1978.

An earlier version of 'The Cantor and the Veteran', a chapter in *Lilith and Other Stories*, trans. A. Goldstein, in *Complete Works of Primo Levi*, Vol. II, pp.1,379-84.

'Ma noi c'eravamo' *Corriere della Sera*, 3 January 1979.

Translated as 'But We Were There' in Belpoliti, *The Black Hole of Auschwitz,* pp.50-1.

'Un Lager alle porte d'Italia' [A Lager at the gates of Italy], *La Stampa*, 19 January 1979.

Translated as 'Concentration Camp at Italy's Door', in Belpoliti, *The Black Hole of Auschwitz,* pp.52-6.

'Chi vuole l'odio antisemita' [Those who want anti-Semitic hatred], *La Stampa,* 13 March 1979.

'Perché non ritornino gli Olocausto di ieri' [So that yesterday's Holocausts do not return], *La Stampa*, 20 May 1979.

Translated as 'No Return to the Holocausts of the Past (Nazi Massacres, Crowds and the TV)' in Belpoliti, *The Black Hole of Auschwitz*, pp.56-8.

'Chi ha coraggio a Gerusalemme?' [Who has courage in Jerusalem?], *La Stampa*, 24 June 1982.

'Il difficile cammino della verità' [The difficult path of truth], *Rassegna Mensile di Israel* [Monthly Israel Review], July-December 1982.

Translated as 'The Difficult Journey of Truth' in *Uncollected Stories and Essays: 1980-1987*, pp. 2,598-605.

'Vecchio io?' [Old, me?], *Stampa Sera*, 15th November 1982.

'Il pericolo viene dal militarismo' [The danger comes from militarism], *La Repubblica,* 11 February 1983.

'Kafka col coltello nel cuore' [Kafka with a knife in his heart], *La Stampa*, 5 June 1983.

'Polvere olimpica' [Olympic dust], *La Stampa,* 14 August 1984.

An earlier version of 'A Long Duel', trans. A. Shugaar in *Other People's Trades*, *Complete Works of Primo Levi*, Vol. III p. 2-281.

'Itinerario di uno scrittore ebreo' [Itinerary of a Jewish writer], *La Rassegna Mensile di Israel* [Monthly Israel Review], Nos. 5-8, fiftieth year of publication, 1984. An essay based on the speech Levi gave at a Rockefeller Foundation conference in Bellagio, 29 November to 2 December 1982.

Translated by Gail Soffer as *Beyond Survival,* Prooftexts, Vol. 4 (Baltimore: Johns Hopkins University Press, 1984). This translation was used by Levi on a lecture tour of the United States organized by the Rockefeller foundation.

'Il giocatore occulto', *La Stampa,* 19 October 1985.

An earlier version of 'The Hidden Player' trans. A.M. Appel in *Stories and Essays, Complete Works of Primo Levi,* Vol. III, pp.2,379-82.

'Buco nero di Auschwitz', *La Stampa,* 22 January 1987.

Translated as 'The Black Hole of Auschwitz', in Belpoliti, *The Black Hole of Auschwitz,* pp.90-2.

4. Works Published in Collaboration

Levi, P. and Marché, P. *Se questo è un uomo. Versione drammatica* [*If This is a Man.* Dramatic Version] (Turin: Einaudi, 1966).

Introductory note translated as 'Note to the Theatre Version of *If This is a Man*' in Belpoliti, *The Black Hole of Auschwitz,* pp.23-6. A full English version (translator not credited) is available on request from the International Primo Levi Study Centre, Turin: Marché, P. & Levi, P., 'If This is a Man: Stage Version', *Italian Theatre Review,* Year 16, No.2, April-May-June 1967, pp.10-56.

5. Speeches, Lectures and Interviews

Public meeting at Palazzo Carignano, Turin, 4 June 1975.
Public meeting at Leo Club of Cuneo, Autumn 1975.
'Esperienze di uno scrittore' [Experiences of a writer], Swiss lecture tour, 8-12 November 1976.
'Lo scrittore non-scrittore' [The non-writer writer], Associazione Culturale Italiana discussion, Carignano Theatre, Turin, 19 November 1976.
RAI 2 interview before the broadcast of his play *La bella adormentata nel frigo* [Sleeping Beauty in the Refrigerator], evening of 13 January 1978.
Appearance on RAI Radio 3, 'Personalmente' [Personally], 23 December 1978.

Conversation with Ennio Cavalli on 'Segnalibro' [Bookmark], RAI 3, 3 January 1979.

Conversation with Nicola Tranfaglia, 'Col sudore della fronte' [With the sweat of one's brow], RAI3, 22 March 1981.

Conversation with Renato Romanelli, Mostra della Deportazione [Deportation Exhibition], Trino Vercellese, 30 January 1982.

Interview given to Guido Lopez, 'Sorgente di vita' [Source of life], RAI 2, 17 March 1982.

Interview given to Anna Maria Rebaudengo, RAI 3 Piedmont Regional Television News, 17 April 1982.

Lecture, Mostra della Deportazione [Deportation Exhibition], Settimo Torinese, April 1982.

Speech at launch event for *Se non ora, quando?* [If Not Now, When?], Einaudi Bookshop, Milan, 4 May 1982.

Public meeting at Libreria Campus di Torino [Campus Bookshop of Turin],Via Ratazzi, Turin, 20 May 1982.

Conversation with Giulio Nascimbeni and Guido Gola, 'Tuttolibri', RAI 1, 24 May 1982.

Remarks at the Campiello prize-giving ceremony, 4 September 1982.

Interview given to Ennio Cavalli on RAI Radio 1 News, 5 September 1982.

Conversation with Daniel Toaff following a return visit to Auschwitz, 'Ritorno ad Auschwitz' [Return to Auschwitz],special edition of 'Sorgente di vita' [Source of life], RAI 2, 25 April 1983.

Conversation with Dina Luce, 'Il suono e la mente' [Sound and mind], RAI Radio 2, 4 October 1982.

Conversation with Beniamino Placido, 'Film Dossier', RAI 1, 27 October 1983.

Conversation with Massimo Mila, 'Bric-à-brac', RAI 3, 29 November 1983.

Interview in front of the science faculty of the University of Turin, RAI 3, Piedmont regional edition, 25 September 1984.

Conversation with Lucia Borgia, 'Rifarsi una vita' [Remaking a life for oneself], RAI 3, 3 February 1985.

Conversation with Enrica Bonaccorti, 'Italia Sera' [Evening Italy], RAI 1, 11 March 1985.

Conversation with Giorgio Bocca 'Prima Pagina', Mediaset Canale 5, 13 June 1985.

Speech for the Montedison Educational Project, 29 January 1986. Published in *Montedison-Progetto Cultura* (Montedison-Educational Project), No.4, 1987.

Speech at conference organized by the Region of Piedmont and Associazione nazionale ex-deportati [National ex-deportees' association], 'Storia vissuta – Dal dovere di testimoniare alle testimonianze orali nell'insegnamento della storia della Seconda Guerra Mondiale' [Lived history—from the duty to testify to oral testimonies in the teaching of Second World War history], Turin, 21-2 November 1986.

Conversation with Ennio Mastrostefano and Paolo Meucci, 'Focus', RAI 2, 22 December 1986.

6. Miscellaneous - unpublished or untitled

'Bozza di testo per l'interno del Block italiano ad Auschwitz' [Draft of a text for the inside of the Italian Block at Auschwitz], typescript delivered to *La Stampa*, 8 November 1978.

Answer to a reader, *Gazzetta del Popolo*, 21 January 1979.

Statement (no title given) reported in *L'Unità*, 10 October 1982, about the Rome synagogue attack the previous day.

Other Works Cited

Alterocca, B. 'Fantascienza in tv con Primo Levi' [Science fiction on TV with Primo Levi], *La Stampa*, 16 February 1977.

Appiotti, M. 'Sulla collina torinese risuonano le voce del Lager di Auschwitz' [On the Turin hills the voices of the Auschwitz Lager resound], *Stampa Sera*,22-23 April 1964.

Arpino, G. 'Non lamentiamoci dei premi letterari' [Let's not complain about literary prizes], *La Stampa*, 17 June 1979.

Baglivo, A. 'Gli ebrei di Torino: non più Olocausti' [The Jews of Turin: no more Holocausts], *Corriere della Sera*, 7 July 1983.

Balbi, R. 'Mendel il consolatore' [Mendel the consoler], *La Repubblica*, 14 April 1982.

Bàrberi Squarotti, G. 'Dio creò il male e lo chiamò Lilìt' [God created evil and called it Lilith], *La Stampa*, 5 December 1981.

Bartoli, E., 'Prima che il sole ci ingoi' [Before the Sun swallows us], *La Repubblica*, 16 August 1983.

Bassani, G. *The Garden of the Finzi-Continis* (Atheneum: New York, 1965).

Beaudelaire, C. *Oeuvres posthumes et corréspondances inédites* [Posthumous works and unpublished correspondence](Paris: Maison Quantin, 1887).

Benzi, R. 'Quel treno per Auschwitz' [That train for Auschwitz], *Gli Altri*, second quarter of 1979.

Bernardi, G. 'Primo Levi traduce Kafka' [Primo Levi translates Kafka], *Il Giornale*, 22 May 1983.

Bertacchini, R. 'Quando le "pecore" colpiscono' [When the 'sheep' strike], *La Notte*, 26 May 1982.

Bertinetto, G. 'La fanta-violenza di Primo Levi' [The fantasy-violence of Primo Levi], *L'Unità*,13 January 1978.

—,'La godibile ironia di Primo Levi' [The enjoyable irony of Primo Levi], *L'Unità*, 27 January 1978.

Bianucci, P. 'Tanti atti di fede nel romanzo' [So many acts of faith in the novel], *Gazzetta del Popolo*, 20 November 1971.

—, '*Olocausto* è brutto ma può servire' [*Holocaust* is bad but it can be useful], *Gazzetta del Popolo*, 25 May 1979.

—,'Sì, anche la mia cultura può essere considerate yiddish' [Yes, my culture too can be considered Yiddish], Interview with Primo Levi after he won the twentieth Campiello Prize, *La Stampa*, 6 September 1982.

Bobbio, N. *Trent'anni di storia della cultura a Torino (1920-1950)*[Thirty years of history of culture in Turin (1920-1950)](Turin: Cassa di Risparmio, 1977).

—, Speech at Primo Levi International Study Days, event organized by Piedmont Regional Council [Consiglio Regionale Piemonte], Council headquarters in Palazzo Lascaris, Turin, 28-9 March 1988.

Boeri, E. 'Quattro chiacchiere con Primo Levi' [A chat with Primo Levi],*Tecnologie chimiche*, December 1983.

Borges, J.L. , ed. Kerrigan, A., (various translators), *Ficciones* (New York: Grove Press, 1962).

Boursier, G. 'Primo Levi rievoca la barbarie dei Lager nazisti' [Primo Levi re-enacts the barbarism of the Nazi Lagers], G*azzetta del Popolo*, 17 November 1966.

Bragg, W. *Concerning the Nature of Things* (London: Bell & Sons, 1925).

Bravo, A. and Jalla, D. (eds), *La vita offesa* [The wounded life] (Milan: Franco Angeli, 1987).

Bruck, E. Speech at Primo Levi International Study Days, event organized by Piedmont Regional Council [Consiglio Regionale Piemonte], Council headquarters in Palazzo Lascaris, Turin, 28-9 March 1988.

Buzzolan, U. 'Come scongelare la bella ragazza dopo cent'anni' [How to defrost the beautiful girl after 100 years], *La Stampa*, 13 January 1978.

—, 'Il diario di un uomo che è tornato alla vita' [The diary of a man who has come back to life], *La Stampa*, 25 April 1978.

—, 'La voce di chi conobbe i crimini nazisti' [The voice of those who knew the Nazi crimes], *La Stampa*, 15 May 1979.

Cacianti, P. 'Primo Levi vince il nuovo Campiello' [Primo Levi wins the new Campiello], A*vanti!* 8 September 1982.

Calcagno, G. 'Primo Levi spiega perché ha accettato la riduzione del suo libro' [Primo Levi explains why he agreed to the adaptation of his book], *Il Nostro Tempo*, 1967, Year XXI, No.47 (published weekly).

—, 'La Terra Promessa dei miei ebrei non è una potenza militare' [The Promised Land of my Jews isn't a military power], *Tuttolibri* (*La Stampa*), 12 June 1982.

—, 'Per i nostri scrittori la montagna non è incantata' [For our writers the mountain isn't magic], *Tuttolibri* (*La Stampa*), 27 November 1982.

—, 'Primo Levi: capire non è perdonare' [Primo Levi: understanding is not forgiving],*Tuttolibri* (*La Stampa*), 26 July 1986.

Calvino, I., trans. Weaver, W., *Cosmocomics* (New York: Harcourt Brace, 1965).

—, 'Le quattro strade di Primo Levi' [The Four Roads of Primo Levi], *La Repubblica*, 11 June 1981.

—,trans. Weaver, W., *Marcovaldo: Or the Seasons in the City* (London: Secker & Warburg, 1983).

—, trans. Weaver, W., *Mr. Palomar* (New York: Harcourt Brace, 1985).

—, trans. Colquhoun, A., *Path to the Spiders' Nests* (New York: Harper Collins, 2000).

Camon, F. 'Ma allora Dio non c'è?' [So then there isn't a God?], *Panorama,* 25 May 1986.

—, 'Se il Lager oltre la vita spezza la dignità' [If as well as life the Lager destroys dignity], *Il Giorno*, 5 June 1986.

—, *Autoritratto di Primo Levi* [Self-portrait of Primo Levi] (Padua: Edizioni Nord Est, 1987).

—, trans. Shepley, J., *Conversations with Primo Levi* (Marlboro: Marlboro Press, 1989).

Canducci, L. 'La cinquantatreesima edizione del Premio Viareggio; parlano alcuni dei protagonisti' [The fifty-third edition of the Viareggio Prize: some of the protagonists speak], *Avanti!* 30 June 1982.

Carrel, A. *Man, The Unknown* (New York: Doubleday, 1935).

Cavaglion, A. Speech at Primo Levi International Study Days, event organized by Piedmont Regional Council [Consiglio Regionale Piemonte], Council headquarters in Palazzo Lascaris, Turin, 28-9 March 1988.

—, 'Argon e la cultura ebraica piemontese (con l'abbozzo del racconto)' [Argon and Piedmontese Jewish culture (with the draft of the story)], in Cavaglion (ed.), *Primo Levi. Il presente del passato* [Primo Levi: the present of the past], (Milan, Franco Angeli, 1991),pp.169-96 (essay), 187-96 (draft).

Cavani, L. (dir.) *The Night Porter* (Joseph E. Levine Productions/Itar Noleggio Cinematographico/Lodar Film Productions, 1974).

Chabad, *Ethics of the Fathers (Pirkei Avot)*, 1.14, available at: http://www.chabad.org/library/article_cdo/aid/682498/jewish/English-Text.htm [Accessed 13 September 2016].

Coletti, E. (Prof.) Speech at Primo Levi International Study Days, event organized by Piedmont Regional Council [Consiglio Regionale Piemonte], Council headquarters in Palazzo Lascaris, Turin, 28-9 March 1988.

Colombo, F. Opening speech, event at Comunità israelitica di Torino [Israelite Community of Turin: now 'Comunità ebraica di Torino' or Jewish Community of Turin], 12 April 1989.

Conrad, J., 'Note to Typhoon', available at: https://ebooks.adelaide.edu.au/c/conrad/joseph/c75ty/preface.html [Accessed 13 June 2016].

D'Angeli, G. 'Il sonno della ragione genera mostri' [The sleep of reason produces monsters], *Famiglia Cristiana*, no. 48, 27 November 1966.

D'Arrigo, S. *Horcynus Orca* (Milan: Mondadori, 1975).

Davico Bonino, G. 'Scusi: le piacerebbe nascere sulla terra?' [Excuse me, would you like to be born on Earth?], *La Stampa*, 22 May 1980.

D'Azeglio, M., trans. Maffei, Count A., *Recollections* (London: Forgotten Books, 2012).

Debenedetti, A. 'Vincitore il romanzo' [The novel's the winner], *Corriere della Sera*, 6 July 1979.
De Kruif, P. *Microbe Hunters* (New York: Blue Ribbon Books, 1926).
Del Buono, O. 'Primo Levi ritraduce Kafka: il nuovo "Processo"' [Primo Levi retranslates Kafka: the new 'Trial'], *Corriere della Sera*, 7 July 1982.
Del Colle, G. 'Attori di sette nazioni per il dramma di Auschwitz' [Actors of seven nations for the drama of Auschwitz], *La Stampa*, 17 November 1966.
Dentice, F. 'Mi travesto da Kafka' [I dress up as Kafka], *L'Espresso*, 24 April 1983.
De Rienzo, G.'In un alambicco quanta poesia' [How much poetry in a still], *Famiglia Cristiana*,no.29, 20 July 1975.
—, 'All'eroe dell'ultimo romanzo di Primo Levi lavorare piace' [The hero of Primo Levi's last novel likes working], *Famiglia Cristiana*, January 1978.
—, 'Come il mio Faussone io celebro la religione del lavoro' [Like my Faussone I celebrate the religion of work], *Stampa Sera*, 29 December 1978.
Di Caro, R. 'Il necessario e il superfluo' [The Necessary and the Superfluous], *Piemonte Vivo*, No.1, 1987, p.53.
—, 'La fatica di scrivere' [The Struggle of Writing], L'*Espresso*, 26 April 1987.
Elliot, G. *Parliamo itang'liano* [We speak *Itang'liano*] (Milan: Rizzoli, 1977).
Éluard, P., trans. Bowen, G., *Unbroken Poetry* (Newcastle: Bloodaxe, 1996).
Faldini, E. 'Primo Levi si sente scrittore "dimezzato"' [Primo Levi feels like a 'halved' writer], *L'Unità*, 4 January 1966.
Fallada, H., trans. Hofffman, M., *Every Man Dies Alone* (New Jersey: Melville House, 2009).
Faurisson, R. 'Le rumeur d'Auschwitz' [The rumour of Auschwitz], *Le Monde*, 29 December 1978.
Ferrero, E. 'Se lo scrittore sapesse che la scienza è anche fantasia' [If the writer knew that science is also imagination], *Tuttolibri, La Stampa*, 21 January 1984.
Ferrero, N. '*Se questo è un uomo* in scena a Torino' [*If This is a Man* on stage in Turin], *L'Unità*, 17 November 1966.
Gagliano, E. and De Rienzo, G. 'La ragione non può andare in vacanza' [Reason can't go on holiday], *Stampa Sera* books column, 13 May 1975
Genius, 'Una domanda a Primo Levi' [A question for Primo Levi], no.4, 4 January 1985, pp.11-12.
Genta, L. 'Così ho rivissuto "Il Processo" di Kafka' [This is how I relived Kafka's 'Trial'], *Tuttolibri* (*La Stampa*), 9 April 1983.
Giacomoni, S. 'Il mago Merlino e l'uomo fabbro' [Merlin the Mage and man the maker], *La Repubblica*, 24 January 1979.
Ginzburg, N., trans. Low, D. M., *Family Sayings* (New York: Arcade Publishing, 1989).
Goldstein, M. (Prof.). Speech at Primo Levi International Studies Days, event organized by Piedmont Regional Council [Consiglio Regionale Piemonte], Council headquarters in Palazzo Lascaris, Turin, 28-9 March 1988.

Goria, G. 'Sono diventato ebreo quasi per forza' [I became a Jew almost by force], *Paese Sera*, 3 May 1982.

Granzotto, P. 'Una chiave d'oro per Levi' [A gold key for Levi], *Il Giornale*, 6 July 1979.

Grassano, G. *Primo Levi* (Florence: Il Castoro/La Nuova Italia, 1981).

Green, G. *Holocaust* (Ealing: Transworld Publishers, 1978).

Guidotti, M. 'Senza sorprese lo Strega a Primo Levi' [No surprises as the Strega goes to Primo Levi], *L'Avvenire*, 6 July 1979.

Il Giorno, 'Bella da sgelare una volta l'anno' [Beauty to be defrosted once a year], 13 January 1978.

Jesurum, S., *Essere ebrei in Italia*[Being Jewish in Italy] (Longanesi: Milan, 1987).

Lammer, E.G., trans. Prati, R., *Fontana di giovinezza* [The Fountain of Youth] (Milan: L'eroica, 1932).

La Repubblica, 'La favola del prossimo secolo' [The fable of the next century], 13 January 1978.

La Stampa, 'A Natalia Ginzburg il Premio Strega' [The Strega Prize goes to Natalia Ginzburg], 5 July 1963.

—, 'Levi sotto falso nome vince il premio Bagutta' [Levi wins the Bagutta Prize under a false name], 15 January 1967.

—, 'Così fu arrestato Primo Levi partigiano' [This is how the partisan Primo Levi was arrested], 21 April 1984.

Laurenzi, C. 'Sei scrittori in corsa per un premio letterario' [Six writers in the race for a literary prize], *Corriere della Sera*, 4 July 1963.

Lerner, G. 'Se questo è uno stato' [If This is a State], *L'Espresso*, 30 September 1984.

Levi, C., trans. Fenaye, F., *Christ Stopped at Eboli* (New York: Farrar, Strauss and Company, 1947).

Longo, T. 'La Lilìt di Primo Levi' [The Lilith of Primo Levi], *La Stampa*, 20 January 1982.

Lo Presti, V. '*Tornare, mangiare, raccontare…*' [Returning, eating, telling…], *Lotta Continua*, 18 June 1979.

L'Unità, 'Il Premio Prato assegnato a Donini e a Primo Levi' [The Prato Prize awarded to Donini and Primo Levi], 13 September 1975.

—,'La parola al chimico' [The chemist's turn to speak], 20 November 1976.

Magalotti, Count L. *Relazione sulla cina* [Account of China] (Adelphi: Milan, 1974). First published 1676.

Mancinelli, L. 'Così ho inventato Gedale, il partigiano che amava il violino' [This is how I invented Gedale, the partisan who loved the violin], *L'Unità*, 8 July 1982.

Manganelli, G. 'Elogio del scrivere oscuro' [Commendation of obscure writing], *Corriere della Sera*, 3 January 1977.

Mangano, G. 'Primo Levi ha vinto lo Strega' [Primo Levi has won the Strega], *Gazzetta del Popolo*, 6 July 1979.

Manzini, G. 'Elogio del libero lavoro' [In praise of free work], *Paese Sera*, 11 December 1978.
Manzoni, A. *I promessi sposi* (Milan: Guglielini e Redaelli, 1842).
—, trans. Penman, B., *The Betrothed* (St Ives: Penguin, 1983).
Massari, G. 'È già stagione di premi, ma chi vincerà la corsa?' [It's already prizes season, but who will win the race?], *La Stampa*, 1 May 1979.
Miccinesi, M. 'Inchiesta sulla letteratura come contestazione' [Inquiry into literature as protest], *Uomini e Libri*,no.18, April 1968.
—, 'La condizione dello scrittore nel contesto politico italiano' [The condition of the writer in the Italian political context], *Uomini e Libri*, no.63, March-April 1977, p.20.
—,'Intervista a Primo Levi' [Interview with Primo Levi],*Uomini e Libri*, Milan, January-February 1979, no.72, p.39.
—, 'Un romanzo storico costruito secondo i modelli classici' [A historical novel built according to the classical models], *Uomini e Libri*, November-December 1982, p.40.
Milani, G. 'Al chimico va stretta la memoria del Lager' [Lager memory constricts the chemist], *Piemonte Vip*, March 1986, p.19.
Mondo, L. 'Dal Lager non si esce' [One doesn't get out of the Lager], *La Stampa*, 19 December 1975.
Nascimbeni, G. 'Campiello '82: dopo vent'anni ancora premiato Primo Levi' [Campiello '82: Primo Levi awarded the prize again after twenty years], *Corriere della Sera*, 6 September 1982.
—, 'Levi, l'ora incerta della poesia' [Levi, the uncertain hour of poetry], *Corriere della Sera*, 28 October 1984.
Orengo, N. 'Su Svevo e *Il Gattopardo* niente da dire' [Nothing to say about Svevo and *The Leopard*], *Tuttolibri* (*La Stampa*), 9 March 1985.
Pacchioni, G. 'Segrete avventure di eroi involontari' [Secret adventures of accidental heroes], *Il Globo*, 13-14 June 1982.
Paglia, G.J. 'Ma davvero un Faussone cammina ancora tra noi?' [But is a Faussone really still walking among us?], *La Stampa*, 6 July 1979.
Pampaloni, G. 'Padri e figli' [Fathers and Sons], *Il Giornale*, 29 December 1981.
Pansa, G. 'Io Primo Levi chiedo le dimissioni di Begin e Sharon. Begin, gli ebrei dicono basta' [I, Primo Levi, ask for Begin and Sharon to resign. Begin, the Jews say enough], *La Repubblica*, 24 September 1982.
Paoletti, P.M. 'Sono un chimico, scrittore per caso' [I'm a chemist, a writer by chance], *Il Giorno*, 7 August 1963.
Papuzzi, A. 'L'Alpinismo? È la libertà di sbagliare' [Mountaineering? It's the freedom to make mistakes], *Rivista della montagna,* year 16, no.61, March-April 1984, pp.106-9.
Pasolini, P.P., trans. Weaver, W., *A Violent Life* (Manchester: Carcanet, 2007).
—, trans. Goldstein, A., *The Street Kids* (New York: Europa Editions, 2016).
Pecora, E. 'Parliamone male ma concorriamo tutti' [We speak ill of them but we all compete], *Tuttolibri (La Stampa)*, 26 March 1979.

Piattelli Palmarini, M. 'Quando il romanzo "parla" la scienza' [When the novel 'speaks' science], *Corriere della Sera*, 17 August 1979.

Pirandello, L., trans. Abba, M., *Diana and Tuda* (New York: Samuel French, 1934).

Pitkin, W.B. *A Short Introduction to the History of Human Stupidity* (New York: Simon and Schuster, 1932).

Poli, F. 'Intervista a Primo Levi' [Interview with Primo Levi], *Il Quotidiano dei lavoratori*, 28 February 1979.

Poli, G. 'L'alfabeto della chimica' [The alphabet of chemistry], *Tuttolibri, La Stampa*, 6 December 1976.

Presser, J., trans. Mussey, B., *Night of the Girondists* (London: Harvill, 1992).

Queneau, R. *Petite cosmogonie portative* [Small Portable Cosmogony] (Paris: Gallimard, 1950).

—, 'Le chant de la styrène' [The song of Styrene], poem written for and featured in Alain Resnais (dir.), *Le chant de la styrène*, documentary film (Les Films de la Pléiade/Péchiny, 1958).

—, trans. Solmi, S., *Piccola cosmogonia portatile* [Small Portable Cosmogony] (Turin: Einaudi, 1982).

—, trans. Calvino, I., *La canzone del Polistirene* [The song of Polystyrene] (Milan:Scheiwiller, 1985).

Raboni, G. 'Riesce a creare suspense col montaggio di una gru' [He succeeds in creating suspense with the assembly of a crane], *Tuttolibri, La Stampa*, 23 December 1978.

—, 'Primo Levi poeta vero ad ora incerta' [Primo Levi a true poet at an uncertain hour], *Tuttolibri* (*La Stampa*), 17 November 1984.

Reggiani, S. 'Diventa sfida il lavoro ben fatto' [Work properly done well becomes a challenge], *La Stampa*, 14 January 1979.

Rizzo, R. '*Olocausto*? Come un western, romanzato e superficiale' [*Holocaust*? Like a Western, romanticized and superficial], *La Stampa*, 25 May 1979.

Roth, P. 'A Man Saved by His Skills', *New York Times Book Review*, 12 October 1986.

—, 'Salvarsi dall'Inferno come Robinson' [Saving oneself from Hell like Robinson], *La Stampa*, 26 November 1986.

—, Il mio western degli ebrei ribelli' [My Western of the rebel Jews], *La Stampa*, 27 November 1986.

—, *Shop Talk: A Writer and His Colleagues and Their Work* (New York: Houghton Mifflin Company, 2001) pp. 1-17.

Sciascia, L. 'A chi giova l'atroce bugia che vuole cancellare le stragi nelle camere a gas del regime nazista' [To anyone pleased by the atrocious lie which seeks to erase the massacres in the gas chambers of the Nazi regime], *Corriere della Sera*, 3 January 1979.

—, *La Strega e il Capitano* [The Witch and the Captain] (Milan: Bompiani, 1986).

—, trans. Thomson, I., *Death of an Inquisitor and Other Stories* (Manchester: Carcanet, 1990).

Shalamov, V., trans. Glad, J., *Kolyma Tales* (St Ives: Penguin, 1994).

Solzhenitsyn, A., trans. Parker, R., *One Day in the Life of Ivan Denisovich* (New York: Dutton, 1963).

—, trans. Whitney, T.P. *The Gulag Archipelago* (place unknown: Harper & Row, 1974).

Spriano, P. 'L'antifascismo al Premio Strega' [Anti-fascism at the Strega Prize], *L'Unità*, 4 July 1963.

—, 'L'avventura di Primo Levi' [Primo Levi's adventure], *L'Unità,* 14 July 1963.

Stabile, A. 'Sì, Israele ha passato il segno, ma non è giusto parlare di nazismo' [Yes, Israel has overstepped the mark but it is not fair to speak of Nazism], L*a Repubblica,* 28 June 1982.

Stille, A. Contribution to the round table at the Primo Levi International Study Days, event organized by Piedmont Regional Council [Consiglio Regionale Piemonte], Council headquarters in Palazzo Lascaris, Turin, 28-9 March 1988. The text used here is abridged from that included in Cavaglion, *Primo Levi: Il presente del passato* [Primo Levi: the present of the past], (Milan: Franco Angeli, 1991),pp.203-11.

Tesio, G. 'Su alcune giunte e varianti di *Se questo è un uomo*' [On some additions and variants of *If This is a Man*], *Studi Piemontesi*, November 1977, vol. IV, issue 2, p. 273.

—, 'Ritratti di contemporanei: Primo Levi' [Portraits of contemporaries: Primo Levi], *Belfagor*, Florence, 30 November 1979, p. 657.

—, 'Le radici di Primo Levi' [Primo Levi's roots], *Nuova Società*, 22 March 1980.

—, 'Le occasioni? La memoria, un ponte, una ragnatela' [The causes? Memory, a bridge, a spider's web], *Tuttolibri* (*La Stampa*), 17 November 1983.

Toscani, C. 'Incontro con Primo Levi' [Meeting with Primo Levi], *Il Ragguaglio Librario*, No. 3, 1972.

Vacca, R. 'Manganelli nell'oscurità', [Manganelli in obscurity], article published in both *Il Resto del Carlino* and *La Nazione*, 15 February 1977.

—, 'Un Western dalla Russia a Milano' [A western from Russia to Milan], *Il Giorno*, 18 May 1982.

Vergani, L. 'Parla Primo Levi, il numero 174517' [Primo Levi, number 174517, speaks], *Corriere della Sera*, 20 March 1979.

Vincenti, F. *Invito alla lettura di Primo Levi* [Invitation to read Primo Levi], (Milan: Mursia, 1987).

Index